ROBERT SCHUMANN
The Man and his Music

BY ALAN WALKER

A Study in Musical Analysis
An Anatomy of Musical Criticism

EDITED BY ALAN WALKER

Frédéric Chopin: Profiles of the man and the musician
Franz Liszt: The Man and his Music

ROBERT SCHUMANN
an oil portrait by Jaeger

ROBERT SCHUMANN

THE MAN AND HIS MUSIC
EDITED BY
ALAN WALKER

FRANK COOPER   JOHN GARDNER
LOUIS HALSEY   ALFRED NIEMAN
LEON PLANTINGA   BRIAN SCHLOTEL
ERIC SAMS   HENRY PLEASANTS
ELIOT SLATER   YONTY SOLOMON
BÁLINT VÁZSONYI   JOSEPH WEINGARTEN
ALAN WALKER

BARNES & NOBLE
BOOKS
10 East 53d St., New York 10022
(a division of Harper & Row Publishers, Inc.)

First published in Great Britain 1972 by Barrie & Jenkins Ltd

Published in the U.S.A. 1974 by
HARPER & ROW PUBLISHERS, INC
BARNES & NOBLE IMPORT DIVISION

© 1972 by Barrie & Jenkins Ltd

ISBN 06 497367 0

Corrigenda

p.2, line 1: *for* 'Ludwig' *read* 'Johann'.

p.4, footnote 3: *for* 'Fleschig' *read* 'Flechsig'.

p.89, line 3: *for* 'Kinderscenen' *read* 'Album für die Jugend'.

p.98, line 8: add '(Ex. 9)'.

p.223, line 24: *for* 'Ex. 30 (a)' *read* 'Ex. 31'.

p.258, footnote 1: *for* 'November' *read* 'August'.

p.259, line 5: add '(Ex. 36)'.

p.259, line 7: add '(Ex. 37)'.

p.317, *for* 'Ex. 45b' *read* '54b'.

p.483, line 23: *add* 324-31.

Printed in Great Britain

Contents

Illustrations

Music examples drawn by
Paul Courtenay

Acknowledgments

I should like to express my thanks

to Dr Martin Schoppe, Director of the Schumann-Haus in Zwickau, for providing photostats and for advice on the Complete Catalogue of Schumann's works;

to Mr Eric Sams, for his unflagging musicological assistance in matters ranging far beyond his own essays;

to Professor Leon Plantinga and Mr Henry Pleasants for their translations of Schumann's prose-writings quoted on pp. 191–99;

to Miss Carol Williams, Miss Jane Kendal and Miss Jane Parks, for their secretarial help;

to Universal Edition (London) Ltd, for permission to quote extracts from Mahler's re-orchestrations of Schumann's symphonies;

to the Royal Musical Association, for permission to re-publish from its Proceedings (Vol. 96) 'The Tonal Analogue in Schumann's Music', by Eric Sams;

to the BBC Music Library and the Radio Times Hulton Picture Library, for the loan of essential materials;

to Mrs Iris French who checked the final proofs.

A. W.

Key to the Abbreviations

The following references, which include some of the basic sources in the Schumann literature, are so frequently referred to that they are usually abbreviated, thus:

GSK = *Gesammelte Schriften über Musik und Musiker* ed. F. Gustav Jansen, Leipzig, 1891; (5th ed. Kreisig, Leipzig, 1914)

NZfM = *Neue Zeitschrift für Musik*

Jugendbriefe = *Jugendbriefe von Robert Schumann*, ed. Clara Schumann, Leipzig, 1885

Jansen = *Briefe: neue Folge* ed. F. Gustav Jansen, Leipzig, 1886

Niecks = *Robert Schumann: a supplementary and corrective biography*, Frederick Niecks, London, 1925

Litzmann = *Clara Schumann: Ein Künstlerleben* (3 vols.), by Berthold Litzmann, Leipzig, 1902–8

Bœtticher = *Robert Schumann: Einführung in Persönlicheit und Werk*, by Wolfgang Bœtticher, Berlin, 1941

Other references are indicated in full.

An asterisk after a name in the text indicates 'see Register of Persons'.

A. W.

Notes on Contributors

(1) FRANK COOPER, pianist and harpsichordist. Professor of Piano at Butler University, Indianapolis. Specialized interests in the music of the nineteenth century. Founder and organizer of the annual Romantic Revival Festival of Music, Butler University.

(2) JOHN GARDNER, composer, conductor, pianist, lecturer and writer on music. Professor of Composition at the Royal Academy of Music, London, and Director of Music at St Paul's Girls' School, Hammersmith. Principal works include an opera *The Moon and Sixpence*, a Symphony, a Piano Concerto and five full-scale Cantatas. Commissioned to write an opera *The Visitors* for the Aldeburgh Festival, 1972.

(3) LOUIS HALSEY, founder and conductor of the Louis Halsey Singers and the Thames Chamber Choir; artistic director of the Thames Concerts Society. Radio producer in the Music Division of the BBC. Specially interested in the music of the Renaissance, Baroque and contemporary periods; has commissioned and performed many new compositions. Other activities include commercial recordings, writing, lecturing, editing and adjudicating.

(4) ALFRED NIEMAN, composer, pianist and lecturer on music. Professor of Composition and Piano at the Guildhall School of Music, London. Works include piano sonatas, chamber music and song-cycles.

(5) LEON PLANTINGA, an Associate Professor of history of music at Yale University. Author of *Schumann as Critic* (1967), and various articles and reviews concerning the music of the eighteenth and nineteenth centuries. During 1971–72 Guggenheim Fellow and Visiting Fellow at University College, Oxford; currently researching into the music of Muzio Clementi.

(6) HENRY PLEASANTS is the American translator of both Schumann (*The Musical World of Robert Schumann*) and Eduard Hanslick (*Music Criticisms 1846–99*). Original books include *The Agony of Modern Music, Death of a Music?, The Great Singers,* and *Serious Music—And All That Jazz!*. London music critic of the International Herald Tribune and London Editor of Stereo Review.

(7) ERIC SAMS, writer and broadcaster on music; read German and French at Cambridge; specializes in the relation of music to language in the *Lied, mélodie*, etc., and in the other works of their composers and poets. Author of *The Songs of Hugo Wolf* (1961) *The Songs of Robert Schumann* (1969), and *Brahms Songs* (1972).

ix

(8) BRIAN SCHLOTEL is a Senior Lecturer in English at Gipsy Hill College of Education, Kingston-upon-Thames, and has a special interest in music education. Educated at Oxford University. Awarded a Fulbright Scholarship and visited USA 1958–59 as lecturer, composer and conductor. Has published compositions in USA. Contributor to musical journals.

(9) ELIOT SLATER is the Editor of the *British Journal of Psychiatry*, and previously Senior Lecturer in the Institute of Psychiatry, University of London. He is the author of books and papers on clinical psychiatry and psychopathy; and he is a Vice-President of the Société internationale de Psychopathologie de l'Expression.

(10) YONTY SOLOMON, South-African born pianist. Graduated from University of Cape Town in music and psychology. Later studied with Dame Myra Hess in London. Recent public performances include Bach's complete 48 Preludes and Fugues, and the complete piano music of Ravel and Debussy. Has a special interest in contemporary music. His chief relaxations are collecting antique glass and growing camellias.

(11) BÁLINT VÁZSONYI, Hungarian-born pianist. His studies were completed mainly at the Franz Liszt Academy of Music, Budapest, where he was admitted at the age of ten. From 1956 he studied with Dohnányi, whose last pupil he was. Later embarked on a concert career which, since 1960, has included most European countries, North America and Africa, and a good deal of commercial recording. Author of a book on Dohnányi, the first definitive biography of this composer.

(12) ALAN WALKER, author of *A Study in Musical Analysis* (1962), and *An Anatomy of Musical Criticism* (1967). Editor of symposia on Chopin (1966) and Liszt (1970). Contributor to Encyclopaedia Britannica. Formerly a producer in the Music Division of the BBC. Since 1971, Professor and Chairman of the Music Department, McMaster University, Canada.

(13) JOSEPH WEINGARTEN, pianist, now a British subject, was born in Hungary, where he studied at the Franz Liszt Academy of Music, Budapest, under Kodály, Dohnányi and Leo Weiner, winning prizes for his interpretations of the music of Liszt, Schumann and Chopin. Professor of Piano at Trinity College of Music, London, and at the Birmingham School of Music. Also a member of the Budapest Trio.

Preface

The case for another major study on Schumann needs no stressing. In recent years, much new information has come to light which radically affects our understanding of both the man and his music. To give a few striking examples. It is still possible to read that Schumann was pursued for half a lifetime and finally killed by a mental disease, most likely schizophrenia, although the evidence for this diagnosis was always scanty. Medical opinion today is firmly of the view that Schumann contracted syphilis; it is now up to his biographers to draw whatever conclusions they can. As for Schumann's music, few things have caused more confusion than the rumour that his metronome was faulty, although the evidence for this belief never even existed. While it persisted, however, it made a performing tradition of his music peculiarly awkward to establish; it is now the turn of Schumann's interpreters to draw whatever conclusions they can. Finally, we have known for a century or more of Schumann's special interest in symbols, codes, crosswords, chess and even acrostics. But the extent to which his most 'romantic', spontaneous-sounding music sprang from these sources, strict, exact, and logical, as they are, is only just beginning to dawn on us. Much detective-work remains to be done, and it promises a rich crop of discoveries.

Ten years ago, when I embarked on my Chopin symposium, I had little idea that it would prompt a similar book on Liszt, and that this, in turn, would lead to the present volume on Schumann. In retrospect, however, this progression appears inevitable. The three composers hang closely together; their lives and their music intertwine; and such is their community of spirit, that a study of any one of them is hardly adequate without a study of them all. Together they represent one of the glorious epochs of music. It is fitting, however, that this series of books (for such it has now become), should end with Schumann. He was the quintessential Romantic. After him, Romanticism had no future, only a past.

Looking through these symposia, I see that more than thirty musicians played their part—performers, composers, scholars and writers. To them I express my sincere thanks. In every case, literary collaboration has been a stimulating experience. And from time to time, it has even yielded me a permanent friend. Not many editors can say that.

ALAN WALKER

London, N.2
August 1972

ALAN WALKER

Schumann and his background

Early Years (1810–28)

ROBERT Alexander Schumann was born on 8 June 1810, at Zwickau in
Saxony. His father, August Schumann, was a bookseller and publisher.
He had settled in Zwickau two years earlier and had soon established a reputation
as a 'scholarly' publisher, bringing out pocket editions of the classics which were
much sought after in their day. Within a short time, the business was thriving
and August had become one of the most respected and influential citizens in
Zwickau. From him, Schumann acquired a life-long interest in literature.

Schumann's mother, née Johanna Schnabel, was the daughter of a municipal
surgeon at Zeitz. There is some evidence to suggest that her father thought the
marriage to August beneath her station, for at first he favoured a wealthier
suitor. The couple eventually married in 1795, and moved to Ronneburg, having
first given an undertaking to go into the grocery business to raise some capital.
The enterprise foundered, and August, risking everything on his interest in
publishing, opened his own bookshop in 1799. The move to Zwickau came in
1808; it was a larger town and possessed a grammar school which created a
demand for books. Altogether, there were five children of the marriage, four sons
and one daughter. Robert was the youngest.

By the time Robert had reached school age, the Schumanns were comfortably
off, and they could contemplate having him privately educated. Of all the great
composers, with the exception of Mendelssohn, Schumann probably started life
with the best material advantages. At first, he had a resident tutor. Later, when
he was six years old, he was placed in a private preparatory school run by Archdeacon Döhner. There, he made excellent progress and was eventually enrolled
as a student at the Zwickau Lyceum where he remained until he was eighteen.
Although the Lyceum specialized in the classics, it also gave students frequent

opportunity for music-making. On its staff was the local organist Ludwig Kuntzsch,★ who gave the young Schumann his first elementary piano lessons. It is doubtful whether Kuntzsch's instruction amounted to much more than correcting the boy's fingering and guiding him through the simpler works in the piano repertory. His chief importance to Robert was to help him release the powerful musical impulses gathering within him.

Soon, Schumann was participating in the school concerts, even playing such things as Moscheles's 'Alexander March' variations, a difficult piece requiring a good deal of agility. Passages like the following pose a challenge, and if the lad tackled them successfully we have to acknowledge that his later ambition to become a virtuoso pianist was not based on a mere whim, but on serious accomplishment.

EX I

Var. : 5   'Alexander March' Variations

Moscheles,★ in fact, was one of Robert's early models. In the summer of 1819 the boy had accompanied his father to Carlsbad where he had attended a recital given by the great virtuoso. The memory of that dazzling occasion never faded. Thirty-two years later, when he wrote to Moscheles to thank him for the dedication of the latter's Cello Sonata, op. 121, Schumann recalled the event: 'At that time I never dreamed that I should ever be honoured by so celebrated a master.'

Music apart, the other great passion of Schumann's youth was literature. In pursuit of his classical studies he devoured Homer, Cicero, Horace and Sophocles;

★ An asterisk after a name in the text indicates 'see Register of Persons'.

among German writers, Schiller and Goethe were his idols. At sixteen, he helped to run a German Literary Society among Lyceum students, asserting that 'it is the duty of every cultivated man to know the literature of his country'. He also tried his hand at poetry. Once, he made an abortive attempt to deliver one of his poems *The Death of Tasso* in public from memory. Halfway through, he forgot it and was left floundering in embarrassment on the stage. (Robert Schauffler suggests that this traumatic incident helps to explain Schumann's renowned taciturnity in later life.[1] Certainly, he had a horror of making public speeches, and he was frequently tongue-tied, even in private.) Another great influence was Jean Paul,[2] whose high-flown literary style made such inroads into Schumann's impressionable mind that he described Jean Paul's novel *Die Flegeljahre* as 'in its own way like the Bible'.[3] *Die Flegeljahre* exemplifies the Romantic literary theory of double personality. Its importance for Schumann scholars lies in the fact that its two characters 'Walt' and and 'Vult' represent the contrasting halves of Jean Paul's own personality, and they give us a vital glimpse into the origins of 'Florestan' and 'Eusebius', two of the 'Davidsbündler' who later peopled Schumann's imagination.[4]

In 1826, Robert's nineteen-year-old sister Emilie killed herself.[5] She was a favourite with August Schumann, who never recovered from the blow. A few weeks later, on 10 August, August himself died as well. Johanna Schumann was away at Carlsbad at the time, 'taking the cure', and the sixteen-year-old Robert had to bear the brunt of the tragedy. The event left a permanent scar on him; thereafter, he was totally incapable of facing the thought of death and funerals. (He could not bear to attend his mother's funeral when she died in 1836; yet the journey to Zwickau from Leipzig, where he then lived, took only two or three hours by post-chaise.) August left his family well provided for. A guardian had been appointed, one Gottlob Rudel, to protect Robert's future and to help

[1] Schauffler: *The Life and Work of Robert Schumann*, New York, 1945, p. 18.

[2] German Romantic writer. His real name was Johann Paul Richter. See 'Register of Persons', p. 435.

[3] Letter to Clara, March 1838.

[4] Eric Sams traces these origins in his essay 'Schumann and the Tonal Analogue'. See p. 390.

[5] By drowning, during an attack of typhus fever. The wretched girl had also contracted a skin disease, the psychological effects of which were so unpleasant that they induced a condition of melancholia. This, the 'official' account, comes to us from Jansen (*Die Davidsbündler*) and it has been followed by Schumann's biographers ever since. However, in C. E. Richter's little-known biography of August Schumann we are told that Emilie died in 1825—that is, a year earlier. Moreover, Eugenie Schumann, the composer's daughter, quotes from an undated letter by Johanna which says: 'I have just spent twelve sleepless nights with much sorrowful weeping in the room where my dear Emilie passed away' (*Robert Schumann: Ein Lebensbild meines Vaters*, 1931, p. 60). This implies that Emilie's death was not by drowning. Whichever version of her death is assumed, there seems to be little justification for thinking that Emilie was insane. Schumann's biographers will have to look elsewhere in their search for hereditary insanity within the composer's immediate family circle.

administer the lad's share of the estate.[1] It was Johanna who, with Rudel's connivance, insisted that Robert pursue a legal career. She referred to music as 'the breadless art'. August Schumann would have disagreed with her. He had always supported Robert's artistic ambitions; at one point, he had even corresponded with Weber about the possibility of his taking Robert as a pupil.

It is instructive to observe the mature way in which Robert handled the situation. There was no attempt at argument; he knew his elders too well for that. Instead, he shrewdly agreed to enrol as a law-student at Leipzig University. Once at Leipzig he could argue from a safe distance. As Niecks points out, he had not the slightest intention of pursuing law.[2] Nothing is more symptomatic of Schumann's strength of character than the manner in which he skilfully cajoles, coaxes, castigates, persuades, and finally converts Johanna to a change of heart.

Leipzig and Heidelberg (1828–30)

Schumann graduated from the Zwickau Lyceum in March 1828. He wrote:

> School is now behind my back and the world lies ahead. As I went out of school for the last time, I could scarcely suppress my tears; but the joy was still greater than the pain. Now the true inner man must come forward and show who he is.[3]

He arrived in Leipzig on 24 March, and at once enrolled as a law-student at the university. Since Leipzig's academic term did not begin until May, Schumann now seized the chance to travel. He made friends with one Gisbert Rosen,* a young law-student who was on the point of emigrating to Heidelberg, and together they went off on a tour of Bavaria, visiting Bayreuth, Nuremberg, Augsburg, and Munich. The trip was not without incident. At Munich, he called on Heine, whose irony and wit were already the talk of Europe. The great poet received him coolly, little guessing that his own name would soon be linked with that of his young visitor on the highest level of artistic creation. Another treasured encounter was with the widow of Jean Paul in Bayreuth, who gave him a portrait of the master which he packed carefully and sent home to Zwickau. The most important event of all, however, was his first meeting in Leipzig with

[1] Robert inherited 8,000 thalers, a tidy sum then. Today (1971) it would be worth about £11,200 (figure provided by the Coin Department of the British Museum, London). See also footnote 4, p. 17.

[2] Niecks, p. 50.

[3] Letter to his school friend Emil Fleschig, on 17 March 1828. *Jugendbriefe*, p. 13.

Friedrich Wieck* and his daughter Clara, then an infant prodigy of nine, whom he heard play the piano part in a Hummel trio 'amazingly well'.[1] The occasion was charged with consequences for all three people; they had no notion of how closely their lives would shortly intertwine. Wieck and Robert discussed the possibility of a few lessons, and laid the foundations for a teacher–pupil relationship which was to persist for several years. Of Clara herself, Schumann's only comment was that her nose was too long and her eyes too large for her face.

Back from his tour, Schumann attempted to settle down to his law books in Leipzig. He quickly grew bored. His thoughts were with Rosen, who, now settled in Heidelberg, kept sending back glowing accounts of university life there. Schumann resolved to join him. But what to tell his mother? He soon thought of a suitable excuse. Thibaut,* one of the greatest experts on jurisprudence, taught law at Heidelberg. He was the author of a *System der Pandektenrechts*, a codification of Roman law as it was practised in Germany, and a man of considerable influence in political circles. He was also a keen amateur musician, and Schumann knew his book on musical aesthetics. A quick visit was made to Zwickau in order to thrash out the matter with Rudel, his guardian, who agreed to sanction the new arrangement, and Robert set out for Heidelberg in May.

Typically, he combined the journey with a holiday, and made his leisurely way down the Rhine, travelling by post-chaise. Among his travelling-companions was Willibald Alexis,[2] one of the best-selling novelists of his time; he took a liking to Robert, and the pair did much of their sightseeing together, visiting Goethe's birthplace in Frankfurt and also calling on Ferdinand Ries, Beethoven's former pupil. Ries had an English wife who captivated Robert: 'When she spoke English it was like the lisping of an angel.'[3] His elated mood was reflected in an elaborate practical joke he played while at Frankfurt. Feeling the need to do some piano practice, he walked into a dealer's showroom claiming to be the representative of an English aristocrat who wished to purchase a grand piano. He was shown to an excellent instrument, and practised solidly on it for three hours, finally telling the proprietor he would return in two days with his lordship's decision. 'By that time, however, I was already in Rüdesheim,

---

[1] According to Niecks (p. 55) the meeting probably took place at a musical party given by Dr Carus on 31 March 1828.

[2] His real name was Georg Wilhelm Häring. His early novels *Walladmor* (1823) and *Schloss Avalon* (1827) were actually written under the pseudonym 'Sir Walter Scott', an author whom Häring admired and whose style he emulated. Later on, he achieved fame on his own account with a series of Prussian historical novels.

[3] Schumann appears to have been attracted to Englishwomen. In a letter to his mother, written on 27 September 1830, he says: 'If ever I marry, it will be an Englishwoman.' *Jugend-briefe*, p. 124.

drinking Rüdesheimer.' Schumann finally arrived at Heidelberg on 21 May 1829, on foot, penniless.

Thibaut* was more impressive even than Schumann had imagined.

> What a difference there is between the Leipzig professor, who stood at his desk at lectures and rattled off his paragraphs without any sort of eloquence or inspiration, and this man Thibaut, who, although about twice as old as the other, is overflowing with life and spirits.[1]

Thibaut became a dominant influence in Schumann's life. Unforgettable hours were spent making music at his house.

> Thibaut is a splendid, divine man, my most enjoyable hours are spent with him. When he has a Handel oratorio sung at his home (every Thursday more than seventy singers present) and accompanies enthusiastically on the pianoforte, two big tears roll down from the fine, large eyes beneath the beautiful silver-white hair, and then he comes to me so delighted and serene, and presses my hand and is silent from sheer emotion. I often don't know how a poor beggar like myself has the honour to be admitted to listen in such a holy house. You can have no idea of his wit, acuteness, feeling, pure artistic sense, amiability, powerful eloquence, and wide outlook.[2]

At Heidelberg, Schumann indulged in what can only be described as 'high living'. He developed a taste for cigars and expensive champagne, and he did the full round of restaurants and taverns, running up large debts. In money matters generally, Schumann must be regarded as irresponsible; at Heidelberg he was a spendthrift, and he regularly exhausted his generous allowance. He became, in Niecks's phrase, a master in the art of writing begging letters, a virtuoso in all styles, and poor Rudel, his guardian, must often have been hard put to it to know how to deal with such demands as: 'How much you would oblige me, most honoured Herr Rudel, if you were to send me as soon as possible as much as possible!'[3]

On Easter Sunday, 1830, Schumann travelled from Heidelberg to Frankfurt to hear the great violinist Paganini.* The event proved a turning-point in his life and brought him to the brink of decision. Diplomatically, yet firmly, he now began to prepare his mother for his true intentions. He wrote to her, euphemistically at first, 'Jurisprudence alone sometimes touches my morning with a nipping

[1] Letter to his mother, 17 July 1829. *Jugendbriefe*, p. 62.
[2] Letter to his mother, 24 February 1830. *Jugendbriefe*, p. 105.
[3] 26 March 1830. Jansen, p. 24.

little hoar-frost,' and added, lest she failed to grasp the point, that in Thibaut's view Heaven never meant him for a lawyer. He also reminded her, for good measure, that his father had clearly perceived that he was destined either for art or for music. To his family he wrote: 'Surely you would all rather see me poor and happy in art than poor and unhappy in the law.' His whole case is presented in a letter written to his mother, dated 30 July 1830.[1] Schumann himself said that it was the most important letter he had ever written in his life.

Good morning, Mamma!

How shall I describe my bliss at this moment? The spirit lamp is hissing under the coffee pot, the sky is indescribably clear and rosy, and the keen spirit of the morning fills me with its presence. Besides, your letter lies before me and reveals a perfect treasury of good feeling, common sense and virtue. My cigar tastes uncommonly good; in short, the world is very lovely at times, if one could only always get up early.

There is plenty of blue sky and sunshine in my life at present, but my guide, Rosen, is wanting. Two more of my best friends, the v. H.'s, from Pomerania (two brothers), went off to Italy a week ago, and so I often feel very lonely, which sometimes makes me happy, sometimes miserable—it just depends. One can get on better without a sweetheart than without a friend; and sometimes I get into a regular fever when I think of myself. *My whole life* has been a twenty years' struggle between poetry and prose, or, if you like to call it so, Music and Law. There is just as high a standard to be reached in practical life as in art. In the former the ideal consists in the hope of plenty of work and a large extensive practice; but what sort of prospect would there be in Saxony for such a fellow as myself, who is not of noble birth, has neither money nor interest, and has no affection for legal squabbles and pettiness? At Leipzig I did not trouble my head about my career, but went dreaming and dawdling on and never did any real good. Here I have worked harder, but both there and here have been getting more and more attached to art. Now I am standing at the crossroads and am scared at the question which way to choose. My genius points towards art, which is, I am inclined to think, the right path. But the fact is—now, do not be angry at what I am going to say, for I will but gently whisper it—it always seems to me as if you were putting obstacles in my way. You had very good reasons for doing so, and I understood them all perfectly, and we both agreed on calling art an 'uncertain future and a doubtful way of earning one's bread.' There certainly can be no greater misery than to look

[1] *Jugendbriefe*, p. 116.

forward to a hopeless, shallow, miserable existence which one has prepared for oneself. But neither is it easy to enter upon a career diametrically opposed to one's whole education, and to do it requires patience, confidence and quick decision. I am still at the height of youth and imagination, with plenty of capabilities for cultivating and ennobling art, and have come to the conclusion that with patience and perseverance, and a good master, I should in six years be as good as any pianist, for pianoforte playing is mere mechanism and execution. Occasionally I have much imagination and possibly some creative power. . . . Now comes the question: 'To be, or not to be,' for you can only do *one* thing well in this life, and I am always saying to myself: 'Make up your mind to do one thing thoroughly well, and with patience, and perseverance you are bound to accomplish something.' This battle against myself is now raging more fiercely than ever, my good mother. Sometimes I am daring and confident in my own strength and power, but sometimes I tremble to think of the long way I have traversed and of the endless road which lies before me. As to Thibaut, he has long ago recommended me to take up art. I should be very glad if you would write to him, and he would be very pleased too, but unfortunately he went off to Rome some time ago, so probably I shall never speak to him again.

If I stick to law I must undoubtedly stay here another winter to hear Thibaut lecture on the Pandects, as every law student is bound to do. If I am to go in for music, I must leave this at once and go to Leipzig, where Wieck, whom I could thoroughly trust, and who can tell me what I am worth, would then carry on my education. Afterwards I ought to go to Vienna for a year, and if possible study under Moscheles. Now I have a favour to ask you, my dear mother, which I hope you will grant me. *Write yourself to Wieck and ask him point blank what he thinks of me and my career.* Please let me have a SPEEDY answer, deciding the question, so that I can hurry on my departure from Heidelberg, although I shall be very sorry to leave it and my many kind friends and favourite haunts. *If you like you can enclose this letter to Wieck. In any case the question must be decided before Michaelmas*, and then I shall pursue my object in life, whatever it may be, with fresh vigour and without tears. You must admit that this is the most important letter I have ever written, so I trust you will not hesitate to comply with my request, for there is *no time* to be lost.

Goodbye, dear mother, and do not fret. In this case heaven will help us only if we help ourselves.

Ever your most loving son,
Robert Schumann

Johanna lost no time in acting on this document. She contacted Wieck immediately, asking for his advice and enclosing Robert's letter. Wieck replied at once, and agreed to accept Robert as a pupil, adding: 'I pledge myself to turn your son Robert, by means of his talent and imagination within three years into one of the greatest pianists now living.'[1] This letter finally convinced Johanna of the folly of continuing to oppose her son's wishes. As Wieck pointed out to her: 'Compulsion is of little use in such matters; we must do our part as parents: God does the rest.'

And so, after a three-year struggle, Robert joined that impressive band of musicians who have abandoned the law for music;[2] and he did so with Johanna's blessing. He left Heidelberg on 24 September, and journeyed to Leipzig to commence his serious music studies under Wieck. He was twenty years old.

Friedrich Wieck (1785–1873)

Before embarking on the next stage of Schumann's career, let us take stock of Friedrich Wieck, the man who had promised to turn him into 'one of the greatest pianists now living'. There have been many attempts to sketch in Wieck's character. He was autocratic, sharp-tongued, categorical, pugnacious even, and he had an obsession for debate which he indulged at the slightest provocation. When crossed, he could fly into a violent temper. He possessed firm convictions about everything, but particularly about piano-playing, a topic on which he had lavished much thought, and had now arrived at definite conclusions.

Wieck was born in 1785. As a youth, he had suffered great privation. Thanks largely to the charity of friends, he had been able to attend the University of Wittemburg, where he had studied theology. He was so poor as a student that he had no money for food, and in his half-starved condition he was obliged to rely upon the 'charity soup' handed out twice a week. These events left an indelible scar on his personality, and may have accounted for his pathological meanness over money matters in later life. In music, he was almost entirely self-taught. As he himself put it: 'Helpless and very poor, I had to rely solely on my self-education, and on the many chances of my destiny.' Finding himself

---

[1] Was this conceit on Wieck's part? In the occasional lessons he had given Robert during 1829, nothing whatsoever had emerged on which he could possibly base such an absurd promise. Wieck had a high opinion of himself, both as a man and as a pedagogue, and he was prone to boasting. He once told Dorn that if only Liszt had had a proper teacher he would have become the finest pianist in the world!

[2] Others have included Handel, Tchaikovsky, von Bülow, Sibelius and Stravinsky. One wonders what the musical profession might have been like without them—to say nothing of the legal profession with them.

unsuited to a theological career, he took a post as a private tutor in the household of an eccentric nobleman, which he held for several years. It was during this period that his interest in the piano was aroused. One of his fellow tutors was Adolf Bargiel, who later became a well-known piano professor in Berlin. The two men were close friends for a time, and Wieck, stimulated by Bargiel's example, became fascinated with the theory of piano teaching. He was twenty-eight when he finally set himself up as a piano pedagogue. His chief qualifications for this task were a keen analytical mind, an unshakeable faith in the rightness of his own views, and a profound belief that he had a special calling for this career. Later events proved these beliefs to be absolutely justified. He was an acute observer of pianists and pianos alike, and his skill as a teacher rested largely on his happy knack of bringing both into a closer and more harmonious relationship. At first, he followed Logier's system.[1] Later, he abandoned it on the grounds that it was 'artificial'. He worked out his own principles of teaching, remarkable for their breadth of outlook and freedom from pedantry. In a virtuoso age, which insisted on bigger tone and stronger muscles, Wieck stood for a 'singing touch' and a quiet manner at the keyboard. He maintained that in order to play the piano you must know something about the art of singing—a point of view which merits a lot of thought. Unlike his great contemporary Karl Czerny, he refused to teach from morning till night, and he restricted himself to a small handful of carefully chosen pupils, maintaining that each lesson required painstaking preparation—not only from the student, but also from the teacher. His approach to the keyboard is explained in his book *Clavier und Gesang* (1853).

In 1816, Wieck married a nineteen-year-old pupil called Marianne Tromlitz. She was a gifted pianist, who made several appearances at the Gewandhaus concerts in the 1820s. The marriage was a failure. After eight unhappy years, during which time Marianne bore Wieck five children, she deserted him, leaving Wieck to look after their young family as best he could. Clara, his gifted daughter, was the second child.[2] It is indicative of Wieck's unbending character that on the day he divorced Marianne he made the five-year-old Clara start a diary, filling in the first entry himself: 'Today my father divorced my mother.' He instilled into Clara the solid virtues of discipline, hard work, thrift and

---

[1] Johann Logier (1777–1846) invented the 'Chiroplast', a contraption which was supposed to aid the student towards a correct hand and arm posture. See 'Register of Persons', p. 433.

[2] The first died young, before Clara herself was born in 1819. The fifth child, Victor, a babe-in-arms at the time, was brought up by the mother. Wieck was therefore left with three young children: Clara, Alwin and Gustav. Shortly after her divorce from Wieck, and by an intriguing coincidence, Marianne married Adolf Bargiel, Wieck's former colleague (see above), and they settled down in Berlin. One of the children of her second marriage was Waldemar Bargiel (1828–97) who became a well-known composer. See Schumann's family tree (p. 418).

unflinching obedience. Under his tutelage, Clara quickly developed into a mag-
nificant pianist, and she made the name of Wieck known across Europe. When
the tours began, in 1831, Wieck made a great deal of money out of her. Yet it must
be said in his defence that he never once exploited the child. Indeed, he had a
low opinion of the uncultivated audiences she was sometimes exposed to, and he
did his utmost to protect her from their depraved artistic tastes. The stupid officials
he had to deal with were given short measure. Once, at the equivalent of a
'press conference', before Clara's Hamburg concerts, Wieck sarcastically noted
the 'seventeen questions which were asked him seven hundred times':

Q. When did your daughter begin?
A. Never.
Q. How old is your daughter *really*?
A. That is written under her portrait.
Q. Do not your daughter's fingers hurt her?
A. You forget that you are speaking of Clara Wieck.

and so on, leading to the absurd climax:

Q. Does your daughter like playing?
A. There is an end of everything—even of answers.[1]

Clearly, a difficult man.

Wieck regarded Clara as his special creation, the outward symbol of his status
as a teacher. When, fifteen years later, she changed her name to Schumann, it
was hurt professional pride more than anything else which poisoned his relationship with his daughter.

Wieck eventually remarried in 1828. His second wife was Clementine Fechner,
the twenty-four-year-old daughter of a clergyman. Presumably he at last found
domestic contentment, since the union lasted until his death in 1873, forty-five
years later. There were three children of this marriage, and, as Clementine
acquired three stepchildren at the same time as she acquired Wieck, this meant
that the Wieck household consisted of a large family of eight. They lived in a
spacious house in Grimmaische Gasse, No. 36, and it was here that Wieck did
all his teaching.

When Robert became his pupil, in October 1830, Wieck was a man of
forty-five. As a 'pupil-in-residence' Schumann saw Wieck almost daily. His immediate aim was to acquire a virtuoso technique. To this end, Wieck laid down a
rigorous course of study. We know virtually nothing of the way Wieck

[1] Litzmann, Vol. I, pp. 80–81.

conducted his lessons. Certainly, he did very little demonstrating, preferring to sit by his pupils, observing, analysing, explaining. He was not a particularly good pianist. But according to A. von Meichsner,[1] he would sometimes accompany his pupils 'as one who had feeling in every finger-tip'.

In pursuing his technical studies, Schumann had continually before him the shining example of Clara Wieck. This eleven-year-old child, with her immaculate technique, must often have given him pause for thought. She was nine years younger than himself, but she already had a wonderful command of the keyboard. Schumann must have envied such fluency; Clara accomplished with ease what he himself still had to struggle over. Perhaps it was at this time that he began to reflect on the possibility of a technical 'short-cut'. Such thoughts were in the air in the 1830s. A whole crop of 'technical aids' appeared, designed to advance the player's technique and thus allow him to by-pass the years of physical drudgery otherwise stretching before him. Wieck, as we have seen, frowned on such methods. But Wieck was not always there; sometimes he took Clara away on tour. Thus, there were periods when Robert was left to work at the piano by himself. It was during one such occasion that a mysterious tragedy overtook Schumann and put an end to his career as a virtuoso.

The crippled hand

The traditional explanation of what happened is well known. In a foolhardy attempt to 'equalize' his fingers, Schumann is supposed to have invented a mechanical contrivance—a kind of sling, designed to keep one finger out of the way while the others were being exercised—the results of which were disastrous. The tendons of his fourth and fifth fingers of his right hand were permanently injured and his pianistic career came to an untimely end. But is the traditional explanation true? Nowhere does Schumann himself specify his injury in this kind of detail. His *Biographische Notizen* simply contains the laconic entry: 'Overdone technical studies. Laming of my right hand.'[2] Thereafter, Schumann's correspondence refers to his damaged hand only in the vaguest terms. The chief source of the 'official' story is Wieck's *Clavier und Gesang* (1853), which merely states that the 'sling' was invented 'by a famous pupil of mine, contrary to my wish and used behind my back to the righteous outrage of his third and fourth fingers'. Wieck does not mention Schumann by name. And when Niecks interviewed Clara Schumann on the topic in 1889, she stated

[1] *Friedrich Wieck and his two daughters*, Leipzig, 1875.
[2] 1831. See Bœtticher, p. 224. Schumann actually writes as early as 1830: 'weakness in my right hand' (Musikalischer Lebensgang).

emphatically that the injury was to Robert's right *index* finger, and that it was caused by practising on a stiff dumb keyboard.[1] Clearly, the evidence is contradictory. So what did cause Schumann's hand injury?

In a fascinating essay,[2] Eric Sams has claimed that Schumann's 'accident' never occurred, at least not in the form generally reported. Mr Sams suggests, instead, that in the course of undertaking a cure for syphilis (Schumann's terminal disease; see pp. 35 and 167), Schumann may have suffered irreversible motor-damage through the absorption of mercury—a substance widely prescribed for syphilis in the nineteenth century. This theory lies well within the bounds of medical possibility (see p. 413), and it has the merit of economy: that is, Schumann's hand injury becomes only one among the various symptoms produced by Schumann (including numbness, speech-difficulty, tinnitus—a ringing in the ears) all of which fit the clinical picture of syphilis. While this explanation must remain circumstantial, it has at least as much to support it as the traditional one which relies largely on hearsay.

Wieck was appalled by the injury. Perhaps he feared for his reputation as a teacher and wished to guard himself against rumours that he 'forced' his pupils. By publicly condemning the finger 'sling' in *Clavier und Gesang* (1853) he made his position clear to the entire world. His significant omission of Schumann's name from this context can mean only one thing: Wieck lacked a reason for including it. To accuse Schumann directly of using a 'mechanical aid', he would have been obliged to rig the evidence. Later commentators have not been so cautious. As for Schumann, the full extent of the tragedy took some time to sink in. A variety of dubious 'cures' was prescribed by his doctors, who urged him to take animal baths (which involved immersing his hand in the secretions of cattle, a procedure Schumann found distasteful since he feared that something of the nature of cattle might pass into his personality) and to sleep at night with his arm in a herbal bandage. 'The cure is not the most charming,'[3] he wrote in a masterpiece of understatement.

As the summer progressed, his anxiety grew. He travelled to Schneeberg for a course of electrical treatment from one Dr Otto. It only made matters worse. By November 1832 he had lost hope.

> As to the hand, the doctor keeps reassuring me; I for my part am completely resigned, and regard it as beyond recovery.[4]

[1] Niecks, p. 102. In 1841–42, Schumann was granted exemption from military conscription on the grounds of his hand injury. He enclosed a medical certificate with his application (from a Dr Reuter) which reveals that both the index *and* the middle finger of the right hand were affected. (Hans-Joachim Rothe: *Arbeitsberichte zur Geschichte der Stadt Leipzig, No. 13 1967.*) See Leon Plantinga (p. 167) for more information on this point.

[2] 'Schumann's hand injury', *Musical Times*, December 1971.

[3] Letter to his mother, Leipzig, 9 August 1832.   [4] Jugendbriefe, p. 194.

For a year, he continued to follow medical advice, but became increasingly frustrated with the results. By June 1833 his situation looked so bleak he started to joke about it, and referred to himself, with grim humour, as 'my nine-fingered self'. His wit was a sure symptom that he had assimilated his misfortune. Moreover, the direction in which his destiny was propelling him was no longer in doubt. Is it fanciful to propose a causal connection between Schumann's hand injury, whatever its origin, and those works he composed soon afterwards? It can hardly be coincidence that one of his first creative reactions to his damaged hand was to embark upon his brilliant 'Paganini' Studies, Op. 3 (1832). They exploit the kind of virtuoso technique which Schumann could now no longer hope to possess. Especially striking is the dazzling *Toccata*, Op. 7 (1830; rev. 1833).

EX 2

It is obsessed with the technical problem of perfect independence between *the fingers of the right hand.* How strange that his hand injury should reveal itself to the world in this way!

*

One of Wieck's pupils-in-residence was an attractive eighteen-year-old girl called Ernestine von Fricken.* Ernestine was the illegitimate daughter of Baron von Fricken and Countess Zedtwitz. She was a talented pianist, and she lived in the Wieck household from June 1834 to about January 1835. Schumann became infatuated with her; before the year was out the couple were engaged. We shall never know the full story behind the brief entanglement. Within weeks the engagement was broken off by mutual consent. It seems that Ernestine may have been less than frank with Schumann about her illegitimacy, and when he discovered the complications in her family background he was hurt by her silence. Several years later, the affair was dragged up by Wieck (who, of course, observed the pair at first hand) in his desperate efforts to blacken Schumann's name and prove his unsuitability as a husband for Clara.

The year 1834 was notable for a quite different event, this time of major significance. Schumann had long been dissatisfied with the low standard of musical criticism in Germany. As early as 1833 he had discussed with friends and musical acquaintances the possibility of establishing a new magazine which would raise the level of criticism and become a mouthpiece for the rising generation of young Romantic musicians in Germany. The *Neue Zeitschrift für Musik* was founded in 1834. At first, Schumann was assisted in the project by Wieck, Schunke* and Julius Knorr* (who was nominated its first editor-in-chief). Within a few months, however, Schunke was dead, Knorr was ill, and Wieck had lost interest. So Schumann took over the entire project himself. The first issue appeared on 3 April 1834. Under Schumann's guidance the journal became the most influential musical publication of its time, with a wide circulation throughout Germany. Such was its success that for many years Schumann was far better known to the outside world as a critic than as a composer.[1]

Robert and Clara (1832–40)

When Schumann took up residence at Wieck's house in 1832, he was twenty-two years old. Clara was thirteen. Despite the nine-year difference in their ages, there sprang up between them a bond of mutual affection. This was hardly surprising; Schumann, who was treated like one of the family, saw Clara almost daily. At first, Robert assumed the role of an elder brother; there were long rambles together in the countryside, hilarious games of blind-man's-buff with her young brother Alwin, and ghost stories told by Schumann with such relish (he was a wonderful mimic) that the children shrieked with fright. Soon there were signs of deeper feelings stirring within them. Then came Ernestine von Fricken. Clara could compete with the older girl neither physically nor intellectually. Throughout the summer and autumn of 1834, while Schumann's affair with Ernestine progressed towards its unhappy close, Clara (as she later confessed in her letters) felt cut off from Robert's affections. It came as a relief to her when Ernestine retired from the scene for good. By November 1835 Clara and Robert had declared their love for one another.

Wieck was not blind to what was going on. Clara was developing into a striking young woman, mature above her years. Robert was now her constant companion. Infatuation was one thing; a love-affair was quite another. Wieck thought it wise to take suitable precautions. In January 1836 he removed Clara

---

[1] The origins of the *Zeitschrift* are dealt with by Leon Plantinga (p. 162).

from Leipzig to Dresden, thinking to break her association with Robert. This was an extreme step, and Wieck doubtless congratulated himself on its effectiveness. But he reckoned without Schumann. While Wieck was unexpectedly called away from Leipzig on business, Robert seized the opportunity to travel to Dresden (about fifty miles away) and visit Clara. On his return, Wieck was informed of the fact, and broke into a torrent of abuse against the luckless pair. He thoroughly frightened Clara by threatening to shoot Schumann if he ventured near the girl again. Then he forbade Schumann to enter his household. Clara was brought back to Leipzig, under strict surveillance. Her mail was opened; she was not allowed out alone; even her bedroom door had to remain unlocked. Small wonder that Schumann, faced with such stringent behaviour, nicknamed Wieck *Rappelkopf*—'crackpot'.

If we wish to understand Wieck's attitude towards Robert, we must first understand his attitude towards Clara. Clara was more than a daughter: she was Wieck's special creation, his life's work. (Even before her birth, Wieck had determined that she should become a great pianist. Her very name 'Clara' was chosen to presage her brilliance in the firmament of music.) For years, he had toiled over her at the piano. Eventually, she had become his star pupil, the finest exponent of his method. Equally important, she had become a valuable commodity, much sought-after. She boosted Wieck's bank balance at the same time as she boosted his ego, and Wieck found the combination highly agreeable to him. Wieck, in short, was professionally involved. His uncompromising character did the rest.

Robert had no notion of the protracted struggle which lay ahead of him. For one thing, he was constitutionally incapable of understanding Wieck's complex make-up. For another, he made the elementary blunder of supposing that it was he, Schumann, to whom Wieck was personally opposed. Nothing could be further from the truth. Wieck would have opposed anyone who threatened his special relationship with Clara. And he would have fought back with exactly the same weapons—invective, deceit, libel, even violence—which he eventually brought to bear against Schumann.

The first hint of the granite-like character Schumann was up against came in September 1837. Schumann gambled everything on a letter to Wieck in which he declared his love for Clara, and requested an interview: 'You owe it to my position, my talent, and my character.'[1] The letter was tactfully delivered to the old man on 13 September, Clara's eighteenth birthday. A few days later, Robert was ushered into the presence. He had not set foot in the Wieck household for

[1] Litzmann, Vol. I, p. 24.

over a year. There was a scene. Wieck was quite implacable. Robert later wrote to Clara:

> My interview with your father was terrible. He was frigid, hostile, confused and contradictory at once. Truly his method of stabbing is original, for he drives in the hilt as well as the blade.[1]

Wieck's chief objection was that Clara was to be a concert pianist, not a Hausfrau. He poured scorn on the idea of 'Clara with the perambulator'.

Now began the long and sordid quarrel between Wieck and Schumann which lasted for three years and culminated in a lawsuit.[2]

Wieck's case rested on the flimsiest grounds. He maintained that Schumann could not afford to marry, and he complained of his 'drinking habits'. Schumann had little difficulty in disposing of both charges. He produced figures to show that his annual income was well above average,[3] and he found witnesses to testify to his sobriety.[4] Far more difficult was to deal with the slanderous gossip Wieck spread through his network of friends and associates in and around Leipzig; it was calculated to do Schumann the maximum harm, and to discredit him in the eyes of the world. Wieck did not hesitate to dredge up the Ernestine Fricken affair, and he tried, in vain, to enlist her help in blackening Schumann's character. He even stooped to encouraging one Karl Banck, a friend of the family, and Clara's singing-teacher, to flirt with Clara, rightly calculating that when Schumann heard about it he would be upset. Since the two lovers had no way of meeting, it was impossible for either one of them to reveal Wieck's mendacity to the other. For a lot of the time Clara was on tour with Wieck; her only means of communication with Schumann was a clandestine correspondence which was in

---

[1] 18 September 1837. Litzmann, Vol. I, p. 126.

[2] That Wieck regarded Clara as an extension of his own artistic personality, and that his 'case' was really a huge rationalization of this peculiar *professional* attachment to his daughter, is very well illustrated by the notorious 'Lehmann' letter. In January 1840, when it looked as if Wieck was about to lose the legal fight for possession of Clara, he forged a letter containing all kinds of accusations against Schumann, which he signed 'Lehmann'. Wieck then arranged for this squalid document to be delivered to Clara on the day of her great Berlin recital, hoping so to undermine her confidence that the result would be an artistic disaster. By this means he thought to teach her a sharp lesson and bring her to the realization that her father's benevolent support was an indispensable factor in her artistic success. Fortunately, Clara's young brother Alwin discovered the plot and alerted Schumann who, in turn, warned Clara of the letter's impending arrival (Litzmann, Vol. I, p. 386). Such acts of callous behaviour are inexplicable, until we see them as attempts to hang on, at all costs, to his *musical* status as Clara's teacher and benefactor, with all the renown this brought him.

[3] The figures are set out in a letter to Clara (Litzmann, Vol. I, p. 225). They show that Schumann was very well off. Between them, the pair were able to muster a working capital of more than 14,000 thalers, worth more than £2,916 in 1838. (The thaler then equalled 4s. 2d.). By today's (1971) values, this is the equivalent of £19,600, a very large sum of money. (Figures provided by the Coin Department, British Museum, London.)

[4] Including Mendelssohn, Ferdinand David and Count Reuss. Litzmann, Vol. I, pp. 386–7.

constant danger of interception by Wieck himself. It soon became apparent to Schumann that in view of Wieck's implacable attitude they would have to go over his head and apply to the law courts for permission to marry. Clara found herself torn between her lover and her father, whom she still deeply respected. It was not until September 1839 that Schumann finally persuaded her to sign the affidavit. She later wrote: 'The instant when I signed was the most important of my whole life. I set my name down with firm resolution, and was boundlessly happy.'

Wieck's reaction was one of frenzied rage; he refused to have her in the house and she went to live temporarily in Berlin with her mother. By his extreme behaviour, Wieck turned himself into a laughing stock. He wrote to dealers advising them not to let Clara play their pianos, else the action might be damaged. He tried to drive away her audiences; he spread reports of her 'shameless' behaviour and described her as 'a miserable, demoralized girl'. And all this from a man who, as Schauffler points out, once wrote in Clara's diary this pious utterance: 'Let your highest goal be the forming of your charge into a good person!' Whenever he met Schumann in the street, he spat in his face. He finally drew up an impossible document setting out five basic conditions under which he would consent to the marriage:

1. The couple must not live in Saxony.
2. The 7,000 thalers so far earned by Clara would be withheld, only $4\frac{1}{2}\%$ of the capital being paid to her.
3. Schumann's statement of income must be guaranteed by the courts.
4. Schumann must not communicate with Wieck until Wieck gave permission.
5. Clara would lose all rights to claim any inheritance from Wieck.[1]

The terms were totally unrealistic. In an attempt at conciliation, the couple sent Einert, a Leipzig lawyer, to present their case in person. The uncontrollable Wieck screamed that he would enforce his will, 'though it meant the destruction of thirty people'—a remark worthy of Caligula. 'What a man!' was Schumann's comment. There was a second attempt at conciliation in December 1839. The parties met in court, and Wieck became so abusive he had to be silenced by the judge. He appears to have had no legal representation, and was thus a perfect example of the old adage that a client who conducts his own defence has a fool for a lawyer. The judge evidently agreed; he threw out Wieck's case, but gave leave of appeal. Matters dragged on until the following August, when the courts,

[1] Litzmann, Vol. I, p. 373-4.

having received no further word from Wieck, gave judgment in favour of Robert and Clara. The wedding banns were published on 16 August, and the wedding ceremony itself took place on 12 September, a day Robert may well have chosen in order to spite Wieck.[1]

★

In the popular imagination, Robert and Clara are frequently depicted as an ideal couple, each one serving as a perfect complement to the other. Yet it is not true that theirs was a relationship without stress. Not even a cursory glance at the evidence will support such a view. There was not only the inevitable tension between them, caused by the ordinary pressures of domestic routine; frequently, there was a serious clash of artistic interests as well, which caused damaged feelings on both sides. Clara's piano-playing was the first casualty. After only five months of marriage, we find her complaining to her Diary: 'My playing is getting all behindhand, as is always the case when Robert is composing. I cannot find one little hour in the day to myself! If only I did not get so behind!'[2] Schumann was well aware of the difficulty, and felt guilty about it. 'I am often

[1] The next day, 13 September, was Clara's twenty-first birthday, after which she would have been free of Wieck's control. 12 September, then, was the last possible day on which Wieck could be legally defied—a parting shot from Robert.

It may be of interest to pursue here, briefly, the relationship between Clara and her father *after* her marriage to Robert, since Wieck traditionally disappears from the story at this point. In reality, of course, he remained very much a part of their lives. The Schumanns set up house in Leipzig, at No. 5 Inselstrasse (in defiance of Wieck's first condition, see p. 18) and they would hardly have been able to avoid all contact with him. Furthermore, in 1840 Robert began a libel action against Wieck for slander, and although this was settled in Schumann's favour, the case dragged on for a year or more (Litzmann, Vol. I, p. 307). Meanwhile, Schumann's genius blossomed and his reputation grew. It was gradually borne in on Wieck that he had seriously under-estimated his son-in-law. Clara then presented him with grandchildren, and he naturally became curious about them. In December 1843 there was a reconciliation, and we shall do Wieck no injustice if, as Litzmann says, we put it down to a return to commonsense on his part. Wieck put out the first feelers, and wrote the following letter to Schumann:

Dear Schumann,
　　Tempora mutantur et nos mutamur in eis.
　　In the face of Clara and of the world we can no longer keep apart from one another. You are moreover the father of a family—what need is there for a lengthy explanation?
　　We were always united where art was concerned—I was even your teacher—my verdict decided your present course in life for you. There is no need for me to assure you of my sympathy with your talent and with your fine and genuine aspirations.
　　In Dresden there joyfully awaits you
Your father
Fr. Wieck

The two families spent Christmas 1843 in Wieck's house in Dresden—where he had recently moved—although the old intimacy, needless to say, was vanished for ever.

[2] January 1841 (Litzmann, Vol. II, p. 15).

sorry that I so frequently hinder Clara in her study, because she will not disturb
me when I am composing.' Worse was to follow, however. In 1841, the couple
went on tour. At Oldenburg an invitation to visit court arrived for Clara alone.
Robert felt the insult deeply; the implication was obvious: Clara was well
known but who was her husband? The incident so marred the tour that
Schumann returned to Leipzig while Clara went on to Copenhagen by herself.[1]
Again, during the Russian tour of 1844, Robert's subordinate position was continually painful to him. While Clara was enjoying a huge popular success at her
concerts, Robert, trailing behind, was introduced to everybody as 'the pianist's
husband'.[2] It is to the everlasting credit of both of them that they were able to
rise above such stresses. Schumann himself saw their peculiar situation with
absolute clarity, and expressed it thus:

> Well, so must it be when artists marry; one cannot have everything; and
> after all the chief thing is the happiness which remains over and above, and
> we are happy indeed in that we possess one another and understand one
> another, understand and love with all our hearts.[3]

[1] Of course, the Diary rationalizes the situation—that the money will come in handy,
that Robert cannot abandon the *Neue Zeitschrift* any longer, that their tiny daughter has been
left in Leipzig, etc. But these reasons were as true before Schumann took offence as afterwards.

[2] Certain incidents suggest that, at times, Schumann even regarded Clara as a threat to
his artistic personality. He became incensed at any suggestion that his works might not have
made their own way without Clara's persuasive advocacy. According to Hirschbach:

> I still remember the evening when Assessor H., an old acquaintance of Schumann's,
> remarked to him that Clara had helped a great deal to smooth his path as a composer
> and obtain a public hearing for his works. Highly insulted, Schumann sprang up, and
> called to me: 'Come on, Hirschbach!' With that, our sitting at Poppe's† was ended for
> the evening.

[3] Litzmann, Vol. II, p. 16.

† A restaurant frequented by Schumann.

FRIEDRICH WIECK (c. 1865)
a photograph

SCHUMANN'S BIRTHPLACE AT ZWICKAU

SCHUMANN'S PARENTS (1810)
oil portraits by Glaeser

Leipzig (1840–44)
Friends and Contemporaries

Leipzig, where the Schumanns first settled, was fast becoming one of the important musical centres of Germany. A city of forty thousand people, and rapidly expanding, its economy was based on light industry, and it was there that the great printing house of Breitkopf and Härtel had its home. A hundred years earlier, Bach had lived and worked there. The St Thomas Church still housed many of his forgotten manuscripts. Soon the 'Bach revival' would get under way and make Leipzig world famous. The Gewandhaus concerts, subsidized by the linen-merchants of Leipzig, and held in their ancient market-hall, had a distinguished history stretching back to the first half of the eighteenth century; they were now approaching their most glorious epoch. Already talk was of founding a Conservatory of Music; within three years, in fact, a group of wealthy businessmen had put up the required capital and launched an institution which was to attract some of the most brilliant names in music. Leipzig was a practical place to be in 1840. Robert and Clara lived there for four years.

At the heart of Leipzig's musical life stood Felix Mendelssohn.* This young genius towered over his contemporaries. When he was only twenty-six years old, and already a composer of European fame, he had been appointed conductor of the Gewandhaus concerts.[1] Under his inspired leadership, the Gewandhaus became a kind of musical shrine at which the faithful gathered regularly to hear the masterpieces of Beethoven, Schubert and Bach brought to life by this incomparable musician. Schumann stood in awe of him, and of his unique gifts; he called Mendelssohn 'the Mozart of the nineteenth century'.[2] In 1843, Mendelssohn founded the Leipzig Conservatory of Music and appointed to its teaching staff such names as Moscheles* (piano), David* (violin), Hauptmann* (theory), and Schumann himself for composition and piano. Through sheer force of artistic personality, Mendelssohn welded together this loose band of musicians and gave them a higher artistic purpose. Within ten years, he had led Leipzig out of its quiet cultural backwater into the mainstream of Europe's musical life.

According to Niecks, Mendelssohn began Schumann's acquaintance with two prejudices which he never quite overcame: 'that against literary writers on music, and that against dilettantism'.[3] Both prejudices were unfair; they could not possibly be applied to Schumann; this did not stop Mendelssohn applying them, however. Mendelssohn's dislike of musical journalists is understandable. He had the creative artist's contempt for people who merely write about art

[1] He held the position from 1835 to 1843.   [2] NZfM, 13 (1840).
[3] Niecks, p. 155.

B

instead of practising it. Unfortunately, in 1835, when the two men first met, Schumann was famous as the journalist-editor of the *Neue Zeitschrift*, but hardly known at all as a composer. This situation was soon to change; but Mendelssohn never entirely forgave him his literary origins. As for Mendelssohn's hatred of dilettantism, this was born of his sense of professionalism, and of his belief that anything less than the absolute mastery of one's craft is the unforgivable sin. Alas, Schumann frequently gave the impression of being a 'dabbler'. There was a certain vagueness about his personality, which was often mistaken for dilettantism by those who did not know him very well. Moreover, Mendelssohn could point to things in which Schumann was obviously deficient. He left a negative impression on the rostrum, for instance, lacking even an adequate stick technique (in which Mendelssohn excelled). It was no accident that when Mendelssohn relinquished the direction of the Gewandhaus concerts in 1843, and the question of his successor arose, Schumann was bypassed in favour of Hiller.*

Another friend of this period was the young English musician Sterndale Bennett,* who arrived in Leipzig in the autumn of 1836 on a visit to Mendelssohn. Bennett had been an infant prodigy. He was spotted by Mendelssohn who happened to be in London in 1833 when the seventeen-year-old Bennett played his D minor Concerto in the Hanover Square Rooms. Mendelssohn immediately invited him to Leipzig. 'If I come, may I be your pupil?' 'No, you must come to be my friend.' Schumann, too, had a high regard for Bennett. The *Neue Zeitschrift* is full of complimentary references to Bennett's compositions. Naturally, it was not long before Schumann introduced him to Clara. Here, Bennett may have blotted his copy-book. She played him her Piano Concerto. Asked for his opinion, he replied: 'It requires weeding.'[1]

Niels Gade* was another member of the Leipzig circle. He had achieved fame overnight, at twenty-four, by winning first prize in a Copenhagen competition with his overture *Echoes of Ossian*. In 1843, he settled in Leipzig, and Mendelssohn appointed him deputy conductor of the Gewandhaus concerts. He became friendly with Schumann who described him as 'a splendid fellow and musician'. Schumann soon observed that the letters of Gade's name are all to be found in the musical alphabet. With his special gift for musical anagrams and puzzles he at once devised the following:

[1] Niecks, p. 165. That Clara was offended with Bennett is beyond question. Her Piano Concerto had just received a poor review in (of all places) the *Neue Zeitschrift*, by K. F. Becker. (Schumann had nobly given him the job, rather than do it himself, to ensure impartiality.) Becker, unfortunately, had dismissed the Concerto on the grounds that it was 'the work of a lady'. Clara, already upset that Schumann had not reviewed her work himself, was incensed by the subsequent issue of the *Zeitschrift* which contained a glowing review, by Schumann, of Bennett's latest concerto. Bennett was blissfully unaware of the delicate situation when he put his foot in it.

EX 3

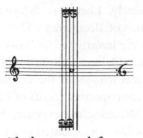

Read it clockwise, starting with the tenor clef.

One of the 'Album for the Young' pieces (called 'Northern Song') is based on Gade's name. It begins:

EX 4

Schumann's relationship with Liszt was more complex. It started out enthusiastically; later it was marred by a foolish quarrel over Mendelssohn. Schumann first met Liszt in 1840, when Liszt, in the middle of those historic European tours which brought him both fame and notoriety, stopped off at Leipzig to give concerts.[1] After their first meeting Schumann declared: 'It is as if we had known one another for twenty years.'[2] Schumann's feelings are reflected in the dedication of his great C major Fantasie to Liszt.[3] Eventually, however, Schumann reacted against Liszt's flamboyant personality. He came to accept Mendelssohn's description of Liszt: 'a continual alternation between scandal and apotheosis'. Clara did not help matters. She called Liszt 'a smasher of pianos'. As Schumann's own involvement with piano virtuosity waned, he, too, came to despise Liszt's spectacular brand of keyboard fireworks. By 1850, the two musicians were hardly on speaking terms.

In order to understand what happened, we have to go back a bit. In June 1848, Liszt paid the Schumanns a surprise visit at Dresden. After some initial irritation at having the domestic routine disturbed, Clara went to considerable

---

[1] They were reviewed by Schumann in the NZfM.
[2] Letter to Clara, 18 March 1840. Litzmann, Vol. I, p. 413.
[3] Which was later struck off by Clara.

pains to arrange a musical dinner in his honour. A time was fixed, and musicians were assembled. Unfortunately, Liszt was delayed. The exasperated players having started a performance of Beethoven's D major Trio in their guest-of-honour's absence, were rudely interrupted as 'Liszt burst in at the door',[1] two hours late. Schumann's Piano Quintet followed which Liszt tactlessly described as 'Leipziger-isch'. There was tension in the air throughout dinner. Then an argument broke out about the respective merits of Mendelssohn and Meyerbeer. Liszt praised Meyerbeer at Mendelssohn's expense. At this, Schumann exploded. He seized Liszt by both shoulders and shouted in a rage: 'Who are you that you dare to speak in such a way of a musician like Mendelssohn?' He then rushed out of the room and slammed the door, leaving the others glaring at Liszt in silence. Liszt rose to the occasion superbly. He turned to Clara and said, 'Madam, please tell your husband that he is the only man in the world from whom I would take so calmly the words just offered to me.'[2]

Leipzig versus Weimar

As we shall see, there was a good deal of background to this 'scene'. It neatly illustrated the historic split between the Leipzig and the Weimar schools. Liszt's continual references to 'Leipziger-isch' were aimed at that band of musicians centred around the Leipzig Conservatory—among them Schumann's friends Rietz, Hauptmann and David. He regarded them as narrow academics, and nicknamed them 'little Leipzigers'. The very year of his quarrel with Schumann (1848), Liszt had settled in Weimar and was now busily turning it into a centre for modern music. Leipzig and Weimar were soon at war, and the struggle between them was to dominate the historical scene for about ten years.

Leipzig, then, was a stimulating environment to be in; Schumann did much of his best work there. In one year alone, that of his marriage, he poured out a hundred and forty songs, including *Liederkreis*, Op. 24, and Op. 39; *Myrthen*; and *Frauenliebe und-leben*. The year after, 1841, he finished his First Symphony (the 'Spring') in B flat major, whose first performance was given by Mendelssohn at a Gewandhaus concert. The year after that, 1842, he ventured into chamber music with his three string quartets and his Piano Quintet in E flat major. To all this composing activity has to be added, from 1843, his teaching at the Leipzig Conservatory, to say

---

[1] Clara's phrase (Diary, June 1848).

[2] Jansen, p. 523. Litzmann gives a slightly different account of the episode (Vol. II, p. 121). Schumann's outburst must be understood in the light of the fact that Mendelssohn had died only a few months previously. Wagner was also at this dinner party (*Mein Leben*, English trans. p. 450) and states categorically that it took place in March, not June, in which case Litzmann mis-read Clara's Diary entries.

nothing of the *Neue Zeitschrift* which he ran single-handed and which kept him in continual correspondence with people all over Germany, and beyond. Clara, too, was musically active; apart from her frequent appearances at the Gewandhaus concerts, she undertook two major tours: in 1842 she visited Bremen, Hamburg, and Oldenburg, and in 1844 she went as far afield as St Petersburg where she played before the Russian Imperial Court. On both occasions Schumann accompanied her.

Schumann suffered two physical breakdowns during this period. The first was in 1842. He put it down to 'overwork', and he and Clara went to relax at the Bohemian spas. The second was much more serious. It began shortly after the Russian tour, in August 1844. The symptoms were ominous. He trembled incessantly, was afflicted by various phobias—such as a fear of heights, and sharp metallic objects—and, worst of all, he suffered severe auricular delusions which made composing impossible. (These symptoms, which have always baffled Schumann scholars, were first described by Dr Helbig, the homoeopathic physician at Dresden, whom Schumann consulted in the autumn of 1844. They form part of a much wider clinical picture, and they have to be considered in the light of Schumann's ill-health generally, and the syphilis which first drove him insane and later killed him. The nature of his illness is fully discussed on pp. 35–40 and 406–14.) In September, Schumann tried to resume his teaching at the Leipzig Conservatory, but his health became worse and he was forced to resign. During some dreadful days in October, while the Schumanns were seeking medical advice in Dresden, Clara, who was at her wits' end, reported that 'Robert did not sleep a single night. His imagination painted the most terrible pictures. In the early morning I generally found him bathed in tears. He gave himself up completely.'[1] Matters were not helped by the arrival of Wieck, who, true to form, attempted to 'rouse him forcibly'.

Convinced that nothing short of a complete change of climate would bring him any benefit, Schumann decided to settle in Dresden permanently. He may have been helped towards this decision by the election of Niels Gade to the conductorship of the Gewandhaus concerts in 1844, which Schumann took to be a slight against himself. Mendelssohn was responsible for the decision. (In the light of Schumann's disastrous encounter with the Düsseldorf orchestra a few years later no one could maintain that Mendelssohn made a mistake.) Within a few weeks, Schumann had severed his connections with Leipzig, including the *Neue Zeitschrift*, whose editorship he now handed over to Lorenz,[2] and after a farewell concert on Sunday, 8 December, Robert and Clara left Leipzig for good.

[1] Litzmann, Vol. II, p. 76.
[2] A year later, the magazine passed to Franz Brende lwho remained its permanent editor.

At Dresden (1844–48)

Whatever illusions the Schumanns cherished about Dresden were soon shattered. Convention ruled all. It was no place for artistic enterprise. Dresden's artistic life was centred around the Royal Court. Here, under the autocratic rule of King Friedrich Augustus II, were gathered painters, sculptors, architects, authors and musicians. Court functions were stifling occasions, governed by rigid protocol; the glittering array of artistic talent which dutifully turned up in support of such events was mostly in the pay of the King, and their liberal outlook stood in bizarre contrast to one of the most reactionary monarchies in Europe.[1] This was an explosive mixture. Five years later, Dresden was rocked by the 1849 Insurrection. Schumann, who had no direct dealings with the Court, nevertheless chafed under its restrictive influence. At first, he actually savoured the shortage of music. He wrote to Ferdinand David: 'Here one can get back the old lost longing for music, there is so little to hear!' Soon, however, he was completely frustrated by the prevailing spirit of provincialism.

By far the most important musician in Dresden was Richard Wagner, then conductor of the Royal Opera. Schumann was quite unable to appreciate this wayward genius. 'He has the most amazing gift of the gab, and is always chock full of his own ideas; one cannot listen to him for long.'[2] Wagner, who could not tolerate Schumann's long silences (and doubtless felt encouraged to fill the vacuum whenever it appeared, as it frequently did, with those long 'philosophical' monologues of his), was quick to return the compliment: 'He was too conservative to benefit by my views.'[3] As Niecks humorously put it, the unwillingness of the one to unburden himself, and the overwhelming need of the other to do so, created a situation in which, after a few preliminary skirmishes, their relationship slid of its own volition towards a full close. Schumann's low opinion of Wagner's conducting ('How is it possible for an orchestra to produce a perfect performance, when the conductor himself does not understand the work?'),[4] was matched only by Wagner's low opinion of Schumann's own ('his peculiar awkwardness aroused my sympathy').[5] It was an odd situation. Two of the great composers of the day were living within a stone's throw of one another.

---

[1] King Friedrich eventually opted out of politics; he was more interested in botany. He distinguished himself by publishing a book on the subject, in 1837, called *Flora marienbadensis, oder Pflanzen und Gebirgsarten.*
[2] *Yearbook*, 17 March 1846.
[3] *Mein Leben* (English translation), p. 386, Wagner.
[4] *The Diary*, 1 April 1849; a reference to Wagner's performance of Beethoven's Ninth Symphony.
[5] *Op. cit.*, p. 385.

And the sole extent of their encounter was a few random remarks in each other's literary jottings.

One of Schumann's few real musical friends in Dresden was Ferdinand Hiller. He had moved there from Leipzig around 1840 and now directed the Dresden *Liedertafel*, an amateur male-voice choral society; he was the only one to extend a friendly hand to Schumann. Before long, the two men had joined forces and were attempting to generate some musical activity in Dresden by organizing subscription concerts, like those at the Leipzig Gewandhaus. It was uphill work, and Schumann wrote despairingly to Mendelssohn[1] that the Royal Orchestra was refusing to embark on them, for fear of drawing away the audiences from the long-established pension-fund concerts. A month later, however, he had actually got them started, much to everyone's surprise. Clara, who was billed to take part in the opening concert on 10 November, fell ill; old Wieck was despatched post-haste to Leipzig to find a substitute and came back with Joachim, then a mere lad of fourteen, who staggered everybody by playing Mendelssohn's Violin Concerto.[2] This was a promising start. As the concerts got under way, however, Schumann saw that his efforts to bring Dresden up to the level of the Leipzig Gewandhaus were unrealistic; there was a basic lack of interest among the Dresdeners, and after a run of two or three seasons the concerts lapsed.

Clara had little patience with the Dresden musicians. She despised them for their lack of enterprise. She was ruthless in her ambitions for Robert, and doubtless looked back longingly to her concert tours, in the days when she had been able to promote so many of his works. Could she not repeat these early successes? In a mood of determined optimism the Schumanns now arranged an ambitious visit to Vienna, the scene of one of Clara's greatest triumphs nine years earlier. The couple set out on 24 November 1846. A gloomy reception awaited them. Attendances were thin, the applause was cool, and, worst of all, receipts were down.[3] After the third concert, Robert discovered that they were out of pocket by nearly a hundred ducats. Clara put on a brave face, and wrote euphemistically in her Diary that Robert's music 'took extremely well', and that he 'was recalled several times'. This was wishful thinking. Hanslick,* who was in the audience, has left a different account. After the concert he went round to the artists' room, where he found Clara 'complaining bitterly of the coldness and ingratitude of

---

[1] On 24 September 1845.   [2] Litzmann, Vol. II, p. 111.

[3] The sensation-seeking Viennese had turned up anticipating a repetition of the glittering bravura concerts Clara had previously given them. They were disappointed. She offered them instead Beethoven's G major Piano Concerto (10 December), Bach's Prelude and Fugue in A minor (15 December), Schumann's A minor Piano Concerto (1 January), and, at the final concert, Beethoven's *Appassionata* Sonata (10 January). The other chief work by Schumann, presented at the third concert, was his Symphony in B flat major (the 'Spring'), which he himself conducted.

the public. Everything that the rest of us said, endeavouring to soothe her, only increased her vexation. Then Schumann said these never-to-be-forgotten words: "Calm yourself, dear Clara; in ten years' time all this will have changed." [1] Disaster now stared them in the face. Their final concert, on 11 January 1847, was still to come. They had to brace themselves to go through with it. Then, out of the blue, Jenny Lind* descended on them and offered her services. As the most famous soprano of her time (she was popularly known as the 'Swedish Nightingale') she had a large following wherever she appeared. The last concert, predictably, was sold out. The Schumanns returned to Dresden with a clear profit of 300 thaler. Grateful as they were to Jenny Lind it had been a chastening experience. Clara wrote: 'I could not get over the bitter feeling that one song of Lind's had done what I, with all my playing, could not do.'

A brighter interlude lay ahead of them, however. In July, 1847, Schumann's native town of Zwickau prepared a two-week festival in honour of her greatest son. Here Schumann saw again some of his childhood friends, and had a moving reunion with his old teacher Kuntzsch who went about, as the Diary puts it, 'Swelling with pride' over his famous pupil. It was welcome compensation for the Vienna setbacks, and both Robert and Clara were satisfied with the recognition accorded them.

In November, Hiller left Dresden to become Director of Music at Düsseldorf, and he handed over to Schumann the conductorship of the *Liedertafel*—the men's choral society. Schumann now had a regular outlet for music-making, the first since he had arrived in Dresden. Within a couple of months, he had expanded the society into a large-scale 'Choral Union' for mixed voices—about seventy strong. The choir met every Wednesday evening, with Clara accompanying at the keyboard. At the first meeting in January 1848, Schumann made a speech in which he told the new society they would make a special study of modern music, while not neglecting the classics. Under Schumann's direction, they sang music by Bach, Handel and Palestrina, while among contemporary works Mendelssohn's *Athalie*, Hiller's *Geist über dem Wasser* and Schumann's own *Paradise and the Peri* featured in their programmes. Altogether, this was a happy and rewarding activity for Schumann. The society often met for social excursions; there was a particularly memorable outing, one hot summer morning, when they all travelled by steamboat to Meissen and sang in the cathedral; an open-air meal followed in the park, to the singing of quartets, and even a thunderstorm could not quench their enthusiasm. As a direct result of the 'Choral Union', Schumann composed a large number of partsongs; they are among his most neglected compositions, but some of them are well worth reviving today.[2]

[1] *Aus meinem Leben*, 1894, Hanslick.   [2] They are discussed by Louis Halsey on p. 352.

Four children were born to the Schumanns during these years: Julie (March 1845), Emil[1] (February 1846), Ludwig (January 1848), and Ferdinand (July 1849). Clara's hands were now so full (together with the two elder children she now looked after a family of six), she had temporarily to abandon her piano playing: As the Diary shows, she accepted her lot philosophically.

What will become of my work?! But Robert says: 'Children are blessings,' and he is right for there is no happiness without children, and therefore I have determined to face the difficult time that is coming,[2] with as cheery a spirit as possible. Whether I shall always be able to do so or not, I do not know.

There were deeper anxieties however. Schumann's health showed signs of further deterioration. His unusual symptoms, first observed in Leipzig (see p. 25), now took a disquieting turn. In May, 1846, he had suffered a severe attack of tinnitus,[3] which made composing impossible. There were ups and downs of mood, too, intense elation alternating with black depression. His fear of heights increased. This last symptom became so marked that by 1850, when he visited Leipzig for a performance of *Genoveva* and was given a bedroom on a high floor, he experienced such terror that he was forced to exchange it for one on the ground level.

These were serious setbacks, and they placed his creative work in perpetual jeopardy. No sooner was he given a respite, starting to revel in his newly-recovered creative strength, than his symptoms broke out again, in Litzmann's phrase, 'as an enemy breaks from an ambush'. Several Schumann scholars, in the light of the great inroads his chronic illness made into his composing, have postulated a 'creative decline'. They see Dresden as a turning-point, and they argue that Schumann never again reached those great expressive peaks depicted in his piano music and his songs. There is a formidable list of compositions, dating from the Dresden years, to challenge their view. Schumann finished his Piano Concerto in A minor, the first performance of which was given by Clara in Dresden on 4 December 1846; that same year, he completed his Symphony No. 2 in C major. A few months later he began his opera *Genoveva* which occupied him until August 1848; the ink was scarcely dry before he began his incidental music to Bryon's *Manfred*, and in the year 1849 he wrote more than twenty works between Opp. 67 and 146, including such major compositions as the Concertstück for four horns and orchestra (Op. 86) and the Introduction

[1] Died in infancy, aged 16 months.
[2] Diary, May 1847. The date makes it obvious that 'the difficult time that is coming' refers to her fifth pregnancy. Ludwig was born eight months later.
[3] A disturbance of the aural nerve in which the sufferer hears illusory sounds.

and Allegro Appassionato for piano and orchestra (Op. 92). True, these works mark a new stylistic departure; but a stylistic departure is not necessarily a 'creative decline'. It would be unreasonable to expect a composer of Schumann's stature to go on repeating himself.

The Dresden Revolution

In May 1849, the Dresden insurrection broke out. Barricades were flung up,[1] and bitter hand-to-hand street fighting ensued. Liberal though he was, Schumann had no stomach for violence. The sight of fourteen corpses laid out in the courtyard of the local Clinic revolted him. Nor could he face the thought of compulsory enlistment. Twice the 'press gangs' came knocking at his door, and twice the distracted Clara denied that he was in. When they threatened to search the house, Schumann fled through the back garden with Clara and his eldest daughter Marie, and stayed with friends at the nearby village of Maxen. Clara showed immense courage by going back the following day, risking the street firing and the patrolling soldiers, in order to pick up the younger children, whom she had left in the house and now found asleep in bed.[2] The Schumanns sought sanctuary in the tiny village of Kreischa, and here Robert withdrew from horrible reality and buried himself in composition. Clara was astonished at the ease with which he cut himself off from the outside world.

> It seems to me extraordinary how the terrible events outside have awakened his poetic feeling in so entirely contrary a manner. All the songs breathe the spirit of perfect peace, . . .

The only mark the Revolution seems to have made on his output, in fact, was the four 'barricade' Marches, Op. 76 and three 'revolutionary choruses' for male-voice choir and military band; they are among his least important works.

Throughout 1849, Schumann's desire for a regular position in the world of music increased. Clara, too, was impatient on his behalf. She longed for him to gain an official post in keeping with his growing status as a composer. In 1847, doubtless as a result of her prodding, he had inquired after the directorship of the Vienna Conservatory which had fallen vacant. Again, shortly after the death of Mendelssohn, he had put out discreet feelers about the conductorship of the Gewandhaus orchestra.[3] Although these moves came to nothing, they indicated

---

[1] They were built to specifications drawn up by Wagner! (Litzmann, Vol. II, p. 191).
[2] Litzmann, Vol. II, p. 188.
[3] It eventually passed to Julius Rietz, who held the post from 1848 to 1860.

his underlying dissatisfaction. When, in the autumn of 1849, he received a letter from his old friend Hiller, about to take up a new appointment at Cologne and offering Schumann the music directorship at Düsseldorf, he decided to accept. The decision was complicated for him by a curious discovery.

> The other day I looked for some notices of Düsseldorf in an old geography book, and among the places of note in that town I found mentioned three convents and a mad-house. I have no objection to the former, but it made me quite uncomfortable to read about the latter. I will tell you how that is: a few years ago, as you will remember, we lived at Maxen. I there discovered that the principal view from my windows was on to the Sonnenstein. At last I perfectly hated the sight of it, and it entirely spoilt my stay there. So I thought the same thing might happen at Düsseldorf. But possibly the notice is altogether incorrect, and the institution may be merely a hospital, such as one finds in every town.[1]

Later events give his morbid observations tragic overtones. Clara, however, was more down-to-earth. She was firmly resolved they should leave Dresden, a town she had come to detest. After fulfilling a round of concert engagements in Bremen, Hamburg and Altona, the Schumanns finally set out for Düsseldorf on 1 September 1850.

At Düsseldorf (1850–54)

From the start, Robert and Clara were given a warm welcome. The Düsseldorfers, anxious to please their new Director and his distinguished pianist wife, laid on an enthusiastic reception for them. The couple were met by a deputation of concert officials, led by Hiller, and escorted to the best hotel in town, where comfortable rooms, decked out with flowers, had been placed at their disposal. Later that evening, they were serenaded by the choir. The following day, while dining in the hotel, they heard the strains of the *Don Giovanni* overture coming from the next room—played by a contingent from the town orchestra. 'It was a most pleasing surprise to Robert,' Clara wrote in her Diary. 'They played everything well, and I think Robert will be able to do something with the orchestra.' Her words have a hollow ring in the light of subsequent events.

Schumann's duties at Düsseldorf were quite simple: to direct the public subscription concerts throughout each season. The forces at his disposal consisted,

[1] Jansen, p. 323.

first and foremost, of the large chorus. There were a hundred and twenty singers, and Schumann was expected to rehearse them once a week. They were all amateurs, but under Hiller they had reached a high standard of excellence. The orchestra, on the other hand, was a professional body, and rehearsals were less frequent. Additionally, Schumann was expected to fulfil certain obligations towards the local Catholic Church services whenever large musical forces were required.

The first concert of the season was on 24 October. A few days earlier, Schumann had appointed Wasielewski,★ his former pupil,[1] as the new orchestral leader, for he was determined to maintain a high level of performance. There was a large audience present, and as Schumann mounted the rostrum he was greeted with a triple fanfare. The programme included Beethoven's 'Consecration of the House' overture and Mendelssohn's G minor piano concerto, with Clara as soloist. Everybody agreed that the concert was an unqualified success, and Schumann had good reason to feel pleased. Why, then, did relations between him and the orchestra sink to such a low level that, within a couple of years, the latter were demanding his resignation?

Schumann was not a conductor. He had neither the training nor the temperament for it. At first, he commanded respect among the players by virtue of his reputation in the wider world of music; but at Düsseldorf, that reputation wore thin. His baton technique was non-existent. He lacked the capacity to express himself clearly and concisely at rehearsals. Moreover, he indulged in the tiresome habit of repeating passages many times without telling the orchestra why he was doing so. There was no quicker way of killing enthusiasm. Soon discipline began to flag; some of the chorus became bored and stayed away from rehearsals. Schumann, oddly oblivious to his own faults, interpreted their action as a personal slight. The first public criticism of his direction of the concerts was voiced in an anonymous article in the local press, at the end of the first season. Schumann was outraged; he believed the writer to be a member of his own Concerts Committee, and he felt they should have closed ranks behind him. Clara fumed into her Diary: 'It is a disgrace that they should quietly acquiesce in such treatment of Robert at the hands of the Düsseldorfers, instead of shielding him in every way as they should do, in order to keep him.' Actually, Clara was the one person who might have saved the situation: she could tactfully have helped Schumann towards a more objective understanding of his function as a conductor. But her blind devotion to Robert left her utterly incapable of

---

[1] Wasielewski became Schumann's first biographer. Much of our information concerning Schumann's Düsseldorf period came from Wasielewski who was in a position to observe it at first hand. See 'Register of Persons'.

accepting any criticism of him, let alone offering it, and so he lurched from one crisis to another. The next two seasons produced a whole crop of embarrassing situations. Once, at choir practice, the sopranos were singing several high A's, and the effect caused such merriment within their ranks that they stopped singing, and the performance just petered out. Schumann noticed nothing and went on conducting. Tausch,* his assistant, who was accompanying, went on playing for a few bars and then decided that he, too, had better stop. Schumann beckoned him to the rostrum. Instead of offering a reproof, however, Schumann merely pointed to a bar in the full score and murmured: 'See, this bar is beautiful!' On another occasion, during Mass, he continued conducting after the music had stopped and the priest had started to intone. Observers said that it was as if he had withdrawn from the performance altogether. Equally bizarre was his way at rehearsals, whenever Clara relieved Tausch of his chores at the keyboard, and Schumann addressed the singers through her. 'My husband says he would like this passage *piano*.' Whereupon Schumann, on the rostrum, would nod approvingly. There were humorous sides to the situation, however. He frequently dropped his baton during performances. Niecks remembered his father telling him that once, after this happened at rehearsal, Schumann came up to him with his baton tied to his wrist with a piece of string, and exclaimed gaily: 'Look, now it can't fall again!'[1]

By the winter of 1852, the Orchestral Committee had had enough. They wrote a stiff letter to Schumann, criticizing his handling of the rehearsals. They implied he should resign. He refused, so the Committee resigned instead. A new Committee was formed. This time, they succeeded in persuading Schumann to hand over the choir rehearsals to Tausch, while retaining the direction of the orchestra and the public concerts himself. This arrangement came into force at the beginning of 1853. It was an uneasy truce. Bad feeling had been aroused on both sides. It required only one major artistic indiscretion on Schumann's part to bring matters to a head, and he quickly provided it. On 16 October he conducted a mass by Hauptmann in St Maximilian's Church. The performance was so bad, the conducting so apathetic, that the public accused the musicians of lacking respect for the Holy Office. Less than two weeks later, Schumann once again led his forces to the brink of disaster. This time, it was a public concert. Joachim was the visiting soloist, and his name had drawn a large audience.

---

[1] Niecks (p. 299) relates this curious anecdote without comment. An obvious explanation why Schumann kept dropping his baton is that he had a crippled right hand and grasped objects with difficulty. His hand injury must have invaded every subsequent practical activity Schumann engaged in. Litzmann, for instance, mentioned his notoriously illegible handwriting, and offers no comment. With one finger straddled across the others (Schumann's description), what else was to be expected?

Schumann's conducting was incoherent; he was quite unable to start the performance and stood with his arms raised, waiting for the players to commence. Eventually, they did so; but they followed Joachim, not Schumann, who was left to grope his way along as best he could. It was the last occasion Schumann ever conducted in Düsseldorf. The Committee insisted that he hand over the remaining concerts to Tausch. On 10 November the Schumanns thankfully left Düsseldorf for a concert tour of Holland. They were glad to get away, if only for a few weeks. It was the most humiliating episode of Schumann's career.

It is easy to blame the long-suffering Düsseldorfers. Was not Schumann one of the great geniuses of his time? And by his immense prestige had he not brought honour to Düsseldorf? That was Clara's view, precisely. The Düsseldorfers had only one reply: they had had nothing to do with Schumann's appointment. They had accepted him simply because Hiller, their outgoing Director, had recommended him. In the event, Schumann had proved inadequate to the task. Were they now expected to sit back silently and suffer the consequences? Moreover, there is clear evidence that Schumann had already entered the final stages of his fatal illness, and was hardly fit enough to fulfil his duties. The symptoms were ominous. In June 1851 he had suffered a series of 'nervous attacks', as he described them. Clara was more specific. She recorded in her Diary that terrible morning in July 1853 when Schumann got up and was seized by a paralytic stroke. His speech disorder, which made his pronunciation sound clumsy and indistinct, dates from this period.

The one shaft of light which brightened an otherwise dark year was the coming of Brahms.* Towards the end of September 1853, at the height of Schumann's troubles with the Committee, the twenty-year-old Brahms appeared, bearing a letter of introduction from Joachim. It was one of the great moments of musical history. Brahms sat down at the piano and started playing one of his compositions. He had progressed no further than a few bars when Schumann, electrified, rushed out of the room and came back dragging Clara behind him. 'Now, my dear Clara,' he said, 'you will hear such music, as you never heard before; and you, young man, play the work from the beginning.' The meeting was to have fateful consequences for all three musicians. Brahms stayed with the Schumanns throughout the month of October, becoming one of Robert's most devoted disciples. Schumann referred to him as 'the young eagle'. He wrote to Breitkopf and Härtel on the young man's behalf, insisting that they take up his music. The final outcome of the encounter was Schumann's famous article 'New Paths', published in the *Zeitschrift*, in which he hailed Brahms as a genius. Schumann reminded his readers that it was ten years since he had contributed to his old magazine, and that 'many new and significant talents' had emerged in the meantime—Joachim, Gade, Heller, Dietrich, etc. He went on:

> It seemed to me, who followed the progress of these chosen ones with the greatest interest, that . . . a musician would inevitably appear to whom it was vouchsafed to give the highest and most ideal expression to the tendencies of our time, one who would not show his mastery in a gradual development, but, like Athena, would spring fully armed from the head of Zeus. And he has come, a young man over whose cradle Graces and Heroes stood watch. His name is Johannes Brahms.[1]

This was lavish praise to bestow on an unknown, twenty-year-old composer. Overnight, it launched Brahms to fame. Brahms was deeply appreciative. He remained a steadfast and loyal friend to Schumann through his days of dark despair, now almost upon him, and he provided solace and comfort for Clara in her hour of need.

The last illness

The medical picture presented by Schumann's last illness is complicated by its wide range of symptoms—auditive disorders, difficulties of speech, partial paralysis and massive memory failure.[2] There have been several attempts to arrive at a convincing clinical diagnosis, but the results are by no means unanimous. Let us look, first of all, at the harrowing sequence of symptoms experienced by Schumann in 1854, which terminated in his death two years later. Then, on the basis of the evidence, we can consider the various medical conclusions which have been advanced to explain them.

On the night of 10 February 1854, Schumann reported a 'very strong and painful aural affection'. Four days later, on 14 February he was sitting in a restaurant with his friend Becker, the violinist. He put down the newspaper he had been reading and said: 'I can't read any more. I keep hearing the note A.'[3] The aural illusions progressed, and Schumann recorded hearing 'magnificent music, with instruments of splendid resonance, the like of which has never been heard on earth before'.[4] Clara wrote in her Diary:

> My poor Robert suffers terribly. All sounds are transformed for him into

[1] NZfM, 39, 1853.

[2] Add to this his unusual habit of walking on tiptoe (as if frightened of being observed), his fear of heights, and his aversion to sharp-pointed metal objects.

[3] Wasielewski, p. 195.

[4] Two doctors were called in: Dr Böger, an army doctor, and Dr Hasenclever, the family physician. To consult one's own physician is normal. The fact that an army doctor was also called in suggests that syphilis might already have been suspected. See pages 39–40.

music. . . . He has said several times that if it does not stop he'll go out of his mind. . . . The trouble with his ears has now got to the point of his hearing great symphonic pieces played right through with the last note held until another piece comes into his imagination.

During the night of the 17th Schumann got out of bed and took down a tune in E flat major which, he said, the angels had dictated to him. On the 18th the angels were transformed into devils which appeared in the form of tigers and hyenas.

> His condition soon became hysterical [wrote Clara]. He cried out in agony, and the two doctors, who luckily were there, could hardly hold him. I shall never forget the way he looked at me; I suffered with him the most cruel torments. After about half an hour he calmed down and said that the friendly voices were making themselves heard again and giving him back his courage. The doctors got him to bed.

Sunday, 19 February was a distressing day. Schumann claimed to be surrounded by evil spirits, 'those superterrestrial and subterranean men,' as he called them, and they persecuted him until nightfall. The following day, he was overcome by feelings of guilt and remorse; he kept repeating that he was a criminal, that he would go to Hell, and that he must never stop reading the Bible. On 26 February he asked to be taken to a lunatic asylum. He feared doing his wife and children an injury. He ate his evening meal in great haste, and went to gather all the things he might require for his journey. Clara and the doctor persuaded him to go to bed instead. Next day, while Clara was preoccupied, Schumann stole out of the house, dressed only in his dressing-gown and slippers, went straight to the Rhine Bridge, climbed on to a parapet, and threw himself into the river.[1] By a stroke of luck, he aroused suspicion at the toll-gate; being unable to pay the toll he had given the keeper his handkerchief instead. He was seen as he fell into the current and was dragged out by some fishermen who carried him home. Marie Schumann, his eldest daughter, has left this moving account of the tragedy. She was thirteen years old.

> I saw my father for the last time the day he went out to take his life. . . . My mother had to talk to the doctor, and I was told to stay in the little

---

[1] Just before he plunged he removed his wedding ring and cast it into the Rhine. A note was later found in his bedroom: 'Dear Clara: I shall cast my wedding ring into the Rhine. Do you do the same. Then the two rings will be united.' Oddly, this action fulfilled a dream Schumann had had sixteen years earlier, in November 1837, during the turbulent days of his courtship, in which he remembered casting his engagement ring into a deep pool.

room and see if my father in the next room wanted anything. I had been standing for a moment in front of my mother's bureau when the door between the two rooms opened and my father appeared in the doorway in his long green-flowered dressing-gown. He was dreadfully pale. Seeing me, he hid his face in his hands, and said: 'Oh! My God!' Then he disappeared again. I stood for a minute rooted to the spot, then, remembering why I was there, I went into my father's room. It was empty; and the door to my parents' bedroom, and the one beyond that to the hall were both wide open. I rushed in to my mother. The doctor was still there, and we searched all the rooms. It was obvious my father had gone out. We tried to find him, my mother telling me to go to Fräulein Leser's to tell her what had happened. In the street I saw people coming towards me talking loudly, and when I was nearer I recognised my father. Two men were holding him up under the armpits, while he held his hands in front of his face.

Clara, on the verge of collapse, was not allowed to see him. Two male nurses were brought in to look after the sick composer. He again requested to be sent to an asylum, and this time Dr Hasenclever complied. Arrangements were made for him to be taken to the private asylum of Dr Richarz at Endenich, near Bonn. The carriage called for him on 4 March and Schumann, apparently in a state of euphoria, and without so much as a word of inquiry after his wife and children, left home for good.

Schumann spent the next two years at Endenich. He thought he would be cured there. That was not to be. His illness slowly increased its hold over him. He would pace the floor of his room incessantly and frequently kneel down and wring his hands. Sometimes, he held imaginary conversations with voices which denounced his compositions as plagiarisms. He would become agitated and exclaim aloud: 'That is not true; that is a lie!' Quite frequently he refused to eat and towards the end of his illness he became emaciated. According to Brahms, who visited him on 14 August, he had suddenly stopped drinking his wine the day before, complaining that it had been poisoned, and he spilt the rest of it on the floor. Once, Joachim visited him. 'When I was about to leave,' Joachim wrote, 'he took me with great secrecy into a corner (although we were unobserved) and told me that he longed to get away from that place; for the people did not understand him at all, nor what he stood for, or wanted.' These symptoms suggest dementia praecox. This was the diagnosis favoured by Möbius[1] and other authorities. As we shall see, however, later medical experts disagree.

He was not incarcerated. Dr Richarz's asylum stood in spacious gardens,

[1] Möbius, P. J.: *Über Robert Schumanns Krankheit* (Marhold, Halle, 1906).

surrounded by trees, and Schumann was free to wander back and forth at will. He made frequent pilgrimages to Beethoven's monument in nearby Bonn, and in his room he had a piano, manuscript paper, and writing utensils, so that he was able to compose.

For six months he felt no urge to communicate with Clara, and did not even mention her name. Then, on his wedding-day (12 September) he asked after her. She wrote to him immediately, and her letter arrived on the 13th, her birthday, 'this day of all days,' as he put it.

> Endenich,
> September 14, 1854
>
> How pleased I was to see your handwriting, dearest Clara. Thank you for writing on this day of all days, and for your loving remembrance of me and that of the dear children. Give the little ones my love and kisses. O, that I could have a sight of you, a word with you all!

A few days later he wrote to Clara again:

> September 18, 1854
>
> What joyful tidings you have again sent me! The birth of a fine boy—and in June, too. .... If you wish to consult me in the matter of a name, you will easily guess my choice—the name of the unforgettable one.[1]

Throughout 1855 Schumann's condition steadily deteriorated. Brahms visited him for a second time in February 1855 and noted chronic memory failure, accompanied by a violent insistence on the reliability of his recollections whenever they were doubted.[2] A few months later, in the summer of 1855, Schumann's biographer Wasielewski listened to him, unobserved, extemporizing at the piano 'like a machine whose springs are broken, but which still tries to work, jerking convulsively'. By the autumn of 1855 Dr Richarz had given up all hope of a recovery. Brahms saw him again in April and June of the following year; on the second occasion, Schumann, who was confined to his bed with swollen feet, scarcely recognized him, being preoccupied with picking names from an atlas and grouping them in strict alphabetical order.[3] On 23 July Clara received a telegram from Dr Richarz: 'If you want to see your

---

[1] Jansen, pp. 397–99. On 11 June, three days after Schumann's own birthday, Clara had given birth to their youngest son Felix. The news had been temporarily withheld from Schumann. The boy was christened after Mendelssohn, 'the unforgettable one'. Brahms was the godfather.

[2] Letter to Clara, dated 23 February 1855. *Briefe*, Vol. I, p. 78, Leipzig, 1927.

[3] *Johannes Brahms im Briefwechsel mit Joseph Joachim*, Berlin, 1908, Vol. I, pp. 130–31.

husband alive, come with all haste.' Clara saw Schumann for the first time in over two years on Sunday, 27 July, 'between six and seven in the evening'.

> He smiled at me, and with a great exertion—for he could no longer control his limbs—put his arm about me. I shall never forget it. Not all the treasures in the world could equal this embrace.[1]

The following day, Clara helped him to take a little wine. Some of it spilt over her hand and Schumann, 'with the happiest expression and real haste', licked it from her fingers. Throughout the 28th his limbs were in almost continuous convulsion. He died the next day, Tuesday, 29 July, at four o'clock in the afternoon. Two days later he was buried in Bonn. Brahms, Joachim and Dietrich,* his youthful admirers, were the honorary pallbearers, and Grillparzer delivered an oration at the graveside. The only other people present at the funeral, apart from Clara herself, were Hiller and members of the *Concordia-gesellschaft* who had serenaded Robert's arrival in Düsseldorf six years earlier.

*

The true nature of Schumann's illness was regarded as a mystery by the medical profession for nearly a century. No single diagnosis accounted for all the symptoms. In 1873, Dr Richarz first aroused interest in the problem when he published his autopsy findings.[2] This revealed (1) sharp bone-growths at the base of the skull, which had partially pierced the outer covering of the brain; (2) concretion of the two inner coverings of the brain, with adherence of the innermost one to the cerebral cortex in places; (3) distended blood vessels at the base of the brain; (4) considerable atrophy of the entire brain, the weight of which was below normal for a man of Schumann's age. An organic disease was indicated, and Richarz diagnosed general paresis.[3] Unfortunately, it was impossible to check Richarz's findings as the hospital notes relating to Schumann's case disappeared from Endenich shortly afterwards. Möbius, in his foundation work on Schumann's illness,[4] suggested that Richarz himself had removed them (a possible reason may shortly emerge) and, after considering all the evidence, he concluded that Schumann had suffered from a series of schizophrenic attacks from his early manhood onwards. This diagnosis was challenged by Gruhle[5] who pointed out that the same symptoms adduced by Möbius could lead to quite a different

---

[1] Litzmann, Vol. II, p. 414.
[2] As an Appendix to Wasielewski's biography of Schumann.
[3] A partial paralysis of the muscles which does not affect sensation.
[4] Möbius, P. J.: *Über Robert Schumanns Krankheit*, Halle, 1906.
[5] Gruhle, W.: *Brief über Robert Schumanns Krankheit, an P. J. Möbius*, 1906.

diagnosis: namely, manic depression culminating in an organic brain disease. Since then, most of Schumann's biographers have hovered uncertainly over the various choices offered them,[1] with the result that while there is general agreement that Schumann's trouble was largely mental, there is some uncertainty as to its precise nature.

It came as a surprise to the world of music when Dr Eliot Slater and Dr Alfred Meyer, specialists in the fields of psychiatry and neuropathology respectively, published a joint paper in 1959 in which they asserted that 'on careful consideration none of these alternatives fits all the facts as well as syphilitic disease'.[2] Their diagnosis was 'a combination of cerebrospinal syphilis and dementia paralytica'. This links Schumann's 'mental' symptoms (such as aural delusions and giddiness) with his physical ones (convulsions and partial paralysis). Is it possible that Richarz himself, who, after all, observed Schumann daily for two years or more, suspected syphilis and suppressed the hospital records to spare Clara further humiliation? We shall never know. Only one thing is certain. If syphilis is now to be regarded as the 'official' diagnosis, Schumann must have contracted it fairly early since one or two of the symptoms on which the diagnosis is based appeared at least twelve years before he died.[3] The most likely period is 1828–29, during his boisterous days as a student. This is a challenge to his biographers which has so far not been taken up.

[1] In 1928 Macmaster confused the issue still further by suggesting tubercular meningitis. (*La folie de Robert Schumann*, Paris.)

[2] *Confinia Psychiatrica*, Vol. 2, No. 2, p. 87. Syphilis had already been mentioned as a possibility by Gruhle (*op. cit.*) who was quoted by Wörner (*Robert Schumann: Ein letzer Zukunftsblick*, Zürich, 1949).

[3] Schumann had first reported auditory symptoms to his physician Dr Helbig in 1844. His first really distressing attack occurred in May 1846, when he experienced 'a constant singing and roaring in the ears'.

YONTY SOLOMON

Solo Piano Music—I
The Sonatas and the Fantasie

Introduction

SCHUMANN'S three sonatas, and the C major Fantasie, represent an intriguing phenomenon. Not only do they reflect a state of mind in vehement protest against current plebian conventionalities, but they also gather together the first positive threads towards recreating and reassessing the dominant form of the Classical era.

During the decade following the last sonatas of Beethoven, a steady and rapid decline set in. As if overshadowed by Beethoven's towering achievement, music appeared which either perfunctorily imitated the older style, or degenerated into vapid 'decomposition' (to use Schumann's own withering description) like the exhibition pieces in vogue in the flourishing Paris virtuoso school. A sudden explosion of miniature forms resulted, and for a time the sonata suffered a serious setback. Virtually everything performed and published was meant to pander to the increasing demand for popular pot-pourris, flamboyant technical studies, and engaging trifles to beguile an undiscerning public.[1] Even Clara, famous for the 'severity' of her taste, continually hectored Robert not to write music which was too 'difficult' and 'inaccessible'.

Sonatas by Spohr, Moscheles and Ries, among the lesser talents, are today relegated to museum archives. That esoteric group of early Romantics, Schunke, Count von Pocci and Berger, are practically unknown.[2] And as for the galaxy

[1] It is symptomatic of such a dismal musical climate that both Schumann and Chopin published as their Op. 1 dazzling sets of variations. But unlike the general tendency, the themes upon which they are based are not excerpts from popular operas of the day by such composers as Meyerbeer or Bellini, but, in the one case, an original pun on the name 'ABEGG', and, in the other case, a classical aria from Mozart's 'DON GIOVANNI'.

[2] Except for the enthusiasm Schumann himself displayed for them in his critical writings.

of keyboard wizards, Thalberg, Kalkbrenner, and Hiller among them, they concentrated on a new genre of virtuoso piano music which was so fashionable it did not survive its own time, let alone survive into ours.

And what of Schumann? His sonatas live on. They have survived every change of fashion. To understand why this is so, let us turn to Schumann himself. Attacking the attempts at sonata composition by composers of both the older and younger generations of his time, Schumann complains bitterly that this noble form was all-too-often treated as a

> refuge to gain the intellectual praise of connoisseurs, donning its cloak too often to disguise meretricious exercises in form, and devoid of any irresistible inward impulse.

In despair, he continues:

> . . . on the whole it looks as if this form has run its course.[1]

Clearly, Schumann saw himself as the guardian of tradition. The Classical ideals of Beethoven and Schubert, which he held so dear, seemed in danger of being lost. Schumann understood his historical position very well, and when he came to write his own sonatas he was conscious of swimming against the tide.

The breakaway movement from sonata composition, with which Schumann found himself confronted, may be explained in several ways. After Beethoven and Schubert, the break-up of tonality jeopardized the inherent principles of sonata structure. It became possible to relate distant keys, to introduce violent contrasts. In a Beethoven sonata movement, the sudden introduction of a remote tonality has a vital, even catastrophic, effect on the overall construction. Thus, in the 'Hammerklavier' Sonata, when the main theme bursts forth in the unexpected key of B minor, the course of the entire movement is changed.

EX I

Allegro ♩ = 138

These are fundamental matters, and they were continually misunderstood by the early Romantics in the first flush of their rapid conquest of the remote tonal regions.

In the Classical sonata, the structural elements, too, are organically charged by the dramatic conflicts between Principal and Subordinate theme-groups. With the Beethoven sonata, no matter how these warring conflicts are intensified and resolved, it is inevitably the First subject which emerges as the victor. The crucial Development section elaborates, juxtaposes and fragments the theme-motifs presented in the Exposition, exploring the dramatic possibilities of this material to the extent that when we eventually arrive at the Recapitulation, we have new and different insights into these fundamental themes. The sonata, with Beethoven, is thus an essentially dramatic form. And Beethoven's structural technique is of such sharply delineated clarity, that the emerging form has all the reality of a piece of architecture.[1] Yet each of his sonatas is different, and poses a fresh challenge. Again, this was misunderstood by the early Romantics; they not only reverted to a stereotyped form (a sort of 'aural blueprint' for building sonatas, which they wrongly thought had been handed down by Beethoven, and which still has some kind of posterity in today's textbooks), but they also lost that dramatic 'clash of opposites' so typical of Beethoven.

Schumann, though he cleaves to the tradition of Beethoven, tends also towards the lyrical freedom and harmonic richness of Schubert. The diamond-hard definition of material in Beethoven becomes, with Schumann, slightly softened and loosened. His forms, like Schubert's, can be said to depend more on the state of his mind than on the state of his matter. His principal themes consist of flowing sequences, of songlike periods and episodes. The juxtaposition of remote harmonies is part of the very fabric of his musical textures, and the overall structure seems in consequence to fluctuate between formal discipline and extended improvisation. The following passage, the first subject of his Sonata in F minor, is typical of Schumann's entire approach to sonata material.

EX 2

[1] If we regard Beethoven as the master architect whose form is precisely determined by his content, we can see plainly why a strict performance of his music, without 'reading

In fact, the ease with which Schumann modulates in prolonged sections sometimes gives rise to an abundance of repeated sequences, a procedure for which
he has been heavily criticized. It is far from the truth to believe that Schumann's
themes are not capable of development by motivic elaboration. They are often
so developed, their rich potential worked out, before the Development section
proper gets under way. (Here again, Schumann shows a deep kinship with Schubert, particularly the Schubert of the late B flat major Sonata.[1]) Thus, the
Development sometimes loses the sheer impact of Beethoven's tight argument
and logic, and in its place Schumann relies, perhaps too heavily, on the transposition of entire periods through increasingly remote tonalities. These are heightened, however, by effective contrasts in the 'orchestration' of the piano writing,
together with fluctuations in the basic tempo—either as written-out rubatos, or
as complete changes of metre.[2] The central episode from the first movement of
the C major Fantasie, Op. 17, (surely a sonata in all but name) which Schumann
marks 'Im Legendenton'—'in the style of a legend'—serves as a prototype of this
kind of 'static' development, which has a self-contained, new, and definite
character of its own (Ex. 3).

When we come to consider the sonatas as a whole we find that it is in his
Scherzo movements that Schumann's imagination is particularly fired. Here, the
master of the *Novelletten*, *Kreisleriana* and *Davidsbündlertänze* brings his mercurial
qualities to the forefront. 'The younger composers have discovered a new movement, the Scherzo,' Schumann once observed. But none of them wrote wittier

---

between the lines , can give as clear a grasp of the overall shape as a more deeply-felt interpretation can. Some musicians, in fact, prefer such an approach.
   [1] Also the first movement of the 'Great' C major Symphony. ED
   [2] See the first movement of the A minor Piano Concerto (p. 250). ED

EX 3

and more epigrammatic examples than Schumann himself, thus demonstrating conclusively that he knew full well that the essence of the scherzo, like that of wit, is brevity. In this respect, is not the Scherzo from the G minor Sonata a worthy successor to second period Beethoven?

EX 4

Schumann is at his most characteristic in his slow movements. Their dreamy world of self-communion captures new emotional fields for music, and happens to give the word 'Schumannesque' its real meaning. Two of the slow movements (in the F sharp minor and G minor Sonatas respectively) started life as songs,

but they fit so happily into the context of their new surroundings that it is
difficult to remember that they also enjoy an independent existence. Of the remaining slow movements, the one in the F minor Sonata comprises a set of
variations, the only occasion Schumann ever included this form in his sonatas.
It is based on a theme by Clara Wieck.

EX 5

The slow movement of the Fantasie is in many respects the most memorable of
all, not least because Schumann hits upon the highly original idea of placing it
last in the order of movements, and it lingers in the mind's ear long after the
music has stopped, so to speak.

The formal organization of these Sonatas obviously posed a greater challenge
to Schumann than his smaller-scale pieces and the suite-forms. This is borne out
by the lengthy revisions, movement substitutions, and other changes precipitated
during the five years (1833–38) that it took to complete them. But the result is a
body of works which not only carries forward the great tradition of sonata form,
as handed down by the Viennese classics, but combines it with the new, revolutionary language of German romanticism. This makes Schumann's sonatas
unique.

Sonata No. 1, in F sharp minor, Op. 11 (1835)

This masterly tone-poem originated in two of Schumann's earlier compositions.
The first was an unpublished 'Fandango' (1831) which became the framework

of the opening movement, the Allegro vivace, and supplied most of its thematic material.

EX 6

The Allegro vivace, incidentally, begins with a motif derived from Clara Wieck's 'Scène Fantastique', one of her Four Characteristic Pieces, Op. 5. In Clara's youthful piece, the phrase is in the treble clef.

EX 7

Schumann, tongue-in-cheek, transfers this to the bass clef in this manner.

EX 8

Then he simply puts the two ideas together to form the first subject.

EX 9

This material dominates most of the first movement. Even the lyrical second subject

EX 10

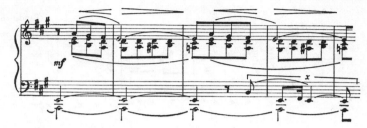

harks back to the 'Clara motif' in its fourth bar (bracket 'X').

The other one of Schumann's earlier compositions incorporated into the Sonata is found in the slow movement, the 'Aria', which is based on an early song 'To Anna' (1828).

EX 11

When Schumann adapted it to his Sonata, he transposed it into A major, and modified the accompaniment.

EX 12

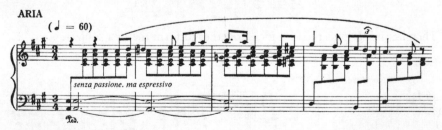

Liszt commented of this slow movement that it was 'one of the most beautiful pages we know, and in spite of its indication "senza passione", it is in fact a song of great passion, expressed with a fullness and calm'.[1]

[1] *Gazette Musicale*, Paris, 1837.

A point of great structural interest now arises. The Sonata is the only one in which Schumann begins with an extended Introduction— a kind of improvisation, eloquent and declamatory. One of its functions (and a truly original one at that) is to offer us a fleeting glimpse of the 'Aria' which is first heard in this form.

EX 13

INTRODUZIONE
Un poco adagio ($\text{\textquotedbl} = 76$)
sotto voce

Compare Ex. 13 with Ex. 12. The effect of the quotation, only four bars in length, is to endow the Introduction with a powerful sense of structural 'integrity'. Did Schumann here discover a new rôle for sonata introductions? There seems to be no precedent for such distant cross-connections.[1]

To Schumann's contemporaries, the F sharp minor Sonata must have come as something of a shock. Critical reactions veered between the extremes of Moscheles and Liszt. Moscheles, one of the most respected pianist-composers of the older generation, was at first perplexed by the Sonata. In a letter to his wife he confessed that he found it 'very laboured, difficult, somewhat intricate, though interesting musically'.[2] Later, after Schumann had invited him to review it for the *Neue Zeitschrift*, he became more enthusiastic. Liszt, on the other hand, recognized its originality and genius from the start, and wrote a perceptive review about it in the *Gazette Musicale* (1837). As for the musical public, they were completely bewildered, and not without reason. Who else would so audaciously have published a work of such spacious proportions, boldness and originality of concept, without disclosing the name of its author? When the Sonata first appeared, it simply carried the declaration 'To Clara, from Florestan and Eusebius'. Who were Florestan and Eusebius? The pseudonyms must have been pretty obvious to the inner circle of Schumann's friends, to those familiar with the Davidsbund; but they were far from obvious to anybody else, and can only

[1] Beethoven, as usual, pointed the way in such works as the 'Pathétique' and 'Les Adieux' sonatas, whose respective introductions play vital rôles in the subsequent structure of their first movements. But there seems to be no case of Beethoven building a bridge from his Introduction to his slow movement in this way. ED

[2] *Life of Moscheles*, by his wife, 1872 (letter of 1 October 1835).

be interpreted as a sly dig at the Establishment. That is how Liszt took it in his review.

> ... the title of the present work is veiled in mystery, a fact which will not endear it to musicians in France where poetry is often confused with eccentricity and criticised as such. In Germany, however, it is a different matter; people are not embarrassed by the fantasies of the artist, and if the work succeeds by its merit and beauty, the sentiments inspiring the composer are respectfully accepted.[1]

It is in every sense a revolutionary sonata. The monumental control with which Schumann dispenses a profusion of ideas, alternating with each other in kaleidoscopic fashion, is admirable. Architecturally, it may lack the impact of those sonatas of Beethoven conceived on a similarly epic scale; but this is Schumann's first published sonata, written at the age of twenty-four, and it embodies so totally his convictions, ideals, and personal commitments that this is probably his most important essay in the form. The late romantic composers discovered in it a model for their own achievements, including Anton Rubinstein, whose performance of the Sonata was perpetuated by Hanslick's criticism.[2] For its time, the actual piano writing must have appeared perplexing. The quicker movements abound in exuberant virtuosity, of which the following passage, from the Finale, is a typical example.

EX 14

Allegro un poco maestoso ♩ = 126

---

[1] *Op. cit.*
[2] 'The slow movement was ideally beautiful—an incomparable transfigured image. The Finale, on the other hand, was overwhelmed in such a manner that even listeners who were

There are constant changes of mood, dynamics and touch. All resources of technique are exploited. The restless succession of repeated notes, octaves, wide skips and clusters of thick chords must have taxed even the most accomplished player schooled in the 'pure' traditions of Hummel, Clementi and Kalkbrenner.

Sonata No. 2, in G minor, Op. 22 (1833–38)

When Clara Schumann published her complete edition of Schumann's works, she felt extremely proprietorial towards this Sonata and conveniently suppressed the original dedication to Schumann's close friend, Henriette Voigt. She did the same with the Liszt dedication of the C major Fantasie. Had her ministrations stopped merely at tidying up Schumann's biography, so to speak, no real harm would have been done. But she left her mark on the Sonata in a more prominent way. She persuaded Schumann to drop the original finale to the work, complaining that it was 'too difficult, and that really the public, even the connoisseurs for whom you write, would not understand'.[1] In its place, Schumann obligingly supplied a totally different, and more conventional Rondo; the original finale he later published as a separate piece, a 'Presto Passionato'. I wish that more pianists would play the 'Presto Passionato'. It is what Schumann originally intended. Its sheer exuberance, and startling originality, are hard to beat. The

thoroughly familiar with it were not always able to keep pace, and often were left to guess at what he actually played.' (Hanslick: *Vienna's Golden Years of Music*—trs. Pleasants.) This last observation has a familiar ring about it when we consider certain present-day performances of this difficult movement.

[1] Litzmann, Vol. I, p. 186.

curious allusion to Beethoven's 'Kreutzer' Sonata makes one wonder at the programmatic motivation[1] (Ex. 15).

[1] Schumann's 'Beethoven quotations', both conscious and unconscious, deserve a separate chapter to themselves. One of the most obvious occurs in the 'Soldier's March' from 'Album for the Young',

a) Munter und Straff

which is clearly modelled on the Scherzo of Beethoven's 'Spring' Sonata.

b) Scherzo: Allegro molto

Another powerful **connection** exists between the 'March of the Davidsbündler' from 'Carnaval',

c) Molto più vivace

and Beethoven's 'Emperor' Concerto.

d) Rondo: Allegro

These likenesses are too striking to be dismissed. They make one wonder whether, as Yonty Solomon suggests in the case of the 'Kreutzer' quotation above, Schumann had some unrevealed programmatic allusion in mind. In this connection, see p. 61 where Mr Solomon mentions the Beethoven 'programme' behind the C major Fantasie. ED

CLARA SCHUMANN (1878)
an oil portrait by Lenbach

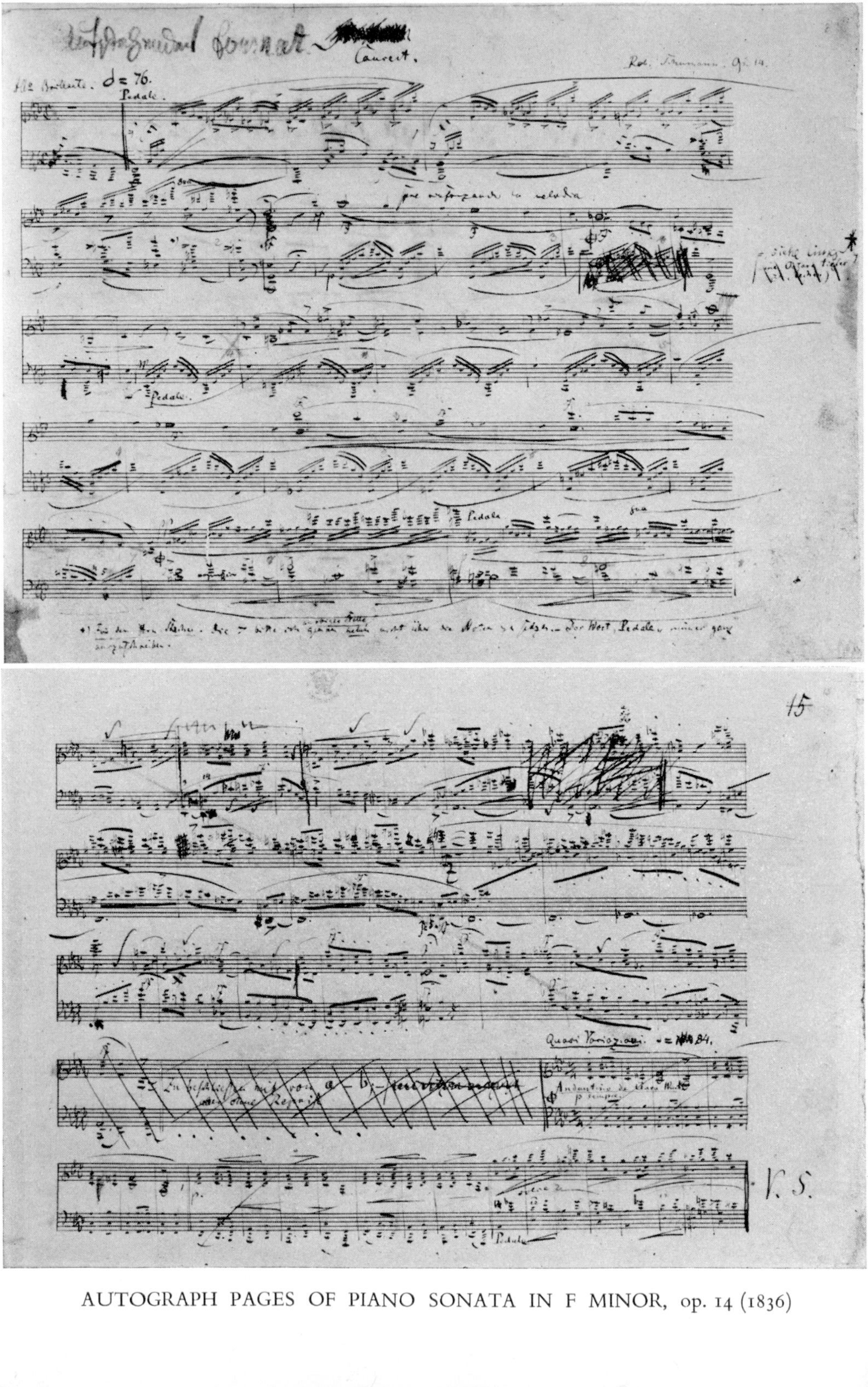

AUTOGRAPH PAGES OF PIANO SONATA IN F MINOR, op. 14 (1836)

EX 15

The unusual dynamic marking *ppp* accompanies the quotation, and the wealth of cross-rhythms pervading the entire movement depicts an aura of spectral fantasy.

The Sonata in G minor, despite its concentrated simplicity, occupied the longest period of creation. Sketches of the Scherzo and the first movement (with a slow-moving opening theme, however), date from June 1833. An early song in E flat major called *Im Herbste* (1828) was subsequently recomposed and became the Andantino; it had also previously appeared as a fragment of a piano piece called *Papillote* (1830). The genesis of the G minor Sonata, then, is not unlike that of the F sharp minor Sonata, and the degree of creative effort which went into the process reflects the seriousness with which Schumann regarded his historical rôle as a 'torchbearer' of the sonata tradition.

The Sonata begins with a brief, introductory flourish, and then plunges straight into its impassioned first subject.

EX 16

A more lyrical, syncopated second Subject, grows out of bracket 'X'.

c

EX 17

The development is concerned chiefly with the first subject; it throws an interesting light on Schumann's methods and the characteristic way in which he tries to create new melodies while remaining faithful to his old ones. The following theme sounds 'new', and hardly part of a development section at all; yet it is clearly related to the first subject.[1]

EX 18

The first movement contains the famous, yet paradoxical marking 'So rasch wie möglich' (as fast as possible), later followed by the impossible 'Schneller' (faster) and the equally impossible 'Noch Schneller'[2] (even faster)! Schumann may have regarded this as a private joke. It may have been a jibe at the tendency of pianists to take quick tempi at break-neck speeds. He counselled Clara before the first public performance in Berlin, 1840, 'not to take the Sonata too wildly; think of him who made it!'[3]

[1] There are many similar examples in Schumann. Nieman discusses this aspect of Schumann's melodic technique on pp. 242–45. ED

[2] See Weingarten (p. 99) on the same point. For a general discussion of Schumann's tempi, see Brian Schlotel, p. 109. ED

[3] The last movement of the Fantasie has an equally perplexing directive: 'Langsam getragen. Durchweg *leise* zu halten'. The indication cannot be taken literally since there are at least

The slow movement, as I have pointed out, originally started life as the song *Im Herbste*. This is what the original looked like.

EX 19

And here is the same passage in its re-composed version for solo piano.

EX 20

two magnificent climaxes. Incidentally, from here onwards (1839), Schumann's tempo indications are almost always in very explicit German, following the tradition of Beethoven's Sonatas Opp. 101 and 110.

There are some exquisite anticipations of Chopin's writing in this movement. Such passages as the following, in thirds and sixths, vividly recall the Polish master, and might have come straight from his G major Nocturne, or even the Barcarolle.

EX 21

The Scherzo is terse, epigrammatic to the point of brusqueness (see Ex. 4, p. 45), while the Presto finale—described as a Rondo—exploits the violent contrasts inherent between the opening theme in broken octaves and the pleading phrases of the second subject (Exx. 22 (a) and (b)).

EX 22

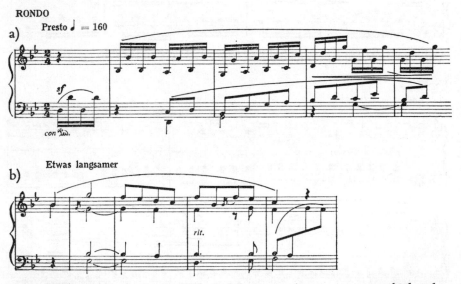

There is a good deal of sequential modulation in this movement, which Schumann is content to repeat in order to fill out his canvas. This has irritated some of Schumann's critics who see in this 'back-tracking' a serious weakness. However, the music sounds so spontaneous, and is so characteristic of Schumann, that the

criticism is rendered almost redundant. This Sonata met with an immediate success when Clara introduced it to the Berlin public, and what Schumann once
wrote of Schubert—'He gives what youth desires: an overflowing heart, daring
thoughts, and swift deeds'[1]—must surely apply to this Sonata as well.

Sonata No. 3, in F minor, Op. 14 (1836 rev. 1853)
'*Concerto without Orchestra*'

The Sonata in F minor was given its first public performance by Brahms in
Vienna, 1862, six years after Schumann's death. It may be no more than coincidence, but the first movement bears some striking resemblances to Brahms's
own F minor sonata, particularly in its dramatic opening, which seems to serve
as a model for the later work.

EX 23

[1] GSK ('Schubert's last compositions').

In 1843, Moscheles (to whom it is dedicated) reviewed the Sonata, but, as in Op. 11, not without caution. The heading 'Concerto without Orchestra' bothered him. 'One wonders what may have prompted the title. The predominant earnestness and passion of the work are incompatible with the expectations of a contemporary concert audience . . .'[1] Actually, the title was added at the persuasion of Haslinger, the original publisher, whose reason was simply 'to whet the appetite of a more curious public'. His ploy does not appear to have succeeded. The Sonata remained one of the least popular of all Schumann's piano compositions. Schumann himself was not entirely happy with it. Writing to Van Bruyck in 1852 he expressed a sense of disillusionment: 'I think you give too much importance to my early works, for example, the Sonatas, whose weaknesses are daily becoming more obvious to me.'[2] The following year, 1853, Schumann undertook a revision of the work,[3] which is why it is now known as the 'Third' Sonata, even though it appeared before the more famous number two, in G minor.

The centrepiece of the Sonata, and the inspired source of the entire work, is the 'Andantino de Clara Wieck', on which Schumann writes a set of variations as his third movement. This single, unifying theme, activates the entire Sonata. Here are just four of its derivations.

EX 24

[1] NZfM, 1843.
[2] Jansen, pp. 355–56.
[3] The manuscript of the first version is now in the British Museum, and bears the date 'June 5, 1836'. It offers an intriguing opportunity to follow alterations to the text prior to Haslinger's first publication, and to compare them with the revised version of 1853.

By such use of his thematic material throughout the Sonata, Schumann created a powerful organic unity. Yet even he cannot avoid a certain monotony of harmony, and he tends to remain fixed in the principal tonality for long stretches. Perhaps the thematic restrictions imposed by the choice of the same basic motif in all four movements was too much for the resulting sonata structure to bear.

The *Davidsbündlertänze* are strikingly recalled by the ancient and solemn flavour of the Scherzo and Trio. It is almost a minuet, with its 'molto commodo' stateliness and characteristic upbeat accents.

EX 25

Much of the writing borders dangerously on that type of parallel 'doubling' with both hands, which was to become so typical a feature in the piano music of Brahms. The Trio passes through a long succession of modulations from D major and B minor, to D flat major and B flat minor, interrupted by sinister references to the Scherzo theme.

The other, second, Scherzo which Schumann composed for the Sonata is much more akin to the *Fantasiestücke*; its F major Trio ominously prophesies thematic details of the Finale. This alternative Scherzo deserves to be performed in its rightful context, even though adding considerably to the duration of the Sonata.

The Variations on Clara's theme are so effectively conceived, that one can forgive the practice of at least one of this century's major pianists to play it as a separate movement. With these most touching and exquisitely-wrought variations, the whole Sonata suddenly springs to life. It is as though one had been brought face to face with the true impetus of the Sonata. Of the six variations in the original, Schumann has left us with four in the revised version, concluding with an eloquent coda. These variations are free and asymmetrical; hence, presumably, the romantic title *Quasi Variazioni*.

The Finale is a fearsomely difficult piece to play, with its displaced accents, its syncopated melodic contours, and at lightning speed too!

EX 26

Alas, this strangely uneven, but important masterpiece, is rarely heard in the concert hall. Audiences experience a curious reserve in accepting it on its own merits. Musically, it is as interesting as its companions, but the repetitious nature of its thematic material appears to irritate a great number of musicians. Perhaps there is some truth in their protestations.

Fantasie in C major, Op. 17 (1836)

The Fantasie in C major, which is dedicated to Liszt, was originally intended as a contribution by Schumann to raise funds for the Beethoven monument in Bonn. A Beethoven Memorial Committee had been set up in the 1830s, and musicians throughout Europe were invited to contribute towards the erection of a monument to the master.[1] Schumann thought that the best contribution he himself could make would be to donate the proceeds from the sales of one of his compositions, and accordingly he began work on a 'Grand Sonata for the Piano-forte'. Shortly afterwards, he dropped this title and called the three movements 'Ruins', 'Triumphal Arch' and 'Starry Crown' because of their programmatic allusions to the life of Beethoven; he even thought of quoting part of the Seventh Symphony in the last movement. These ideas in turn were abandoned, and the work was eventually published by Breitkopf and Härtel as a 'Fantasie', headed by this motto from Schlegel:

[1] It was eventually unveiled in Bonn, in 1845, the 75th Anniversary of Beethoven's birth.

> Through all the tones
> In Earth's many-coloured dream
> There sounds one soft long-drawn note
> For the secret listener.[1]

Ever since, Schumann scholars have asked themselves what the quotation means. The prevailing view is that it is a veiled reference to Clara. Indeed, Schumann himself says as much. In a letter to Clara, he writes:

> Tell me what occurs to you when you hear the first movement of the Fantasie? Doesn't it stir many memories? The melody

> is my own favourite. Are you not the 'note' in the motto? I almost believe you are.[2]

Schumann's reference to Clara's being the 'note' in the motto refers to the 'long-drawn note' in the Schlegel quotation. But the Clara connection is further enhanced by the well-known use that Schumann made of a thematic quotation from Beethoven's song-cycle *An die ferne Geliebte* ('To the distant beloved'), in the first movement of the Fantasie. The quotation, which was first pointed out by Hermann Abert,[3] is more than a topical tribute to Beethoven.

EX 27

[1] 'Durch alle Töne tönet
   Im bunten Erdentraum
   Ein leiser Ton gezogen
   Für den, der heimlich lauschet.'
          —Fr. Schlegel
[2] 9 June 1839. *Jugendbriefe*, p. 303.   [3] *Robert Schumann*, Berlin, 1920, p. 69.

The words of Beethoven's setting, 'Accept, then, these melodies that I sang for you, my love,' reinforce the view that Clara herself was 'the distant beloved' in Schumann's imagination. Abert also pointed out the thematic connection between the main motif (Ex. 28) and Schumann's favourite melody quoted in the above letter; while Robert Schauffler[1] suggested that the five-note falling themes which resound through the piano sonatas and the Fantasie were *all* a tribute to Clara. More recently, Eric Sams[2] has suggested that these and other Clara-themes identified by later commentators all derive from a private cipher-system of Schumann's own; and that it is indeed the use of these themes, woven into the very fabric of the musical material of the Fantasie, and other works, which explains Schumann's frequent mysterious references to Clara, such as the one quoted above.

The Fantasie does not exploit the piano in the 'flashy' style of Schumann's contemporaries. Rather it draws from the instrument some hidden, magical substance. It is a confessional document, a deeply personal utterance, at once agonized and ecstatic; it is private, not public music. For this very reason, it is difficult to bring off in the full glare of the concert hall, particularly on a modern grand, with its heavy action and thick-sounding textures. The work begins in such a way as to suggest that the music commenced some time before the piece itself actually started.

EX 28

Durchaus phantastisch und leidenschaftlich vorzutragen ♩ = 80

---

[1] *Florestan*, New York, 1945, p. 297 *et seq.*

[2] 'Did Schumann use Ciphers?', *Musical Times*, May 1966; 'The Schumann Ciphers: a Coda', *Musical Times*, December 1966.

Here is to be found some of Schumann's most idiosyncratic 'scoring' for the piano; the shimmering, veiled clusters of sound seem to transform the instrument into some kind of sustaining medium, and lend it a higher, visionary quality. It is a touchstone of Schumann's style.

One of the most interesting accounts of the Fantasie comes from Liszt, whose interpretation of the work has been handed down to us in a fascinating account by one of his pupils, who had just played the work to the great master.

> . . . it seems to me that everybody, not you alone . . . has a totally wrong conception of the opening movement. I suppose you know that Schumann wrote the Fantasie especially for me, and more than once I had the pleasure of playing it to him. It is a noble work, worthy of Beethoven, whose career, by the way, it is supposed to represent. But everyone plays this opening movement in too vigorous a style. It is pre-eminently dreamy, 'träumerisch', as he expressed it in German, and altogether the reverse of noisy and heavy. I do not mean that it should be played at all apathetically, for of course here and there are phrases which demand vigorous execution; but the whole outline of the movement preserves more of the dreamy character than it is usual to depict in it.
>
> I remember the first time I played it to the great composer. He remained perfectly silent in his chair . . . which rather disappointed me. So I asked him what impression my rendering of the work had on him, and what improvements he could suggest, being naturally anxious to hear the composer's ideas as to the reading of so noble a composition. He asked me to proceed with the March, after which he would give me his criticism. I played the second movement and with such effect that Schumann jumped out of his

chair, and with tears in his eyes, cried 'Göttlich, our ideas are absolutely identical as regards the rendering of these movements, only you with your magic fingers have carried my ideas to a realisation'.[1]

Structurally, the first movement falls into the three main sections of sonata form. Here the Development corresponds to the C minor episode marked 'Im Legendenton' ('In the style of a legend').

EX 29

This idea has been skilfully metamorphosed from a subsidiary theme in the Exposition, and is not the 'new episode' it sounds at first. Compare Exx. 29 and 30.

EX 30

As for the Recapitulation, this appears to begin daringly in the 'wrong' key of E flat major.

EX 31

[1] Strelezki, Anton: *Personal recollections of chats with Liszt*, London 1893.

But when we examine the structure more carefully, we see that Schumann has merely by-passed his opening pages and come in at a later stage of the main idea. The 'missing' stage turns up in the Coda.

The second movement, the great March with which Liszt so impressed Schumann, contains some of the most difficult keyboard music Schumann ever composed. Its main theme runs like this.

EX 32

Clara's reactions were mostly about the March. 'I have already learnt the March from the Fantasie, and revel in it! It makes me hot and cold all over.'[1] Her extreme changes of temperature are quite understandable, since this exciting movement demands a special, fearsome virtuosity. The overwhelming climax of the Coda, with its dangerous leaps and awkward hand positions, holds terrors for practically every pianist.

EX 33

¹ Litzmann: Vol. I, p. 351.

The Finale is unorthodox. It is a slow movement of such a broad and spacious conception that we have to go back to Beethoven's Op. 111 to find a matching spiritual calm after the upheaval of the preceding drama. Here is created an illusion of time suspended.

EX 34

Langsam getragen, Durchweg Leise zu halten (♩ = 66)

As we have seen, Schumann's real contribution to sonata form was to strip away the superficial embellishments with which his generation had cluttered up a noble form, and give it purpose by returning once more to the generating principles of Beethoven and Schubert whom he regarded as the true founders of Romantic music. Perhaps because of these unshakeable beliefs, the Sonatas may seem at times old-fashioned. But the music has a freshness, a directness, and an intensity of feeling which will ensure for it a permanent place in the sonata literature.

BÁLINT VÁZSONYI

Solo Piano Music—II

The Piano-cycles

A LEADING position among aesthetic fallacies is occupied by our habit of sorting music, composers and performers into neatly labelled pigeon-holes. This is particularly true in the case of the nineteenth century. Here we have decided to establish two diverse groups of composers, and to use the term 'conservative' for one, 'revolutionary' for the other. Merely for the sake of recapitulation: Schubert, Mendelssohn, Schumann, and Brahms are the out-standing names in the former; Berlioz, Chopin, Liszt, and Wagner in the latter group.

On the face of it, the classification seems justified. During certain periods of their lives some of these men openly proclaimed their differing aims; also, they brought allegiance to their own, and opposition to the other school. But many of them lived in the type of close, competitive confinement which all too often distorts the view. Music, like everything else, was a highly emotional affair in the nineteenth century. Nowadays we take great pride in our cool, detached approach to history generally and, within that, to music. It seems uncertain, at best, whether or not the application of this approach to music is justified or, indeed, desirable. While it lasts, however, we might as well utilize it in order to make a fresh assessment of the entire problem.

For the time being we may dispense with Schubert, who died before the emergence of the basic issues; Berlioz, who remained somewhat distant from this basically Central-European battle; and Wagner, whose output has little relevance to the subject at hand: romantic piano music. Like so much else, this, too, started with Beethoven—and not only in its substance. The classical sonata form was first expanded, then brought to unsurpassable perfection and, finally, its stable frame was broken, demolished by the forces generated from within—all this during Beethoven's own development. Thus, he already faced the problems which were to divide the masters of the nineteenth century.

The Sonata, the hard core of piano music in the Viennese Classics, had proved increasingly weak. Beethoven, in his last period, pointed the way. He shifted the weight from the first movement (traditionally, the corner-stone of the sonata with its multitudes of themes) to the last, based on *monothematic* principles. In some cases he compressed sonata form into minute proportions (Op. 101, Op. 109, Op. 110 for example), but in all cases he devised a final movement based on one of the two monothematic forms—fugue and variation—which was to carry the main burden of the entire work. Simultaneously, he laid down the foundation for short character pieces ('scènes mignonnes'[1]) in his Bagatelles. The problem Beethoven's new paths presented was that what might have started as an experiment, was always fully resolved by him, thus leaving little room for continuation.

To continue or to break with the past—that was the problem apparently facing the nineteenth century. The point of departure, however, was Beethoven in all cases. And as Beethoven pointed the way in *every* direction, it could not really be a 'break with the past'. Take any one of the composers mentioned earlier, and you will find the direct influence of Beethoven, as well as a reaction against him; take any *two* of these masters and you will find several aspects which form a tie between them, while detecting just as many characteristics which keep them apart. Only the most superficial observer would find a true similarity between the florid piano passages of Chopin and Liszt; only the casual listener would find much in common between Schumann's *Fantasiestücke* and the Intermezzi of Brahms.

Schumann's Revolution

The word 'revolution' has been abused to such an extent in our time that we might do best by abolishing it—at least in music. However, so long as we use it, Schumann must receive his due.

Let us separate two separate issues right away: the 'message' on the one hand, and the 'means' on the other. The 'revolution of the message' so to speak, was shared by all the great romantic composers of the nineteenth century. Indeed, it would be difficult to prove that anyone composed piano music more romantic than Schumann's own. There have been plenty of great artists (among them Dohnányi, one of the all-time great Schumann-interpreters[2]) who regarded

---

[1] The subtitle of Schumann's *Carnaval*.
[2] Unfortunately he made few gramophone records; one has to rely, therefore, on authori-

Schumann's music as the prototype of romanticism While each of us is free to choose his own 'prototype', no one will maintain that, for example, Chopin's *Polonaise-Fantasie* is more romantic than Schumann's *Études Symphoniques*. We can therefore narrow down the differences, if there be any, to the second issue: the 'means'. It is not only the second issue: it is also secondary. Nobody can deny that analysing the means provides a constant pre-occupation for professional musicians, but it has proved itself to be incidental to the fate of great music and the acceptance of such music by posterity.

'New flasks for new wine'—demanded Liszt. He himself certainly provided them. So did some of those who rallied around him and took up the call. His proclamation makes the process of identification easier for us. But what about the 'opposite' camp? Did they continue to use the 'old flasks'?

Let us try to draw up a list of requirements which we have come to expect the Romantic Composer to fulfil. First of all, he has to be highly individualistic. He has to spend a certain amount of his life in a dreamworld and his experiences there should be placed before us in an unashamed manner, his innermost emotions, frustrations likewise. He is expected to find highly individual ways to express his message, thereby creating new forms, new language and some means of unmistakable identification. Extra-musical inspirations such as poetry, the visual arts or philosophy, should be favoured from time to time. Does Schumann not answer this description? Do any of the great romantics provide some important addition to the list?

With regard to piano music, we can state that the reign of Vienna was equivalent to the reign of the Sonata, which achieved ultimate fulfilment with Beethoven. Schumann may not have said so in as many *words* as Liszt, but his music—just as telling—testifies to that effect. None of Schumann's so-called Sonatas was conceived originally as such, certainly not in the classical sense.[1] And before, during, and after these experiments he gave us an arsenal of piano works, which we can call, for want of a better term, his 'Piano-cycles', and which are, indeed, unlike anything else created by any other composer of any period. The only parallel that comes to mind is the *Lieder* of Schubert. Here Schubert created a form of expression which hardly existed before him and which, although continued by subsequent masters, including Schumann himself, never achieved quite that same perfection, never acquired that same central rôle as in his own œuvre. In the Piano-cycles, however, Schumann created something completely

tative personal testimonies. These, however, exist in plenty and one can still obtain his recording of *Kinderscenen* (RLP 199 43) in order to form an opinion.

[1] The true classical sonata was conceived as a single utterance in several movements. Schumann's Sonatas often contain movements composed individually at some other time and for some other purpose. See pp. 47–48 and p. 55 ED.)

his own, never really continued, that proved to be the perfect means of expressing himself and which must be regarded as the hard core of his output, despite the many other works he left us.

A sweeping statement—yes. I am not certain that I can prove it, although I shall try. The chief handicap is that an alarming number of professional musicians exist to whom Schumann does not seem to speak. And if his music does not succeed in speaking to you directly, no amount of verbal comment will make up for your loss.

Perhaps the most unique quality of Schumann's writing is that it always projects a sense of the *unreal*. Not because he often refers to his pieces as 'Fantasies'; Brahms labelled his Op. 116 this way and nothing could be more real. Within two bars Schumann can place us in the middle of a scene, tell a story, and continually interrupt it with a sigh or a phrase of innermost longing. And, somehow, the whole work—be it one page or thirty minutes—acquires a strange unity, and for no other reason than that all of it was projected by one spirit. There are plenty of short piano pieces—standing individually or tied together in sets—written in the last one hundred and fifty years. But it would be difficult to find a 'suite', lasting a good half hour and having no other unifying force than the composer's musical personality, as is the case in *Kreisleriana*.

Was this the reason why Schumann was not in search of fresh unifying agents—as Liszt was with his all-pervading 'metamorphosis of themes' technique? Schumann's unique blend of epic, lyric and dramatic music apparently provides it for him. In most artistic creations these three basic qualities can be identified with some degree of certainty. I would be happy to discover, however, which of these is the overriding factor in 'Promenade' in Schumann's *Carnaval*.

I have already observed that Schumann's 'message' was something new. Even a brief glance at the 'means' will be sufficient to show that these are unique as well. Thus, even before we take a closer look at these 'means' we can answer the question of the 'old flasks'. True, in his written statements Schumann often appeared to cast his eyes backwards, and he considered the perfection achieved by his predecessors paramount among his artistic ideals. But what he *composed* was as new as anything in the nineteenth century. Do revolutions always have to clamour?

And now let us begin with what, I submit, is Schumann's most personal phrase. Basically, it consists of a turn and a sigh of longing and resignation:

EX I

It is a phrase truly designed for the piano; the *rubato* treatment it requires would never sound quite so natural on another instrument. The reason for presenting it as Schumann's most personal phrase is simple: it appears in passages where the composer speaks in the first person singular, without a shadow of doubt. Here are a few telling examples. Consider first 'The Poet Speaks' from *Kinderscenen*.

EX 2

The 'Epilogue' from the *Arabeske* Op. 18, which stands almost completely outside the piece, could again be called 'The Poet Speaks' had Schumann not used this title earlier.

EX 3

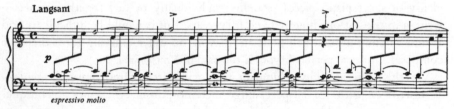

The fourth piece in *Kreisleriana* stands out as the centrepiece of the set—the calm eye of a violent hurricane; it is virtually built around the same phrase.

EX 4

And, finally, a non-piano work of special importance: *Widmung*. The phrase is not so comfortable for the human voice, but here Schumann had the opportunity of coupling it with certain words, thereby giving us a clue to its meaning.

EX 5

'Mir beschieden' means something like 'bequeathed to me'. It was the Heavens that bequeathed Clara to him—according to Rückert's poem, which he decided to use for the purpose. It causes one to wonder. There is, undoubtedly, quiet happiness, touching tenderness at this particular moment. But is there not some of the *resignation* we have come to recognize in this phrase ever since 'The Poet Speaks'? Schumann was not in the habit of quoting himself (or others) by accident. This might prove to be an interesting aspect of his deep-seated sentiments toward Clara for those who enjoy discussing Schumann's music primarily in the light of his love-affairs.

In a sense, one could say that Schumann taught the piano to speak. This is not meant to be disrespectful to all previous composers of keyboard music. There is, however, an element in Schumann's piano texture which resembles human speech more closely than music before or after him. Was the source of this his highly accomplished literacy? He might have been unconsciously thinking in words while composing music,[1] just as he was obviously thinking in terms of

---

[1] See Eric Sams, p. 390. ED

pure music while setting a poem. Critics of Schumann frequently refer to the
'limited range' of his piano writing. True, much of what he tells us lingers around
the middle of the keyboard. But surely, it is most difficult to induce the high
treble or the low bass to speak with a *vox humana*. A prime example of the
'speaking piece' is *Carnaval's* 'Eusebius':

EX 6

Bracket 'A', incidentally, is another typical calling-card to which Schumann
devotes an entire Lied ('Süsser Freund') in *Frauenliebe und-leben*. The 'parlando'
aspect of this piece is its life-blood. Indeed, there is little else that would make
it viable music. The same can be said about 'Almost too serious' from *Kinderscenen*:

EX 7

One would suspect that the idea of starting and stopping throughout the
piece—never getting off the ground, so to speak—hardly allows for good listening, but here the suspicion is unjustified. Schumann has done something similar
in 'Entreating Child' from the same set of pieces,

EX 8

where the plea just fades away at the end in a dominant seventh chord, to be answered only in the following piece.

'Entreating Child' points to another special quality of Schumann's. This little piece consists of four sections (each repeated), the last being the same as the first. It is important, however, to note that the last section is not just a return of a conventional *A* in an *ABCD* form. Much more significant is that the musical idea is just as suitable for the opening as it is for the ending, and it sounds quite different in its respective rôles. The ability of a composer to create ideas with 'open ends', i.e. motifs which can be placed at any point of a sentence or phrase, is not common. Mozart was the unequalled master of this technique, and we might look at an example to illuminate the point:

EX 9

My quotation comes from the last movement of Mozart's Piano Concerto in B flat major, K. 595. As we see, bracket 'A' is first used as an antecedent, and then as a consequent, in this eight-bar sentence. In its second function, it opens the door for a completely different continuation:

EX 10

Probably the innocent listener does not even realize that he has heard the same two-bar idea twice. He is merely aware of something which endowed the music with a kind of heavenly continuity.

One naturally feels cautious of comparing anyone with Mozart. Still, Schumann did have the rare gift of 'open-end' ideas. He employed them more often and more successfully than, perhaps, any other composer after Mozart. The opening phrase of *Warum?*, for instance, is also its ending.

EX 11

It is both an antecedent and a consequent. Music flows *out* of this idea as smoothly as it flows *into* it. Or take the 'Prophet bird' in *Waldscenen*:

EX 12

This idea probably created a school for pieces that do not end. A more complex example of the technique occurs in *Faschingsschwank aus Wien*. Observe how 'A' appears three times: it can serve as a beginning, as a double-phrased arrival/departure, and just as happily as a close.

EX 13

While on the subject of *Faschingsschwank*, I should like to embark on a some-what lengthier discussion of its layout. The work always struck me as one of exceptional logic and cohesion, although I had not attempted to analyse it in the past. As half-a-dozen distinguished pianists with whom I have discussed its form, and who have been intimately acquainted with it for some years, seem to have overlooked its underlying logic, an analysis needs no further justification. For, having taken a closer look at this remarkable work, I am tempted to believe that it could be considered Schumann's most successful Sonata.[1]

The subtitle of *Faschingsschwank* is, as so very often in Schumann, 'Phantasie-bilder'—'Fantasie Pieces'. This subtitle is misleading, particularly if we associate it with free, *ad hoc* construction. At first glance, the suite appears to be a random collection of longer and shorter pieces. The first movement—its longest—is easily mistaken for a loose mixture of ideas with a recurring theme thrown in for good measure. Neither observation is true; indeed, the work is more elaborately constructed than most.

The Allegro opens with this strong recurring idea:

EX 14

Note the rhythmic pattern of the marked bar. The first episode in G minor con-tinues this rhythmic pattern beneath a counter-melody superimposed in larger note-values. It is this which helps to give the episode its continuity.

EX 15

---

[1] Significantly, Schumann himself described it, in a letter to its dedicatee, Simonin de Sire, as 'a great romantic sonata'. Since the finale is, in fact, the only movement which is actually in sonata form, and the first movement is a free rondo, the work is really a sonata seen *the other way round*. ED

This is followed by the first return of the recurring theme, (Ex. 14) arriving naturally because of its identical rhythm. The second episode, in E flat major, brings a complete change of metre. It moves by way of one long, and one short, chord—a continuous chain of suspension and resolution.

This episode, incidentally, illustrates Schumann's lifelong habit of writing rhythmic patterns across the bar line. Critics have pointed out that the sensation of syncopated rhythm is often lost because of the long, uninterrupted chain of such patterns in Schumann's music. Is prolonged syncopation ever audible? I think one can regard extensive syncopation as the rhythmic counterpart of that vastly increased use of suspension in harmony which occurred in the nineteenth century. Metrically, it performs the same rôle as the seemingly endless strings of unresolved suspensions in Wagner's music. Of course, it will be effective only if the performer does not take the easy way out: by this I mean the arbitrary 're-distribution' of the metre. By adding pedal on the tied-over first beat, and by concentrated, one could almost say, hypnotic, projection of the correct metre, it *is* possible to preserve the bar lines as they appear in the score.

The recurring theme of *Faschingsschwank* (Ex. 14) naturally cannot 'float in' at the end of this syncopated episode; it arrives in the manner of a fresh start. Then it plunges into the third episode—again in G minor.

EX 17

As we can see, the rhythmic pattern of the recurring theme is again continued, and this new episode—again with a superimposed counter-melody—thus forms a counterpart to the first episode (Ex. 15). It is, however, much longer than the first episode (which was a simple A–B–A pattern), and is a miniature rondo in itself. The recurring theme arrives again naturally at the end, aided by the identical rhythm, and it is worth while looking at a tiny jewel of Mozartian finesse: the arrival of that theme after the first episode had stopped the quaver movement on the last beat.

EX 18

Here, as a device of additional fluency, it continues into the third beat, thereby overlapping the completion of the episode-motif with the beginning of the main idea.

EX 19

It is only now that we arrive at a full-stop in the flow of the music. A central section follows with a completely fresh set of ideas, in fact the real *Faschings-schwank.*

EX 20

This section contains the much-quoted quotation of the *Marseillaise*;[1] (Ex. 20 (a)); more importantly, it modulates over a wide range of keys, thus conveying the feeling of a development. (Modulation was the one and only requirement imposed on a development, an English term for this section which is highly misleading.) The repeated sequence of modulation is especially noteworthy: once again it shows not only genius, but mastery as well.

A further—fifth—appearance of the recurring theme after this section would not only threaten with over-use, but it would also weaken the impact of its final appearance. Schumann introduces an ingenious solution: a section follows which brings back the home key, the rhythmic pattern of the recurring theme and an ever-increasing resemblance to it; thus providing a recapitulation without a recurrence.

EX 21

Episode four appears. It is in E flat major and moves, again, by way of one short and one long chord—obviously the counterpart of episode two (Ex. 16). The chords are distributed in the metre in a somewhat different manner which also slightly changes the sensation of the suspension-resolution pattern.

EX 22

This episode is more elaborate than its predecessor, leaving no doubt that the relationship between episodes two and four forms a perfect parallel to episodes one and three. It demonstrates conclusively that Schumann was an undisputed

---

[1] Which helps to explain the work's full title 'Carnival jest from Vienna'. The 'jest' is the reference to the *Marseillaise*, which was banned at that time in Vienna owing to the delicate political situation. ED

master of the episode, and frequently bestowed upon it the vital function of sustaining large-scale structures.

The final appearance of the main idea is delayed by a noteworthy transition which combines the elements of both episodes two and four:

EX 23

Despite its coherent pattern, the striking feature of this section is its chromaticism which conveys an unmistakable feeling of transition.

The Coda which follows the final statement of the recurring theme uses the motif of the second episode over a dominant pedal as well as the 'substitute recapitulation' that had preceded episode four with some fresh 'farewell' material in between.

There are many more points of refinement which deserve to be mentioned (such as the marvellously different modulation pattern in the second appearance of the recurring theme), but let us take a look at the movement as a whole. It offers a unique solution for replacing the first-movement-form of the traditional sonata, providing a perfect vehicle for Schumann's own brand of romanticism. We would not overstate the case by calling it his own 'new flask'. Comparing it with the Viennese forms, it comes closest to the sonata rondo, but the Second Group has been replaced by interlocking episodes. Also, the proportions have been transformed by placing only one (though long) episode after the 'development' section. The movement thus resembles a kind of 'golden section' which creates a satisfactory balance despite a shifted centre of gravity. Thematically, the recurring idea draws on the monothematicism of late Beethoven, while the contrasting episodes preserve the polythematic aspect of the earlier sonatas, striking a happy balance between these two possibilities.

Turning now to the set in its entirety, we find a satisfying slow movement in the 'Romanze'; the 'Scherzino' is placed perfectly in the centre of the work and provides the brightest colours of the Suite; the fourth movement, 'Intermezzo', shows symptoms of the sonata principle in its key structure. Incidentally, this idea continued to haunt Schumann until he recomposed it as 'Schöne Fremde' in his *Liederkreis* Op. 39. (Ex. 24). The 'Finale' is in definite sonata form and would be acceptable as the closing movement in any sonata.

Summarizing the whole suite, are we not perhaps justified in calling it Schu-

EX 24

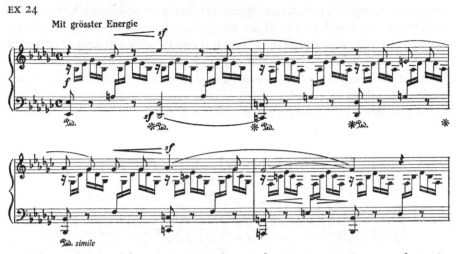

mann's most successful sonata? Two substantial outer movements carry the main burden of the form. Here Schumann reversed the process which led to the late Beethoven sonatas, by making the first movement the corner-stone once again and by allowing the 'Finale' to be—a finale. Three inner movements—all contrasting to all others—contribute the links. By extending the number of movements to five, Schumann achieves new and perfect proportions; this is also reflected in the key structure of the suite: B flat major—G minor—B flat major—E flat minor—B flat major, which is derived—another masterstroke—from the identical key structure of the first movement.

Such statements are, of course, always open to criticism, but one could say that *Faschingsschwank* presents as satisfactory a solution to the big 'structural problem' of the nineteenth century as any of the more readily recognized works. This is particularly true of the intricate and ingenious first movement.

On the more technical side, we can turn to the *Études Symphoniques* (Op. 13). Each of these twelve Études introduces something new into the vocabulary of the piano, each one sheds fresh light on the virtually unlimited inventiveness of the composer, which has frequently been placed in doubt. Apart from its obvious musical value, the *Études Symphoniques* can be seen as a perfect exercise in the arts of variation, counterpoint and colouring. Special importance should be attached to the superb mastery of variation form exhibited in this set,[1] for this was the

[1] To compose a set of twelve studies for the piano was not a new idea. But to combine them in the form of a set of variations was startlingly novel. The result is a unique contribution to the history of musical structure, and it has had no succession. Schumann's own title is: '*Études en forme de variations*'. The theme was by Freiherr von Fricken, Ernestine's adoptive father, who was an amateur flautist. ED

only form among the ancient, time-spanning types of composition which received
merely an occasional tribute from the great nineteenth-century musicians,
Brahms being the sole exception. Études I, II and IV offer a great deal of insight
into Schumann's highly individual approach to counterpoint. Consider the
beautiful 'orchestration' of the second Étude, where the distance between the
outer voices allows for complete clarity of counterpoint, while the inner voices fill
in the harmonies, providing continuity of sound and a truly 'symphonic' effect.[1]

EX 25

Then there is the simple, but ingenious canon of the fourth Étude,

EX 26

where, once again, we see yet another aspect of Schumann's gift for 'open ends
in operation (the only way to end this Étude is by merging it into the next one).
But one of the most convincing examples of Schumann's polyphonic writing is
in bars 7 and 8 of the theme itself:

EX 27

[1] See also Joseph Weingarten, p. 94. ED

Looking, however, for the really significant contributions Schumann made to the history of piano music, one finds that they can be accommodated in two distinct areas: colour and technical demands. In the former, he vastly expanded the means then available and opened the door to a world of unsuspected possibilities; in the latter, he pushed the limits well beyond what then seemed possible, adding the handicap of low rewards for the performer. The third Étude serves as an illustration of all these points.

EX 28

At first glance, the Étude can only be performed by a string trio, consisting of violin, viola and 'cello. As it is, the pianist must be able to evoke these instruments simultaneously on a dead keyboard, coming up to a near-perfect violin *spiccato*, among other things. The instrumentation is as economical as it is perfect, the pedal effect of the bass line aiding the sustaining of the tenor melody. The figuration for the right hand is as revolutionary as anything in the nineteenth century, even if it is ascribed to the appearance of Paganini (to whom credit seems to be given nowadays for practically the whole of nineteenth-century piano literature). The technical demands placed on the performer are, obviously, enormous. And, as if this opening page did not suffice, Schumann provides a hair-raising addition to the recapitulation:

D

EX 29

It is here that we find the true technical difficulty of playing Schumann. Only pianists can appreciate it. This impossible bar must be performed as purely lyrical music, without the slightest trace of visible effort. Even the professional musician, if uninitiated, would listen to it unsuspectingly. As I mentioned before, there is no public reward. Many of Liszt's rhapsodies present much less of a problem than this single bar, and a just-above-the-mediocre performance of those is sufficient to bring an audience to its feet.

Another good example both for new colours and for vast, unsuspected technical problems is the eleventh Étude.

EX 30

The magical sound of this variation comes from a special pedal effect. Looking at the entire piece we observe that every long note in the right hand appears simultaneously—and repeatedly—in the left hand figurations. As the note in the melody is among the harmonics of its lower counterpart, the sound is sustained (one could say, constantly infused with fresh life from below), producing a unique effect. Playing the left hand figuration with utter evenness, and with only the slightest hint of a constant humming, is not easy. Even more difficult is to meet the demand placed on all pianists whose hand does not extend to two octaves! (Ex. 31).

EX 31

The absence of an arpeggio mark would almost seem to indicate that Schumann indeed expected the impossible. And, as usual, the whole Étude has to impress the listener in the way of effortless, sublime lyricism. Even the *Toccata*, a work which by nature should appear primarily as a technical feat, impresses chiefly with its grand manner, vivaciousness and beauty. Only pianists know what it takes to survive this type of passage with elegance.

EX 32

Carnaval is well known. Equally well known is the fact that four letters of the alphabet (A—S—C—H) form the point of departure in each piece.[1] We have come to accept this as a curiosity, and some of us spend a lot more time discussing Ernestine's rôle in the Wieck household, Robert's passing affection for her, and Clara's possible jealousy, than marvelling at the wealth of music flowing from a fleeting idea of three or four notes. Consider the fact that these notes do not form a part of any diatonic scale.

[1] 'Asch' was the name of a small town in Bohemia where Ernestine von Fricken★ (to whom Schumann became engaged for a time) was born. These four letters also happen to coincide with the only four musical letters in Schumann's own name. In German, 'H' is B natural; 'S' (as pronounced 'es') is E flat; while 'As' is A flat. Ex. 33 shows all the derivations.

EX 33

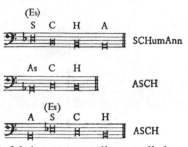

In a way this was helpful, but one is still compelled to admire the wide range of keys: no fewer than seven of them (A flat major, E flat major, B flat major, G minor, C minor, F minor and D flat major) offer wholly convincing settings for the central idea. Not since the bass theme of the 'Eroica' have four notes yielded such a vast canvas of ideas.

EX 34

a) Reconnaissance

b) Lettres Dansantes

c) Arlequin

d) Florestan

e) Chiarina

f) Estrella

g) Promenade

In that sense, *Carnaval* is unique. The same can be said of many other sets of Schumann's piano pieces. The word 'unique' is nowhere more justified, however, than in reference to the *Kinderscenen*. Throughout the nineteenth century this was the only instance of a great composer taking the trouble to sit down and write a treasure-trove of first-rate piano pieces for children. Schumann enabled youngsters at the earliest age, to grow up on truly great romantic music. This volume (and *not* the *Kinderscenen*, which—contrary to popular belief—was intended only for mature artists) offers the perfect link between similar pieces of Bach and Mozart on the one hand, and those of Bartók on the other.

An earlier statement in my essay presumed the piano-cycles to be the hard core of Schumann's output. This was based simply on the recognition that there is hardly another *genre* to which the same words of admiration could be applied *en bloc*; these works assumed the rôle of the power-house in his œuvre, and in them Schumann shows a degree of originality rarely found elsewhere. The volumes of Lieder constitute a notable exception; however, nowhere is the radiation coming from the piano works more strongly felt than in these very volumes. As for the other areas of composition: chamber, orchestral, and choral, the language developed in the piano music lived on and proved to be a fruitful stimulus—if a limited one. As we know, Schumann was not always as successful in solving the creative problems posed (say) by his orchestral music as he was in the piano works. One reason might have been that his life long habit of 'thinking in terms of a piano' later proved as much of an obstacle as it had earlier been an aid. Whatever the reasons, magic failed to carry him through, unlike in the piano cycles. For although one can sense the shape of a sonata in *Faschingsschwank*, the principle of variations in the *Études Symphoniques*, and the all-pervading four-note link in *Carnaval*, there is no denying the notion that most of Schumann's piano-cycles are held together by sheer magic. Most of them can be considered successful, and each is different. Certainly, there are the flaws, the failings. But they are fewer and farther between in these piano works than elsewhere. And it is not without interest that all the great nineteenth-century composers failed more often than those of eighteenth-century Vienna. There was a general instability in the atmosphere, and this was one of Schumann's problems.

Schumann and Posterity

In his 'Abegg' Variations, Op. 1, Schumann was on his way to becoming a German version of Chopin. Perhaps his instincts told him that there could be no such thing. He left that path with surprising speed and turned his back on it for good. In idolizing the more distant, and rejecting the more recent past, he embarked on a course which was—and still is—mistaken by many for a sideroad; it is frequently pointed out that he kept looking behind him, while Liszt and Chopin were casting their glances ahead.

We have already established, however, that Beethoven was the point of departure for every major composer of the nineteenth century. Schumann's piano-cycles, above all, could not be described as 'old flasks'; they were as new as anything in the Romantic era. The question raised at the beginning of this essay has thus been answered, except for one important aspect: the future. By this we mean, of course, the future of nineteenth-century music. And this is where we have the final proof. Liszt's Weimar, with its emphasis on 'the music of the future' maintained that there was no posterity for the 'old' school. In saying this they could have meant one of two things: either that this kind of music would not survive, or that it could not offer a point of departure for generations of composers to come. Possibly, they meant both. They could not have been more wrong. The music of Schumann, and his greatest successor Brahms, has survived in an overwhelming manner. Their works are not performed any less frequently than those of the 'revolutionaries'; in some countries they are performed more frequently. So much for the first assumption. The matter of continuation is a less tangible question. In this pseudo-intellectual age, any zealous supporter of contemporary experiments can submit a straight line of descent from Palestrina to, say, John Cage. All such 'historical' theories, therefore, must be regarded as suspect. The following thoughts come into the same category.

It is widely held that the dissolution of tonality began with Wagner (though more probably with Liszt), thereby making respectable one of the more spectacular developments of modern music. Even so, tonality is but one aspect of music. Liszt and Wagner, of course, exercised a powerful influence on subsequent generations. But did not Schumann as well? Brahms was an obvious continuation, but a true contribution to the future should go beyond these forty years. And it does; it seems sufficient to ask Bartók. In every one of his *Curriculi Vitae* Bartók wrote that he began composing under the influence of Brahms and Dohnányi. In many ways, both these influences transmit the heritage of Schumann—Dohnányi himself began composing under the almost exclusive spell of Schumann. But this might seem too indirect. Fortunately, some of Bartók's early music is even more revealing than his later statements. There we find a *Scherzo oder Fantasie*, which begins thus:

EX 35

We also find an Adagio with this middle section:

EX 36

Schumann, quite clearly. In later years Bartók thought that he went beyond these youthful inspirations as soon as other influences (Liszt, Wagner, and Strauss in particular) entered his world. His music stands as testimony that he never altogether discarded the Schumann–Brahms strain. Bartók's intellect demanded organization in music. The quickest way to satisfy it was to retain that influence. And this is not confined to Bartók's approach to form or his harmonic thinking. Schumann has often been criticized for his persistent, even obstinate rhythms which create too much tension. In Bartók's music we consider this an asset. I do not wish to determine whether either of these views is right or wrong. I cannot, however, fail to notice a bearing of the older master on the more recent one.[1]

For the sake of supporting these submissions one should have recited a much more detailed list of Schumann's innovations in piano technique, pedal effects and the ability to create an instant change of 'scenery', all of which exerted an influence on the future. A close look at all these could not be accommodated in a short essay. My intention was simply to draw attention to a basic problem and,

[1] This applies also to the writing of rhythmic patterns across the bar lines, composing four volumes of pieces *For Children*, and much else.

at the same time, to suggest respectfully a revised evaluation of nineteenth-century music in general. We ought to regard each master as an individual—his aims, his merits, his failings—irrespective of the 'school' to which he subscribes. At the same time, we can look at the total scene as a giant kaleidoscope, perhaps the most colourful in the history of music. Taking the first approach, and looking still for the revolutions of the nineteenth century, we will be certain to find one which came from the unlikely location of Zwickau—though it was undeclared and quiet.

JOSEPH WEINGARTEN

Interpreting Schumann's Piano Music

APPRECIATION of Schumann, like that of many other outstanding personalities, whether they be philosophers, artists, political or social leaders, varies with the changing social climate of the time. In a period of equilibrium, when emphasis is laid on order, logic and tradition, music such as Schumann composed is less well thought of, or less fashionable. But in an age of exuberant self-analysis, self-expression and continuous revolt, his kind of music comes into its own. Hence today there is an ever increasing interest in Schumann, the man, the critic, the composer. Yet to many a musical listener, and even to many a public performer, the idea that there might exist problems concerning the interpretation of Schumann's piano music may seem far-fetched, if not pedantic.

So many of the compositions for the instrument are made up of delightful miniatures, as for example *Papillons, Carnaval, Kinderscenen,* all written in what often superficially appears to be a not too difficult style, and to have seemingly self-explanatory titles reminiscent of programme-notes, that they have a wide and instant appeal; nor do they seem to require any penetrating study. It would be an unusual and provocative musician who would promote the works of Schumann to the same level as those of Bach, Mozart, Beethoven or even Brahms. Yet I believe that there are problems involved in the successful interpretation of Schumann's piano music which it would be interesting and useful to both listener and performer to examine. Music, unlike other arts save drama, does not actually come into being until it is performed, and the reproducing of Schumann's piano music in its noblest form makes very heavy and exacting demands on the pianist. This is undoubtedly true if he wishes to play the works as the composer intended or as they were played by Clara Schumann. In comparing her playing with that of a French pianist, Anna de Belleville, he wrote: 'The playing of the Belleville is technically the finer of the two; Clara's is more impassioned. The tone of the Belleville flatters, but does not penetrate the ear; that of Clara reaches the heart. Anna is a poetess; Clara is poetry itself.'

Robert Schumann was a born musician, a musician by compulsion, whose first love was the piano. He made a deep and detailed study of the instrument, as he himself shows in his preface to Op. 3, his arrangements of some Caprices by Paganini. He writes:

> But behind the light-heartedness which should characterize it [the Caprice], thoroughness and serious study should also be evident, for therein lies genuine mastership. For this reason the editor [Schumann] furnishes a very precise and carefully considered fingering, this being the primary foundation of all thorough playing. The student should, consequently, pay most earnest attention to the point. But if the execution is also to appear technically finished, the player should aim at buoyancy and mellowness of tone in the touch, at finish and precision in the individual parts and at fluency and lightness in the whole.

The result of this study was a new development in writing for the instrument. In Schumann's hands the piano sought to reproduce not only the polyphony of the orchestra, as in the *Études Symphoniques*, Op. 13, but a vast scale of tonal effects not previously conceived.

EX I

In 'Des Abends' from *Fantasiestücke*, Op. 12, he creates, as if by magic, a perfect impression of a quiet evening: nature at rest.

EX 2

To deal with the wide range of pianistic devices which the composer employs, the performer must possess a highly developed technique. All too often, the performer's preoccupation with technical difficulties prevents him from fulfilling the musical intention. For example, in 'Reconnaissance' from *Carnaval*, the right hand has to execute a smooth cantabile while at the same time continuously repeating in a staccato manner, and very softly, semi-quavers of the same note an octave lower. Involvement in overcoming this problem destroys the atmosphere of joyous delight which is the essence of the music. I personally prefer to make repeated use of the thumb for the semi-quavers, and only to the lucky possessor of hands with an unusually large span would I recommend the alternating 2–1 or 1–2.

EX 3

Comparatively few passages, however, in Schumann's piano music demand
the technical skill comparable to that required by Liszt's 'Transcendental Studies';
but even if the composer himself had had only a limited experience as a concert
pianist, he nevertheless had known from the beginning of his life as a serious
musician the internationally renowned pianist Clara Wieck, who later became
his wife. In fact, many of his works were written not only as an expression of his
feeling for her, but in the expectation that they might be included in her repertoire.
In a letter to Heinrich Dorn, written in 1839, he writes: 'The concerto, the
sonata, the *Davidsbündlertänze*, *Kreisleriana* and the *Novelletten* she, almost alone,
brought about.'[1] However, technical *tours-de-force* do occur, as in the Coda of
the second movement of the *Fantasie*, Op. 17,

EX 4

and the ability merely to recognize and surmount them is not enough for a great
performance. Technically, a great artist must never be at the end of his resources,
and must always be in such command of his fingers that he is at no time deflected
from the musical intention behind the digital manœuvres. Schumann, in the
previously quoted preface to Op. 3, writes: 'When he [the performer] has overcome all these external difficulties, his imagination will have freer play, enabling
him to impart life, light and shade to the work and more easily to perfect whatever may still be lacking in freedom of interpretation.' There is much more than
mere pedantry in distinguishing between a brilliant performance and a great
interpretation. Although the work of a skilled craftsman is always to be admired,
in music, technical brilliance in itself, while often momentarily spell-binding,

1 Jansen, p. 170.

leaves the listener, in the long run, unfulfilled. Moreover, as far as Schumann is concerned, this was the very defect that he and his fellow Davidsbündler were fighting against. He described as 'insipid virtuosity' the antics of the popular nineteenth-century pianist-composers, such as Henri Herz, Franz Hünten, Karl Czerny, Friedrich Kalkbrenner, and a host of others, and wrote of them: 'Before Herz and Czerny I doff my hat—to ask that they trouble me no more.'[1] Not that Schumann was opposed to virtuosity itself; but it had to be combined with musicianship and inspiration.

If, therefore, we take keyboard expertise and excellence for granted, what else as far as technique is concerned is necessary for an outstanding interpretation of Schumann? I think that the music asks for considerably more than what one critic has called 'a performance on top of the keyboard'. The playing must have a fullness and roundness of tone, a fine control capable both of a singing splendour as well as of delicate nuances and subtle contrasts, together with a firm and virile touch, for even in the lyrical and tender passages there are no traces of effeminacy.

EX 5

In particular, there must be a thoughtful approach to the question of pedalling. Schumann used the sustaining pedal generously, sometimes in order to give the instrument an increased power of varying tonal shade by adding sonority, as in the final bar of the Introduction of the F sharp minor Sonata, Op. 11;

EX 6

sometimes to enrich the harmonic effects, as in the Allegro of *Faschingsschwank aus Wien*;

[1] NZfM, 1834

EX 7

and sometimes to blur the outline of the context and to produce in sound the effect of mistiness, shimmer, or even of fading away, as in this example from the *Études Symphoniques*, where the desired effect is produced by half-pedalling.

EX 8

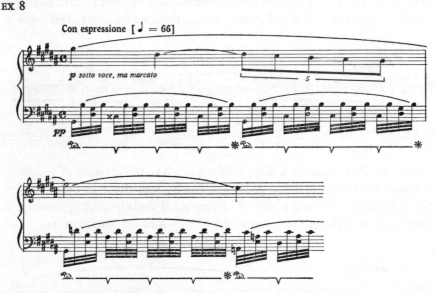

In the last movement of the C major Fantasie, Op. 17, there is a passage in which the left hand maintains the dominant C major in ascending broken chords, while the right hand has a diatonic scale-like melody played without lifting the sustaining pedal. Here the purpose of the pedal is to produce an atmosphere of remoteness and withdrawal.

Schumann frequently used metronome or tempo marks to indicate the speeds he wanted, but here a fundamental point arises. Sometimes tempi have to be altered to suit the acoustic conditions of the hall; sometimes because the performer's concept of the work as a whole demands some variation; although strictly

EX 9

speaking the very structure of the composition dictates its true tempo, each piece having, as it were, from its inception its own natural pace. Schumann himself is not always thoughtful, or even logical, when indicating his tempi. One of the best known examples is the first movement of the G minor sonata, Op. 22, in which he calls for a 'so rasch wie möglich' (as fast as possible), later 'schneller' (faster), and finally 'noch schneller' (even faster). Clearly, this cannot be done.[1]

EX 10

[1]See Yonty Solomon ,p. 54. ED

Both intelligence and musical sensitivity assure us that he is not asking for a tempo in which notes jostle one another so remorselessly that the musical sense is damaged. Each note is part of the composer's intended expression, and, like each word in a verse of poetry, has a significant part to play. It should never be lost in a welter of sound. Perhaps it is not entirely out of place to state the obvious. The terms 'fast', 'slow' are always relative, relative to speeds conceivable at any given time or epoch. Between 1830 and 1840, when Schumann was composing his great piano works, railways were in their infancy and the supersonic jet as yet science fiction. The personal conception of pace has altered since Schumann's day, and music has not remained immune. Obviously the maximum speed of any performer cannot be greater than his own digital facility and the action of the instrument he is using.

Exaggeration of tempo is equally out of place in slow passages.

EX II

Schumann himself noted, 'Dragging and hurrying are equally grave faults.' It is not uncommon to hear performances where the tempo of adagio movements is so slow that the musical thread is broken. Continuity of idea is the very essence of communication, and communication is the only really valid reason for a performance. Moreover, an exaggerated ritenuto or ritardando can destroy the essential character of a piece, as in 'Träumerei' or 'Bittendes Kind' from *Kinderscenen*, where the aim is to capture the simple and ephemeral moods of childhood.

EX 12a, b

This slowing down of tempo is one of the marked characteristics of Schumann's compositions, and appears in many works. Intelligent discrimination must be used when playing these passages to avoid over-emphasis and lingering sentimentality. A good performance should embody the right proportion of enthusiasm and restraint.

It is at this point, I think, that the problem of the length of the pause between sections, so important in considering the playing of Schumann's piano works, should be broached. In his piano-composing period Schumann wrote many works consisting of a dozen or more linked movements. Themes seemed to spring from his fingertips the moment he put his hands on the keyboard. (At this time he composed mainly at the piano, although later he condemned the practice. In a letter to Friedrich Wieck he wrote, 'If only you knew the ardour, the ferment that is in me and how I should have already arrived at opus 100 with my symphonies, if only I had written them down.'[1]) Early compositions such as the 'Abegg' Variations, *Papillons, Carnaval, Kinderscenen* are all a series of miniatures strung together like beads on a necklace to form a single chain. Here the dedicated performer has two problems to solve. Each miniature is complete in itself, with its own particular musical structure, tempo and atmosphere. Moreover they vary in length, and it is this richness and variety of musical imagination which give them their perennial appeal and fascination for both performer and audience. For the former there is the added excitement of giving to each cameo its own distinctive qualities which have to be captured instantaneously and incorporated in the whole: any change of approach during the playing will distort the picture. But it is not enough to produce a series of perfect miniatures, for both in spite and because of their contrasts they are facets of a whole. Unless this unity is apparent, the pieces will dissolve into brilliant fragments like mercury and lose their intrinsic value. Too long a pause will weaken the sense of continuity or, where the pieces are of opposing style and tempo, of contrast. Too short a pause will cause overcrowding and blur the impact. Each pause both links and separates, and has to be just long enough to allow the listener (and this includes the player) to gain a complete impression of one miniature before his interest becomes involved in its equally enchanting neighbour.

[1] Heidelberg, 6 November 1829.

Of special importance are the time intervals between the movements of the major works such as the *Fantasie*, *Études Symphoniques* and the sonatas. Some world-famous pianists leave such long time gaps between the movements that the musical relationship between them is lost and each becomes a separate piece instead of an essential chapter of a major work. Of course, it does happen during concerts that circumstances outside the player's control such as late-comers or a restless audience are responsible for these extended breaks; but although these disturbances are outside the performer's control, and therefore exonerate him from responsibility for the consequences, they still prevent a perfect interpretation.

With many of the composers of the eighteenth and early nineteenth centuries, the pianist has no great need to understand them as human beings in order to interpret them as musicians. Their music speaks for itself, for the works of Bach, Haydn, Mozart, and Beethoven have a clearly defined form of harmonic and melodic structure. They are composed in an accepted idiom and use a known musical 'language'. When, however, we come to the Romantic movement of the nineteenth century, which naturally affected music as it did other forms of art, an understanding of the personality of the composer becomes much more important, for the striving for originality and individuality was one of the chief characteristics of the movement. I believe that it is insufficient just to study the music, and that it becomes much more desirable to find out in what mood the composition originated, what influences acted upon the composer, and most of all to understand the personality of the man himself.

The Romantic movement is the term generally used to describe those years during which the expression of the artist's emotion in all its facets, as opposed to its control by reason and tradition, was of primary importance, and during which the accepted forms became more often notable for their absence than for their presence. The artist turned inwards rather than outwards; he explored both himself and the world around him in relation to himself. He then sought to express his reactions to his discoveries in whatever medium his genius prompted him. In spite of Schumann's sensitivity about being labelled a 'romantic', by 1839 he was widely known as one of the leaders of the romantic composers. Few composers have been so insistent on stressing the impact on their work of day-to-day experiences: moods, books, emotions, weather, and human relationships. He has written much on this theme. In 1838 he wrote to Henrietta Voigt,* 'My writing is part of my thoughts, my thoughts are part of my character. In short I cannot write and compose otherwise than you know me.'[1] And in a letter to Clara Wieck he states: 'Everything that happens in the world affects me: politics,

---

[1] 13 April 1838.

literature, people. I think it all over in my own way, and then it has to make room for itself and find an outlet in music.'[1]

In Schumann's case the fundamental understanding of the man may seem difficult. To say that, like many geniuses, he embodied two contrasting beings, Eusebius and Florestan (perhaps what he was and what he would like to have been, respectively) is to over-simplify the matter. In many ways he was all of a piece. He was sincere and dedicated right through, in his actions as in his thoughts, in his music as in his writings: and whether his feelings were happy, passionate, dreamy or sorrowful, he was able, in fact he was compelled by his inner self, to find release for them in his music. Primarily this was his means of communication. In expressing himself at the piano he opened up that aspect of his personality which his conscious self was incapable of revealing. So he found himself.

Schumann, as a pioneer of the Romantic movement, and in particular of a new style of piano music, used his own musical language, rather than the commonly accepted 'lingua franca' of the earlier so-called 'classical' composers. Their musical idiom can be likened to the universal Latin of medieval Europe, and like medieval Latin had become debased and no longer capable of expressing the host of new ideas with which early nineteenth-century Europe was teeming. This use of a personal 'idiom' makes it considerably more difficult to interpret the music, unless the artist understands the language. Symptomatically, Schumann frequently uses German instead of the accepted Italian for many of his musical directions, and it is not easy to understand his exact intention unless the performer has a really good knowledge of German. When Schumann does use Italian, the superscriptions are not always exact.

There are in existence pianistically excellent recordings of Schumann's works by world famous pianists, which command respect but leave the listener indifferent and musically unfulfilled, because the artist played with Olympian detachment and failed to involve either himself or the listener in the composer's intimate world. I believe that to know Schumann, it is of the greatest importance to understand this intimate world. (Incidentally, in spite of his reiterated emphasis that everything including politics affected him and therefore his music, since these two were inseparable, there is surprisingly little evidence anywhere in his works that the stirring events in Germany in the 1830s, 1840s, and especially in 1848 when the whole land seethed with revolution, had any obvious impact on him!) It is to this inner world that he retreated to escape the over-harsh reality of everyday living. It is a fascinating world, full of striking contrasts and charged with the outpourings of pent-up passions and emotions. Here we are introduced to his

[1] *Jugendbriefe*, p. 282.

dual self: Florestan, the quick, impetuous, impatient, bouncing extrovert that he could never be in real life

EX 13

and Eusebius, the melancholic, shy, rather timid dreamer, his more real self (see Ex. 5).

We find, too, his friends and musical contemporaries, Chopin (sketched in a superbly sensitive reproduction of that composer's style)

EX 14

and Paganini, whose dazzling virtuosity on the violin is now transferred to the piano.

EX 15

It is the world of make-believe, of masked balls, of carnival and romance. It is also the world of the 'Davidsbündler', where the new enlightened generation of young musicians challenges and defeats the defunct, but still enthroned, establishment of the old musical world, the 'Philistines'. It is a world full of the careless joys and innocence of childhood, as well as one in which are to be met unfulfilled love, despair and bitter anger. It is the created world of a lively, inventive genius, who saw and enlarged the possibilities of the piano as a solo instrument, because he had the compulsive need to express on it not only his feelings, but also the ideas, often wraithlike and elusive, which the ordinary events of daily life engendered in his very sensitive being. To give the fullest meaning to such music, the performer has to be able to join Schumann in this fantasy, to enjoy with him the frolics of his chosen companions, to laugh at their antics (he had a playful sense of humour, which he used to advantage in the opening and throughout the twelfth section of the *Davidsbündlertänze*) and to join in their revels.

EX 16

But he must be capable of sharing the composer's ever changing moods: rejoice with him in his hopes, commiserate with him in his disappointment, share his impatience of mediocrity and dislike of hypocrisy. He must share, too, the fear of the ever-widening gulf in a divided personality. Much of the above is there openly in the music for all, who will, to hear, for the music has a life of its own; but Schumann's works are so full of inspiration that it is often necessary to delve below the surface to mine the wealth of impression which lies hidden in the rich texture of sound. Having unearthed the treasure, the performer has then the exacting but rewarding task of displaying it to the listener. For although Schumann's piano music by no means reveals his full artistic nature, it is perhaps the fullest revelation of a personality in musical composition.

What of the impact of the personality of the performer himself on Schumann's piano music? It hardly needs saying that he must be a pianist who is thoroughly convinced of, and unquestioningly accepts, the idea that the piano can be made to express feeling. He must also have the musical intelligence and artistic finesse to know how and when to use each of its special effects to fulfil the composer's intentions. But I also believe that a really great interpreter of any form of art needs to be, in spiritual quality and experience of life, at least of the same calibre as the creative artist whose work he seeks to reproduce, and that with Schumann's music this is a particular need. For him, music was a vision and he spent his life in its pursuit. 'Music,' says Schumann, 'is the ability to express emotions audibly; it is the spiritual language of emotion.' Moreover, he repeatedly emphasized the spirituality of music. 'The art in art is to spiritualize matter so that everything material is forgotten,'[1] and he endowed with this quality some of his noblest compositions, as for example the 'Im Legendenton' section of the first movement of the C major Fantasie.

EX 17

No one would expect or even want the interpreter to have the same personal characteristics or to have endured the same experiences as the composer; but the former ought to have known sufficient difficulty and inner conflict to enable him to appreciate the frustrations and struggles of another. He must be aware of the profundities of life; of the heights where the euphoria of success abides, the joys of love fulfilled, the solace and delight in natural beauty; of the depths when despair gnaws the spirit, when the deadly monotony of sameness numbs the imagination and induces a palsied indolence. Above all he must be able to cast aside his earth-bound self and soar with Schumann in the latter's moments of spiritual exaltation and union with the Divinity. Failure to respond to these demands will always, I believe, preclude a great interpretation; for while it is possible to play music perfectly at a highly rarified and artistically satisfying level just by playing the music as it is written, this type of playing runs the risk of failing to achieve the intimacy and common humanity, two of the well-springs of Schumann's music, and therefore of failing to communicate them to the listener. Schumann once said: 'Try to produce the same impression with a composition as that which the composer aimed at; no one should attempt more; anything beyond it is a mere caricature.'

In spite of the above dictum, I believe that a performer of the stature I have

[1] NZfM.

outlined cannot fail to make his own mark on the music he is playing, even though he sincerely thinks of himself as the vehicle through which the composer speaks. Something of himself will, in spite of everything, be interwoven in the music. Many years ago, I was rudely jolted by the casual remark of a friend, an educated and dedicated lover of music. 'Above a certain perfected and polished standard of playing, I am completely incapable of determining the greatness of the performance. I can only say what pleases me and what does not.' To me, a performing musician, this statement was outrageous; but maturity of thought and years of playing and listening have made me realize that there is much truth in the remark. Once a supremely high standard of keyboard mastery and musical understanding have been reached, what distinguishes one pianist's interpretation of a given work from another's is the difference in their spiritual and musical concepts. Each will appeal to that group of listeners most in tune with his interpretation.

So when I am asked, as I frequently am, what, in my opinion, are the requisites for a great interpretation of Schumann's piano music, I reply that, in addition to all the above mentioned considerations, it is a matter of having the 'Geist', the inborn gift, that quality of the spirit which instinctively senses and records, rather than a talent which develops through sheer dedication, devotion and study. Let me hasten to add that dedication, devotion and study are not only important, but essential to perfection.

If, however, this 'Geist' is missing, then I feel that one is much more likely to give a poor interpretation of Schumann's piano music than of, say, Beethoven's, or even Chopin's. Beethoven's music, like Shakespeare's plays, transcends human failings and even a humdrum performance cannot seriously mar its greatness. Chopin's music too is more single-minded than Schumann's and his style allows the music time to develop and move inevitably towards its logical conclusion. One is always aware of its shapeliness. This opinion of mine is based on the following observations.

Schumann was fundamentally 'a child of his time', that is of the romantic period of the early nineteenth century. Our own age, while having certain superficial resemblances such as the breaking away from tradition, the search for new idioms and the emphasis on individuality, is different not only in its social and political structure, but also in its climate of thought and feeling. Music, besides expressing the hidden emotions, must also have a moral influence. Music has a spiritual quality and the composer is the servant of God. Schumann writes: 'The artist through viewing the wonders of God, is able to perceive phenomena which otherwise would remain imperceptible.' I would not care to estimate the number of people, artists included, who would accept this idea today.

He was subject not only to the dual nature of Florestan and Eusebius, but to nervous feverish attacks, and moods of bitter passion and despondency. He was consumed by music; it wore away his nervous energy. In 1838 he wrote to Clara, seven years after the injury to his right hand: 'Oh, Lord, why did you do just this to me? In me the whole of music is so complete and alive that I can only play painfully, with one of my fingers straddling the others. It is terrible and I have suffered agonies from it ever since.' It needs a superbly sensitive and imaginative artist to transfer such mental agony to the keyboard.

Inspiration and emotion permeate his works. Above all his music is personal, an unburdening of self. It demands spontaneity, and no pianist, however gifted, can unfailingly recreate this mood. This explains why so many modern large-scale performances seem artificial and contrived. It is never very satisfactory to pour out one's innermost self to a large public gathering, at a specified time on a given day. For this reason I agree with the suggestion that Schumann's music sounds best in the salon or drawing-room in an atmosphere of intimacy.

Paradoxically, if the performer's personality is so extrovert and dominating as to command easily the attention of a large audience, it is not very likely to be compatible with that of Schumann, who lived largely within himself and through his music. On the other hand, the pianist so in sympathy with him as to be his other self, may be more influenced by the immediate conditions and circumstances surrounding his performance, and find himself attuned to these rather than to the needs of the music. The resolution of this paradox is one of the chief difficulties in Schumann interpretation.

When all is said and done, the great interpreter, like the great composer, is born, and neither taught nor made. My master, Ernst von Dohnányi, the famous Hungarian pianist-composer, who had a control of the piano rarely equalled, at least in modern times, was quite unable to explain in words what the music meant to him, or even how his superbly satisfying performances were achieved. Like Schumann, words failed him. He rarely, if ever, gave exactly the same interpretation twice; but each performance was not only true to the composer's intention, but authentic and convincing in its entirety. Schumann would have been satisfied.

BRIAN SCHLOTEL

Schumann and the Metronome

SCHUMANN took considerable trouble to add metronome indications to his works. The great majority of his piano pieces, chamber works, orchestral and choral works have them. The only considerable area of his work in which he dispensed with them was in his Lieder; here he no doubt felt that the poem, and the singer's personal reaction to it, would be sufficient guide to the interpretation of the general tempo marking at the head of each song. Furthermore, in the first editions of his music, Schumann seemed to take particular care over the metronome marks at the proof stage. In many manuscripts (for example, *Kinderscenen*, *Kreisleriana*, and *Nachtstücke*, which among others can be seen at the Schumann-Haus in Zwickau) there are no metronome marks, though these appear later when the work is in print. In other manuscripts, their provision is foreseen but not yet added, thus ($\boldsymbol{\mathsf{J}} =$). In yet others, they are already indicated in pencil, no doubt pending further checking, and then altered in the published edition.

There was apparently no suggestion in Schumann's lifetime that his metronome was faulty. Yet within a few years of his death the rumour was being widely circulated. This is strange in view of the fact that Schumann often heard or conducted rehearsals and performances of his own works in which the players had the printed editions in front of them with Schumann's own metronome markings, and could easily have pointed out discrepancies. Moreover, these markings never seem to have been queried in the regular correspondence about performances of his works that Schumann maintained with other conductors such as Dr D. G. Otten in Hamburg, Liszt in Weimar, or Verhulst* in Holland. That Schumann certainly felt his own metronome was in order is seen from this letter to the composer Ferdinand Böhme who had sent him a new quartet:

Düsseldorf,
February 8, 1853

Dear Sir,

. . . the composition does you great credit, and I was very pleased at your intention of dedicating it to me.

Have you a correct metronome? All the tempi appear to me far too quick. Mine is correct. It always gives as many beats to the minute as the number on which the weight is placed. For instance, if the number is 50, it gives 50 beats to the minute; if 60 = 60. And, as far as I know, this is the test of correctness. Perhaps you would try your metronome in this respect.

Robert Schumann[1]

Martin Schoppe, Director of the Schumann-Haus, has told me that no metronome belonging to Schumann has survived to the present day, and that he does not know of any metronome of Schumann's ever being scientifically tested.[2] (Possibly, though, Schumann may have tested his own, and he was certainly aware that its scale represented the number of ticks per minute—as is shown by the letter to Ferdinand Böhme quoted above.)

The possibility that his metronome was defective may first have been suggested after his death by Clara Schumann. Certainly in April 1861 she was discussing with Brahms her plan to revise the metronome markings of her late husband's works.[3] But it was von Bülow (who was friendly with Brahms and perhaps heard the idea from him) who seems to have been the first to make the suggestion in print. In the preface to his edition of Cramer's studies, published in 1869, Bülow writes: '. . . it is generally held that Schumann used a defective metronome for an entire creative period'. Soon von Bülow's qualified and rather tentative suggestion became hardened into 'fact'. Thus Gustav Jansen, who had obtained Clara's permission to publish an edition of Schumann's letters, stated quite categorically in the first edition of 1886 that Schumann's metronome was not correct, 'as was proved after his death. Consequently many of his works are wrongly metronomised.'[4] Perhaps the idea would not have persisted were it not for the fact that, in her later editions of Schumann's music, Clara made extensive

---

[1] *Robert Schumanns Briefe: Neue Folge*, ed. F. Gustav Jansen.
[2] Letter dated Zwickau, 26 April 1971.
[3] Litzmann: *Clara Schumann—Johannes Brahms Briefe aus den Jahren 1853-96* (letter from Brahms, 25 April 1861).
[4] Jansen: *Briefe von Robert Schumann*, p. 309, footnote.

changes in his metronome markings, which seemed to set the seal upon the theory that Schumann's metronome had been faulty.

Between the years 1879 and 1893 the publishing house of Breitkopf and Härtel brought out a Complete Edition of all Schumann's works (running to twenty-nine volumes) with Clara Schumann and Brahms as joint editors. Then in 1887, also with Breitkopf and Härtel, Clara published her 'Instructive Edition' of Schumann's piano music 'based on the manuscripts and the personal tradition of Clara Schumann'.

Brahms fully foresaw the difficulties that Clara would have in revising the metronome markings. He advised her that as she would have the work in hand for at least a year she should try each piece through several times, and each time record her speed of playing. She would find, Brahms predicted, that she had played it each time at a different pace, but if she then took the average it would do well enough.[1] One letter of Clara's makes it clear that her method was to use a watch with a second hand, rather than a metronome.[2] Presumably she would play for a minute exactly, and then stop and count how many beats she had played. Clara described the task to Brahms as 'pure torment'.

Strange to say, in spite of this prodigious labour, when the volumes of the Complete Edition appeared, only five piano works (Sonata in F minor, *Kinderscenen*, Fantasie in C major, *Nachtstücke* and *Waldscenen*) had changes—and these were of a very slight order, while virtually none of the orchestral works, choral works or chamber music had any changes made in their metronomization. Did Clara feel they were a reasonable guide to what her husband had wanted?

However, in her other editorial work, the Instructive Edition of the piano pieces, 'based on the personal tradition of Clara Schumann', she made extensive changes in Schumann's metronomization. We shall shortly see that they do not point to any fault in Schumann's metronome that could possibly be imagined. Here is a comparison of the markings for *Papillons*, *Davidsbündlertänze*, *Kinderscenen*, *Kreisleriana*, *Arabeske*, *Faschinesschwank*, and a few later works with the figures specified in Schumann's own first editions on the left, and those specified by Clara in her Instructive Edition of 1887 on the right.

[1] Litzmann, *op. cit.* Letter from Brahms, 25 April 1861.
[2] Litzmann, *op. cit.* Letter from Clara, 7 May 1878.

Papillons, opus 2

	Robert	Clara
No. 1	♩ = 120	♩ = 138
No. 2	♩ = 116	♩ = 116
No. 3	𝅗𝅥 = 120	♩ = 144
No. 4	♩. = 108	♩. = 108
No. 5	♩ = 80	♩ = 80
No. 6	♩ = 152	𝅗𝅥. = 84
No. 7	♩. = 58	♩ = 58
No. 8	♩ = 132	𝅗𝅥. = 63
No. 9	♩. = 112	♩. = 112
No. 10	♩. = 108	♩. = 104
No. 11	♩ = 112	♩ = 112

Davidsbündlertanze, opus 6

	Robert	Clara
No. 1	♩ = 160	♩ = 152
No. 2	𝅗𝅥 = 138	♩ = 96
No. 3	𝅗𝅥. = 60	♩ = 152
No. 4	𝅗𝅥. = 80	𝅗𝅥. = 88
No. 5	♩ = 116	♩ = 96
No. 6	♩. = 132	♩. = 120
No. 7	♩ = 92	♩ = 96
No. 8	♩ = 100	♩ = 100
No. 9	♩ = 112	♩ = 126
No. 10	𝅗𝅥. = 80	𝅗𝅥. = 88
No. 11	♩ = 80	♩ = 88
No. 12	♩ = 104	♩ = 96
No. 13	♩ = 144	♩ = 152
No. 14	♩ = 138	♩ = 100
No. 15	♩ = 160	𝅗𝅥. = 56
No. 16	♩ = 160	♩ = 132
No. 17	♩ = 126	♩ = 100
No. 18	♩ = 152	♩ = 136

(Schumann's first edition of opus 6, published in 1837, has no metronome marks. The first column of figures above is taken from the revised second edition which Schumann published in 1851)

Kinderscenen, opus 15

		Robert	Clara
No.	1	♩ = 108	♩ = 108
No.	2	♩ = 112	♩ = 132
No.	3	♩ = 138	♩ = 120
No.	4	♪ = 138	♪ = 88
No.	5	♪ = 132	♩ = 72
No.	6	♩ = 138	♩ = 120
No.	7	♩ = 100	♩ = 80
No.	8	♩ = 138	♩ = 108
(1) No.	9	𝅗𝅥. = 80	𝅗𝅥. = 76
No.	10	♩ = 69	♪ = 104
No.	11	♩ = 96	♩ = 108
No.	12	♪ = 92	♪ = 80
No.	13	♩ = 112	♩ = 92

Kreisleriana, opus 16

	Robert	Clara
No. 4 Molto Lento	♪ = 66	♪ = 66
No. 6 Lento assai	♪ = 84	♪ = 108

Arabeske, opus 18

	Robert	Clara
Leicht und zart	♩ = 152	♩ = 126
Minore I	—	♩ = 112
Minore II	♩ = 144	♩ = 120
Zum Schluss	𝅗𝅥 = 58	𝅗𝅥 = 58

Faschingsschwank, opus 26

	Robert	Clara
Allegro	𝅗𝅥. = 76	𝅗𝅥. = 76
Romanze	♪ = 92	♪ = 69
Scherzino	♩ = 112	♩ = 112
Intermezzo	♩ = 116	♩ = 104
Finale	♩ = 138	♩ = 138

[1] For opus 15 no. 9 Schumann's first edition has 𝅗𝅥 = 80, but for this piece in 3/4 time this is an *obvious* misprint, and is corrected here to 𝅗𝅥. = 80.

Album für die Jugend, opus 68

	Robert	Clara
No. 23		
Reiterstück	♩. = 100	♩. = 112
No. 34		
Thema	♪ = 84	♪ = 72

Waldscenen, opus 82

	Robert	Clara
No. 5		
Freundliche Landschaft	♩ = 160	♩ = 144

Second Sonata for the Young, opus 118, No. 2

	Robert	Clara
3rd Movement	♩ = 50	♩ = 63

With the *Papillons* four of Clara's speeds are faster, one is slower and six are the same; with the *Davidsbündlertänze* seven of Clara's speeds are faster and ten are slower—one dramatically so; with the *Kinderscenen* one piece is considerably faster, two others faster, while nine are marked slower. And so on—with each work containing some pieces left unchanged.

Now the metronome consists basically of a pendulum with a movable weight swinging in line with a graduated scale. If calibrated incorrectly it could tick too fast, or too slowly, at any part of the scale, but it is impossible to conceive of one of these comparatively simple instruments being as eccentric as these tables make out Schumann's to be—sometimes too fast, sometimes too slow, sometimes correct, and each of these at every part of the metronome's scale, and during the composition of one work. It is difficult to escape the conclusion that by 1887 Clara preferred to play many of her husband's works in a different way from that which he had intended. For instance, the *Arabeske* taken at Robert's speeds evokes a much more fanciful, exotic picture than the homely mood engendered by Clara's much slower tempi.

During his lifetime and after, Clara always showed the greatest and most unswerving loyalty to Schumann and his music, and one can be quite sure that her editorial work was undertaken with the highest motives and in the sincere conviction that she was offering helpful advice to performers. But Clara was an independent artist in her own right, and already famous all over Europe before her marriage to Schumann at the age of twenty. Also in her long widowhood after the age of thirty-six, it is only reasonable to suppose that she developed as an artist and pianist. Clara's marks are undoubtedly welcome when they are supplied for those piano works for which Schumann published none himself,[1]

[1] Notably opp. 4, 5, 8, 9 and 12.

and also when they exactly confirm Schumann's own indications.[1] But where they are available, Schumann's metronome marks are the ones which a performer should primarily go to for guidance, and publishers for their part should make quite clear whose markings they are using. An appalling muddle exists over this in many modern editions—one well-known English edition of the *Kinderscenen* has Clara's speeds for nos. 2 to 11 and Robert's for nos. 12 and 13, without a word of explanation or even acknowledgment of the two differing sources.

For the pianist or conductor who wishes to check the metronome marks in his scores, the best authorities are the editions of his music that Schumann himself saw through the press; and fortunately for the English researcher the British Museum has a large collection of Schumann first editions.

*

How far is the metronome a reliable guide at all to interpretation? This is a highly controversial question, and some composers such as Brahms and Sibelius have zealously avoided using it for tempo guidance in their scores. 'Idiot! do you think I want to hear my music always played at the same speed?' Brahms is said to have snapped in justification of this. Wagner, too, wrote in his book *On Conducting* that in his earlier operas he had thought the correct tempo fixed beyond doubt by the metronome marks he had furnished. But whenever he had heard an unsuitable speed, as for example in a performance of *Tannhäuser*, performers always parried his recriminations by saying that they had followed his metronome marks! Eventually, Wagner tells us that in his compositions after *Tannhäuser*, because of the uncertainties of musical mathematics, he gave only general verbal instructions for the main tempi.[2] But other great composers have felt the metronome to be a most useful guide, and Berlioz for example clearly stated the case for the metronome in his Treatise on Instrumentation:

> If the conductor has not had the opportunity of receiving instructions on tempi directly from the composer, or if the times have not been transmitted to him by tradition, he must have recourse to the indications of the metronome and study them well; the majority of composers having nowadays the precaution to write them at the head and in the course of their pieces. I do not mean by this to say that it is necessary to imitate the mathematical regularity of the metronome; all music so performed would become of freezing stiffness, and I even doubt whether it would be possible to observe

---

[1] As in opp. 13, 19, 21, 28, 32, 56 and 111.
[2] Wagner: *Über das Dirigiren—Gesammelte Schriften und Dichtungen*, vol. 8, p. 342 (Leipzig, 1873).

so flat a uniformity during a certain number of bars. But the metronome is nonetheless excellent to consult, in order to know the original time, and its chief alterations.

Berlioz continues by saying that if the conductor possesses neither the composer's instructions, nor tradition, nor metronome indications, he has no other guide than vague terms, and his own feeling of the composer's style. And he concludes:

> We are compelled to admit that these guides are too often insufficient and delusive. . . Composers therefore ought not to neglect placing metronome indications in their works; and orchestral conductors should study them closely. The neglect of this study on the part of the latter is an act of dishonesty.[1]

Beethoven, who was one of the first great composers to champion the metronome after it had been invented in 1815, took pains, in 1817, to prepare and issue metronome markings for the eight symphonies he had then composed, and soon after that for his first eleven string quartets. And in December 1826 we find him sending a new composition to the publishers Schotts Söhne and saying: 'The metronome markings will be sent to you very soon. Do wait for them. In our century such indications are certainly necessary.'[2]

But a number of Beethoven's marks are felt by experienced musicians to be impossibly fast, and many theories have been advanced to explain this—that Beethoven was reading the scale along the *lower* edge of the weight of his metronome, that his metronome was out of order, that he sometimes put his metronome on the floor beside his piano while he was playing and then read the scale inaccurately because of the sharp angular perspective. Far more comvincing than any of these, however, is Tovey's explanation, in discussing the very fast metronome marks of Beethoven's 'Hammerklavier' Sonata:

> The composer's natural impulse is to set the metronome at various paces until the bare ticking sounds as energetic as the music in question. It is quite possible to do this without suspecting that the real music will not squeeze into such a tempo.[3]

[1] Berlioz: *A Treatise upon Instrumentation and Orchestration* (English edition, London 1856), p. 246.
[2] Emily Anderson: Letters of Beethoven, Vol. III, p. 1325 (London, 1961).
[3] Beethoven Sonatas for the Pianoforte, with commentaries and notes by Donald Francis Tovey Vol. III, p. 136 (London, 1931).

AUTOGRAPH SKETCH OF
'HUMORESKE', op. 20 (1838–39)

AUTOGRAPH PAGE OF 'SCENES OF CHILDHOOD' (1838)

AUTOGRAPH SKETCH OF
PIANO SONATA IN F SHARP MINOR, op. 11 (1835)

Tovey went on to recall that Max Reger had spent some time in carefully metronomizing all his works but then had to issue a warning that his marks are to be regarded merely as setting the extreme permissible upper limit of speed.

It is relevant that Beethoven, Reger and other composers such as Chopin have all been criticized for their metronome marks at times being *too fast;* but, so far as I am aware, no composer has been criticized for putting the metronome marks which are *too slow.* This lends support to Tovey's idea; unless a metronome mark is carefully checked, or tested against a live performance, it may tend to be on the fast side.

Schumann, too, seems to have sometimes succumbed to the usual hazard amongst composers of putting his speeds too fast. An example of this carelessness is surely the Finale of the Second Symphony whose breathtaking speed of ♩=170 would certainly ruin the Symphony's effect even if players *could* take the semi-quaver swirls at that pace. However, as Tovey implied, it is possible to imagine a performance at that speed against the ticking of the metronome. And the conductor, if he likes, can start his preparations from there. Another very difficult mark is the ♩=84 at the head of the Piano Concerto. For the first pages it seems impossibly fast. One can only wonder if this is intended to refer to the Animato in which the movement settles down from bar 67; for this it is perfectly satisfactory.

Metronome indications seem peculiarly liable to misprints, and modern editions of Schumann's music have their share. Thus one miniature score has the opening of the 'Rhenish' Symphony as ♩=66, whereas the first edition, published by Simrock in 1851, which was seen through the press by Schumann himself, has ♩.=66, and this is confirmed in Clara Schumann's Complete Edition. Again an English publisher's piano arrangement of the Second Symphony has ♩=76 for the slow movement, whereas Schumann's own first edition has ♪=76, again confirmed by Clara's Complete Edition. In the first case, the omission of a dot means a 33% decrease in speed; in the second, the omission of a quaver tail means 100% increase in speed. Another appalling carelessness is the mark of ♩=96 at the head of a well-known English Edition of the *Blumenstück.* Both Robert's and Clara's editions agree that this should be ♩=69.

Schumann's metronome marks, although a useful guide to finding a judicious tempo, are not necessarily there to be slavishly adhered to at all times. Differences in the size of the hall, the mood of the day, the ability of the players, all need to be taken into consideration for any particular performance. Nevertheless his metronome marks are useful in showing intending interpreters the kind of tempo he had in mind. This can be illustrated by the following table comparing the speeds used in five typical, though well differentiated, performances of the

E

'Spring' Symphony. Schumann's own metronome speeds are taken from the first edition of the full score, which was seen through the press by the composer himself, and published by Breitkopf and Härtel in 1853.

Schumann	Boult[1]	Fricsay[2]	Klemperer[3]	Koussevitzky[4]	Szell[5]
I.					
Introd.	70	60	61	46	70
♩ = 66					
Allegro					
♩ = 120	134	132	120	122	124
II.					
Larghetto					
♪ = 66	60	52	48	56	64
III.					
Scherzo					
♩. = 88	88	72	70	78	73
Trio I					
♩ = 108	140	120	110	126	135
IV.					
Finale					
♩ = 100	108	126	96	120	97

[1] Boult conducting the Philharmonic Promenade Orchestra, Nixa NCT 17004.
[2] Fricsay conducting the RIAS Symphony Orchestra, Berlin, Heliodor 478141.
[3] Klemperer conducting the New Philharmonia Orchestra, Columbia SAX 5269.
[4] Koussevitzky conducting the Boston Symphony Orchestra, HMV DB 3983/6.
[5] Szell conducting the Cleveland Orchestra, Columbia SAX 2475.

As is to be expected, from these five conductors, with their differing temperaments, backgrounds, generations and nationalities, there is a wide interpretive variety in speeds. But in each movement there is at least one conductor who adopts a speed almost identical to Schumann's own precise suggestion, while many of his speeds meet with wide agreement. Thus in the Symphony's introduction Schumann's indication is central to four of the speeds, with Boult and Szell conducting the merest fraction faster, and Fricsay and Klemperer the merest fraction slower. The extremely grandiose reading of Koussevitzky is the only interpretation which is not reasonably near the metronome mark. In the ensuing Allegro Klemperer adopts Schumann's tempo exactly, with impressive results, while Koussevitzky and Szell are so close that the difference is almost unnoticeable. In the Larghetto Schumann's speed is rather too fast compared with the consensus, but Szell conducts at this speed almost exactly. Similarly Boult in the Scherzo and Klemperer in Trio I virtually adopt Schumann's speeds.

Berlioz's caution about avoiding imitating the freezing stiffness of the metronome's beat should above all be borne in mind by interpreters of Schumann. And if it is, Schumann's metronome marks do, despite all, give a useful guide to how he wanted his music played.

ERIC SAMS

The Songs

Antecedents

THE *Lied*, or song for voice and piano, in which poetry is recreated as music, is an essentially nineteenth-century ('Romantic') art-form which can be arbitrarily defined as beginning with Schubert's first songs (1812) and ending with Wolf's last (1897). It had ancestors in North Germany and Austria;[1] it soon had siblings in Russia and France; it now has descendants everywhere. But its new, individual voice belonged to an emergent German-speaking middle class; and its musical language fell midway between the courtly diction favoured by the nobility of the Hapsburg empire and the freer expressive vernacular of the people.

All this had necessarily been preceded by a similar development in German poetry; the art of Hölty for example, like that of Goethe himself, contained a new ferment of feeling which broke down classical thought and metre into simpler stanzas suitable for singing. At the same time, the pianoforte had developed into an accompanying instrument which could provide not only supporting chords, like the homely guitar, but independent melodic lines and enriched tone-colour, like the court orchestra. Similarly the social milieu of the *Lied* was neither the homestead nor the palace, but the drawing room. It was made for small intimate fellowships rather than large societies, whether humble or noble; it remains the ideal art-form for friends or lovers.

So from its earliest beginnings it expresses the emotions and aspirations of the individual. Ideally, indeed, the same person could be its poet, composer, pianist and singer, all in one. This tradition of the lutenist or troubadour was being revived in a sharply labour-dividing society; and in practice the new art, like that society, was better served by specialization. Yet its essence remained in-

[1] Maurice J. E. Brown. *Schubert Songs*, pp. 6–11, London, 1967.

divisible; in its music as in its poetry it deals electively with the feelings of one particular character, man or woman, real or imagined, at a given time; and usually in circumstances or surroundings which serve to set off or intensify those emotions. It is no mere hazard that the first great *Lieder* are about a girl's concern for her lover (*Gretchen am Spinnrade*), a father's fears for his son (*Erlkönig*), each imagined against a background of scenes and moods apt for quasi-dramatic recreation in sound. In this art-form words and music, lyric and drama, speech and action, mood and character, are fused into one substance; and many of its elements derive directly from the main influences absorbed and transformed by the young Schubert—the courtly wisdom of Mozart opera, the simple immediacy of popular song.

Schumann in his turn was at first influenced by the mastery of Schubert and by the popular songwriting of his own day, including the work of Spohr (1784–1859) and Weber (1786–1826), as well as such minor figures as Gottlob Wiedebein (1797–1854). But his own dozen juvenile essays in that form (1827–29) proved unrewarding, and he soon abandoned it for the expressive piano-cycle or suite, which became his constant preoccupation from his eighteenth to his twenty-ninth year. At first this seems perplexing. His verbally-oriented mind made him a born song-writer. Yet not only did he write no song of any consequence until his thirtieth year, in 1840, but as late as 1839 we find him writing to a friend that he had always considered song an inferior art-form and ranked it below instrumental music.[1] There is no reason to doubt his sincerity. From 1834 onwards he could have written about any topic he chose in the *Neue Zeitschrift für Musik*, the journal he helped to found and later edited. But he wrote rather seldom on song, and then without any notable enthusiasm; he was generally content to leave (indeed, to delegate) that topic to others.[2]

A study of his own writings in those years helps to explain this view. He believed that music was a form of language, and that the duty of the song-writer was therefore to translate verse into music. For mere musical illustration, however (even in Schubert and Loewe), Schumann had a special distaste.[3] Music ought not to be brought down to the level of words. Such a feeling would reflect his own personality and position. As a critic and composer, he was a leader of contemporary thought; despite the injury to his right hand, he retained a virtuoso's grasp of keyboard music. Besides, his own piano music already had speech and language of its own; poetry would be at best an irrelevance, at worst a rival.

Yet by the end of 1840 Schumann had sufficiently overcome his objections to

[1] F. Gustav Jansen. *Robert Schumanns Briefe*. 1904, p. 158.
[2] Jansen, pp. 104, 120, 130, 199.   [3] GSK, Vol. I, p. 270.

become the world's greatest living songwriter, with about 130 songs, including all his best-known masterpieces. Only Schubert in 1815, and Wolf in 1888, can match this for sustained inspiration; and each of them at the time was a practised songwriter. Schumann, the inspired layman, crammed his life's best work in the song form into a few months of memorable mastery. So profuse and violent a flowering must have been seeded early and deep in his creative mind.

Influences

No doubt it began with Schubert, whose instrumental music, as well as songs, always seemed to Schumann to be verbally expressive. His essay on Schubert's great C major symphony,[1] which he had himself located in manuscript in Vienna, reaffirms those qualities. The stimulus of that experience may well have prompted the further exploration of Schubert's posthumous songs, then (1838–1839) being published in Vienna.

Beethoven, too, was a source of inspiration; his *An die ferne Geliebte* is freely quoted and adapted throughout Schumann's C major Fantasie, op. 17 (1836), which was written as 'a deep lament' for Clara Wieck.[2] He must have played and sung Beethoven's song-cycle of the distant beloved very often, and in the most impressionable of moods. No wonder its pianistic style and cyclic form dominate his own love-songs.

Another clear influence was Mendelssohn. Schumann's review of *St Paul*[3] (1837) praises the 'union of word and tone, language and music'; while in discussing a set of the *Songs without Words* he gives an unconsciously prophetic description of his own songwriting style, thus:

'Who has never sat at his piano in the twilight . . . and quietly sung to himself a tune while improvising? If you happen to play the melody and accompaniment together, and if (more to the point) you also happen to be a Mendelssohn, the result will be a beautiful *Song without Words*.' The resulting piano song is a concept explicitly avowed and defended in Schumann's own critical writings. He described a set of songs by Kirchner as 'self-contained instrumental pieces . . . often like translations of the poems into keyboard terms . . . like *Songs without Words*, but inspired by words . . .'[4] He also explained that the identification of piano and vocal lines, although admittedly limiting for the singer, comes naturally to a composer who has begun with instrumental composition and proceeded thence to songwriting.[5]

[1] GSK, Vol, p. 459.   [2] See Yonty Solomon, p. 61. ED
[3] GSK, Vol. I, p. 323.   [4] GSK, Vol. I, p. 98.   [5] GSK, Vol. II, pp. 83, 123.

Hindsight reveals how and when Schumann himself came to take that turning. By early 1839 he was chafing at the limitations of the keyboard. 'I could smash the piano,' he writes; 'it constricts my thinking. One day I shall master orchestral technique, though I've had little experience of it as yet.'[1] Perhaps he never really broke with the piano. His symphonies may have been conceived in keyboard terms; the 1840 songs certainly were. But at least songwriting, like his forthcoming marriage, offered some escape from an increasingly convoluted world of private fantasy. Clara herself had suggested that his piano music was too cryptic for the general public.[2] Then, as now, vocal music was more widely popular. So Schumann in his marriage year of 1840 needed a more accessible form of musical communication, for the sake of both love and money. In each respect he was to be outstandingly successful. The songs made him a good profit and a good name; and they also persuaded Clara that he was the finest living musician (an impressive tribute from one who knew Chopin, Liszt and Mendelssohn).

There may have been earlier subconscious impulses to songwriting. In 1838 we hear of a work called *Maultreiberlied*[3] (Muleteer's song), now lost. It was perhaps a piano piece; but it is the first work even to be called 'song' for ten years, and is thus of some historical interest. More evidentially, we can hear the piano music of 1839 adding a new voice, written on a third stave, as in the

EX I

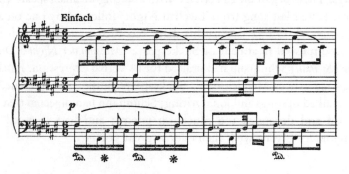

Romanze in F sharp major, op. 28 no. 2, or the *Humoreske*, op. 20, where it is described as an 'innere Stimme', or inner voice (Ex. 2).

It seems likely that at least one of the 1839 piano pieces, the *Scherzo*, op. 32 no. 1, was later converted into the song *Ich wandre nicht*.[4] At the same time, Schumann's prejudices against songwriting were fading. The discipline of

[1] Jansen, p. 153.
[2] e.g. Berthold Litzmann: *Clara Schumann*. 1906, Vol. I, p. 311.
[3] Wolfgang Bœtticher. *Schumann in seinen Briefen und Schriften*. 1942, p. 210.
[4] Eric Sams. *The Songs of Robert Schumann*. 1969, pp. 83–84.

EX 2

regular critical writing may have helped him (as it did Hugo Wolf) to a closer understanding of the inner life of words. By 1839 his prose is better integrated; the quotations and allusions, at first merely scattered on the surface, become absorbed in his own style. By 1838, he was reading and writing verses in homage to Clara[1]. By then, too, he had reviewed a number of songs and studied several others (as editor of a journal which regularly published a vocal music supplement).

Thus strong forces and pressures were at work clearing a channel for song and diverting Schumann's spate of piano music into it. His self-erected dam of *a priori* objections would no doubt have been overwhelmed in any event. But there is evidence[2] that it was independently broken down; hence the flood of 1840 songs. These began on 1 February with a setting of Shakespeare (*Schlusslied des Narren*, Feste's last song from Twelfth Night) followed by one on a Biblical theme (*Belsatzar*). On 31 January his diary recorded a meeting with Mendelssohn, whose musical treatment of Shakespeare (*Midsummer Night's Dream*) and the Bible (*St Paul*) Schumann had praised for its verbal expression. Furthermore, that first song echoes Mendelssohn's Shakespeare music. The inference is plain. They had talked of songs and songwriting; Schumann had objected that the form was hybrid and depended too much on poetry; and had received the self-evident rejoinder—'very well; then choose great poetry'.

Poetry

As. t happened, Shakespeare and the Bible were not the right elements for Schumann song. But they were certainly the right catalysts; the chain reaction was all but uncontrollable. Its source of energy was always music. We could have inferred this from Schumann's prose-writing as well as his songwriting.

[1] Litzmann. Vol. I, pp. 255–258.
[2] Eric Sams. 'Schumann's Year of Song.' *Musical Times*, February 1965.

His choice of imagery for words and music instinctively awards pride of place to the latter; the poem is to wear the music as a wreath, or yield to it like a bride.[1]

So he treats poetry as a means to an end. Thus it can be altered or repeated to make a small-scale musical form or grouped to make a larger one. It is selected to correspond with Schumann's own mood; hence the main choice in 1840 of Rückert or Heine and their sweet or bitter love-poetry. This is then added to piano music expressive of verbal ideas and thus converted into a song. Some examples may make the process clear. The *Davidsbündlertänze*, op. 6, of 1837 contained 'wedding thoughts' of Clara and were 'dedicated to her more than anything else of mine'.[2] That work is structured by a five-note running theme in B minor which (for whatever reason) was closely associated with Clara.[3] An entirely typical example begins op. 6 no. 11.

EX 3

By the beginning of 1840 this melodic idea had been turned bodily into a song of impatient waiting, with the piano melody doubled in the voice part. The full chords are hurried along in both hands to convey a sense of urgency and strain.

EX 4

---

[1] GSK, Vol. I, pp. 495, 272.
[2] Litzmann, Vol. I, pp. 169, 179.
[3] As first shown by Roger Fiske in 'A Schumann Mystery', *Musical Times*, August 1964.

By May 1840 the same material had been reworked into the more complex patterns of *Dichterliebe*; again the piano part matches the poetic imagery.

EX 5

So music and words interact in Schumann to make a more varied texture than in any previous songwriting. Even so, his songs are simpler in essence than his piano music. The melodies are essentially stepwise and modest in range, varied with recitative elements (e.g. *Belsatzar, Zwielicht*) and decorations (e.g. the turns in *Lied der Suleika, Er der Herrlichste*). The harmony is usually diatonic with contrasting sections in, for example, the supertonic or mediant, held firmly within the tonic frame; the miniature form is too slender for long-range tonal contrast. Time-signatures mainly conform to the natural duple or quadruple scansion of German iambic verse. Repeated rhythmic patterns are used sparingly (as Schumann himself recommended to aspiring songwriters).[1] Piano techniques are undemanding.

Against this general background the exceptions stand out as serving an expressive purpose. Remote key-signatures convey complex emotions (again, as Schumann himself advocated).[2] The melodies have a quasi-instrumental compass in songs of wide emotional range (e.g. *Ich grolle nicht, Stirb, Lieb' und Freud'*). A true modulation is always significant; a change of key-signature represents a complete change of mood; chromatics convey blurring and confusion. Complex or unusual time-signatures are a way of translating a special quality in the poem; thus Chamisso's quadrimeter is allotted a slow CC in *Die Löwenbraut*, but a quick 2/8 in *Die Kartenlegerin*, to match the sense of the poem and the movement of the verse. Rhythmic patterns recur wherever the text warrants, as in *Im Rhein*. They are usually illustrative, like the turning figurations which suggest the carriage wheels in *Mein Wagen rollet langsam*.

[1] GSK, Vol. I, p. 432.   [2] GSK, Vol. I, p. 106.

EX 6

The piano sometimes suggests another instrumental timbre, e.g. lute (*Mein Herz ist schwer*), horn (*Der Knabe mit dem Wunderhorn*), violin (*Der Spielmann*), bell (*Auf das Trinkglas*), or indeed a whole orchestra (*Das ist ein Flöten und Geigen*). Complex piano writing is an expression of the poem, as in Ex. 5 above. Arpeggios suggest the natural movement of wind or waves as in *Der Nussbaum* or *Im Rhein*; the depths of the left hand speak of darkness or solemnity as in *Mondnacht* (cf. Ex. 20). Such musical equivalents (novel though many of them are) can be inferred from Schumann's own prose writings. Thus he tells us that poetic *contrasts* can be well expressed in music.[1] He even suggests specific equivalents; for example that a question in a poem might aptly be expressed by the dominant chord.[2] This features in his own work, as at the end of *Frage* (A Question), op. 35 no. 9. More intense interrogations are posed by dominant sevenths, as at the end of *Im wunderschönen Monat Mai* and *Die Nonne*; and more intense still by diminished sevenths, as in *Lied der Braut I* and *Rätsel* (the latter is answered in Ex. 17).

Similarly, Schumann praises a song which begins in C minor and ends in

EX 7

[1] GSK, Vol. I, p. 268.   [2] GSK, Vol. II, p. 408.

A flat major 'exactly reflecting the sense of the poem, which has itself become more keyed-up'.[1] In a review of an *English Sailor's Song* by Mme Malibran he writes 'we can feel quite clearly the "wide and silver'd sea", the evening lying spread out over it, the waiting ship with hoisted sails. However, this is not crude depiction but the image of an emotion (Seelenbild).'[2]

Like many other composers he could sense that words and tones are complementary; the former are at their most precise where the latter are at their most abstract, and conversely. No music can define seas or ships or sails as such; but it can evoke the nature of such qualities as expanse, brightness, serenity or tension in a given context. Even Mme Malibran's modest compositional skills offer enough intuitive response to language to impress Schumann: the two different wave motions, deep swell and surface ripple, the melody augmented and sharpened for breadth and brightness, are inarticulate but expressive utterances in Schumann's own native tongue.

EX 8

Of course there is no one-for-one correspondence between music and language. But Schumann himself clearly believed not only that the two forms could be congruent, but also that the essence of songwriting lay in expressing that congruity. How his mind worked is best shown by the best-documented example.

[1] GSK, Vol. I, p. 270.   [2] GSK, Vol. II, p. 302.

A Typical Lyric

In March 1840 he wrote to Clara:[1]

'Do you remember how you felt after that first kiss, Clärlein? I'll tell you how.' He went on to quote a poem by Rückert. 'The jasmine bush was green when it went to sleep last night. But when breeze and sunlight woke it this morning it was snowy white. What has changed me overnight? it wonders. Well, this is what happens to trees that dream in springtime.' He added 'This lyric always makes me think of our first kiss. I'll be sending you the music for it very soon'; and on the margin of his manuscript he wrote 'really much too difficult to set to music, if the secret stirrings of nature in the poem are somehow to be matched. But consider it as an attempt'.

We would expect this song to be in essence piano music inspired by Clara, and very possibly containing a musical allusion to her, as in op. 6. Schumann's own testimony also suggests that he will also try to distil the poem into music, phrase by phrase. If so, the music may well betray its verbal origins and thus become as it were a Rosetta stone or bilingual inscription, from which other meanings may be inferred; perhaps this was what Schumann meant when he said that his early songs 'offer a deeper insight into the inner workings of my music'.[2] *Jasminenstrauch* (The Jasmine Bush) is illustrated entire as a typical Schumann lyric of 1840.

EX 9

[1] Litzmann, Vol. I, p. 412.　　　　　　　　　[2] Jansen, p. 203.

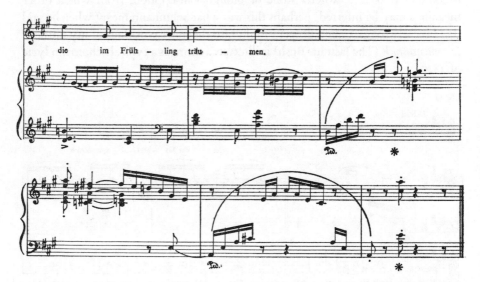

Its one-bar prelude of upward arpeggio in a bright A major, redolent of colourful grace and vitality, would be self-explanatory even without the parallel in the first bars of *Der Nussbaum* (The Walnut Tree) which had flowered only a few weeks earlier (Ex. 10).

Next, the A major colouring is tinged with Clara's B minor theme as in Exx. 3–5 above; perhaps more than coincidence. Note also the characteristic

EX 10

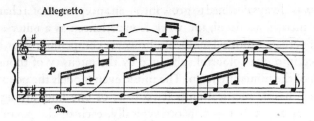

piano-song construction; the opening vocal melody is already contained in the right hand. The decorative variations may in a sense be taken literally; if music is to have symbolic meaning, then it seems apt that grace-notes should signify beauty, in this Schumann song as in many others.[1]

The rhythmic movement in these two bars is also meaningful. The arpeggios are made to sway and droop at the word 'schlafen' (sleep); the music is heard nodding off. Then the texture is imperceptibly lightened by the continued omission of the decorative motif in the second half of bars 6–7 and 9–11, making an image of half-awareness to match the poetic idea of gradual awakening from sleep. Against this background, the half-motif is set sighing at 'Morgens Hauch' (breath of morning) and 'aufgewacht' (awake). It is then rounded off and enlivened, for the only time in seven bars, at the word '(Sonnen) lichter' (rays of sunlight). Meanwhile a new harmonic idea has dawned. The first five bars had stated, quitted and re-established the tonic—a brief separate introduction like the first two lines of the poem, which also end in a full stop. Then follows a six-four chord of the relative minor, with a slight but insistent accent, giving an effect of mild surprise; again, just as in the poem. Is this F sharp minor to remain a chord or become a new key? The listener shares the poem's uncertainty which in bars 12–13 is further transformed into amazement. As shown in Ex. 7a and b, the diminished seventh is a rhetorical question. Here the effect is enhanced by the downward arpeggio, which is heard as a negation of the confident feeling in the prelude and also as a mysterious counterpart to the natural movement of bar 5. All this is blurred by the piano into the sense of confusion and trance implied by the words 'Wie geschah mir in der Nacht' (What has happened to me overnight?), where the voice part diverges from its melody into a recitative, as if absent-mindedly lapsing into speech. Then finally the last four bars for voice and piano reassuringly affirm the home tonic as a natural conclusion. It's all right, the harmony says; this is how it was *meant* to be. And to resolve any lingering doubts the postlude goes over the same ground again. The springing arpeggio of upward elation is checked, troubled, reassured, perplexed again, resolved and

[1] Eric Sams, *op. cit*, p. 22.

finally restored and complete, all in a handful of notes. The last bars illustrate what the prelude was always destined to grow into—an apt epitome of a charming song.

For all its meticulous detail, the work is experienced as a unity and not as a succession of verbal or musical moments, however compelling. Words and music are here fused into one colourful substance by the intensity of thought and the compression of the miniature form. The music even models the poem's thought-structure; each has its metrical units (two bars, or one line) arranged into the same pattern of 2 + 3 + 1 + 2. More typically, each of the poem's facets has a corresponding musical motif. Thus Schumann's songwriting builds up mosaic patterns or pictures of feeling in every imaginable colour and form, ranging from frank imitation through conventional scene-painting to music of inward action and gesture, and finally to the 'image of emotion' or *Seelenbild*. From this kaleidoscope some seventy fairly definable patterns may be isolated.[1] Some twenty are melodic, twenty-five contrapuntal or harmonic, and ten rhythmic, while the other fifteen relate to piano texture or register. This distribution may help to confirm Schumann's own feeling that his songs were less complicated, more melodious than his piano music. The addition of words precipitated lighter and brighter elements which cohered and interacted to form new expressive compounds which could in turn be combined into song-cycles made to symbolize whole new worlds of personal feeling.

Personality

Four main aspects of Schumann's complex character are reflected in his song-writing. First comes his cyclic disposition, fluctuating between extremes of elation and depression. Next is the quite different (but equally marked) duality which Schumann himself called Florestan and Eusebius, the active or passive voices of his outgoing or inward moods. On these two innate dualities his life superimposed a pattern of growth and decline. Betrothal and marriage in 1840 brought maturity and responsibility. Thereafter his world, and hence his music, was no longer composed solely from his own intensely personal feelings. Finally the organic disease which destroyed his mind in 1854 must surely have already damaged his creativity at an earlier stage.

Liederkreis, op. 24

These four variables give all Schumann's music a great depth and contrast. But the *Lied* is essentially a lyric form; so it is not surprising that his fame in this

[1] Eric Sams, *op. cit*, pp. 11–26.

genre rests almost wholly on the lovesong cycles written for Clara in their marriage year. These begin with the *Liederkreis*, op. 24 (completed in February, 1840, but perhaps sketched much earlier), on poems by Heine, to which Schumann's strong stream of self-expression often runs counter. His main mood is that of a successful thirty-year-old, deeply in love; the poems express the desperately unhappy passion of a very young man. Schumann seizes on the element of love-longing and enhances it by changing or repeating the words, on which he also imposes his own unity of key-structure. Conversely the poems though immature already have the typical dash of Heinesque bitters which brings new tang and substance to the fluid blandness of the *Davidsbündler*-type piano music whence Schumann fashions his accompaniments. The words also give the melodic line a new expressiveness deriving from transient dissonances or appoggiature. For example the word 'klage' (lament) in no. 1 yields this:

EX II

Again, a phrase like 'da hauset ein Zimmermann schlimm und arg' in the fourth poem, where Heine likens his heartbeat to the hammering of a carpenter making a coffin, freezes the freeflowing melody into an awe-struck whisper, while in the accompaniment a dark shadow falls and the heart misses a beat.

EX 12

Nothing so graphic and verbally responsive had been heard on this miniature scale in German song before, not even in Schubert, whose influence is evident throughout, for example, in the constant images of movement as in *Winterreise*. Schumann also brings to the *Lied* a thesaurus of expressive devices compiled from ten years of piano music. Thus the footsteps of the first song, about walking in a day-dream, have this pattern among others.

EX 13

which is then urged along, as in Ex. 4, to suit the impatience of the second song, and then again relaxed

EX 14

for the dreamy amble of the third, before breaking into a run in the sixth song about flight and pursuit.

EX 15

The seventh is about the Rhine and its waves; and Schumann responds in a Schubertian flow of semiquavers. In the postlude we hear for the first time his generalized expression for the undulating movement of water or of wind-stirred leaves (see also Ex. 10 and the first and penultimate bars of Ex. 9).

Myrthen, op. 25

With such musical equivalents of life and movement he can now animate poems about nature and fulfilled love, which is the central idea of his next cycle *Myrthen*, op. 25 (that is, myrtles or traditional bridal finery; they were his wedding present to Clara). The twenty-six poems were hand-picked for the purpose; and their significance perhaps goes even deeper than intended.

First we hear Schumann himself in the Florestan vein; independent, confident, active (*Freisinn, Höchländers Abschied, Niemand*). He was making money, gaining popularity, being more industrious than ever. But all this took its toll ('tired out', 'unwell', 'exhausted', says the diary); and these equally characteristic feelings also infiltrate the music (*Mein Herz ist schwer, Was will die einsame Träne?*). In other moments of involuntary candour Schumann's choice of poem tells of his fondness for wine (*Sitz' ich allein, Setze mir nicht*) and women (*Zwei Venetianische Lieder*) as well as song. *Rätsel* shows his lifelong penchant for enigma. The text is a riddle to which the answer is 'the letter H'. The voice's last word, 'Hauch', meaning a breath or an aspirate, is omitted so that the piano can have the last word—on the German note 'H'.

EX 17

To this self-revelation Schumann adds his own vision of Clara: devoted (*Lied der*

Suleika, Lieder der Braut), brave (*Hauptmanns Weib*), lonely (*Die Hochländer-Witwe, Weit, weit*), maternal (*Hochländisches Wiegenlied, Im Westen*), and above all beautiful, like a flower (*Die Lotosblume, Du bist wie eine Blume*). This last is in A flat major, Schumann's ceremonial key (as also in e.g. *Stirb', Lieb' und Freud'*), conveying the tones of organ voluntary and marriage service. In the first and last songs these same tones offer a solemn harmonic unity; alpha and omega, till death do us part. Best of all perhaps is the sweet kernel of longing in the songs of separation and assuagement, *Aus den östlichen Rosen* and *Der Nussbaum*. In each we hear the piano part set free for a moment to make an image of leaves in springtime, just as in *Jasminenstrauch* (Ex. 9), and again this independent use of piano texture provides new expressive device.

Liederkreis, op. 39

The next song-cycle, the Eichendorff *Liederkreis*, op. 39, combines elements of the first two; the imagery of nature and movement is inter-stressed with the ideas of lovesong and personal self-revelation. Again we can cite direct testimony. Spring came early and profusely to Leipzig in 1840. Schumann wrote to Clara[1] 'This springtime has amazed me; everything is in full bloom already. I thought about the "Jasmine Bush"'; and on the next day 'I expect your head like mine is still quite dizzy with the happiness of our time together; I can't calm down'. In the music too the external world, hardly glimpsed in the earlier piano music, and seen with growing awareness in opp. 24 and 25, is now suddenly in full flower. Schumann turns instinctively to Eichendorff, the poet of the German rural scene and its seasons. He chooses lyrics that sing of place and time, of slow or swift change, of sky or forest quick or serene with the flight or song of birds; in spring or summer, at dusk or nightfall, with stars or moon. Again his letters to Clara testify to this new mood of almost mystic exaltation. 'Such music I have in me that I could sing the whole day through';[2] or 'I'm having to sing myself to death like a nightingale'.[3] At the same time he had thoughts of an opera. So the poetry too is conceived scenically or dramatically. There are sound-effects ranging from imitation (e.g. the horns swelling and dying in the forest in *Waldesgespräch*) through suggestion (the processional six-eight rhythm for wedding and hunting parties in *Im Walde*) to metaphor (the way in which the arching leaf-music of the lonely woods in *In der Fremde I* is topped with fronds of rustling sound at the word 'rauscht'), thus

---

[1] Bœtticher, p. 332.   [2] Bœtticher, p. 338.   [3] *Jugendbriefe*, p. 314.

EX 18

Then there are deeper associative levels, such as the creeping files of single notes ushering in an ominous twilight in *Zwielicht*, while the voice has not only recitative effects but such graphic devices as the falling octaves for the depths of the heart at the end of *Im Walde*.

EX 19

There may also be an expressive use of cipher. The word 'Ehe' (marriage) had been noted by Schumann in a letter to Clara as 'very musical',[1] (meaning that it could be written in notes, since H in German is the note B, as in Ex. 17). Those notes appear like a litany throughout *Mondnacht* in the left hand of the piano part;

EX 20

and that song begins with an image of the marriage of earth and sky. A striking feature of this cycle is the use of sequences to show how time passes and in what moods; slowly for the acceptance of fate as in the modal or mediaeval tones of *Auf einer Burg*

[1] *Jugendbriefe*, p. 281.

EX 21

or swiftly for the **excitement** of change as in *Frühlingsnacht*

EX 22

or blending both as in *Mondnacht*. In these last two songs the piano part moves into a higher register to suggest the reaches of the night sky. This insistent and intense fusion of music and meaning throughout op. 39 also affects other techniques; thus the piano prelude is often an integrated and inseparable part of the song (nos. 6, 8 and 12). Even the key-structure (beginning on F sharp minor and ending on F sharp major) plays its part in creating the illusion of a change from winter into spring.

Dichterliebe, op. 48

In op. 39, scene and drama are pantheistic and impersonal. The personal hero reappears in the complementary masterpiece of *Dichterliebe*, op. 48, also written in May 1840. Its title envisages an artist's love as especially sensitive and vulnerable and hence capable of extreme elation and despair. Heine's fine poems also add their own imagery of nature, movement, time, life itself.

Like the earlier Heine cycle, op. 24 (with which it shares themes, Exx. 4–5), *Dichterliebe* is an alloy of music and poetry rather than one single substance. Heine's verse now recalls past happiness in present grief, an added sorrow; hence its bitter irony. Schumann's music recalls past suffering in present bliss, an added joy; hence its innocent exaltation. So the two interlock in a fusion of contrasts. Thus in Heine *Im wunderschönen Monat Mai* is a poem of pure delight. The setting however is all hesitancy, nostalgia, regret; it begins with a grieving dissonance

EX 23

and ends uniquely on the dominant seventh of a tonic which is never once heard. Similar contrasts are manifest in the interplay of voice and piano throughout. In sixteen songs, only six of the voice parts end unambiguously on a tonic. Elsewhere the tensions often have to be resolved by an extended piano postlude, often using new material. This happens typically, here as in other song-cycles, where the poem is about thoughts too deep for words. Thus the piano muses on an inexpressibly sweet hour in *Ich will meine Seele tauchen*, an ineffable beauty in *Im Rhein*. Speechless rage and despair end *Und wüssten's die Blümen* and *Das ist ein Flöten und Geigen*. The postlude of *Hör' ich das Liedchen* expresses a sorrow, and of *Die alten bösen Lieder* a love, for which not even the poet can find words. When Heine is silent, Schumann speaks. Again, the key-structure is expressively related to the cycle of fifths which Schumann himself had suggested as apt for the expression of far-reaching emotion.[1] The voice is stretched to cover two full octaves (highest at 'heart' in *Ich grolle nicht*, lowest at 'tears' in *Allnächtlich im Traume*); the piano spans nearly six octaves (from the dark depths of 'grave' in *Die alten bösen Lieder* to the rarefied heights of the postlude to that song and *Am leuchtenden Sommermorgen*); the rhythmic and dynamic contrasts are correspondingly wide and graphic. Other musical imagery is also more vivid and varied than ever. In *Und wüssten's die Blumen* the demisemiquavers flutter and twinkle as birdsong and starshine. In *Im Rhein* the semibreves stand like stone in the left hand while time and the river flow past in the right, as the cathedral is mirrored in the Rhine. In *Das ist ein Flöten* the bass notes are obsessively repeated as the hated dance music (at the loved one's wedding) wheels and whirls in the

[1] GSK, Vol. I, p. 106.

jealous mind. In the ominous *Ich hab' im Traum geweinet*, the cortège creeps past in a pall of E flat minor, always a deathly key to Schumann (see Ex. 12). The final song creates a climactic processional march of giants; and so on.

Again (as in the *Liederkreis*, op. 39) the sequence in voice and piano have both structural and expressive function. They are here associated with the idea of involuntary love, as in the first song at the words 'love rose up in my heart';

EX 24

da ist in mei — nem Her — zen   die Lie — be auf — ge — gan — gen

and similarly throughout the lovesong *Ich will meine Seele tauchen*. Compare also *Im Rheim* at the mention of 'her eyes, her lips and cheeks'; *Ich grolle nicht* at 'love lost for ever'; *Hör' ich das Liedchen* at 'a dark longing drives me out to the high hills'; and so on.

Finally in *Dichterliebe*, as in its predecessors, there are the unifying five-note linear themes so dear to Schumann which (whether one calls them 'Clara themes' or not) are heard throughout the piano music of 1835–39 as well as the songs of 1840. To give just one example of one such link in its B minor form: each of the song-cycles thus far considered has a song which (like *Jasminenstrauch*, Ex. 8) is in A major with B minor overtones—no. 7 of op. 24, no. 9 of op. 25, no. 2 of op. 39, no. 2 of op. 48.

Frauenliebe: the Ballads

In this respect as in many others, the next song-cycle *Frauenliebe und -leben* (A woman's life and love) is quite different. We can hear that Schumann's creative mind has taken a new turn. Personal passion has changed to concern for the loved one, for others, for the world at large. His music had always been responsive to external circumstance. As he wrote to Clara in 1838: 'Everything that happens affects me; politics, literature, people—I think it all over in my own way, and then it has to find an outlet in music'.[1] Such a reaction was possibly the source of his songwriting, which began with a ballad and a character-sketch. This was not the right road at the time. But it remained open; and Schumann's thoughts often turned in that direction. It was then the modern trend; and it also led directly to his own development towards much larger forms as symphony and opera. At first, even his ballads and stories and characters in music were subjective or self-expressive. For example *Die Grenadiere* is so vivid because Schumann's own hero-worship for Napoleon marches in step with his own dread of defeat and oblivion, making fine dramatic end as the triumphant strains of the *Marseillaise* turn into a dying fall.

EX 25

We can compare Wagner's postlude in his contemporary setting, which while embodying the meaning and drama of the poem lacks the contrasting lyric elements which are the essence of the *Lied*, even in its ballad form.

Another Heine ballad, *Die feindlichen Brüder*, is about two brothers who fight to the death for love of the lady Laura, which will surely not be unrelated to the fight by Florestan and Eusebius for the hand of Clara. And certainly the ideas of rivalry and jealousy are deeply ingrained in the songs, with Heine as the prime source of texts, as in the trilogy *Der arme Peter* and in *Es leuchtet meine Liebe*, omitted from *Dichterliebe*. In other separate songs the driving force is nature in all its moods; examples range from the pallid watery arpeggios of *Lorelei* to the finely graphic *Abends am Strand* which contrasts places and people and brings them all under the sway of the sea, in undulating quaver lines and deep bass notes (as also in *Frühlingsfahrt*). As in many another song where the sea of the Rhine is mentioned, much of this music reflects the darker depths of Schumann's own nature, and foreshadows his own despairing leap from the bridge at Düsseldorf in the first onset of his madness in 1854.

[1] *Jugendbriefe*, p. 282.

den Kai — — ser, den Kai — — ser zu schü — tzen!

But of course there was also the lighter side. The clown's ditty which began
the 1840 songwriting was the forerunner of many in gayer mood; dancing or
drinking *in propria persona,* as in *Niemand* or the two *Divan* songs, or adventuring
in mask and cloak as in the two Venetian songs, all in op. 25. As in the Ballads,
all this music is full of images of action and gesture. Schumann's lyric impulse
was preparing to absorb these ideas into a new dramatic music. Nothing had
come of the proposed opera; perhaps fortunately, since the time was not yet
ripe. But the urge to more objective forms found some outlet, in the male voice
quartets, op. 33 and the duets, op. 34. In the latter we hear for almost the first
time in Schumann's work the idea of colloquy or dialogue (*Liebhabers Ständchen,
Unterm Fenster*) or even of shared family life (*Familiengemälde*).

At the same time he was thinking of character-studies of women, a further step
towards objectivity, as in *Hauptmanns Weib* (which he thought 'very novel and
Romantic'[1] meaning no doubt precisely the elements of realism and characterization) and the two *Lieder der Braut,* op. 25, which serve as sketches for *Frauenliebe.*
This, the next and last of the great song-cycles (July 1840), is both continuation
and contrast. It focuses on the interior world through the verse of Chamisso,
the indoor poet of nature and dream. There is only the one scene—a room in a
house. But there is a strong and clear story, and a supporting cast. For the first
time in a Schumann song-cycle we learn (as in both of Schubert's) something

[1] Bœtticher, p. 331.

about the protagonist. She is young, with even younger sisters. Her lover, whose lot is ceaselessly and unaffectedly contrasted with her own, is presumably old, rich and famous (if only in comparison with her own more modest station). The girl herself grows from a hero-worshipping child in the first three songs to a woman, a mother, and finally a widow (and in the last poem, omitted by Schumann, a grandmother). At each stage the past is seen through older and wiser eyes. The verse has been sharply criticized for its sentimentality and convention. The latter at least has been misunderstood. Chamisso's aim (whatever its success) is to describe an actual relationship for better or worse in a real world. Schumann's music embodies his and Clara's mutual love, which commands respect. Thus considered, op. 42 is as much a masterpiece in its kind as its predecessors; but its kind is significantly different. It is not only an expression of emotion but an attempt to see life through another's eyes. So the music changes its attitude. The untranslatable direction 'innig' appears on four songs out of eight (as compared with five out of sixty-three in the other cycles) which suggests that inwardness is a sign of objectivity in Schumann. This inward mood matches the interior quality of the scenes and emotions described. Sharp keys yield to flats; voice and piano have a modest compass, a rhythmic sameness. But the cycle is also notable for its frequent changes of tempo within the same song; now hesitant, now impetuous. The idea of musical movement, previously experienced, is now observed. Thus the first song *Seit ich ihn gesehen* has reluctant but inevitable progress, as if being drawn along despite itself. A stepwise walking movement sidles ingratiatingly into the second song, *Er der Herrlichste*, at the words 'go your ways' with a canonic hint of following on behind.

EX 27

The same motif marks the transition from childhood to maturity in *Du Ring an meinem Finger*; and by the fifth song, *Helft mir, ihr Schwestern*, it has become caught up into a wedding march. The musical sequences are more marked and

expressive than ever. There is an ascending flight expressive of outright adoration
at 'let me but hold you close and closer'

EX 28

while a more modest upward glance accompanies the idea of admiration from
a distance, e.g. as in Ex. 27 above, or at the words 'I will live for him, serve him'
in the fourth song.

EX 29

A more gentle questioning—'do you not know why I weep?'—is even more
restrained musically, rising no more than a third in five bars:

EX 30

But when the words speak of humility, the sequences incline downwards, as at 'nur in Demut' etc., following Ex. 27; while for the later moments of entire selfabnegation in that second song—'I will bless the exalted woman of your choice'—the figures bow more deeply than ever in obeisances soon made even lower still as the self-denial deepens into self-sacrifice at the words 'what matter though my heart should break, so long as he is happy?'

The music is more aware of duality than ever before, even in the duets. The piano has separately expressive motifs, e.g.

EX 31

which was first heard in Ex. 27 and recurs three more times, the last of which coincides with the key word 'weinen' (weep). All these devices are heard throughout the cycle. For example in Ex. 30 above and the few preceding bars we find accompanied recitative, separate piano motifs, the expressive appoggiature, sequence, canon, and true modulation (a great rarity in these 1840 songs). The whole motivic vocabulary is being deployed to create story, scene and character as well as mood.

All of these components reappear in the varied settings with which Schumann followed *Frauenliebe*, for which we are again indebted to Chamisso. First, there are three more poems of women and their emotional life. *Die Löwenbraut* is a Grand Guignol ballad of jealousy and revenge; *Die rote Hanne* a solemn study of poverty and fidelity; and *Die Kartenlegerin* a deft and gay picture of childish petulance. In all three, Schumann's art becomes plastic; his Galateas come to life. The world is seen realistically through sombre eyes in *Der Soldat* and *Der Spielmann* (again about betrayal and jealousy) and is depicted in dark hues in *Muttertraum* and the other Andersen songs of op. 40 (in Chamisso's translation). But other songs don full costume and produce stage effects in the colourful Geibel settings of July 1840; *Der Page, Der Knabe mit dem Wunderhorn* and especially *Der Hidalgo*, where the piano and voice sing love duets. In the same month the duets as such resume, also to words by Geibel, and also with scenes of the outside world; *Ländliches Lied, In meinem Garten*, and the lively vocal quartet *Zigeunerleben* with triangle and tambourine. This last is a vivid if naïve presentation of scene, character and costume, all in the open air; it might well have been the opening chorus of an opera, and is worth a revival. More pressing however was the dénouement of Schumann's own drama. After much frustration and misfortune he finally married Clara Wieck on 12 September 1840, the day before her twenty-first birthday. Of course the first music thereafter was a set of duets,

op. 43 (one of which, *Wenn ich ein Vöglein wär*, later appeared in the opera
Genoveva). In the months after his marriage, Schumann's balladwriting culminates in three songs which (consciously or not) express his own hopes and
fears, as in the earlier lyrics. They even foretell his own fate. In *Frühlingsfahrt*
two brothers set out to seek their fortune; one finds home and family, the other
disaster and despair. That theme is itself divided into two other songs. *Blondels
Lied* tells of the successful quest for a loved one, while in *Der Schatzgräber* the
treasure-seeker is buried alive and smothered to death. Again the musical images
are physical in origin; the leading figures in the music sing as they wander,
intone as they delve. Finally the single songs end with two more character-
studies of single women, *Die Nonne* and *Mädchen-Schwermut*, both very unhappy.

Thus through all that long flowering of song from spring to autumn the two
faces of Schumann's music had slowly unfolded to the external world. There too
the last song-cycles belong.

The Reinick Songs

Indeed the successor to *Dichterliebe* and *Frauenliebe* might well have been called
Malerliebe, since the words are taken from Reinick's *Lieder eines Malers* (Songs
of a Painter). Again Schumann strives to depict the world. Certainly music and
verse are alike illustrative, full of line and colour. But the result lacks depth and
perspective. The key-structure is less taut and controlled. The musical impulse
slackens too. Schumann's original fears are now being realized; the settings faithfully reflect the essential dullness of the verses. Of course there are fine moments.
The idea of a serenader's guitar-music helps to make *Ständchen* enchanting; the
idea of billowing clouds buoys the long-flighted melodic line and gently-moving
accompaniment of *Liebesbotschaft*. But *Sonntags am Rhein* with nearly five-
hundred continuous quavers, and *Nichts Schöneres*, nearly as repetitive, convey
only too well the plodding metre and pedestrian thought.

This outcome must have disturbed the composer himself. If he was to go on
writing songs he needed at this stage texts full of character and incident to
stimulate him to fresh invention. One solution was deliberately to seek particular
kinds of verse; and this he had tried. 'Bring me the Kerner poems' he wrote to
Clara,[1] 'Lend me the Geibel volume' to a friend.[2] Another possibility was to
abandon songwriting in favour of larger instrumental forms, in which the
musical construction itself provides dramatic contrast and interplay of themes.
This impulse was already active; in mid-October 1840 we hear of symphonic

---

[1] Bœtticher, p. 339.   [2] Unpublished MS.

sketches,[1] no doubt the beginnings of the First, in B flat major. This may be why the letters in August and September suggest a subconscious resentment against songwriting; 'I can't stop writing songs' . . . 'I can't free myself from vocal music', together with further talk of an opera and larger forms in general.[2] The impulse that had seemed so unexpected and marvellous in February was now outstaying its welcome. But once Schumann's mind had clenched there was no prising it loose; it could only relax of its own accord, slowly. And it still had two more song-cycles within its grasp.

The Kerner Songs

First came the promised Kerner. This group is interestingly titled *Eine Liederreihe*, a row or series of songs, as distinct from the previous *Zyklus* or *Kreis*, a cycle or circle, as if to confirm that the music is now open-ended. The outside world of nature is the main motivic force. The typical soft, slow music in flat keys makes a fine autumnal afterglow to the 1840 songs. The poems are chosen as a counterpart to *Frauenliebe*, to hint at a similar story of love and loss, with nature as final solace. The evocations of scene and character are memorable, as in *Stirb, Lieb' und Freud'*. So is the background of external nature; the storm in the valleys in *Lust der Sturmnacht*, the green freshness of the interludes in *Erstes Grün*, the touching nostalgia of *Sehnsucht nach der Waldgegend*. Whenever the music is outward bound or forward looking its impulse is vital; but when it looks inward (e.g. at the room from the storm in *Lust der Sturmnacht*) or backward (e.g. the home thoughts from abroad in the middle of *Wanderlust*) then the inspiration seems to falter.

The Rückert Songs

At this dramatic turning point the curtain is about to fall on Schumann's first and finest year of mature songwriting and to rise without intermission on his first and finest year of mature orchestral music. As usual there is a linking theme. The first symphony, known as the 'Spring', was of one birth with the song-cycle, op. 37, from *Liebesfrühling* (Love's Springtime) by Rückert. Their constant harping on seasonal renewal seeks to unite love and nature in a cosmic flowering. After opp. 39 and 48 this should have inspired another masterpiece. But as in the Reinick songs the sweet sentiment of the verse cloys the music. Union with

[1] Bœtticher, p. 351.   [2] Jansen, pp. 193, 197, 198.

Clara is being overdeliberately expressed by her collaboration in Schumann's work as in his life. A letter to a publisher says that the lovesongs and duets of op. 37 were written together (sic) with his wife;[1] and this may have been meant literally. Certainly three of them (*Er ist gekommen, Liebst du um Schönheit, Warum willst du And're fragen*) were acknowledged as Clara's and published as her op. 12; but they have an occasional master-touch which is not hers. Conversely some of the other songs have an atypical woodenness, for example in the opening bars of *O Sonn' ,O Meer* and *So wahr die Sonne*.

Developments 1840–48

It was clearly time for Schumann's musical material to be taken out of the domestic song frame and put to more colourful and expansive use, as instrumental music. The First symphony's opening call to awaken is drawn from op. 37 no. 7 at the opening words 'lovely but brief is the festival of springtime'.

EX 32

The symphony theme becomes first the subject of the opening allegro and then the melody of the slow movement, which itself recalls the most deeply felt of the songs, in which rose, sea and sun paint a springtime picture of the loved one.

EX 33

[1] Jansen, p. 431.

AUTOGRAPH SKETCH OF 'PAPILLONS', op. 2 (1831)

CLARA WIECK (1832)
a lithograph by Fechner

The symphony's poignant harmonization of this passage is also drawn from the song, bar 9. More objectively, the contrary motion of *Die Kartenlegerin* skips into the symphony (first movement, bar 120 *et seq.*), creating its own special impression of independent and engaging wilfulness. Later the picaresque rhythms of *Der Knabe mit dem Wunderhorn* reappear in the next orchestral work, the *Overture, Scherzo and Finale*, op. 52, while the soliloquy in the postlude of *Dichterliebe* is re-enacted in the cadenza to the A minor Piano Concerto, op. 54. One of the themes associated with Clara (Exx. 3–5) becomes in its retrograde form the motto-theme of the work which Schumann said would depict her and would be called his 'Clara' Symphony[1] (the D minor op. 120 in its 1841 version). Further, two of the songs yield material for the quartets of 1842; the dramatic encounter of *Es leuchtet meine Liebe* is retold in the scherzo of the A minor Quartet, op. 41 no. 1, while the character-study of *Mädchen-Schwermut* is replayed in the second movement of the one in A major, op. 41 no. 3.

While the stream of song was running underground Schumann was visited in successive years by symphonic music, chamber music, an oratorio (*Paradise and the Peri*) and then in 1844 by a grave nervous breakdown, with tinnitus and giddiness. If his final breakdown and deterioration to death were indeed caused by syphilis (see p. 413) then these will be the first recorded symptoms (as with Smetana).[2] From these barren depths Schumann was lifted by the therapeutic C major symphony of 1845–46, which again begins with a signal of re-awakening. At this time song makes a brief strange re-appearance with *Auf dem Rhein*, which begins and climaxes with the Clara-theme of the D minor symphony, and is inscribed 'to his dear Clara; the first sound of song after long silence'.[3] The poem is clearly chosen for the deep personal significance of its image of love as a closely-guarded secret treasure hidden in the bed of a river— an eeried echo of the 1840 ballads *Der Schatzgräber* and *Frühlingsfahrt*, and an even more ominous foreshadowing of Schumann's own attempted suicide by drowning, having first thrown in his wedding ring as a deranged sacrament. But the song itself is retrogressive in its feeble subjectivism. A welcome return of his dramatic powers led to the opera *Genoveva* (1847–50) and also in May 1847 to a brief resumption of songwriting at the logical stage of character-studies of women, the zenith of his second 1840 style. They still reflect the contrasts of his own temperament; elated in *Die Soldatenbraut*, despairing in *Das verlassene Mägdlein*. They may again illustrate Schumann's sensitivity to people and ideas. These two Mörike settings follow a visit by Robert Franz, notable for his own Mörike songs, just as the Leipzig songs began with Shakespeare after a visit from

---

[1] Litzmann, Vol. II, p. 30.
[2] Brian Large. *Smetana*. 1970, pp. 393, 220, 244, etc.   [3] Unpublished MS.

F

Mendelssohn. By this time the Schumanns had moved to Dresden, and 1847 was an unusually happy and contented year. Yet both songs, grave and gay, have new harmonic tensions; and the music is technically much more knowing and effective (although the basic attitude to songwriting remains unchanged, with the poem subordinated and the voice sharing the piano's melody). In particular the influence of Bach, heard earlier in *Muttertraum*, is now unmistakable. The new contrapuntal style had been freely exercised by a great deal of choral music in 1846–47. Its subject matter too is less romantically individual. The themes are social and purposeful; hunting and fighting, freedom and conscience, in tune with Schumann's own radical sympathies in these years. In the revolutionary year of 1848 came three 'freedom' choruses, prudently left unpublished, and also the famous *Album für die Jugend* for piano solo. Once again the 1840 pattern of vocal music, based on piano music, is ready to recur. Since then Schumann had made only a few passing references to songwriting in his letters and reviews. In 1841 he had complained of being relegated by a critic to the second class of songwriters; with genuine humility, he thought he had claims to a special place of his own, though not of course a leading one.[1] In 1842 he had written to a friend that he could not with confidence look forward to any better performance in the song field than he had already achieved, with which he was on the whole satisfied.[2]

In 1843 he had published his famous review of songs by Franz including a summary of the history of the *Lied*. He felt that songwriting had been the only genre in which progress had been made, and that this had been due to historical circumstances—a new technical development in the piano, a new impulse in German lyric verse.[3]

The 1849 Songs

All these remarks sound in their contexts like obituary notices and funeral orations. He felt that his own works had been forced from an intense inner ferment which could never recur. But in 1849 he wrote more music than ever before in his life in a single year, including nearly as much vocal music as in 1840. This abnormal productiveness may have been a symptom of his condition. The choice of poem as well as the music expresses the older Schumann. The young lover is now the middle-aged paterfamilias; the pianist is a practised composer in every instrumental and vocal form; the style is more distanced, less personal; the harmony is more complex. All these points are well illustrated by the choral works with which the 1849 outburst began. Opp. 67, 69, 75, 91, 145

[1] Jansen, p. 206.   [2] Jansen, p. 216.   [3] GSK, Vol. II, p. 147.

and 146 for mixed or women's voices *a cappella* were mostly written in March of that year. The poets are those already known to Schumann from 1840—Burns, Eichendorff, Goethe, Kerner, Rückert, Reinick—but the themes are predictably ballads and character-sketches rather than lovesongs. The outgoing phase is again approaching the full. With renewed brightness and power it strives to illuminate not only characters but whole societies, classes, nations. As ever, Schumann's music was a reaction to his own reading and experience. In those years the attention of all Europe was still focused to burning-point on social questions. Schumann wrote sociably for chorus or vocal group; his choice of text favoured popular folk poetry of all nations. The famous anthology *Das Knaben Wunderhorn*, used once in 1840, now becomes a favourite source; so does translation. The newcomers among the poets are those most strongly influenced by folksong, e.g. Mörike and Uhland. Even such old favourites as Eichendorff and Geibel now appear as translators from the Spanish. All these were consciously exploited as sources for new musical thoughts and forms as revolutionary as the epoch itself; Schumann wished to be popular in every sense. His letters at this period often mention his involvement with the times, the originality of his work, its arrangement for dramatic effect, and its relation to the drama of the outside world.[1]

Spanisches Liederspiel: Liederalbum: Minnespiel

One example he gives is the *Spanisches Liederspiel* or Vaudeville, op. 74, which treated Geibel's translations (for no very obvious textual reason) in quasi-dramatic form for vocal quartet, duet or solo with piano accompaniment. In his enthusiasm he began a second set straightaway, op. 138, for the same voices but this time with piano duet. The poems later inspired Wolf and the genre Brahms. The style is novel; there are syncopations in the accompaniment and bold declamation in the voice, with free-ranging melodies, chromatic harmonies and independent piano parts. All this is often expressly related to the sense of the words. Yet the music is still basically conceived in piano terms. Here are some illustrations of these points from *Melancholie*, op. 74 no. 6 (Exx. 34 and 35).

Mixed with this new creative vigour there are some ominous signs, which will soon become more disturbing still. The new techniques have no place for fresh melodic invention; indeed, they might have been devised to compensate for its absence. The music lacks rhythmic unity; in *Melancholie* for example no two bars are alike. There is an undue reliance on broken-chord accompaniments

[1] e.g. Bœtticher, p. 444; Jansen, pp. 457-8.

EX 34

which sound like a jaded echo of the vocal line instead of a shared melody as in the earlier songs; and there is a curious trick of shifting briefly from a two-quaver to a triplet-quaver rhythm just to yield such an echo, e.g. from the same song.

EX 35

Thus the creative excitement can easily decline into fatigue. It is as if Schumann's personality is beginning to split under the strain. He needed some respite; if not a rest then at least a simpler style. This was achieved in the five pieces for 'cello and piano in folksong vein; and their return to naiveté and melody, together with his feeling for the oppressed and weak, brought Schumann back again to the world of childhood with the *Liederalbum für die Jugend*, op. 79.

But there, although the style was more relaxed, the mood was still tense and the tempo hard-driven—at the rate of about a song a day. Then on 3 May came the numbing shock of revolution knocking on Schumann's door in Dresden itself. It was bloody and cruel, and was as brutally put down by Prussian troops.[1] Schumann took refuge in a new home in the countryside. Some of his op. 79

[1] See p. 30. ED

echoes this remoteness, with bugle calls blending into cuckoo calls, battle songs
into spring songs. As a lifelong radical, he must have felt the incongruity of this
response. But when he has a scene to imagine, a picture to paint, he is still a fine
composer, as we can hear in the serenity of *Sonntag*, the delicacy of *Der Sand-
mann*, the playfulness of *Marienwürmchen*, which all reflect the innocence of an
ideal childhood. Again, he is comfortably at home in the salon music of *Er ist's*
or *Schneeglöckchen* or the cosy domesticity of the next group *Minnespiel* again
for vocal quartet, duet or solo with piano accompaniment. But by now the
inevitable reaction had set in. Schumann's mind lived through dark days in that
radiant summer of 1849; the diary records,[1] 'lovely day' but 'stupid obsessions';
'sunshine' but 'hypochondria'. A revealing entry for 10 June, his thirty-ninth
birthday, says simply 'Die gute Clara und meine Melancholie'. *Mein schöner
Stern*, in reflecting that ray of hope, far outshines the rest of op. 101. In that song
the whole man speaks whole-heartedly. But elsewhere in the cycle the mood
cracks into saccharine or acrid, each with its own characteristic harmony and
tempo—whether (*a*) sweet as at 'süsse' in no. 1 or (*b*) sour as at 'mit Bitterem'
in no. 6.

EX 36

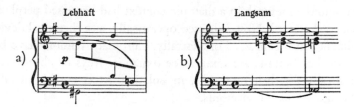

The Wilhelm Meister Songs

This duality seems to have been exacerbated by the Dresden uprising. Schumann's
feelings in 1848–49 had been embodied in pious and paternal music preoccupied
with the fate of others. The *Song Album for the Young* had ended deliberately
with just such a setting—Goethe's famous *Kennst du das Land?*, a lyric sung by the
doomed child Mignon in the novel *Wilhelm Meister*. That choice, as Schumann
himself later explained,[2] was designed to symbolize the end of youth and the
threshold of a fuller emotional life. In his disturbed mind that symbolism shifted,
after the carnage in Dresden, to a more fatal end, a more ominous threshold.
'With Clara through the town; all the signs of a terrible revolution'[3] says the

[1] Bœtticher, p. 449.   [2] Jansen, p. 324.   [3] Bœtticher, p. 448.

diary in May. On 27 June we read 'still thinking of the Song Album'. The next entry, on 2 July, records 'sketches for the *Requiem für Mignon*'. Her fate had so obsessed Schumann that here he even chose Goethe's prose description of her obsequies, for his musical setting. Next he returned to his *Faust* music, choosing those scenes that presage the fate of the hapless Gretchen, who was also to die young. It was natural to continue with more settings from *Wilhelm Meister*, a rich source especially memorable for the interspersed lyrics sung by Mignon and the mysterious Harper. Neither knows that she is his child by his own sister; this sin has sent him wandering crazed through the world. His harp-songs are heavy with remorse and despair; Mignon's lyrics brim with secret grief. Schumann's music, though couched in dramatic terms, is clearly an expression of his own personal feeling. The crazed and fated musician had already figured by chance in his 1840 songs (*Der Spielmann*); so had the sorrowing and lonely girl (*Mädchen-Schwermut*). Now his own dread of death and madness, his fears for Clara, speak with his own voice in the Goethe songs. The words chosen for emphasis and repetition betray his distress; 'all guilt is avenged here below', 'I cannot tell my secret' and so on. This new pitch of expression demands new techniques. The vocal lines move in semi-tones, to catch the moaning inflections of fear and despair. This leads to enhanced chromatics in the piano part. In earlier songs the diminished seventh in a diatonic context had expressed perplexity (as in *Jasminenstrauch*, Ex. 8). Now it is used operatically, as a rhetorical device; the accompaniment too is conceived orchestrally. Chromatic tensions have become the norm; so the contrasts are textural or dynamic. Keys or chords are used impressionistically for their own sake, in isolation. Most notable of all is the novel and conscious use of leitmotifs.

All this can be illustrated from one song, Mignon's *Heiss mich nicht reden*, about a fatal and ineffable secret. This is contrasted in the poem with the inevitable release of sunrise after darkness, the eventual ascent of subterranean rivers into the light, illustrated with a rising motif in the piano part.

EX 37

Later the words tell of lips sealed by a vow, 'from which only a god can release them'. 'God' is darkened by a sombre E flat minor chord, meaning death (as throughout *Ich hab im Traum geweinet*). The interlude brings a moment of peace in a chord of D flat major. But then the 'release' motif reappears, reduced to a diminished seventh, with an effect of wordless straining for speech; and this is followed by a silent cry of dumb agony in a grinding dissonance. Meanwhile the voice has intoned its chromatic recitative; the left hand has conjured up 'cellos and basses; the right hand's repeated chords suggest woodwind, while the climax clamours for brass. The whole passage (Ex. 38) is strikingly more dramatic and intense than anything in Schumann's own opera *Genoveva*; it challenges comparison with the Wagner of 1849, and indeed anticipates the *Ring*.

Wagner was very much on Schumann's mind and conscience at the time, not only as a musician but as a revolutionary active at the barricades in Dresden

Ex 38

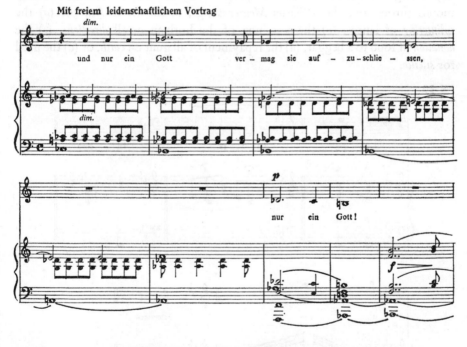

while Schumann was in his country retreat. So this new proto-Wagnerian song-style may have been moulded by special psychological and social pressures as well as normal artistic development. At the same time, the freshness of his youthful style is far from spent, as we can hear from the sprightly melody of *Philine* (the song of the soubrette in *Wilhelm Meister*).

So in the summer of 1849 Schumann was perhaps the most richly endowed of any living musician in expressive force and variety. These Goethe songs should have been towering masterpieces. Yet plainly they are no such thing. They are rarely sung, rarely praised. The ominous signs noted in the earlier 1849 songs are beginning to proliferate. Unmotivated triplets intrude. The thought rambles and becomes incoherent. The motifs are sporadic and tend to be overlooked or forgotten, for example in *So lasst mich scheinen*, where a motif appears three times in the first five bars and then vanishes. In that song's 54 bars, no two are rhythmically analogous. The same expressive progression does duty for several dissimilar moods throughout the *Wilhelm Meister* songs, as shown in Ex. 39; (*a*) the *splintering* of lances, (*b*) the searching of the horizon in all *directions*, (*c*) the *donation* of food to a beggar, (*d*) the repayment of all guilt on *earth*, or (*e*) the need for *silence*.

EX 39

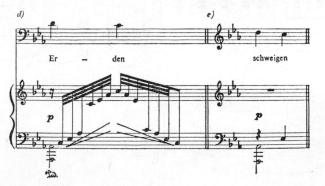

These five ideas have in common only a certain pathos and the fact that each word consists of two syllables. Soon the resemblances begin to appear in wholly unrelated songs. If the illness which was to destroy first Schumann's reason and then his life in a few more years was in fact an organic disease of the brain, then this music may record the first faint signs of its insidious onset. A typical mood-change is exemplified by the next set of songs, the Byron settings of op. 95, written in December 1849. The texts brood over the same themes; the death of a girl, the death of a hero, a mood of inconsolable melancholy. They are a pallid echo of the *Wilhelm Meister* themes—musical as well as literary—with accompaniment for harp or piano, as if the Harper's music were still sounding like a tinnitus. Each song consists of a threefold repetition of a dull idea. In six months the pendulum had swung from frenzy to lethargy.

The 1850 Songs

This was characteristic enough of Schumann's cyclic temperament all his life. But thus far his spirits had always regained their previous heights. In his carefree youth he had no need to compose in the depressive phase; but as a family man he was compelled to force out music for sale, and this ceaseless strain cannot have helped his condition. Yet by 1850 those marvellous powers were again returning, in the instrumental music at least. It would be hard to find signs of decline for example in the E flat major symphony, written in November–December 1850. But songs are quite a different matter. There above all the work of art is itself a hybrid. The music not only contains words and ideas but derives from them and embodies them. Schumann's mind from 1850 onwards is steadily drifting away from an external world definable in words and language into a vague personal world of dumb emotion. We recall that his speech centres were already destroyed some months before he died in 1856, as Brahms recorded in a distressed letter to Joachim.[1]

In the last years the songs are slowly sapped of verbal substance, as they decline in quantity and quality. In his truly inspired songwriting period, the twelve months beginning in February 1840, Schumann had completed at least a hundred and thirty-five songs, many of them durable masterpieces. In his four last years of songwriting, 1849–52, the tally runs 47, 33, 21 and 7; and very few are performed or remembered.

After the great crest and trough of mood change, in 1849, the song-music of 1850 at first sounds curiously quiet and tired. There is little question of character-

[1] Johannes Brahms. *Briefwechsel mit Joseph Joachim.* 1908, p. 131.

study or drama; the subject-matter reverts to a meek and usually doleful lyricism. The keys and tonalities become flat and minor; so does the poetry. For the first time in Schumann's creative life he repeatedly turns to sentimental magazine-verses notable only for their bombast or bathos (e.g. those of 'Wielfried von der Neun'[1] and Elisabeth Kulmann respectively). Worse still, he gravely enthuses over their supposed musical or philosophical qualities.[2] Perhaps worst of all, he lavishes on them the wealth of technical invention newly-devised for the Goethe songs. Indeed, he goes further; and creates the principle of thematic unity in song by means of a consciously expressive and varied leit-motif. Take for example the text of the 'von der Neun' song of May 1850, *Es stürmet am Abendhimmel*, which offers a typically fustian allegory; a cloud in love with the sun is blown dismally away by an ill-disposed storm. In Schumann's music the techniques are as original as the ideas are banal; while his hand is acquiring new skills his mind is losing its old grasp. Ex. 40 tells the story in detail. A rising semitone is associated with the idea of the storm as tragic fate or doom, much as in the Goethe songs (*a*). Semitones loom and lour in every bar. In the prelude the bass growls ominously; thunder (*b*). Octaves sidle up ingratiatingly, still in semitones; a plea (*c*). Then they come storming up; a great wind (*d*). Part of that idea is turned into tremolando chords; sighs of love (*e*). Then suddenly the theme is blown together in diminution (*f*), blown out in augmentation (*g*), and blown apart in disconnected fragments (*h*); yet it somehow survives long enough to give an offstage moan (*i*) before taking a final curtain in emphatic octaves to pronounce doom on life and love in the postlude (*j*). Wolf was later to work wonders, with this technique to hand and fine poetry in mind (as in *Auf einer Wanderung*). But here,

EX 40

[1] i.e. of the Nine (Muses); the typically pretentious pseudonym of one Wilhelm Schöpff.
[2] e.g. Jansen, p. 324; and the fulsome commentary to the first edition (1851) of the Kulmann songs, op. 104.

and in other songs of Schumann's last period, it is applied to banal music and trivial verse.

At the same time he continues to write the same music over again in different and apparently unrelated contexts; sometimes within a month or so,

EX 41

from Op. 83, No. 1, April 1850

from Op. 96, No. 3, July 1850

sometimes within a day or so

EX 42

from Op. 89, No. 3, 11 May 1850

from Op. 89, No. 6, 12 - 18 May 1850

to cite only two such parallels among many. Alternatively the music contains echoes, again apparently subconscious, of earlier and better songs. Often this involves an involuntary association of ideas, the postlude to *Abschied von Walde*, for example, which recalls a melody from *Hör' ich das Liedchen klingen*; both are about lamentation in the woodlands. Sometimes this trait makes the music tolerable, even admirable, as in the Lenau songs of August 1850 where the mellow beauty of some of the verses (e.g. in *Meine Rose*) shines through the music in a lingering afterglow of the old diatonic style, briefly dispelling the gloom and anxiety of the surrounding chromatics. But even in this set the treatment of the poetry is becoming more and more confused. Rhyming words are absentmindedly omitted, as in *Kommen und Scheiden*; the repetitions destroy the poetic sense, as in *Meine Rose*. Another symptom already noted in the Goethe songs now becomes chronic, namely, the constant shifts and quirks of rhythm, despite the obvious striving for rhythmical unity; thus *Der Gärtner*, for all its smiling charm, suffers from intention tremor.

The Last Phase

Most daunting of all is the choice of poetic theme. The tide of musical invention continues to flow unabated; for example, the piano textures have not only orchestral effects but string quartet textures, as in *Resignation* of April 1850. But the words are already on the turn; resignation is their main theme. Then their life begins to ebb. By July 1850 the verbal features of the songs seem to be composing themselves for death. From then to the end of that year Schumann wrote 20 songs; four are about death, six about sorrow, and two about both. In 1851 he was outwardly happy and active; but of the twenty-one songs in that year, four are about sorrow and nine about death, varied with blood, killing, madness and prayer.

In 1852 he was again cheerful and busy; but of his seven songs all save one are about prayer or death, again with killing and blood. So the sad story continues, with the alienated mind eerily active to the last. For example the form of the large-scale declaimed ballad with piano accompaniment which Schumann had invented with *Schön Hedwig* in 1849, had two successors in 1852; one, *Der Haidenknabe*, op. 122 no. 1, is about death by murder, and the other, *Die Flüchtlinge*, no. 2, is about death by drowning. The last solo songs, in December of that year, are settings of texts allegedly by Mary Queen of Scots. The symbolic figure of that doomed heroine intones Schumann's requiem with her own. The five songs say, in pathetic broken chords, 'I am going away; look after my new-born child; we must submit to fate; I must die; Christ have mercy on my soul.' Sometimes this music is resurrected, presumably as an act of piety. But it would surely be a greater piety to leave its acrid dust undisturbed, and to remember Schumann the songwriter at his greatest.

The Heritage

Then he was the rightful heir of Schubert, adding his own powerful expressive device, the independent keyboard, to the *Lied*. In the hands of Brahms and Wolf, this crowned the whole art-form. Schumann's choice of poetry was similarly influential; his translations from the Spanish were continued by Wolf, and his use of folksong by Brahms (who was able to borrow from Schumann's actual library of verse) and by Mahler. Schumann's instrumental music also had its effect on all their song-styles. His fluctuating melodic lines (e.g. in the slow movement of the Trio, op. 63) foreshadow Wolf's subtle declamation; while the idea of two-piano works with vocal quartet led straight to Brahms's masterly *Liebeslieder*; the ironic scherzo of *Das ist ein Flöten* is very Mahlerian.

Brahms and Wolf, opposites though they were, were united in this indebtedness—each to the extent of actually setting to music not a poet's authentic text but the altered version of it that Schumann had used: Wolf in *Das verlassene Mägdlein*, and Brahms in *Mondnacht* and *In der Fremde*. Each of those influences extends, by widely diverse routes, to Richard Strauss.

Among indebted contemporaries was Robert Franz, in whose neglected songs we have a treasury of work which, if not as fine as Schumann's best, is nevertheless often comparable with the songs of 1849 or later. It also seems entirely possible, as Christopher Headington has perceptively suggested[1] that it was Schumann who inspired Liszt to begin songwriting; and certainly the latter's Heine settings date from the year, and almost from the day, on which he first met Schumann, then engaged on his first Heine settings.

Further, Schumann's friend Gade had spread his name and works through Scandinavia; Grieg was conscious of that debt and readily acknowledged it. The songs were known and admired in Russia by 1859,[2] that is before any of Mussorgsky's mature songs were written; and their influence on the French *mélodie* has been brilliantly documented by Olivier Alain.[3]

When the definitive history of the *Lied* comes to be written, Schumann as creator and innovator will surely be accorded the status he modestly claimed—'a special place of my own'. Indeed; at the heart of the *Lied*.

[1] In *Franz Liszt, the man and his music*, ed. Alan Walker. London. 1970, pp. 222, 224.
[2] D. Chitomirski, in *Sämmerlbande der Schumann–Gesellschaft*. 1961. p. 27.
[3] *Ibid., Schumann und die französische Musik*, pp. 53–60.

LEON PLANTINGA

Schumann and the Neue Zeitschrift für Musik

THE major composers of the nineteenth century did a great deal of writing about music. Before Schumann there was Carl Maria von Weber, who began his two careers as a public writer of music and prose at about the same time, at the age of fourteen; his first published essay was a spirited rejoinder to a review of his first opera, *Das stumme Waldmädchen* (Freyberg, 1800). Beginning in 1809, Weber was a frequent contributor to the *Allgemeine musikalische Zeitung* of Leipzig, and his articles and reviews appeared regularly, as well, in German belles-lettres journals such as the *Journal des Luxus und der Moden* (Weimar), the *Zeitung für die elegante Welt* (Leipzig) and the *Morgenblatt für gebildete Stände*—including, in this last, some rather vitriolic criticism of Beethoven's Fourth Symphony. But best known, perhaps, of Weber's writings are the unfinished novel, *Das Künstlerleben*,[1] and the astute but partisan assessments of new operas in the *Dramatisch-musikalische Notizen* of the Prague and Dresden years.

When Berlioz was elected to the Institute in 1856, the *Revue des deux mondes* complained, 'The Institute has not chosen a musician, but a journalist.' And Berlioz was certainly a journalist; for forty years—beginning in 1823, with a piece called 'Polémique musicale' published in *Le Corsaire*—he supplied the periodical press of Paris with literally hundreds of witty and often substantive articles, reviews, and feuilletons. Many of these things reappeared in Berlioz's 'composite' books, *Les Soirées de l'orchestre* (1853), and *À Travers Chants* (1862), and some of them were taken up by periodicals outside France; Berlioz's writings from the *Journal des débats*, for example, were reprinted in translation on a regular basis in Schumann's *Neue Zeitschrift für Musik* of 1840.

The prose writings attributed to Liszt (how much of this Liszt actually wrote

[1] Cf. Gerald Abraham's instructive discussion of this and other of Weber's writings in *The Musical Quarterly* XX (1934), 27–38.

himself is still unclear) come to nine volumes in the German edition of 1880–82; Wagner's ponderous and propagandistic treatises tended to appear in large bunches around the turn of each decade from 1840 to 1880, and together with the poems they comprise as many as sixteen volumes in the edition of 1912–14. And in our own century the best-known composers have continued to write, in various ways, and with varying degrees of intelligibility, about their art: witness Debussy, Schoenberg, Stravinsky, Hindemith, and (of a later generation) Babbitt, Boulez, Stockhausen, and Cage.

It would not have occurred to most active composers of earlier times to invest such prodigious amounts of time and energy into writing words about music. From the eighteenth century only a few exceptions come to mind, such as Rameau and C. P. E. Bach. And before that we know of almost none (a possible exception is Philippe de Vitry). There are, of course, various plausible explanations for the unprecedented amount of writing nineteenth-century composers did. One is that European music had become ever more public in character; composers no longer addressed their work primarily to patrons whose tastes were well known to them, but to a large, diverse, and anonymous audience; and this audience could not necessarily be counted upon for understanding and appreciation. Hence much of the prose composers wrote in that century and ours has an apologetic, explanatory, or didactic purpose. Wagner the author (to cite an extreme case) existed almost exclusively for the sake of Wagner the composer. Much of Schumann's writing is equally propagandistic, but it is not nearly so self-serving; Schumann was an apologist less for himself than for a point of view, and for any musician who seemed to share it.

Another explanation for the extraordinary literary productivity of nineteenth-century composers is simply that the burgeoning musical periodical press, itself a symptom of the public status of the art, provided an outlet for it. The *Allgemeine musikalische Zeitung* of Leipzig (hereafter abbreviated *AmZ*) first appeared in 1798. Its varied mixture of articles on musical subjects, reviews of published scores and concerts (and, occasionally, books), correspondence reports, musical supplements, and publishers' advertisements quickly established the pattern for a host of musical journals that sprang up in all the principal cities of Europe. Some borrowed not only the format, but even the name of their prototype from Leipzig: an *AmZ* was founded in Vienna by Ignaz von Mosel in 1817, and Adolf Bernhard Marx began his journal of the same name in Berlin some seven years later. *The Quarterly Musical Magazine and Review*, first of the influential English musical periodicals, appeared in 1818, and the long-lived *Revue et gazette musicale de Paris*, which was to include among its contributors Berlioz, Liszt, and Wagner, was founded in 1835. Some idea of the enormous vogue of musical journals in the earlier nineteenth century can be gained from a dry statistic or two: Wilhelm Freystätter's bibliography lists only forty-seven musical periodicals between Mattheson's *Critica musica* of 1722–25 (the earliest of them all) and the founding of the *AmZ* in 1798; the recent catalogue of nineteenth-century musical journals by Imogen Fellinger logs two hundred and sixty-two new ones established from 1798 to 1848.[1]

Most of the musical journals of the eighteenth century represented individual efforts, and were addressed to professional colleagues. Mattheson's *Critica musica* was little more than a vehicle for his own learned and irritable polemics; Scheibe's *Critischer Musicus*, with its well-known censure of J. S. Bach, was similarly professional, and the work of one man, as were the various journals of Marpurg. The *Wöchentliche Nachrichten* of J. A. Hiller, more popular in tone, and much better-tempered, was intended for both *Kenner* and *Liebhaber*, and it showed something of the direction musical journalism was to take in years to come. For the characteristic musical periodical of the nineteenth century was not intended principally for professional musicians or men of letters, but for the musical public at large, and it was put out, not by a single person, but by a music publishing firm. Thus the *AmZ* was the house journal of Breitkopf und Härtel, the *Caecilia* of Schott in Mainz, the *Allgemeiner musikalischer Anzeiger* of Haslinger in Vienna, the *Revue et gazette musicale* of Schlesinger in Paris, and *The Musical Times* of Novello in London. These commercial connections often had unfortunate results, and this was a crucial factor in Schumann's decision, in the early 1830s, to take the singular step of establishing and editing a journal of his own.

Schumann had just turned twenty in the autumn of 1830 when, after delicate negotiations with his family, he abandoned his ostensible study of law at Heidelberg to return to Leipzig and devote himself to a career in music. His letters from that period reveal an intelligent, somewhat self-indulgent student, careless of his work, with tastes that ran more to fine clothes, good cigars, long walks in the Neckar valley, young English ladies, and rapturous improvisation in music and prose. This last he practised in letters to his mother (probably much to her mystification), and his style of writing was most high-flown when his need for money was greatest. But whatever his shortcomings, the young Schumann's intellectual talent and training were considerable. His school-friend Emil Flechsig recalls the Zwickau years:

[1] W. Freystätter, *Die musikalischen Zeitschriften seit ihrer Entstehung bis zur Gegenwart*, München, 1884; and Imogen Fellinger, *Verzeichnis der musikalischen Zeitschriften des 19. Jahrhunderts*, Regensburg, 1968. Some allowance should be made, perhaps, for the greater thoroughness of the latter work.

First came a bout with philology—in this he was weakest—and my Schellers Lexikon that I bought from him still shows a great many erudite annotations in his hand from that time. Next in turn came heraldry, and he pursued this with similar zeal. Later we plunged into German poetry, there to remain; for composing verses and writing German he had a decided talent, as his collected writings on music clearly show. There was abundant opportunity to become acquainted with literature; the whole Schumann house was full of classics, and we were allowed to take home the soiled volumes.[1]

That 'bout with philology' was serious enough to include editorial work with the *Forcellini Totius Latinitatis Lexicon* (the German third edition) put out by the Schumann family publishing house. And in his later *Materialen zu einem Lebenslauf* Schumann claims that as a boy in Zwickau he made extensive translations from ancient writers, both Greek and Latin. His favourite modern authors were Klopstock, Schiller, Hölderlin, Byron, and most important, Jean Paul. Flechsig describes Schumann's year at Leipzig University (1828–29):

As a rule he never entered a lecture hall . . . But there was always the newest literature: Heine's travel portraits, Menzel's German history, and especially a great deal of Jean Paul, whose style and manner he unfortunately imitated too much in his own writing—which he practised several hours every day.[2]

A fair number of these early writings have survived: aphorisms, fragments of novels, and essays on various subjects; much of this looks like a schoolboy's imitation of Jean Paul, sometimes done with an air of sophomoric pretentiousness—but it shows a facile and imaginative literary bent.

Schumann's immediate plan, upon returning to Leipzig in 1830, was to devote himself to the piano; Friedrich Wieck, with whom he had studied sporadically in 1828–29, now promised to make of him within three years 'one of the greatest pianists now living'—a most sanguine prediction, considering that by all accounts his playing at this time was still at an amateur level. A letter from the following spring shows continuing indecision, but self-confidence:

There can be only four goals for me: conductor, music teacher, virtuoso, and composer. Hummel, for one, combines all of these. I shall probably

[1] W. Bœtticher, ed., *Robert Schumann in seinen Schriften und Briefen*, p. 8.
[2] *Ibid.*, p. 14.

settle for the last two. I shall be glad when I can be master of something, instead of doing just a little of everything, as has unfortunately been my habit.[1]

At this time Schumann's credentials as a composer were not yet very impressive: of his early compositions—he had completed a psalm setting, a few short pieces for piano, some songs, a piano quartet, and the 'Abegg' Variations—none had been either published or performed in public.

In August 1831, after less than a year under Wieck's tutelage, Schumann was clearly dissatisfied with his progress, and applied to Hummel in Weimar for piano instruction; Wieck became furious, and nothing came of this plan. Then, at this time of uncertainty, Schumann abruptly struck out in a new direction. In September he brashly wrote to Gottfried Wilhelm Fink,* editor of the *AmZ*:

> If you should be interested in a young collaborator to lighten the burden of your possibly overwhelming literary labours, I wish to offer my services. The enclosed pages could be followed by a long series of similar *Caeciliana*; but you should not judge the later ones, which will be theoretically more penetrating, by these which are only intended to reproduce my first impression of a recent composition of genius. Since I have every reason to be modest, I ask you to delete whatever you wish, or whatever offends you . . . Finally, may I ask you for a single-line answer as to whether and when these *Caeciliana* could appear in the *AmZ*, and, in case the style and plan of the whole doesn't displease you, whether I should send some more, or less.[2]

The 'recent composition of genius' was Chopin's *Là ci darem* Variations, and the 'Caeciliana' Schumann sent Fink was of course his famous review of it.

Fink was in no hurry to reply, and Schumann sent off another letter the following month, asking him to publish the piece or return it.[3] Fink settled on a kind of compromise; he printed half of the review—this is the only part that has survived—sent the other half back to the author, and regarded the matter as closed. And Schumann's subsequent attempt to have the article published in its entirety in the Vienna *Allgemeiner musikalischer Anzeiger* failed as well; it gradually became clear that getting his mystifying, fanciful, novelistic writings printed in any of the established musical journals would be difficult if not impossible.

Schumann's letter to Hummel of August 1831 certainly suggests that his pro-

---

[1] *Jugendbriefe*, p. 144.   [2] *Jugendbriefe*, pp. 154–55.
[3] The review is discussed in detail by Henry Pleasants, p. 180 f. ED

gress toward a virtuoso's career left something to be desired. And less than a year later this matter was settled. Schumann tells his mother in June 1832 of a 'curious misfortune', and Clara Schumann, in a footnote to this letter, identifies it as 'laming of the index finger of his right hand'.[1] The cause and exact nature of the disability remain a mystery,[2] but its effect on the course of Schumann's career has surely been much exaggerated. For by the early summer of 1832, when the 'curious misfortune' was first reported to his family, it must have seemed rather unlikely that Schumann would become a concert pianist; he had hardly ever performed in public up to this time, and he seemed more and more preoccupied with other pursuits. He was composing at a brisk pace, and his music was beginning to see the light of day: the 'Abegg' Variations, op. 1, had appeared in mid-1831, the *Papillons* in early 1832. The Études after Caprices of Paganini were finished in June of that year, and the *Intermezzi* op. 4 one month later. The pattern Schumann's life was to take was becoming clear; the hand injury merely confirmed it.

During 1831–33 the editors of the principal German musical journals came to know Schumann well. Besides sending them his literary efforts for publication, he bombarded them with correspondence about his music and their reviews of it. Four editors received elaborate advance explanations of the literary connections of *Papillons* when it first appeared, lest they misunderstand. When a rather favourable review of *Papillons* and the 'Abegg' Variations appeared in the Vienna *Allgemeiner musikalischer Anzeiger*, Schumann thanked the editor warmly and enclosed a review copy of the Études after Paganini—together with more explanations. He quarrelled a bit with the crotchety Ludwig Rellstab* about his assessment of *Papillons* in *Iris im Gebiete der Tonkunst*, and took the precaution of explaining to him that the harmonic mistakes in the Études (a copy was included with the letter) were Paganini's fault.

[1] *Jugendbriefe*, p. 184.
[2] There has recently been a new flurry of interest in the question of what was wrong with Schumann's hand. In an article in *The Musical Times* of December 1971, Eric Sams has argued persuasively that the disability resulted not from a specific accident or injury, but from mercury poisoning brought about by attempts to treat symptoms of syphilis. Specific information on this point was published in 1967 by Hans-Joachim Rothe in the *Arbeitsberichte zur Geschichte der Stadt Leipzig* (no. 13); it has been summarized by William Newman in *The Piano Quarterly* (Summer 1971). Rothe cites a detailed report of Schumann's disability from archival documents, *viz.* the military conscription records of Leipzig for the years 1841–2. This report—a retrospective one, as Schumann's symptoms had appeared ten years earlier—describes a total paralysis of the middle finger of the right hand and partial paralysis of the index finger. There was, it says, a single identifiable injury (in October 1831), one inflicted by a mechanical device.

But the Leipzig documents may none the less support Sams's independent conclusions. For the device in question, which held the fingers extended toward the back of the hand for periods of time, was intended not for pianists, but for people with lame hands. It did not *cause* Schumann's paralysis, but exacerbated a condition (described as a 'congenital weakness' of those two fingers) already present.

One editor seemingly wanted nothing to do with Schumann: Fink of the *AmZ*, after printing his Chopin review in December 1831, did his best to ignore him. Schumann had sent Fink copies of all his published music (op. 1 went with his letter of 10 November 1831 even before the composition was released to the public) together with the usual helpful commentary by the composer. Fink, after repeated prodding from Schumann, finally printed his review (unfavourable, but restrained) of op. 1 and opp. 3–5 on 11 September 1833, and this was the last time Schumann's name was to be mentioned in the *AmZ* for many years to come. For in the meantime he had attacked the *AmZ* and its editor in a local belles-lettres periodical, *Der Komet*; Schumann's rift with the largest and most influential of German musical journals was now irreparable.

Schumann's quarrel with the *AmZ* was not only a personal one. In his articles of 1833, printed in *Der Komet* under the title 'Die Davidsbündler', he lashed out at the 'damnable German politeness' and 'shoulder-shrugging' that plagued music criticism of the time; he did not say so, but it was clear that he was thinking particularly of the *AmZ*. Like many other musical journals, the *AmZ* seemed under Fink's direction to bow increasingly to the commercial interests of its publisher. The music reviews usually carefully avoided anything like censure (exceptions could be made for composers like Chopin and Schumann), and often they looked more like advertisements than critiques. Schumann's colleague Karl Banck said of the *AmZ*.

It is clear throughout that the criticism of this paper carefully avoids recognizing genius or spirit, and it similarly avoids any open opposition to mediocrity and the talentless. Its policy is one of greatest tolerance, equally far removed from enthusiastic praise and forthright condemnation.[1]

Schumann felt that German musical taste in the early 1830s was in a lamentable state; since the later years of Beethoven, he claimed the concert and opera stage in Germany was awash with 'foreign hackwork'. In the Introduction to his *Gesammelte Schriften* of 1854, he reminisced, 'Rossini still reigned supreme in the theatre; among pianists Herz and Hünten had the field pretty much to themselves.'[2] The musical periodical press ought to have put up resistance to this situation, Schumann thought, but instead most of the journals, which cared more for money than music, encouraged it. And worst of the offenders, in Schumann's eyes, was the local *AmZ*. When Franz Hünten, one of the most insipid of the Parisian virtuoso-composers, came out with yet another set of four-hand varia-

---

[1] *Neue Zeitschrift für Musik* I (1834), 183.
[2] For an extensive quotation from this *Introduction*, see Henry Pleasants, p. 182.

tions (Schumann called them 'decompositions'), the *AmZ* described them this way:

> A euphonious Introduction, that engages the efforts of both players very nicely, leads to the beloved theme of the universally known Marseillaise; and even as a theme, it is prettily handled. The well-mixed variations are even more so. They provide all types of concertato passagework that nevertheless falls well under the fingers, and is not very difficult; they offer agreeable entertainment, and promote enjoyable playing. The entire composition consists of four variations and a rather extended Finale. For those who like to play the earlier music of this composer, this volume will quickly become a favourite; it is among his best works.[1]

This kind of music criticism was rather normal for the time, and the young Schumann had absolutely no patience with it.

One journal that Schumann knew well was different: Rellstab's *Iris im Gebiete der Tonkunst* dispensed praise and blame, Schumann said himself, in a ratio of about one to five. But this rigour was not particularly easy for Schumann to appreciate; in a review of some piano pieces by J. C. Kessler, Rellstab gives an example of his opinions:

> We have frequently complained that young composers of recent times have no real composition teachers, and hardly even teachers of thorough-bass, so without study or guidance, they just compose away. We thought this situation was already disastrous. But more was yet to come. Now not only do they lack instruction in what is good, but they even have systematic instruction in what is bad—they make a study of folly. For this young talent [Kessler], Chopin's most recent compositions have obviously served as a model, as a bad example.
>
> So now there is a tendency to strive for unprecedented instrumental effects, however trivial and trite the musical ideas may be. Unfortunately we are witness to the formation of a whole school for error; we could recognize it recently in Chopin, then in Schumann and others, and now also in this young composer.[2]

So in the early 1830s Schumann felt it was almost impossible for serious, progressive composers to get any kind of hearing in Germany. The public seemed preoccupied with music for superficial entertainment, and most of the musical

[1] *AmZ* XXXIII (1831), 697.   [2] *Iris im Gebiete der Tonkunst* V (1834), 91.

journals were not in the least inclined to interfere with their preferences. A few critics like Rellstab and F.-J. Fétis did their work with more integrity, but their sensibilities, Schumann felt, belonged to an earlier generation. Schumann was impatient with the reception accorded composers like Chopin and himself by either type of critic, and he was frustrated in his attempts to air his own views in the established musical press. This was the background of Schumann's determination to begin his own journal, and in June of 1833 we hear him mention it for the first time:

> A group of cultivated young people, mostly music students, have formed a kind of circle around me, and I have in turn drawn it about the Wieck house. For the most part we are preoccupied with the notion of a major new musical journal. Hofmeister will be the publisher, and the prospectus and announcement of it will appear within the next month.[1]

This group of 'cultivated young people' included the pianists Julius Knorr and Ludwig Schunke, the organist and music critic Ernst Ortlepp, and the deaf painter and novelist J. P. Lyser; their meetings took place either at Wieck's house (as Schumann implies), or at the nearby Gaststätte, Zum Kaffeebaum—where the little corner room they occupied can still be seen, purportedly unchanged since the 1830s.

Founding a journal turned out to be a great deal more difficult than Schumann and his friends foresaw. First Hofmeister, the prospective publisher, began to see that the kind of paper these young idealists had in mind was not likely to further the interests of his music publishing house. When he withdrew, Schumann turned to his brothers Karl and Eduard, who were carrying on the family publishing business in Schneeberg and Zwickau; but they too remained unmoved by his most eloquent pleas. It was not until March of the following year that a publisher was found (C. H. F. Hartmann) and the editorial staff settled, *viz.*, Schumann, Schunke, Wieck, and the editor-in-chief, Julius Knorr. On 3 April 1834 the first issue of the journal appeared, 'published by a society of artists and friends of art', with the title *Neue Leipziger Zeitschrift für Musik*.

Things had not gone as Schumann had hoped. It is clear that from the beginning he, more than anyone else, had supplied the impetus for founding the journal, and he had certainly expected to be its principal editor. And during the course of 1834, it was again Schumann who had to assume most of the responsibility for the affairs of the paper. On 2 July he complained to his mother that 'our editor, Knorr has been absolutely unable to work for eight weeks because

---

[1] *Jugendbriefe*, p. 209.

of ague, so that I must take care of everything—correspondence, proofreading, manuscripts', and later in the same letter,

> Just now I must devote all my energies to the journal. The others are not to be depended upon—Wieck is always away on his travels, Knorr is sick, and Schunke does not understand very well how to use a pen. So who remains? But the journal is such a success that I work away at it with enthusiasm and profit. Up to now we have received 300 subscriptions.[1]

Towards the end of the year Schumann managed through persistent negotiations —probably involving some of his inheritance of 8000 thalers—to gain official control of the journal. The first issue of 1835 was put out as *Neue Zeitschrift für Musik*, 'published in collaboration with a group of artists and friends of art, under the direction of R. Schumann'. And so it was to remain for almost ten years.

In some ways the *Neue Zeitschrift* looks like many other musical journals of its time. Like the *AmZ* and the *Revue et gazette musicale*, it consists of a varied procession of articles on musical subjects; reviews of published music, concerts, and occasionally books; correspondence reports from other cities; and, in a separate *Intelligenzblatt*, advertisements. The journal appeared twice weekly, and from the beginning it had a surprising number of contributors, the regular ones usually signing their articles with pseudonyms such as Schumann's 'Florestan', 'Eusebius', and 'Raro', or with ciphers—a common practice in journals of the time.

Though its format was apparently modelled directly after that of the *AmZ*, in other ways the fledgling journal had little in common with its venerable rival. Each issue began with an epigraph, taken from Shakespeare, Goethe, Hölderlin, Jean Paul, or some other of Schumann's favourite writers. These quotations reflected a 'literary' predilection of the *Neue Zeitschrift*, and, more particularly, they reflected Schumann's own literary tastes. The very first one announces the serious intentions of the journal with some words from the prologue of Henry VIII:

> Only they
> That come to hear a merry bawdy play,
> A noise of targets, or to see a fellow
> In a long motley coat guarded with yellow,
> Will be deceived.

And the special literary character of the *Neue Zeitschrift* can also be seen in the content of its articles. A Prospectus printed in the first issue for 1834 promises, among other things, 'belletristic writings, short musical narratives, imaginative

[1] *Jugendbriefe*, pp. 239, 242.

pieces, scenes from life'; this promise was to be fulfilled, during 1834, in contributions by Lyser, Karl Banck, and others.

But it was in its style of criticism that the *Neue Zeitschrift* differed most radically
from the *AmZ* and most other musical periodicals. In his New Year's editorial
of 1835, just after he assumed full control of the journal, Schumann explained,

> The age of idle compliments is gradually dying out, and we were not
> interested, we confess, in contributing to its revival. When you have no
> confidence to attack what is bad, you defend the good only half-way . . .
> We do not see why we should behave differently from practitioners of the
> other arts and sciences, where factions align themselves openly and war
> against each other. Nor do we see how true criticism and the honour of
> music can be associated with tolerance or indifference toward these arch-
> enemies of our art and every other: the talentless, the dime-a-dozen talent,
> (we find no better word for them), and the talented, facile scribblers.[1]

The *Neue Zeitschrift* certainly showed a new rigour and partisanship. In the first
volume, for example, Ludwig Schunke reviewed a 'Rondo militaire on an air of
Serment' by Henri Herz, one of the most famous piano virtuosi of the day:

> There is absolutely nothing new in this piano piece by H. Herz . . .
> Naturally enough, since he has gained fame writing music that is pianistic,
> vulgar in tone, and well received in many quarters because it is so ordinary,
> he has endeared himself to music publishers as a facile and favourite tran-
> scriber. And conversely, he understood that this was the field where, by
> means of a routine already mastered, he could quickly achieve success—in
> other words, make a fortune . . . It is said that Herz has understood his
> times. Yes, he has properly celebrated its insipidness, and the masses have
> embraced him. But may he also understand his times now; let him not
> mistake a sunset for dawn, and may he forgive his generation for bestowing
> upon him laurels he did not in the least deserve.[2]

Schumann himself intended, in the beginning, to specialize in what the Prospectus called 'belletristic writings'—imaginative, impressionistic essays, like his
Davidsbündler articles published in *Der Komet*. But this was impossible, principally
because the burden of writing music reviews fell increasingly upon him. To the
first volume he contributed a short commentary on a recent article in the *Caecilia*,
'The Comic in Music', a review of three other musical journals under the rubric
Journalschau, and a group of aphorisms. But most of what he wrote, from the
beginning, consisted of reviews of published music. So Schumann simply adapted

[1] *Neue Zeitschrift* II (1835), 3.   [2] *Neue Zeitschrift* I (1834), 166–67.

his unorthodox, novelistic style of writing, as he had done in the earlier Chopin review, to this purpose. A review of Hummel's Études op. 125, appearing under the caption *Die Davidsbündler,* is cast as a discussion between Eusebius, Florestan, and Raro; and even the half-column notice of a monodrama by J. Brandl pretends to be a description of a dream about a country fair. It was only for a short time that Schumann indulged in this sort of thing. His fondness for the excesses of late romantic literary style soon waned, for one thing, and as he assumed the full editorial duties of the ˙ournal, there simply was no time to make everything 'poetic'.

For nearly ten years—the years of his greatest productivity as a composer—Schumann exercised a close editorial control over the *Neue Zeitschrift*; he conducted a mountainous volume of correspondence in its behalf, did much of the proofreading himself, and tirelessly browbeat his contributors into writing as he thought they should. And he himself contributed in the neighbourhood of one thousand pages of copy for the journal: reviews, editorials, articles, and commentary on countless issues in the musical life of his time. In the pages of the *Neue Zeitschrift,* during all these years, he articulated his ideas about music with integrity and passion. With equal conviction he excoriated the Grand Opera and its fashionable appendages, belittled all things Italian, and exalted the canon of romantic musical heroes, from Bach to Beethoven, Schubert, and a number of select contemporaries.

If a reading of the journal reveals an astute critic with a profound insight into the musical culture of his time, it also certainly shows Schumann's abiding weaknesses: a rather provincial chauvinism, and a tendency towards impulsive enthusiasms. He disliked Rossini without really knowing him, and he decided in advance that Hermann Hirschbach's quartets must be good because the composer's views about things were so right. As Henry Pleasants mentions elsewhere in this volume, some have doubted Schumann's critical acumen because he championed not only Schubert, Chopin, Berlioz, and Brahms (all of these, at the time, virtually unknown), but also, on occasion, composers who have since slipped into oblivion: Ferdinand Hiller, for example, William Sterndale Bennett, and Schumann's colleague Ludwig Schunke. But one cannot avoid the suspicion that Schumann's critics may not be very familiar with the music of Hiller, Bennett, and the rest, but have simply relied upon the judgment of posterity—if a composer hasn't turned out to be famous, Schumann shouldn't have praised him.

Such an implicit faith in the good musical sense of all the generations between Schumann's and ours may be misplaced; the question of whether or not Schumann erred in assessing his contemporaries must be judged, surely, case by case. Let us take a moment here to consider just one utterly forgotten musician Schumann admired: Norbert Burgmüller. August Joseph Norbert Burgmüller was born in 1810 in Aachen, studied with Spohr and Moritz Hauptmann, and was befriended by Mendelssohn. An epileptic, he lived only to the age of twenty-six, but managed to produce two symphonies, a piano concerto, a piano sonata, several string quartets, and four collections of lieder. Schumann became acquainted with Burgmüller's music only after the composer's death (most of it was published posthumously), and in 1839 he wrote an emotional and somewhat belated eulogy in the *Neue Zeitschrift*. It begins:

> After Franz Schubert's premature death, none could be more painful than Burgmüller's. Fate, instead of decimating the ranks of the mediocre, camps in hordes on all sides, takes from us our most talented field commanders. Franz Schubert was at least somewhat appreciated in his time; Burgmüller enjoyed not even the beginnings of public recognition. He was known in only a small circle, and even there, perhaps more as a 'curious fellow' than as a musician. So it is our duty to accord to the deceased the honour we could not show him (and in this he himself may have been partly to blame) while he yet lived.[1]

Schumann then launches into an appreciative resumé of Burgmüller's work, ending with some comments about his most recent book of Lieder (op. 6—actually only the second of the four collections):

> The volume of Lieder that has most recently appeared is not in the least inferior to the earlier one in richness and content. The texts have been chosen with a discerning eye, and they accord well with the melancholy, agitated temperament of the composer: 'Wer nie sein Brot mit Tränen ass' (Goethe), 'Hell glühen die Sterne im dunklen Blau' (Stieglitz), 'Ich schleich' umher, betäubt und stumm' (Platen), 'Wundes Herz, hör' auf zu klagen' (I. Schopenhauer), 'Ich reit' ins finstre Land hinein' (Uhland). We find here everything that could be asked of a Lied: poetic interpretation, lively detail, a happy coordination of voice and accompaniment and, overall, discrimination, insight, and the warmth of life.[2]

The last-named song of this set is Schumann's favourite—'a more masterful realization could hardly be imagined'. This splendid song begins with an agitated, chromatic figure in the piano illustrative of the blustery landscape described in the first lines of the poem (Ex. 1).

---

[1] *Neue Zeitschrift* XI (1839), 70.   [2] *Ibid.*, p. 71.

EX I

When the poetry turns contemplative in the following lines, the rushing in the piano ceases, and a prolonged pedal point, later reinforced in the upper register, provides a static harmonic effect convincingly suited to the 'nostalgic remembering' of Uhland's text (Ex. 2).

EX 2

In this case, Burgmüller's music seems to justify Schumann's enthusiasm, and the same can be said, I believe, for several other works of this composer, his *Winterreise*, for example (another Uhland song), and his Sonata op. 8. Succeeding generations probably did not prove Schumann wrong when they ignored Burgmüller; they may have confirmed, merely, that excellence alone provides no guarantee of lasting recognition.

Among the major composers, Schumann was unique in the degree of his involvement with musical journalism; none other was ever editor of a journal, or took responsibility, as Schumann did during a whole decade, for evaluating a substantial and representative selection of European music. Schumann's extraordinary undertaking had certain important consequences, in his own career, surely, and even in the workings of the musical culture of which he was a part.

The immensely influential *AmZ* was forced to change editors and revise its policies largely as a result, it seems, of pressure from the *Neue Zeitschrift*. In 1841 Fink took leave of his editorship with a theatrical announcement in the *AmZ* indicating clearly that Schumann and his rival journal had a great deal to do with this decision. He was immediately replaced by Karl Ferdinand Becker, a friend of Schumann's, and a regular contributor to the *Neue Zeitschrift* since its inception. The impudent student who annoyed Fink with his bizarre contributions and suggestions in 1831 had now succeeded in toppling his regime altogether, and thus one of the dreariest chapters in the history of German musical journalism was brought to a close.

There can be little doubt, furthermore, that Schumann's efforts on behalf of certain romantic composers paid off. The *Neue Zeitschrift* played a leading role in keeping the memory of Schubert alive, and Schumann personally arranged for the performance and publication of the Great C Major Symphony—commemorating the event, as well, with a memorable essay. The favourable publicity Berlioz was given in the *Neue Zeitschrift* (by Schumann himself, Heinrich Panofka, and others) surely had something to do with the fact that he was widely known in Germany, and better received there than in France. Chopin's fortunes in Germany, too, must have been improved by the advocacy of the *Neue Zeitschrift*—if for no other reason than that, beginning in 1831, Schumann's violent partisanship brought to light a pronounced division of opinion about the Polish composer's music. It was perhaps largely because of Schumann's writing that Chopin ever became such an issue in Germany.

In the 1830s Schumann's music was for the most part piano music. The accepted method for a piano composer to present his work to the public was by performing it himself; but for Schumann, of course, this was impossible. It is doubtful that he could have achieved any other than a local reputation in those years had it not been for the *Neue Zeitschrift*. In fact, like Berlioz, he was better known, during most of his career, as a writer than as a composer. Chopin, Berlioz, and Liszt, for example, all came to know him first as editor of the *Neue Zeitschrift* (and later, as the husband of the vastly more famous Clara Wieck). And upon Schumann's death in 1856, the *Neue Zeitschrift* (now under the editorship of Franz Brendel) recalled that 'until his retirement from this journal he was admired, by the overwhelming majority, primarily as an author'.[1]

If the world got to know about Schumann through the *Neue Zeitschrift*, the converse was equally true. Schumann's duties as a critic forced him to study literally hundreds of compositions that otherwise he might never have known, and as editor he was obliged to take notice of issues in music that extended far

[1] *Neue Zeitschrifte* XL (1856), no. 7.

beyond his little corner of Germany. In this way the *Neue Zeitschrift* contributed immeasurably to the composer's continuing education, and to the broadening of his horizons. As critic and editor, Schumann finally achieved a kind of cosmopolitanism—enough so, at least, to be widely recognized as Europe's foremost apologist for romantic music.

HENRY PLEASANTS

Schumann the Critic

SCHUMANN, as music critic, has many distinctions, none more extra-ordinary, certainly, than the fact that he is remembered primarily, by all but specialists, for his very first and his very last notices. In the one he heralded the genius of Chopin, in the other the promise of Brahms.

The auguries themselves are astonishing, based as they were on the scantiest of omens. The Chopin notice, published in the *Allgemeine Musikalische Zeitung* of Leipzig (7 December 1831), was concerned with nothing more than the Variations for Piano and Orchestra on 'Là ci darem la mano' from *Don Giovanni*, an Opus 2, composed in 1827 when Chopin was seventeen. All that Schumann knew of Brahms when he wrote the subsequently celebrated 'New Paths' for the *Neue Zeitschrift für Musik* twenty-two years later, in 1853, was opp. 1–5, none of which had been published at that time.

In respect of the Chopin review, the only comparable example of precocious prescience that comes readily to mind is Hanslick's confident description of Wagner, in 1846, as 'the greatest dramatic talent among all contemporary composers'. Hanslick was then twenty-one, as was Schumann in 1831; but Hanslick was reviewing *Tannhäuser* and was already familiar with *The Flying Dutchman* and *Rienzi*. To match Schumann's feat he would have had to discern Wagner's genius in nothing more advanced than *Das Liebesverbot*.

But prophecy is not the principal concern of music criticism; which is just as well, since critics generally, and young critics particularly, are given to hyperbole, and are remembered more frequently and more vividly for their misses than their hits. Schumann was lucky. His hits were spectacular. But among those familiar with the whole body of his critical production he has been taxed with immoderate and, in retrospect, undue enthusiasm in the cases of such composers as William Sterndale Bennett, John Field, Niels Gade, Stephen Heller, Adolf Henselt, Hermann Hirschbach, etc.

Schumann's 'An Opus 2' is remarkable for more fundamental attributes than those which go to make a talent scout. It is an original, imaginative and, for its time, a uniquely picturesque approach to music criticism. In heralding a young Polish composer it also introduced, if it could not so quickly establish, a young German critic as extraordinary in his own way as Chopin. Schumann's subsequent fame as a composer has overshadowed his literary and propagandistic accomplishments of the decade 1834–44, when he was first a co-founder and then almost immediately the editor and a principal contributor of the *Neue Zeitschrift für Musik*. Chopin's variations can hardly have been more startling to those who first heard them than was the lead of Schumann's notice to the unsuspecting readers of the stodgy *Allgemeine Musikalische Zeitung*:

Eusebius dropped by one evening, not long ago. He entered quietly, his pale features brightened by that enigmatic smile with which he likes to excite curiosity. Florestan and I were seated at the piano. He, as you know, is one of those rare musical persons who seem to anticipate everything that is new, of the future and extraordinary. . . . This time, however, there was a surprise in store even for him. With the words 'Hats off, gentlemen, a genius!' Eusebius spread out before us a piece of music.

We were not allowed to see the title. I turned the pages idly; there is something magical about this secret enjoyment of music unheard. It seems to me, moreover, that every composer has his own musical handwriting. Beethoven looks different on paper from Mozart, just as Jean Paul's prose differs from Goethe's. Here, however, it was as if I were being stared at oddly by strange eyes—eyes of flowers, basilisks, peacocks, maidens. In certain places it became clearer—I thought I could discern Mozart's 'Là ci darem la mano' being woven through a hundred chords, Leporello winking at me, and Don Giovanni hurrying by in a white cloak. . . .

The review continues in that vein, linking the variations to characters and incidents in the opera.

The Adagio is in B flat minor, to be sure, but I [Florestan] can think of nothing more appropriate. It seems to imply a moral admonition to the Don. It's naughty, of course, but also delightful, that Leporello should be eavesdropping—laughing and mocking from behind bushes; that oboes and clarinets should pour forth their charming seduction and that B flat major, in full bloom, should signal the first amorous kiss.

And it closes with Julius, the pseudonymous narrator, bidding Florestan good night and observing:

> These private feelings may well be praiseworthy, if rather subjective; but obvious as Chopin's genius may be, I, too, bow my head to such inspiration, such high endeavour, such mastery!

As is true of much of Schumann's critical writing, and especially of his encomiums, we learn a lot more about Schumann in this little literary excursion than we learn about Chopin and his variations. This fact was not lost upon G. W. Fink,* editor of the *Allgemeine Musikalische Zeitung*, who found the piece so fanciful and so wanting in both sobriety and specifics[1] that he bracketed it with a second notice of the same work by 'a reputable and worthy representative of the older school', who supplied the specifics, including musical examples, but found in them only 'bravura and figuration'.

Among the essential things we learn about Schumann is the impressionable character of his approach and reaction to music and the many-sided nature of his complex and elusive personality. Schumann's own awareness of a persistent ambivalence is reflected in his invention of the Davidsbund, whose charter members we meet here: the impulsive, impatient, decisive and effusive Florestan, the moderate, cautious, slower, sometimes sceptical Eusebius and the mature, detached, paternal Master Raro.

And in the reference to Jean Paul there is a clue to Schumann's literary tastes and predilections. Jean Paul (Richter), along with E. T. A. Hoffmann, was his principal model; and Jean Paul may be held responsible for Schumann's frequent excessive use of high-flown metaphor, obscure allusion, coy disguise and evasion, trivial mysteries and riddles, and ambiguous syntax. This tendency to rhetorical extravagance diminished over the years. The Davidsbund and the feverish articulation of its members gave way to a more sober—and also more conventional—style of criticism. With it went much of Schumann's charm as a writer and critic. But it never vanished entirely; and it re-emerged in all its former uninhibited exuberance, appropriately, possibly, but also appallingly, in the 'New Paths' heralding Brahms in 1853:

> Seated at the piano, he [Brahms] began to disclose most wondrous regions. It was also most wondrous playing, which made of the piano an orchestra of mourning or jubilant voices. There were sonatas, more like disguised symphonies; songs whose poetry would be intelligible even to one who

---

[1] See Leon Plantinga (p. 166) who discusses the background to this review. ED

G

didn't know the words, although a profound vocal line flows through them all; a few piano pieces, partly of a demoniac character, charmingly formed; then sonatas for violin and piano, string quartets, etc.—all so different one from another that seemed to flow from a spearate source. And finally it seemed as though he himself, a surging stream incarnate, swept them all together into a single waterfall, sending aloft a peaceful rainbow above the turbulent waves, flanked on the shores by playful butterflies and the voices of nightingales. . . .

The term 'Davidsbund' (League of David) does not occur in 'An Opus 2', although its members do. It made its debut in two essays published in *Der Komet* in 1833. The concept, of course, was a circle of high-minded idealists and enthusiasts united against the Philistines as represented by the current vogue of virtuosity, especially of the keyboard variety. The Davidsbund existed largely in Schumann's imagination, and he retained for himself the characters of Florestan and Eusebius; but the term, as he used it, or the Bund, was extended to include others of his musical and literary persuasion, some of whom became co-founders with him of the *Neue Zeitschrift für Musik* or contributors to its pages.

When Schumann published a collection of his own contributions in 1854 as *Gesammelte Schriften über Musik und Musiker*, he recalled the circumstances and discussions that had led to the periodical's founding:

Toward the close of the year 1833 a group of musicians, mostly young, living in Leipzig, established the custom of nightly gatherings. The meetings were informal, as if purely by chance, and primarily social, although they obviously also served the exchange of ideas about the art which was food and drink to them all—music! The state of music in Germany at that time can hardly be said to have offered any grounds for rejoicing. Rossini still reigned supreme in the theatre; among pianists Herz and Hünten had the field pretty much to themselves. And yet only a few years had passed since Beethoven, Carl Maria von Weber and Schubert had lived among us! Mendelssohn's star was, to be sure, in the ascendant, and wonderful things were spoken of a Pole named Chopin; but their enduring influence would not be established for some years to come.

One day these young hotheads were seized with an idea: Let us not sit idly by; rather let us do something to improve matters, to restore the poetry of the art to its rightful place of honour! Thus emerged the first pages of the *Neue Zeitschrift für Musik*. The pleasure of a firm and close association of young talents was of short duration. Death claimed one of our dearest associates. Some of the others left Leipzig for a time. The enterprise was on the point of dissolution when the musical visionary of the group, who heretofore had spent more of his life dreaming at the piano than with books, undertook the direction of the magazine and continued as its editor for ten full years, until 1844.

Even here, Schumann was romanticizing. As Leon Plantinga has emphasized in his book, *Schumann as Critic*, Schumann was more solidly grounded in literature than in music; and literary predilections had been apparent from his earliest childhood. The son of a book dealer and publisher in Zwickau, he grew up with books. His education was classical. He was translating from Greek and Latin at fifteen, and was widely versed in German literature. Even before going off to Heidelberg he was writing aphorisms and fragments of novels. His musical grounding, by comparison, was superficial and haphazard.

This tardy maturation of a latent musical genius may help to explain the conspicuous change in Schumann's literary style after the first two or three years of the *Neue Zeitschrift für Musik*. It seems reasonable to suppose, in retrospect, that with the flowering of his compositional talent, music replaced literature as a vehicle for his poetic imagination. What remained of the writer was a solid professional, producing music criticism of a far more conventional cast than one would ever have expected from the author of 'An Opus 2'.

The mature criticism was also more conventionally German. That Schumann's early idols included Chopin, Berlioz and William Sterndale Bennett would seem to suggest an international or cosmopolitan disposition and experience. But Schumann was not, in fact, so disposed. He was, on the contrary, a thoroughly provincial German, ill-travelled even in Germany, with characteristic German attitudes toward the outside world, and especially toward the Latin world. He rated Italians as capable of nothing more than sweet melody. And Paris, in his view, was a halfway station where the frivolous gathered to applaud Meyerbeer and Thalberg while awaiting passage to purgatory.

Thus, one of the most celebrated and most extended of Schumann's critiques— the appreciation of Berlioz's *Symphonie Fantastique* in 1835—emerges as an anomaly. It is not, really; for Schumann obviously sensed in Berlioz a kindred idealist rebelling against all that Schumann detested in what he knew, or thought he knew, about musical life in Paris, and one prone, moreover, to the kind of visionary fancy so characteristic of his own aesthetic predilections.

Berlioz and Schumann had much in common, both as composers and critics. History has tended to view them as prototypes of the nineteenth-century romantic and as pathbreakers, Schumann in his picturesque and colouristic employment of the piano, Berlioz in his exploitation and refinement of the new resources of the orchestra. And this is accurate enough—up to a point. Certainly they shared a graphic approach to music, although Schumann objected to the scenario of the *Symphonie Fantastique*. He was easily capable, as his review demonstrated, of providing a scenario of his own. 'The German,' he observed smugly, 'with his sense of tact and his distaste for intimate detail, does not welcome such explicit instruction.'

But what united them even more fundamentally than an over-active fantasy life, was, paradoxically, a deeply rooted conservatism. Their contempt for Rossini and Donizetti, and for the glittery virtuosity of the keyboard matadors of the day, was motivated by a reverence for the masters of the past, whose memory they felt violated in the fashionable music of the time. Berlioz's early idols were Gluck and Spontini. Schumann's were Beethoven and Schubert. They were both traditionalists. What attracted Schumann to Berlioz's symphony was the fact that it was—a symphony!

'With Beethoven's Ninth Symphony,' he wrote, 'the greatest of all purely instrumental works in respect of sheer size, it seemed that the ultimate had been reached in terms of both proportion and objective. Now, in an obscure corner of France, a young medical student has thought up something new. Four movements are not enough for him. He prefers the full five-act form of the theatre. . . .'

Schumann found in Berlioz, in other words, a reassurance about the continued vitality of the idiom, just as he would find a similar reassurance nearly twenty years later in the symphonic implications of Brahms's early piano sonatas and string quartets. Like Berlioz, he had little patience with those whom we regard as the true radicals, or progressives, of the nineteenth century, Wagner and Liszt. Granted, during the decade of his activity as a critic, Wagner had not yet emerged and Liszt was still in the virtuoso phase of his career. But when Schumann heralded Brahms in 1853 he had heard *Tannhäuser*, and was aware of *Rienzi*, *The Flying Dutchman* and *Lohengrin*. Plantinga notes pertinently that in a list of promising composers of the time, appended to the 'New Paths' panegyric, the name of Wagner is missing.

One is tempted to note a certain contradiction implicit in the conservatism of Schumann's taste as opposed to the bold originality of both his compositions and his criticism. His originality as a critic is most conspicuous in what may be termed an inferential approach to music appreciation. Schumann habitually heard music in terms of persons, pictures, experiences, incidents, reminiscences, dreams, etc. Before his time, criticism had been concerned primarily with craftsmanship. The critic assessed the musician's accomplishment, whether as composer or executant, in technical terms against conventional criteria of performance.

Schumann, more than any critic before him, listened to music and evaluated it with the ears and imagination of a poet. His wide reading doubtless had a lot to do with this; and his literary enthusiasms speak for themselves, notably Jean Paul and E. T. A. Hoffmann.

Hoffmann's famous appreciation of Beethoven's Fifth Symphony in the 4 July 1810, issue of the *Allgemeine Musikalische Zeitung* was the prototype of this new kind of creative, or interpretive, criticism. It is often offered as evidence by those at pains to prove that Beethoven was not the misunderstood and neglected genius of legend. For that there is weightier evidence, including J. F. Rochlitz's articles on the *Eroica* and the late piano sonatas and quartets, also in the *Allgemeine Musikalische Zeitung*, whose editor he was from 1798 to 1818. The importance of Hoffmann's article lay rather in the substance and manner of the exegesis. And no one knew better than Hoffmann that his appreciation of Beethoven was compelling him into a new area of critical enterprise and critical endeavour.

> The reviewer has before him, [he wrote] one of the most important works of the master whose pre-eminence is denied by none. It is permeated through and through with that subject which is paramount in the reviewer's thoughts, and thus no one should take it amiss if he the [reviewer] transgresses the normal bounds of criticism in his effort to encompass in words what he experienced in the study of this composition.

Carefully distinguishing pure instrumental music from all other forms as the ideal medium for the expression of the romantic spirit, Hoffmann first salutes Haydn and Mozart as forerunners of Beethoven who also breathed the same romantic spirit, and then hails Beethoven as the man who 'disclosed to us the region of the colossal and the immeasurable'. What this region contained, for Hoffmann, at least, is then spelled out in a prose whose density cannot be pruned without damage to its innate characteristics:

> Radiant beams penetrate the dark night of this realm, and we become aware of gigantic shadows, weaving up and down, embracing us ever more tightly, crushing all within us except the pain of endless longing, in which every sensual impulse first surges upward in joyous tones, then falls and disappears, leaving nothing but this pain which, consuming love, hope and pleasure, destroys nothing, but seems rather to burst our breast with a full-voiced polyphony of every passion—and we live on and are enchanted disciples of the spirit world.

No one was more enchanted than Schumann. This inferential, or interpretive, approach to criticism, so boldly adopted by him at the outset of his career as a critic in 'An Opus 2', is illustrated vividly in many of Schumann's subsequent articles. His account of a performance of Mendelssohn's *Meeresstille und glückliche Fahrt* under the composer's direction in Leipzig in 1835 provides as good an example as any. It is in the form of a notional letter to Chiara:

> Do you remember that evening when we drove along the Brenta from Padua? The oppressive Italian night air sent us off to sleep. And then in the morning there was a sudden cry: '*Ecco, ecco, signori, Venezia!*'—And the sea lay stretched out before us, motionless and monstrous; far out on the horizon a distant tinkle, as if the little waves were conversing in a dream. Thus it coils and shimmers in 'Meerestille'. One dozes, more lost in thought than thinking. Beethoven's chorus, also based on Goethe, with its accentuation of every word, sounds almost rough compared with this sounding spider-web of the violins. A harmony is unleashed toward the end that seems to suggest a daughter of Nereus casting a seductive eye at the poet, as if to lure him down. But then, for the first time, there comes a higher wave, and little by little the sea grows everywhere more sportive, and sails flutter in the breeze, and gay pennants, and now away, away, away!

Schumann was not alone, of course, in this inductive propensity. It was Karl Friedrich Ebers, in the periodical *Caecilia*, in 1825, who had read into Beethoven's Seventh Symphony a village wedding—Schumann enthusiastically enlarged upon this dubious conceit—and Friedrich Wieck, Schumann's future father-in-law, significantly, contributed to *Caecilia*, in 1831, a review of Chopin's opus 2 very similar to Schumann's. It was Wieck's article, not Schumann's, incidentally, that excited Chopin's scorn. But Chopin would probably have reacted similarly to Schumann's.

This way of listening to music was simply in the air, so to speak, prompted, no doubt, by the dramatic, philosophical and picturesque implications of Beethoven's masterpieces. It would shortly lead to a new 'interpretive' approach to performance and to a kind of composition which was either explicitly programmatic or which assumed an 'interpretive' performance.

It has persisted in music criticism to the present day, especially in the approach of sympathetic critics to the major works of Brahms, Bruckner, Mahler and Sibelius. And it has a curious descendant in the 'inferential art' of our own time, which goes one better than Hoffmann and Schumann by putting the creative responsibility upon the listener, or onlooker, totally. A work of art, according to this aesthetic philosophy, is what you make it.

Schumann would not have concurred. He was a fanciful listener and a fanciful writer. But he was also both a fine musical craftsman and an admirer of fine craftsmanship. The often extravagant, sometimes farfetched character of his inferential exercises has called attention to itself at the expense of a vast amount of sober, expert comment on the work of fellow composers by one who knew what he was talking about.

Indeed, it was in his craftsman's appreciation and assessment of craftmanship that Schumann stands pretty much alone. Other critics have written imaginatively and have espoused worthy aesthetic ideals. Other critics have had a wider range of interest and have written from a wider range of experience. But none has had a better grasp of the sheer craft of composition. In any case, the relative brevity of his preoccupation with criticism rather disqualifies him as a contender for a place in the history of criticism alongside such career practitioners as Burney, Chorley, Davison and Newman in London, Rochlitz in Leipzig, Rellstab in Berlin, Hanslick and Kalbeck in Vienna, Berlioz and Fétis in Paris, and Krehbiel, Aldrich and Henderson in New York. He is to be numbered more appropriately with Hoffmann, Hugo Wolf, Shaw, Debussy, Dukas and Virgil Thomson among those brilliant, perceptive and articulate individuals for whom criticism was an avocation rather than a calling and who would probably have ranked among the great critics had they devoted their lives to it.

Of the trinity constituting Schumann's complex personality it was Florestan who made the biggest impact and who lingers in the memory. It was through Florestan, too, that Schumann spoke for his own time. But Eusebius and Master Raro were always at Florestan's elbow, ready to restrain their impetuous comrade, to leaven his fancies with a becoming sobriety, to encourage reverence for tradition and to inspire the quest of perspective.

ROBERT SCHUMANN

Aphorisms, Maxims and Quotations

Advice to Young Musicians[1]

Play always as if a master listened.

Seek among your comrades those who know more than you.

The world is large. Be modest! You have not yet discovered and contrived what others before you have already imagined and found out. And even if such should be the case, look on it as a gift from above to be shared with others.

Reverence what is old, but have a warm heart also for what is new. Indulge no prejudice against unknown names.

Be diligent in the study of life, as well as of the arts and sciences.

The laws of morality are also those of art.

By industry and endurance you will always rise higher.

From one pound of iron, which cost but a few pence, many thousand watch-springs are made, and the value is increased a hundred thousand fold. Make faithful and profitable use of the pound that God has given you.

Without enthusiasm nothing genuine is accomplished in art.

Art does not exist for the acquisition of riches. Aim ever at becoming a greater and greater artist; everything else comes to you of itself.

[1] Originally intended as a preface to *Album for the Young* (1848), but finally published in 1850 in the NZfM (supp. 36). ED.

Only when the form grows clear to you, will the spirit become so too.

Perhaps it is genius alone that understands genius.

There is no end to learning.

'Dumb keyboards' have been invented; practise on them awhile to see that they are worthless. The dumb cannot teach speech.

As you grow older, converse more frequently with scores than with virtuosi.

Industriously practise the fugues of good masters; above all those of J. S. Bach. Let the '48' be your daily meat. Then you will certainly become an able musician.

You must practise scales and other finger exercises assiduously. There are, however, many people who fancy they attain perfection by spending, even until an advanced age, several hours daily in mechanical execution; that is as if a person should exert himself to repeat his A.B.C. faster and faster. Employ your time better.

The study of musical history, reinforced by hearing the actual performance of the masterpieces of different epochs, will prove the most rapid and effectual cure for conceit and vanity.

Neglect no opportunity of practising on the organ. There is no other instrument which inflicts such prompt chastisement on offensive and defective composition or execution.

Listen attentively to popular songs; they are a mine of the most charming melodies, and afford an insight into the character of different nations.

If everyone would play first fiddle, no orchestra could be got together. Let each musician keep his proper place.

Do not be deterred by the words Theory, Thorough-bass, Counterpoint, etc. Approach them as a friend, and their response will be most cordial.

All that is merely fashionable goes out of fashion in its turn; and if you continue to cultivate it till you are old, you will become a simpleton whom no one values.

Read poetry with diligence, as a relief from your musical studies. Take frequent exercise in the open air.

On Criticism

The music critic's noblest destiny is to make himself superfluous! The best way to talk about music is to be quiet about it![1]

Even the most hard-hearted critic sometimes feels an urge to *praise*.[2]

A significant indication of the present level of talent was provided by the Vienna Prize Award. Say what one will, such contests can only be helpful; they can do no harm. And he knows little about creative impulses who imagines that they are not encouraged by inducements, even prosaic ones. Had someone offered a prize of precious diamonds—such as are to be found in royal and imperial treasuries—while Mozart, Haydn and Beethoven were still alive, I bet that the masters would have done their best to get it. But then, of course, who would have judged?[3]

Critics always want to know what composers cannot tell them, and critics often hardly understand a tenth part of what they talk about.[4]

In no other kind of criticism is it so difficult to prove one's point as in music. Science argues with mathematics; poetry has the decisive, golden word; other arts have nature herself as arbiter, for they borrow their forms from her. But music is the fair orphan whose father and mother no one can name.[5]

Now it is absurd that the musical journals try to open the eyes of the world to what they call 'agreeable' talents, such as Kalkbrenner, Bertini, etc. We can already see through glass; for this we need no boring interpreter.[6]

The vocabulary of disparagement has a million more words than that of praise.[7]

---

[1] GSK, Vol. I, p. 147.   [2] NZfM, 13 (1840).   [3] GSK, Vol. I, p. 424.
[4] NZfM, 10 (1839).   [5] NZfM, 2 (1835).   [6] NZfM, 4 (1836).
[7] NZfM, 5 (1836).

On Composition

The first conception is always the most natural and the best. Reason errs, but never feeling.[1]

The philosophers are clearly wrong when they think that a composer working with an idea sits down like a preacher on Saturday afternoon, schematizes his theme according to the usual three points, and works it out in the accepted way—to be sure, they are wrong.[2]

The stimulation of the composer's imagination is such a delicate matter, that once the track is lost, or time intervenes, it is only by a happy coincidence that in a later rare moment it can be recovered. For this reason, a work discontinued and laid aside is seldom completed; it would be preferable for the composer to begin a new one, and give himself over completely to its *Stimmung*.[3]

To get to the core of a composition, it should be divested first of all its adornments. Only then will it become apparent whether it is really beautifully formed; only then will it become clear what its essence is, and what art added. And if a beautiful melody still remains, and if it embodies a healthy, noble harmony, then the composer has won and deserves our applause. This requirement seems so simple, yet how seldom is it successfully fulfilled![4]

In his 'Pastoral' Symphony Beethoven sings simple themes such as any child-like mind could invent. Yet surely he did not merely write down everything presented by the initial inspiration, but made his choices from among many possibilities.[5]

Talent labours, but genius creates.[6]

Everything that happens in the world affects me, politics, literature, people; I reflect on all of this in my own way, and then whatever can find release in music seeks its outlet.[7]

It is not surprising to me that you cannot compose now, since there may be so many people coming in and out of your house. To create, and to do so successfully, requires happiness and profound solitude.[8]

[1] GSK, Vol. I, p. 25. [2] NZfM, 18 (1843). [3] NZfM, 11 (1840).
[4] GSK, Vol. I, p. 409. [5] NZfM, 3 (1835). [6] GSK, Vol. I, p. 21.
[7] *Jugendbriefe*, p. 282. [8] Letter to Clara, March 1838.

Among all artists, travel is the least profitable for musicians Our great composers always have dwelt quietly in one and the same place, for example, Bach, Haydn, Beethoven, although a view of the Alps or of Sicily might not have harmed them.[1]

Tell me where you live, and I will tell you how you compose.[2]

A genuinely musical art form always has a focal point towards which all else gravitates, on which all imaginative impulses concentrate. Many composers place it in the middle (like Mozart), others reserve it for nearer the close (like Beethoven). Wherever it lies, the effect of any composition is dependent upon its dynamic influence.[3]

Everything beautiful is difficult, the short the most difficult.[4]

I do not care for the man whose life is not in harmony with his work.[5]

Genius creates empires, whose smaller states are distributed by higher authority among Talents. To the latter falls the task of organizing and perfecting details while Genius remains preoccupied with grander productions.[6]

A certain hot-head (now in Paris)[7] likes to define the term 'fugue' as denoting 'a composition where one voice races away from the others—and the listener from them all'. He himself, he would add, made it a point to talk loudly when such things were played in public, and to mutter insults.

In fact, he understood very little about it, rather resembling the fox in the fable; that is, he could not write one himself, no matter how much he secretly wished to. Those who can, of course, define a fugue differently—choir directors, graduate music students, etc. According to them, 'Beethoven never wrote nor could have written a fugue; even Bach allowed himself liberties at which one can only shake one's head. The best instruction is to be found in Marpurg', etc. How different again, is the view of still others, myself included, who can revel for hours in the fugues of Beethoven, Bach and Handel and who have reached the conclusion that—with the exception of diluted, tepid, miserable, patchwork stuff—fugues can no longer be written.[8]

The anti-chromatic school should remember that, once upon a time, the seventh startled just as much as the diminished octave now does and that, through the

---

[1] GSK, Vol. I, p. 415.   [2] GSK, Vol. I, pp. 183–84.   [3] GSK, Vol. I, p. 147.
[4] GSK, Vol. I, pp. 389–90.   [5] GSK, Vol. II, p. 262.   [6] GSK, Vol. I, p. 147.
[7] Heine? ED
[8] GSK, Vol. I, p. 247. Schumann went on to make an exception of Mendelssohn.

development of harmony, passion received finer nuances by means of which music has been placed among those high mediums of art which have language and symbols for all spiritual states.[1]

Nature would burst should she attempt to produce nothing save Beethovens.[2]

It is inadmissible to appraise an entire life on the basis of a single deed. An instant that threatens the overthrow of a system may often be explained and excused by reference to the totality of which it is but a tiny part. Disassemble a Beethoven symphony with which you are not familiar and see whether even the most beautiful idea is effective as an isolated phenomenon. This is truer of music than of the graphic arts, where a single torso can establish the master. In music everything is dependent upon the relation of the individual part to the whole. This applies to the individual composition, whether large or small, and it applies, also, to the artist's whole life. One often hears, for instance—false and impossible as it may be—that Mozart had only to write *Don Giovanni* to be the great Mozart. He would, to be sure, have gone down in history as the composer of *Don Giovanni* but he would be far from having been Mozart.[3]

On Programme Music

Beethoven was well aware of the dangers involved with his 'Pastoral' Symphony. In the few words with which he prefaced it, 'more the expression of emotion than tone-painting', there lies an entire aesthetic for composers. It is ridiculous that a painter should represent him in portraits sitting at a brook, his head resting on his hand, listening to the splashing.[4]

I always say, 'first of all let me hear that you have made beautiful music; after that I will like your programme too'.[5]

[On the origins of *Papillons*]
I must mention that I added the text to the music, not the reverse—for that would seem to me a silly beginning. Only the last, which by strange coincidence formed an answer to the first, was aroused by Jean Paul.[6]

[On the origins of *Carnaval*]
I attached the titles afterwards. Is not music always in itself sufficient and expressive? 'Estrella' is a name, such as is placed under portraits, to grasp the picture

---

[1] GSK, Vol. I, p. 22.   [2] GSK, Vol. I, p. 22.   [3] NZfM, 1 (1834).
[4] NZfM, 2 (1835).   [5] NZfM, 18 (1843).
[6] Letter to Henrietta Voigt, *Briefe*, p. 54.

more firmly; 'Reconnaissance' a lovers' meeting; 'Aveu' a confession of love; 'Promenade' a walk, as one does at German balls, arm in arm with one's lady-friend. All of this certainly does not have any artistic value.[1]

It is certainly wrong to believe that composers take up pen and paper with the tortuous intention of expressing, of portraying, of painting this or that. Yet outward accidental influences and impressions should not be underestimated. Unconsciously, along with the musical image, an idea continues to operate along with the ear, the eye; and this latter, the ever-active organ, perceives among the sounds and tones certain contours which may solidify and assume the shape of clear-cut figures.[2]

On Musical History

Mozart and Haydn had but a partial and one-sided knowledge of Bach. No one can guess how Bach would have influenced their productivity, had they known him in all his greatness.[3]

Do you know Bach's Passion music according to St John, the so-called little one? But of course you do. I wonder if you agree with me that it is much bolder, more powerful and poetical, than the St Matthew version? The St Matthew seems to me . . . rather drawn out in places and of excessive length; in the St John what terseness, what inspiration, especially in the choruses, and what consummate art.[4]

[In 1847, Franz Brendel founded a 'Universal German Society of Musicians' and invited Schumann to participate at its first convention. Schumann was unable to be present, but in a letter to Brendel[5] he requested that the following points be presented on his behalf. They disclose an enlightened attitude to what a later generation called 'musicology'.—ED]

First, I think it desirable that a section should detach itself from the Convention to consider *the protection of Classical music against modern adaptations*.

I should then like to propose that another section be formed for *the research and restoration of corrupted passages in Classical works*.

I should next like to raise the question of *the use of French for titles*, also *the*

---

[1] *Robert Schumanns Briefe*, ed. F. Gustav Jansen (Leipzig, 1914).
[2] GSK, Vol. I, p. 84.
[3] *Briefe*, pp. 177–78.
[4] Letter to Director D. G. Otten, Dresden, 31 May 1849 (Storck, London, 1907).
[5] Dresden, 8 August 1847 (Storck, pp. 256–58, London, 1907).

misuse of Italian for marks of expression, by Germans in their own compositions. I should be glad if you would move *the abolition of French titles,* and *the rejection of such Italian expressions as may be rendered as well, if not better, in German.*

Finally, the Convention should consider by what means their future meetings ... may be made *to benefit and encourage youthful composers especially.* [Schumann's italics.]

The whole so-called 'Romantic School' (of course, I am speaking of Germans) is far nearer to Bach in its music than Mozart ever was; indeed, it has a thorough knowledge of Bach. I myself make a daily confession of my sins to that mighty one, and endeavour to purify and strengthen myself through him. And then, however honest and delightful Kuhnau may be, one can hardly place him on a level with Bach. Even if Kuhnau had written *The Well-Tempered Clavier* he would still be but a hundredth part of him. In fact, to my mind Bach is unapproachable—he is unfathomable.[1]

It may well be true that great fathers seldom beget children who grow great in the same art or science, but still those are fortunate who are chained to their talent through birth and whose calling is never in doubt—Mozart, Haydn, Beethoven, etc. whose fathers were simple musicians. They drank in music with their mother's milk, learned it in their childhood dreams; with the first emerging awareness they felt themselves members of the great family of artists, into which others often have to purchase admittance with sacrifices.[2]

On his Contemporaries

Hector Berlioz:
Berlioz does not try to be pleasing and elegant; what he hates, he grasps fiercely by the hair; what he loves, he almost crushes in his fervour.[3]

Richard Wagner:
Wagner has just finished another opera (*Tannhäuser*). He is certainly a clever fellow, full of crazy ideas and audacious to a degree. Yet he is really incapable of conceiving and writing four beautiful bars, indeed *hardly good* ones, in succession. That is where they are all wanting, in pure harmony, skill in four-part chorale writing. What lasting good can come of it? And the score lies before

[1] Letter to Keferstein, 31 January 1840.   [2] NZfM (1837).
[3] NZfM, 3 (1835). Review of the *Symphonie Fantastique.*

us, beautifully printed, with all the fifths and octaves, and he would like to alter and erase—too late![1]

[Schumann later changed his mind about the work]
About *Tannhäuser* . . . I must withdraw much that I wrote to you after reading the score; on the stage everything works out differently. I was greatly affected by much of it.[2]

Felix Mendelssohn:
He is the Mozart of the nineteenth century, the most brilliant musician, the one who sees most clearly through the contradictions of this period, and for the first time reconciles them.[3]

Alexander Dreyschock:
Has the young virtuoso no friend to tell him the truth, no one who can disregard his clever fingers and point out to him how vapid, how utterly negligible it all is? There is a rumour afoot that he is the sworn enemy of Beethoven and can see nothing in him. We don't know; but his composition gives us no reason to doubt it. If he would just learn from Beethoven! Or not even that! He can learn something from third and fourth-rate masters, from Strauss and Lanner![4]

Frédéric Chopin:
Chopin could publish everything anonymously. One would recognize him immediately. This implies praise and censure at once—the one for his talent, the other for his aspirations. Inherent in everything he does is that significant originality which, once displayed, leaves no doubt as to the master's identity. He produces, moreover, an abundance of new forms which, in their tenderness and daring alike, deserve admiration. Always novel and inventive in externals, he remains the same in the construction of his compositions and in special instrumental effects, so that one fears that he may not surpass what he has already achieved. The latter, to be sure, is enough to enter his name ineradicably in the history of modern art, although his influence is restricted to music for the piano. With his gifts he could have achieved more, and have extended his influence upon the further growth of our art in general.

[1] Letter to Mendelssohn, 22 October 1845.
[2] Letter to Mendelssohn, 12 November 1845.
[3] NZfM, 13 (1840).
[4] NZfM (1841). Dreyschock (1818–69) was a typical piano virtuoso, noted for his powerful left hand. Heine once remarked of him that when he played in Cologne, and the wind was in the right direction, you could hear him in Paris.

Let us be thankful for what we have. What he has accomplished has been so fine, and he still gives us so much! Certainly we would congratulate any other artist who had accomplished half as much.[1]

William Sterndale Bennett:
He is no Beethoven, with years of struggle behind him; no Berlioz, preaching revolution in heroic accents and leaving horror and destruction in his wake. He is rather a quiet, lovely spirit, who, whatever may be raging inside him, works alone and above, like a star-gazer, tracing the course of the planets and absorbing the secrets of nature.

His name is the one which appears above, his fatherland is the home of Shakespeare, whose Christian name he also shares. Indeed, it would be strange if the arts of poetry and music were such strangers to one another that the celebrated country that gave us Shakespeare and Byron could not also produce a musician! Old prejudices have been weakened by the names of Field, Onslow, Potter, Bishop, etc; they should be further shaken by this individual, at whose cradle a kindly providence stood watch.[2]

Niels Gade:
A French newspaper reported recently: 'A young Danish composer is making something of a sensation in Germany; his name is Gade. He travels frequently from Copenhagen to Leipzig on foot, his violin strapped to his back. He is said to be the living image of Mozart.'

The first and the last sentences are correct. Some fiction has crept into the middle. The young Dane did, indeed, arrive in Leipzig a few months ago (although not on foot), and his Mozart-like head, with its shock of hair, looking as if it had been carved from granite, blended well with the sympathy previously aroused in local musical circles by his 'Ossian' overture and his First Symphony . . . Nothing quite like him has come our way among the younger composers for a long time.

It would be a great mistake to assume from his physical resemblance to Mozart a corresponding musical affinity, as truly striking as the former may be. We have here to do with an entirely new musical personality.[3]

Rudolph Willmers:
Willmers has already made a name for himself as a brilliant pianist and gifted composer . . .

[1] NZfM, 15 (1841).　　　　　　　　　　[2] NZfM, 7 (1837).
[3] NZfM (1843). Gade (1817–90) was a Danish composer who came to Leipzig in 1843. See pp. 22–23, also Register of Persons, p. 430.

We have only one fear: that it will not last long. The public itself pulls apart the wreaths it has plaited in order to plait them anew and in a different shape for someone who knows how to be more amusing. He should ponder all this, and change his ways while there is still time. It is possible to fritter away even the goodwill of one's colleagues, and then it is twice as hard to clamber back, to regain respectability. He should think it over . . .[1]

Franz Liszt:
No matter how many important artists have passed before us in the last year; no matter how many artists equalling Liszt in many respects we ourselves possess, not one can match him in energy and boldness. People are fond of comparing him with Thalberg. But a look at both heads decides the question. I remember the remark of a well-known Viennese cartoonist who said of his countryman's head that it resembled 'that of a handsome young countess with a man's nose'; while of Liszt he observed that 'he might sit to any painter as a Greek god'. There is a similar difference in their art.[2]

Joseph Kessler:
One cannot judge the power of Mount Etna by the size of the stones it discharges; but people do gaze upwards in astonishment when its pillars of flame leap up towards the clouds. There is an admonishment here for Kessler, for having produced (in the metaphor) mere stones; for myself, too, for having picked them up and examined them without awaiting the greater eruption.[3]

Henri Herz:
About Herz one can write (1) sadly, (2) gaily, (3) sarcastically or, as now, all three at once. One can hardly believe how cautiously and shyly I avoid any discussion of him, and how I try to stay at least ten paces away from him, lest I praise him too loudly to his face . . .

What more does he wish than to amuse—and grow rich? Has he ever implied that those who like him should therefore like Beethoven's last quartets less? Does he ever ask that his own compositions be compared with them? . . .

We should not forget that he has kept millions of fingers busy, and that the public, by playing his variations, has achieved a dexterity which can be employed to advantage in the performance of better and even diametrically opposed things . . .

[1] NZfM, 18 (1843). Rudolph Willmers (1821–78) was a piano pupil of Hummel in Weimar.
[2] NZfM, 12 (1840). Review of Liszt's Leipzig recitals.
[3] NZfM, 1 (1834). Kessler (1800–72) was a pianist and pedagogue.

Herz's Second Concerto is in C minor, and is recommended to those who liked the first. Should it by chance be placed in a programme also containing a certain Symphony in C minor, one prays that the symphony will follow the concerto.[1]

[1] NZfM, 4 (1836). Herz (1803–88) was Professor of the pianoforte at the Paris Conservatoire from 1842 to 1874. He made a fortune from the sale of his piano compositions.

JOHN GARDNER

The Chamber Music

THE chamber-music of the Classical era was dominated by the string quartet, which was established by Haydn and brought to its zenith in his mature works and in those of Mozart and Beethoven. Until this time a keyboard instrument had been used in every ensemble, whether vocal or instrumental, for about 150 years, not so much as a colouristic addition, but as a filler-in of the harmony implied by the polyphony of the other parts. Only occasionally was the keyboard *obbligato*; yet its absence would at once be noted, often by a weakening of the harmonic progression or by top-heaviness of texture. Typically, Baroque chamber-music is for a trio of two violins and cello with an additional harpsichord continuo; while classical chamber-music is for a string quartet with a viola on the hitherto absent 'tenor' line, which in the past would have been supplied *ex tempore* by the keyboard player.

In the late eighteenth century, therefore, a new self-sufficient polyphony arose, but not for long. The piano was developing in power and range and was gradually superseding the harpsichord. By the end of the first quarter of the nineteenth century, notably in Beethoven's last period and in the works of Schubert, it had become a household orchestra. It was, however, essentially an instrument of suggestion, of make-believe. On it one could pretend to sing like a human voice, to chirrup like a bird, to sound like a horn, to articulate like a violin, to strum like a harp. In reality, of course, one could do none of these things, for the piano's notes were no sooner struck than they faded away. Yet it was in this tonal evanescence that, paradoxically, the piano's strength lay, for it could call to mind imaginable sounds—an illusion which was further enhanced by the invention of the sustaining pedal with its suggestion of limitless depth and density of texture. The piano became the romantic instrument *par excellence*, beloved alike of composers and listeners. Its solo repertoire grew, and it claimed the attention of specialist composers like Chopin and Liszt. No longer did it enter into chamber-music subserviently in the manner of a *continuo*, but with a clear domination of the ensemble. Schumann's own account of a typical contemporary piano trio, 'a fiery player at the piano, and two understanding friends who accompany softly', hits the nail on the head, and is a pretty fair description of much of his own chamber-music. This is not to say that it is necessarily badly written. The famous and popular Piano Quintet, for instance, has excellent and effective string parts despite the predominance of the piano; and there are such movements as the canonic *Scherzo* of the F major Trio or the Third Fairy Tale, op. 132, which are, by any standards, exquisitely scored for their chosen medium.

Three String Quartets (1842)

In using the piano in the bulk of his chamber-music Schumann was being no more than typical of his generation. There are, in fact, only three chamber-works of his without piano: the three String Quartets, op. 41, written, amazingly, within the space of a few weeks in 1842, an *annus mirabilis* during which he produced, amongst other important pieces, two of his biggest chamber-works with piano: the Quintet and the Quartet. He had been studying counterpoint and fugue, and immersing himself in the quartets of the classical masters. The effect of this upon him was not exactly inspiriting. In a review of a prize-winning string quartet, by one Julius Schapler, he wrote in this very year 1842:

> . . . the quartet has come to a standstill. Who does not know the quartets of Haydn, Mozart and Beethoven, and who would wish to say anything against them? In fact it is the most telling testimony to the immortal fresh-ness of their works that yet after half a century they gladden the hearts of everyone; but it is no good sign that the later generation, after all this time, has not been able to produce anything comparable. Onslow alone met success, and later Mendelssohn, whose aristocratic-poetic nature is particu-larly amenable to this genre.[1]

Schumann's Quartets, in fact, owe more to the limpid style of Mendelssohn (to whom they were dedicated) than to the huge, involved structures of late Beethoven. Furthermore, as a composer with a highly individual genius, he was critically selective of the lessons to be learnt from his great models, for he had his own things to say in his own richly personal musical language. The String Quartets are unmistakably the work of Schumann, despite the wide variety

[1] NZfM, 16 (1842), 142–43.

of forms and moods they encompass. In each of them he faces fresh challenges. Progressive tonality,[1] monothematicism,[2] the introduction of new material in the course of a movement,[3] fugal development,[4] transits through remote regions of tonality,[5] a new kind of variation form with more than one theme,[6] and so on. Each situation is dealt with boldly, imaginatively and with mastery. What a tragedy that he wrote no more String Quartets before his powers began to fail!

It is a pity that our professional players act on the assumption that the only one of Schumann's Quartets worth playing is the first in A minor, and that not very often. Maybe its string writing is somewhat less influenced by keyboard style than that of its successors;[7] maybe it is the best of the three in other respects, having a stronger Finale than No. 2, a less prolix one than No. 3. I do not necessarily agree with this judgment. The three Quartets constitute such a rich mine of uniquely beautiful music that to approach them with a view to picking the winner is to be distracted by irrelevant frivolity. There is only one way to enjoy them; to explore and experience to the full their manifold variety.

The first movement of the First Quartet has the distinction of being apparently in the wrong key. A slow introduction in A minor, based upon a continuous imitative stretto, which never recurs later in the work in an overtly recognizable form,

EX I

leads to an Allegro in F major, in which key the movement ends.

[1] First movement of No. 1; finale of No. 3.
[2] Finale of No. 1.   [3] Finale of No. 1.
[4] Finale of No. 1.   [5] Slow movement of No. 3.
[6] Slow movement of No. 2.   [7] Schumann invariably composed at the piano.

EX 2

Only later events tell us that the home key is, and always was A minor/major.

Can we detect the effect of Schumann's recent study of Bach in this Introduction? It is, in fact, utterly unlike anything Bach ever wrote, though not unlike other passages in Schumann, who loved to write music upon an ostinato fragment:[1] in this case the semi-quaver motif of the first bar, which recurs in each of the next eighteen bars. The mood reminds us of the cadenza to the A minor Fantasie for Piano and Orchestra, written the year before and later amplified into the Piano Concerto. (See p. 251, Ex. 18(a).) It is very much a controlled Introduction, however, with little feeling of the improvisation which befits a cadenza. Furthermore it strays less from its tonic region than the cadenza does, for Schumann would not wish to weaken the home key at this point, since the subsequent Allegro is going to be cast, unprecedently, in the sub-mediant region, and the whole work's tonic region has to be established beyond doubt before this innovating step is made.

The second movement, a Mendelssohnian Scherzo in the home key, has a gracious Trio in the mediant; the third, an extensive, passionate Lied, returns to the submediant of the first Allegro. The Finale is, of course, in the tonic, moving to the mediant at the double-bar. It is tautly monothematic. Schumann derives his second subject, in reality a 'closing theme',

EX 3

from his main theme:

EX 4

whilst an inversion of part of the latter (see Ex. 3) permeates the link section.

EX 5

A surprising and original stroke towards the end plunges the music into the tonic major in a slower tempo and introduces a 'new' theme. Structurally, at this point, we are in the Coda after a sub-mediant recapitulation of the second subject and a further tonic recapitulation of the main theme. The 'new' theme, however, (see Ex. 6) is a musette-like transformation of Ex. 5.

The Second String Quartet, in F major, is chiefly remarkable for its beautiful slow movement, an 'Andante, quasi variazioni' in the key of the flattened mediant major. The form of these variations is unique to Schumann. The first two variations are, in reality, a mere continuation of the opening theme (see Ex. 7);

EX 6

EX 7

whilst the third and fourth variations are based upon a somewhat different melody, related to the first theme only in its later stages. At bar 90 the opening theme returns for the first time to suggest a kind of ternary structure. Schumann's

own description, 'quasi variazioni', cannot be improved upon. The ensuing
Coda relates to variation 2, and with its arpeggios it prepares the listener for
the Scherzo's theme, which is also arpeggiated.

It has been said, with justification, that Schumann is overfond of writing
pianistic arpeggio formations for his string instruments. The Development of the
first movement, and the opening theme of the Finale of the Second Quartet,
certainly show this propensity; one can almost hear Schumann delightedly
trying over the latter on his piano.

EX 8

The Third Quartet in A major, on the other hand, has little arpeggiation and,
in some respects, is the loveliest of the three works. Its first movement is based
upon one of those epigrammatic themes peculiar to Schumann which manage to
keep their identity amidst a multitude of different structural functions.[1]

EX 9

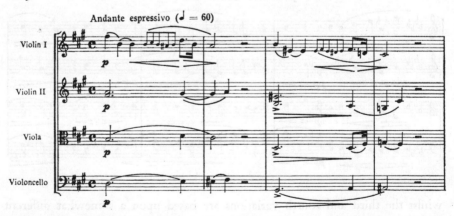

[1] See Bálint Vázsony (pp. 75–77) who discusses this aspect of Schumann's composing technique in detail. ED

This phrase, already adumbrated in the Introduction, occurs no less than nine times in the Allegro molto moderato. And this only includes full statements of the phrase. In fact, its initial falling fifth permeates the entire movement and forms an essential feature of the second subject. (See bracket 'X', Ex. 10.)

EX 10

Schumann creates an unconventional modification to the classical sonata-form by starting his Development with the first subject (Ex. 9) *in the tonic key*. (Haydn and Beethoven normally only did this when they were, rarely, not repeating the Exposition. See, for example, Haydn's Piano Sonata no. 51, in D major.)[1]

The Quartet's second movement consists of four variations and a Coda on what appears to be this restless, sighing off-beat theme.

EX 11

In retrospect, it turns out to be the first of three variations which Schumann ingeniously discloses in advance of the theme on which they are based. Not until the 'Un poco adagio' do we hear the theme itself in all its fullness, and Ex. 11 merely as its tentative outline. (Compare Exx. 11 and 12.)

The slow movement which follows is a rondo with a developing episode, which recurs once, and whose restless tonality contrasts excitingly with the more predictable harmonic inflection of the main theme. It uses two main motifs: one drawn from the main theme, the other based upon the same melodic shape as Ex. 11.

The Rondo Finale, as relaxedly sectional as any Strauss waltz, anticipates the

[1] Compare, also, the first movement of Brahms's Symphony in E minor. ED

EX 12

EX 13

progressive tonality of the Finale of the Piano Quintet. Beethoven, in the Finale of his second 'Rasumovsky' Quartet, gave us a theme which approached its tonic (E minor) from the sub-mediant region of C major. In the Third String Quartet Schumann takes the practice of his predecessor a stage further by giving us a tune which, though centred around its tonic in its first four bars, moves into the sub-dominant region in the fifth bar and, by its subsequent course, makes us hear the opening tonic as the dominant of the sub-dominant and, therefore, to interpret the D major cadence at the end as being in the home key. A uniquely subtle manipulation of tonality! (See Ex. 14.)

EX 14

Certain general features of Schumann's style emerge clearly from a study of the String Quartets. In his first movements he favours a repeated Exposition and a full, regular Recapitulation. His repeat signs should always be obeyed, for not to do so can lead to partial incomprehensibility. For example, in the first movement of the A minor Quartet Schumann composes a closing idea within the first-time bracket which is never heard if the repeat sign is ignored; its subsequent recapitulation at the end of the movement sounds new, an effect Schumann did not intend. The tendency to cap his Expositions with a version of the *main* theme in the *second* key is, in fact, a common practice with Schumann, as also is his un-Beethovenian tendency to make his first themes complete and, in a sense, finite. Almost always are we aware in Schumann of the bridge-section to the second subject as a separate and distinctly identifiable event, often containing its own theme and usually beginning after the main theme has full-closed in the tonic. Conversely, Schumann's second-subject groups, unlike Mozart's, rarely contain a fully-fledged lyrical theme. More often are they a series of incomplete and complementary phrases, transiting through many regions, perhaps, but coming to rest with the customary cadencing phrases of the classical style.

Schumann's developments are often based upon modulating sequences, organized sometimes on the largest scale, and frequently introducing apparently new material. Like Schubert's before him, they are full of transposed repetition and when he is adding a lengthy coda (found in none of the String Quartets, in fact) he is liable to give us a further transposition of parts of the development section so that the coda becomes, as it were, a recapitulation of the development.

The slow movements are invariably 'songs without words' organized into rondo-type structures, such as A–B–A or A–B–A–B–A. The Scherzos, which come as second almost as often as third movements, often have a second trio, an interesting extension of Beethoven's practice of two statements of one trio. Sometimes these Scherzos are anxious rather than relaxed (e.g. the Third Quartet and Second Piano Trio), but almost without exception they have a compound time signature, sometimes changing to a simple metre for the trios, a precedent for which exists in the Ninth Symphony of Beethoven.

The completeness of Schumann's first subjects may sometimes give a rondo-ish quality to his sonata-form finales (e.g. those of the First Piano Trio and Violin Sonata). On the other hand the Finale of the First String Quartet combines Schumann's typical pithiness with a classical incompleteness which bears the listener inexorably onwards without pause for rest to the very end of the exposition in the *prima volta* bars.

In only one of his ten chamber-works in sonata form, the A minor Violin Sonata, does Schumann drop the Scherzo to produce the three-movement work, nor does he anywhere, as his successor Tchaikovsky did, depart from the classical model of fast outer movements. Everywhere in the chamber-music there stands out his belief in the structural self-sufficiency of each individual movement based nearly always upon unity of time-signature and tempo. Only once does he interlink movements (in the D minor Piano Trio), though occasionally he will in the closing stages of a movement clearly anticipate the main theme of the movement to come (e.g. the Scherzo of the D minor Violin Sonata). The conscious use of motto-themes, as in the Fourth Symphony, is not his normal practice,

EX 15

(a)
Mov. I : Mit Energie und Leidenschaft

(b)
Finale : Mit feuer

though he may attain unity by subtler, less conscious means as, for instance, in the D minor Piano Trio where the main ideas of the outer movements are plainly cognate in origin (Exx. 15(a) and (b)).

The Violin Sonatas

The violin sonatas have never attained the same place in the repertory as those of Beethoven and Brahms. In 1945 the British pianist and violinist Harold Bauer, in bringing before the public a new performing version of two of these sonatas, in which the parts had been redistributed, many doublings eliminated and the texture clarified, wrote:

> Schumann's greatest admirers will hardly deny that the two violin and piano sonatas suffer from ineffective handling of the technical resources of the respective instruments. Passages which seem to call for violin tone are frequently given to the piano, and *vice versa*. The same notes are frequently doubled by both piano and violin, causing a dull tone which forbids the requisite dramatic intensity; and since many highly expressive passages are cast in the most unfavourable violin register, the pianist is compelled to subdue the tone to a disproportionate degree, thus giving a wrong impression of restraint within an impassioned mood.

Bauer goes on to claim that he has not changed the composition itself 'in the least' and has retained 'both the melodic line and the harmonic structure . . . absolutely intact', an assertion that cannot go unchallenged, for, highly skilled though his versions are, they are marred by a tendency to touch up the harmony: to add a ninth to a seventh, for example, or to remove a typical asperity. On the other hand, no one would deny, in an aural comparison of the Ur-text and the Bauer versions, that there has been a great improvement on the original in the direction of audibility, and that this improvement is, by implication, a valid criticism of the composer's craftsmanship. Certainly the Bauerized texts can be commended to performers for serious consideration, provided that they are, here and there, revised in the light of a detailed comparison with the original texts. One might then get the best of both worlds, with Schumann's pristine thoughts emerging in the clarity of their original conception.

Another reason for the neglect of the violin sonatas lies in the fact that they are, in the true sense of the term, *Hausmusik*, written for two players in close and inward-looking communion with little opportunity for concert-platform projection. There is, in fact, an especial feeling of oneness in these duos, and this quality may well lessen their appeal to solo violinists. Furthermore, only a player of the most peculiar sensibility, able to nuance a continuously unostentatious yet deeply expressive melodic line with infinite gradation of dynamic and tempo, should attempt to play such music as the slow movement of the A minor Sonata, op. 105, well described by Joan Chissell as 'coming as near to human speech as music ever can'.[1]

The D minor Sonata, op. 121, is the more considerable of the two works. Its stormy first movement, thematically and emotionally, reminds us of the Piano Trio in the same key. Its main theme is especially strongly constructed: a six-bar phrase on the violin, restated with a two-bar overlap by the piano, crowned by a magnificent final six-bar phrase on the violin.

The other three movements of the D minor Sonata comprise a Brahmsian Scherzo (of a less than Brahmsian stature), a lovely Air with variations and episodes (culled from the Scherzo, as is the Air itself), and a quick Finale which reaches a somewhat overbright and unconvincing conclusion in the key of D major.

Schumann's remaining essay in this medium was a Sonata in A minor, two movements of which were written as a birthday tribute to Joachim upon a motto-

[1] *Robert Schumann* (Master Musician Series), p. 167, London, 1967.

theme 'F.A.E.' representing the intial letters of Joachim's personal motto: *Frei aber einsam* ('Free but alone'). These movements originally formed part of a composite sonata (known as the 'F.A.E.' Sonata) by Schumann, Dietrich and Brahms, the latter pair contributing the first movement and Scherzo respectively. Later, Schumann turned his contribution into a full-scale sonata, which was only published for the first time in 1956. Though shot here and there with a remarkable intensity of feeling, it is decidedly inferior to its two predecessors, with which it shares a lack of effectiveness due to a generally opaque texture. Its highlight is undoubtedly the *Intermezzo* (part of the original 'F.A.E.' Sonata), in which the motto is used as an *idée fixe*.

EX 18

Regrettably, the other movements do not reach this level, despite an impressive introduction to the first movement, a valiant attempt at a fiery Scherzo, and a conscientious injection of fugal development into the finale, in which Schumann's hard-won, and usually successfully-applied, contrapuntal skill degenerates, alas, into a series of inept gestures.

The Piano Trios (1847–51)

The three Piano Trios, unlike the String Quartets, were written over the space of several years and show the gradual decline of the powers of their composer.

The greatest of them, the first in D minor, op. 63 (1847), is a magnificent specimen of the romantic trio, on a par with one of its obvious models, Mendelssohn's in the same key. Amongst its many strokes of genius is the appearance, in the development of the first movement, of a new theme in a slower tempo.[1] Its inspirational highpoint, and one of the peaks of Schumann's inventiveness, is the theme of the slow movement.

EX 19

The close connection between the themes of the first and last movements of this Trio has already been pointed (see Ex. 15(a) and (b)). Comparison of Ex. 19 with these will demonstrate the no less deep kinship with the slow movement.

The Piano Trio No. 2, in F major, op. 80 (1847), though in my opinion inferior to the D minor, is none the less a remarkable and beautiful work. The first movement has generous proportions. One of its many highpoints is a beautiful middle theme at bar 106, whilst the development section which follows has some of the tautest, imitative counterpoint in Schumann's works (Ex. 20).

It cannot be denied that this Trio has its gaucheries of texture and, at one point at least, of harmony. I refer to the curious passage through the 'forbidden' region of the supertonic major in the first movement's second subject; forbidden

[1] The structural model for this was undoubtedly the famous 'episode' in the first movement of Beethoven's 'Eroica' symphony—arguably the most influential turning-point in the history of form. ED

EX 20

in the sense that the Classical masters normally avoided this key, except in its function as the dominant's dominant. Schubert, before Schumann, had managed to cadence in it with strangely beautiful effect during the main theme of the slow movement of his C major Quintet; Schumann, more boldly, moves directly to it in the first strain *via* the mediant minor. The effect is odd and, to me at least, unsatisfactory.

EX 21

At bar 80, however, in the continuation of this theme the richness is **more** digestible; but then, he avoids the crudity of D major.

EX 22

The Piano Trio in G minor, op. 110 (1851), which is dedicated to Niels Gade,★ belongs to the period of Schumann's increasing mental instability and shows a sad decline from the standard of the D minor Trio, written four years earlier. It is, however, unmistakably the work of a genius at such moments as the close of the first movement where there occurs one of Schumann's typical closing themes, which gradually loses its energy and passion until it becomes a mere suggestion on the piano.

EX 23

Too much of this Trio is bedevilled by Schumann's growing insensibility to instrumental timbre (e.g. in the Scherzo *passim*), and by his declining inventiveness (e.g. the creaking *fugato* in the development of the first movement, which introduces insignificant new material, a rarity for Schumann, who had an especial genius for significant new ideas at precisely the right moment). Almost throughout, the piano pegs away in its middle register (so beloved of Schumann, but so disastrous to him when he hadn't urgent things to say in it). One longs for the heights, for air, for silence; there is scarcely a rest from beginning to end! Yet it is impossible to dislike the work if one loves the man who wrote it, and there is not a phrase in it, good or bad, which is not manifestly the work of Schumann.

Piano Quartet in E flat major, op. 47 (1842)

Most musicians rate the Quartet below the Quintet. Yet is has many beauties, ranging from its Beethoven-ish introduction,

EX 24

interwoven into the subsequent Allegro—after the manner of Beethoven's own op. 127 Quartet—

EX 25

to its exquisite, if drably scored, Scherzo with two trios, the second of which is a typically Schumannesque essay in a metre so syncopated that the off-beats sound as on-beats.

EX 26

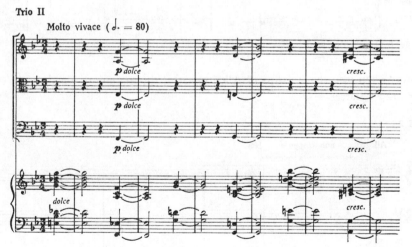

Its slow movement is famous for the direction to the 'cellist to tune his C string down to B flat ('Hier stimmt das Violoncello die C-Saite einen ton tiefer nach B'), which enables Schumann to produce the following beautiful harmonic progression, underpinned by a 'cello pedal.

The fugued Finale begins with a motif descended from another, greater fuga
Finale: that of the 'Jupiter' Symphony.

EX 28

The Finale of the Piano Quartet is a particularly original and successful attempt
to blend freedom of action with exactness of repetition in a way which leads us
right to the very core of Schumann's structural principles. It is an example of the
kind of prolongation of the proportions of sonata-form first achieved by Beethoven in such movements as the Finale of the Eighth Symphony and the First
Movement of op. 132, and, though it may be convenient to pigeon-hole all
that happens after bar 222 as 'coda', such unimaginative, procrustean efforts at a
uniformity of formal approach do scant justice to the extensive, noble proportions of Schumann's structure, for the classical form has here been extended into
something new by presenting us with an early solution of that ever-present
nineteenth-century problem: how to write longer movements without a lessen-
ing of comprehensibility, an obsession which reached its culmination in the vast
structures of Mahler's Symphonies.

Piano Quintet in E flat major, op. 44 (1842)

The Piano Quintet is one of the finest and most celebrated creations of what Niecks, Schumann's biographer, called 'the chamber music year', 1842. The String Quartets were finished in August; in September and October he wrote, in what must have been the white heat of inspiration, the Quintet. In December it was first performed, domestically, at the house of his friends the Voigts. Owing to Clara's being unwell,[1] the piano part was read, at sight, by Mendelssohn, who criticized the second trio as lacking liveliness. Schumann obliged his friend by later replacing it by another (see Ex. 40). The Quintet (and the Quartets) received considerable critical acclaim. Hauptmann, Cantor and Musical Director of St Thomas's School at Leipzig, and the foremost German critic of the day, wrote that 'these compositions are without reservation among the finest that recent times can show in this department . . . we have to admire anew the freedom and security with which he (Schumann) moves in a branch of composition new to him, as if he had been long accustomed to it'.

Most illuminating of all critical appraisals of the Quintet is, however, that of Tovey, who wrote:

> Schumann is writing an altogether new type of sonata-work; a kind that stands to the classical sonata somewhat as a very beautiful and elaborate mosaic stands to a landscape picture. In the mosaic the material and structure necessitate and render appropriate an otherwise unusual simplicity and hardness of outline and treatment, while at the same time making it desirable that the subjects should be such that this simple treatment may easily lend them subtlety of meaning—just as, on the other hand, the costly stones of which the mosaic is made have in themselves many exquisite gradations of shade and tone, though the larger contrasts and colours of the work as a connected whole are far more simple and obvious than those of a painting.[2]

The 'costly stones' of Schumann's mosaic form a chain of interrelated aphorisms organized into sonata and rondo structures. The broad, almost orchestral style of the string writing and the massive, dominating piano part seem so suitable a medium for what Schumann has to say that it is easy to forget that not only did he create in his Quintet a new kind of musical form, but also a new kind of instrumental style. As Tovey goes on to say in his remarkable essay: 'the orches-

[1] She was five months pregnant. Her second daughter, Elise, was born the following April. ED
[2] Tovey: Essays in Musical Analysis (Chamber Music, p. 150), London, 1944.

tral string parts of his concertos are, strangely enough, more exacting to play than those of the Quintet, so big is the sweep of the latter, so simple its method of rigid sequence and exact repetition.'

Schumann, so often ill at ease with a real orchestra, gives us in the Quintet that first real taste of an orchestra in the home which was to be a dominant aim of nineteenth-century chamber-music. That this was so may be due in part to the fact that, just as baroque orchestral and chamber-music share the same style (being in effect both chamber-like in texture), so the monumental symphonic style of the nineteenth century had to be reflected in *its* chamber-music. As usual in musical history, a multitude of factors—social, economic, mechanical, expressive and idiomatic created the situation; and it is illogical, therefore, to isolate one factor and make it responsible for musical style. None was more a child of his age than Schumann, and none wrote more typically contemporary music than he.

The piano in the Quintet provides not only the 'missing' wood-wind, brass and timpani parts, but also the concerto soloist. Yet it does so without descending into the accompanimental extravagances of Tchaikovsky's Trio in A minor, or rising to the virtuosic heights of Ravel's Trio, or getting involved in the stupefying complexities of Taneiev's Piano Quintet which contains perhaps the most exhaustingly responsible piano part in the whole literature of chamber-music. After all, Schumann knew better than anyone the piano's peculiar fitness for providing a background, discreet yet expressive, to lyrical melody. This attitude lies behind the Quintet. Look, for example, at those short telling introductory and linking piano phrases in Ex. 30(a) and Ex. 34, where the piano addresses the strings as if to say: 'I can only suggest it; you can actually do it.' The greatest moments in piano literature are often found in such passages of modest self-effacement.

The Quintet begins with a bold statement of the main idea, which is to dominate so much of the first movement.

EX 29

This theme, incidentally, is destined to return at the very end of the Quintet where it reappears in dazzling combination with the *Finale's* first subject (see Ex. 49).

Schumann's ability to invent new aphoristic forms of previous statements (one of the secrets of his method of development) is nowhere better exemplified than in the Quintet's first movement. The first subject not only yields a transition theme with an unmistakable family resemblance,

EX 30

but the transition theme itself goes on to produce a second subject (Ex. 32) with which it shares a common background. Compare its second and third bars with the piano's subsequent anticipation of the second subject,

EX 31

a theme which is immediately taken up in dialogue between 'cello and viola.

EX 32

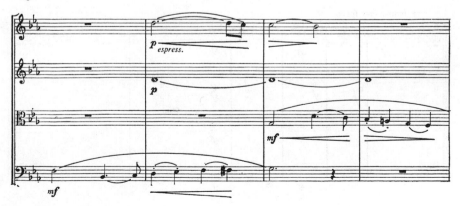

This, in turn, gives way to yet another off-shoot of the main idea, which exploits the octave motif first heard in Ex. 30.

EX 33

Seen in this light, Tovey's 'mosaic of costly stones' takes on a significant meaning, and suggests that Schumann pointed the way to a completely new type of melodic development.

The development section begins with an ominous transformation of the first subject by rhythmic variation and octave transposition. As usual with Schumann's sequential developments, the music strides through a wide gamut of keys; it is based exclusively on the first subject which, when treated in diminution, yields such 'new' piano figurations as this:

EX 34

The recapitulation is full and regular, a normal practice with Schumann.

The Second Movement 'In modo d'una marcia' is a rondo with sharply contrasted episodes. The rondo theme is in binary form and has an introductory phrase of peculiar poignancy which serves as a refrain and a coda to it as well,

EX 35

The melody of this section is based entirely upon a four-bar phrase of remarkable pithiness, even for Schumann. The sharp-eyed (and eared) may note the tell-tale falling fifth motif and compare it with the transition (Ex. 31). They may also remark that the theme of the first episode (functionally, the typical *maggiore* trio of any funeral march) is a kind of rhapsody upon the latter part of the Rondo theme.

EX 36

Like the Rondo theme itself, the melody of this episode is entirely based upon statements of one note-pattern of eight bars, and is cast in a similar binary mould.

The second episode is itself quite openly based upon a diminution of the Rondo theme used as an *idée fixe*.

Its stormy mood affects the next statement of the Rondo theme by leaving the piano still playing triplet quavers and interrupting the viola's statement of Ex. 35 with Ex. 37 on violin and 'cello. Schumann also reveals its strong sub-dominant colouring by allowing the key-signature of four flats to persist, despite the tune still being in C minor. At bar 132 the first episode (Ex. 36) returns in the *sub-dominant* major, as if to confirm our suspicions. It is as if consolation, which in the tonic major seemed too immediate to be convincing, is now too distant to be of much effect. The whole restatement, in fact, has something of the quality of reminiscence rather than direct experience.

The final appearance of the Rondo theme is, in fact, pitched unequivocally in the sub-dominant key to begin with, and only manages to reach the tonic C minor at the end of its first strain. One 'neapolitan' stab of remorse on the second fiddle (at bar 187) prevents the coda from achieving complete tranquillity in the tonic major.

The opening theme of the Scherzo consists of a simple scale pattern of two-bars length repeated incessantly throughout, and occasionally set against a descending trochaic phrase, whose short notes are sometimes tied over to the long ones to produce a characteristically Schumannesque syncopation.

EX 38

The first Trio, canonic in texture, is based mostly upon the motif of a falling fifth, already observed so often in this work,

EX 39

Trio I

and the second Trio (itself a miniature five-section rondo), by filling out the fifth with semi-quavers, creates a contrasting episode of great vigour and character.

EX 40

The Scherzo is unvaried on its two restatements, but Schumann adds a coda which, in its last six bars, harks back to the theme of the first Trio (Ex. 39) and looks forward to the main theme of the Finale (Ex. 42(a)) which is just about to break upon us.

EX 41

The Finale, a sonata rondo, is one of the earliest examples in music of 'progressive tonality', that is, a structure which moves from one key to another, rather than on an excursion to and from the home key. Later romantic composers, particularly Mahler and Nielsen, were to use this device as a rule; in the early nineteenth century it was still exceptional, though there are one or two examples of themes which reach their tonic from a neighbouring region—for example, those of Mendelssohn's 'Wedding March' and the finale of Beethoven's second 'Rasumovsky' Quartet. In such cases, it is, of course, a much less drastic extension of the principle of 'progressive tonality' than that of basing a whole movement on such a device. Schumann only reaches his tonic *qua* tonic at the third appearance of his main theme, since both previous appearances have given it the effect of being in a secondary and contrasting key. It is doubtful whether in a single, detached movement Schumann would have used such a scheme. In a work of several movements, however, where the listener has been firmly orientated towards an E flat tonic, there can be no kind of bafflement, merely a delighted surprise at the freshness of the G minor theme with which he begins his Finale. Furthermore, a musical listener will positively enjoy the battle for the establishment of the tonic.

The main theme has two chief, alternating ideas: one in the mediant minor (Ex. 42(a)), and the other in the tonic (Ex. 42(b)), which here sounds like the submediant region of G minor.

EX 42

These two ideas are at once restated in the keys of D minor and B flat major respectively, further eroding our sense of the home key of E flat, which is, in fact, not to be established until the recapitulation.

The second subject appears, without a transition. It has two elements: the first (Ex. 43) derived by diminution from Ex. 42(b);

EX 43

the second (Ex. 44) by inversion.

EX 44

Both are pitched clearly and unequivocally in the key of G, which strikes us, as far as the course of this movement hitherto is concerned, as the region of the tonic major (!).

The exposition closes in G major with a restatement of the first part of the main theme, in rondo fashion, in the key of B minor (G major's mediant) and immeasurably distant from the home key of the whole work. A new idea (Ex. 45) is now introduced, a solemn cadencing phrase in B major based upon a major form of the root progression underlying Ex. 42(a).

EX 45

There follows a wonderfully poetic transition which takes us into a restatement of the viola theme of Ex. 44 beneath a new melody on the violin.

EX 46

Of course this melody is not new, only apparently new. A glance at the first violin's part in the transition passage shows us its evolution: two cells at bars 102 and 105

EX 47

which come together at bar 115 to form Ex. 46. The next appearance of the main theme is in the key of G sharp minor (B major's submediant). The former alternating course of this tune is altered by an unexpected transposition of Ex. 46 into the local dominant (D sharp minor), which enharmonically is, of course, the tonic minor (E flat) and smooths the way for the second subject in the home tonic (at last!).

Schumann still plays upon our tonal senses, however, for the next appearance of his main subject is back in the key of G minor in which it first appeared. But not for long. He is reminiscing, and roughly casts us back into the tonic a few bars later. Then comes one of those inspired 'new' themes so often introduced by Schumann in his codas.

EX 48

This has the gavotte-like metre of all the material of this movement, but perhaps belongs most closely to the family of Ex. 46 though it bears traces of Ex. 42 too.

The Finale culminates in a highly original fugato, which draws in the threads of the entire Quintet. It is heralded by a grand dominant pause, and we hear the main theme of the first movement sounding as a kind of *cantus firmus* against the main theme of the last.

EX 49

The effect is of the closing stages of a three-voice *fugue d'école*: stretto, pedal point and so on. The tonic is never far distant. Schumann shows exquisite judgment, however, in not finishing fugally, for that would have been out of character with the work as a whole.

*   *   *

In conclusion let us consider the total importance of Schumann's chamber-music in terms of the influence it had upon his contemporaries and successors. Schumann was, perhaps, after Wagner and Liszt, the greatest single influence in nineteenth-century music, and despite the fact that he was so often considered inexpert in the art of writing for instruments other than the piano, this influence is nowhere more clearly demonstrable than in the case of his chamber-music. There is a case to be made for the view that, if his own chamber-music had not been so piano-thick, and his own influence not so immediate and dominating, his nineteenth-century successors might have come more under the sway of the limpid textures of Beethoven and Mozart. In fact, they had no choice but to seek inspiration from Schumann, because he had shown them a way to write music in a contemporary manner, contact with which could bring none other than immediate enslavement. *His* sonata-forms, rather than Beethoven's, were the model for Tchaikovsky, Smetana, Grieg, Fauré and a host of lesser composers. They had to be, because, in adopting Schumann's lyrical style and, with it, a tendency to compose in aphorisms, they (no doubt unconsciously) found themselves unable to think in terms of the classical sonata. The fascinating exception is Schumann's great friend Brahms. Though in terms of texture, mood and idiom clearly much influenced by the older composer, he alone of Schumann's disciples was able to make a compromise with the classical sonata method with its emphasis on the complete whole, the indivisible total melody, rather than on a series of intense but musical statements.

It has sometimes been said that the predilection of so many nineteenth-century composers for writing almost entirely in four-bar phrases was due to Schumann's example. A study of Schumann in depth, however, shows him to have depended less upon the four-bar phrase-length than might previously have been supposed. It is true that his best-known chamber-work, the Piano Quintet, depends almost entirely on phrasing in multiples of four bars; but many of the other, lesser-known works contain all kinds of fascinating inflections of this basic, commonplace, but not necessarily banal procedure. A study of the Five 'cello pieces, Op. 102, is enough to show how interested Schumann was in all kinds of phrase-length, and there are other examples quoted in this essay. Schumann is, in fact, no small, one-method composer. He is one of the greatest geniuses of the nineteenth century, albeit a flawed one. His faults, however, are inseparable from his virtues. That which made him cling to the middle compass rather than the extremities of an instrument also gave him his homely eloquence, his gentleness. His lack of virtuosity in scoring likewise enhances the *intrinsic* value of what he has to say; and his occasional ineffectiveness forces our attention upon the actual content of his musical message. In an era which had more than its fair share of charlatans, Schumann's essential goodness and honesty shone forth like a beacon for all to see. That was the opinion of his contemporaries, certainly; for what other composer was beloved alike by Mendelssohn, Liszt, Alkan, Grieg, Tchaikovsky, Brahms, Debussy and Mahler? One thing to all men. That is Schumann.

ALFRED NIEMAN

The Concertos

Introduction

APART from the Piano Concerto in A minor, Schumann's works for
solo instruments and orchestra have not generally been given the place
at least four of them deserve. The Concertstück for four horns and orchestra
(1849), a brilliant concerto despite its name, and the posthumous Violin Concerto
(1853), are cruelly neglected. True, the Cello Concerto (1850), which is still a
great work despite its flaws, is more often given an airing; but the splendid
Introduction and Allegro Appassionato for piano and orchestra (1849), one of
Schumann's masterpieces, seldom finds a place in any programme whatsoever. The
Violin Concerto, in fact, has been held up to a curious kind of scorn, probably
because it is judged (as a leftover from the nineteenth century) in terms of
Beethoven, or worse, against the determined craftsmanship of Brahms. Such an
attitude is guaranteed to miss the flow of intimate poetry of which Schumann was
a master, for the key to his strength lies in his deep lyric impulse enriched by a
sensuous awareness of the half-lights in harmony.

It would not be illogical to consider these works as belonging to a 'second
period' when Schumann was attracted to the challenge of big forms, the first
period embracing the unique piano works composed before his marriage in 1840.
Those early pieces lived freely, and timelessly, in a vivid crystallization of childhood's fantasy images. They reacted sharply against the traditional Germanic
background of solemn, square shapes and folk-song influences. Later, even in the
discipline of sonata form, they still retained the quintessence of his evocative
imagination. But what of the concertos, the 'challenge of big forms'? They represented a completely new departure for Schumann, and there are still musicians,
even among his most ardent admirers, who maintain that these works reveal a
creative decline. Many reasons are advanced in support of this observation—his

association with the 'Leipzig School', the influence of Mendelssohn, Clara's insistence on turning him into a 'symphonist'—but perhaps none is more foolish than the fact that, by an unhappy coincidence, they were all composed during the last decade of his life when he was in the grip of a long, distressing, and ultimately fatal illness, which, from time to time, undoubtedly paralysed his creative faculties and was at least partly responsible for a 'falling off' in quality of certain works. Anyone who is intimately acquainted with these concertos, however, will find them difficult to reconcile with the 'falling off' theory, which seems to have been put about by those critics of Schumann's later style who, disappointed that the master was not content to go on repeating his early successes, are only too happy to blame his mental decline for the appearance of works they themselves fail to understand. Is it not irrational to go on looking for the earlier master in the later one? The concertos represent a new stylistic direction for Schumann which is there to be understood.

The chief argument in the past against Schumann's large-scale forms, like those of Chopin, was really based on the recognition of the tremendous achievement and significance of Beethoven—particularly the Beethoven of the 'Eroica' Symphony, with its epoch-making first movement, which carried motivic development to new heights. In fact, the whole nineteenth-century tradition of intense, organic development has sprung from the 'Eroica', and only in the new music of today, in the Post Webern School, are new concepts replacing this. Every textbook since Beethoven has emphasized the need for small motifs, ideas and figures, to be worked out in sonata form. Tunes are a disadvantage: they offer little scope for the organic process of development. As almost every composer up to Webern has followed this line, historians tend to take organic development for granted, and anything else as weakness. The Viennese Classics have become a religion, and the creative idea of integrating large *melodic* concepts into sonata form some kind of heresy. Yet, ironically, the success of Schumann's Piano Concerto lies, as much as anything, in the strikingly unconventional use of melodic variation in the development section. Consider his first subject,

EX I

and the way it is then 'developed' in what is practically a monothematic composition.

EX 2

This is melodic re-creation, hardly 'development' in the conventional sense. It means, most of the time, side-stepping the principle of small motifs 'worked out' textbook-fashion, in favour of long melodic lines which largely avoid the rhythmic possibilities inherent in small motifs. Even the Concerto's 'second subject' is merely a different version of the same idea.

EX 3

If Schumann was split between Florestan and Eusebius, he was also a genius struggling with the angel of tradition. He approached the concerto with respect, and lamented the fact that his contemporaries treated such a noble form so casually. Once, when reviewing a concerto by Döhler, he wrote: 'If one works with so great an art form, before which even the best in the land are timid, he should know what he is doing.'[1] Schumann, like Schubert before him, in fact, had to strive to re-create the Classical past in terms of his Romantic present. And the past can be a source of inspiration only when sufficiently absorbed to be forgotten, which creatively is its only value. His reward was to find a large-scale synthesis between past and present which makes the piano and violin concertos, and the Introduction and Allegro Appassionato unique. At the heart of this synthesis is full-blooded melodic material, and its re-creation. This aspect of Schumann's creative character has suffered much criticism mostly in the finale of the Violin Concerto. As we shall see, the variety and ingenuity of presentation to be found there, as well as the irresistible charm of the material, weakens such criticism which itself will soon run the risk of being misunderstood.

[1] NZfM, 4 (1836), 83.

It is in the important aspect of thematic unity that Schumann's concertos differ markedly from the classics. Unity within diversity is intuitive with all good composers. But Schumann went further in *consciously* integrating themes from one movement into another, using them as links, and transplanting them from one movement to another. The Cello Concerto provides a telling example, the first movement's main idea

EX 4

returning to haunt the closing bars of the slow movement.

EX 5

A more subtle example, frequently overlooked even by professional analysts, occurs in the Violin Concerto. The slow movement begins with this syncopated 'rocking' theme in the 'cellos.

EX 6

Later on, in the Finale, Schumann transforms this theme into a counterpoint to the second subject.

ROBERT SCHUMANN (*c.* 1835)
an unidentified oil portrait

ROBERT SCHUMANN IN
SILHOUETTE

ROBERT SCHUMANN (1847)
a lithograph by Kaiser

EX 7

Schubert had already shown the way in the 'Wanderer' Fantasy. This new dimension of *conscious* overall unity found its logical outcome in the thematic 'metamorphosis' of Liszt's concertos and, ultimately, in Schoenberg's technique of 'developing variation'. But let us be clear in pointing out Schumann's historic role in all this.

Concerto for Piano and Orchestra in A minor, Op. 54 (1845)

It would be impossible to guess, on musical grounds, that the first movement of the Piano Concerto was ever a separate piece. Yet Schumann composed it four years before the rest of the work in 1841, and aptly called the result a 'Fantasie'. It was not until 1845, in Dresden, during May and July, that the two additional movements appeared, forming the Concerto we now know.[1] He must surely have carried the whole work unconsciously in his head, in embryo, waiting for the right time to give it birth.

For Schumann, and for his time, the Concerto represents the boldest kind of

---

[1] Clara gave the first performance at a Gewandhaus concert in Leipzig on 1 January 1846.

I

experiment. There is no orchestral exposition, no new second subject. In one sense, the work is almost monothematic. Schumann throws the burden of the entire structure on to the opening melody of the first movement. Added to this is his imaginative use of chamber-musical elements in the scoring, which throughout is masterly.[1] Above all, this is not a virtuoso's concerto, but a musician's. It is Schumann's 'reply' to the nineteenth-century's 'gladiators of the keyboard' and their empty showpieces, a form of music-making which was rife in his day, and which he detested.

Immediately after the fiery introduction

EX 8

which is to show itself again in the Development, the principal subject enters in the orchestra, to be answered, and completed, by the soloist.

EX 9

[1] In a prophetic article on piano concertos which Schumann had published a year or two earlier in the *Neue Zeitschrift*, he wrote: 'And so we must await the genius who will show us in a newer and more brilliant way, how orchestra and piano may be combined, how the

A haunting, unforgettable subject; and how interesting! There is so much rhythmic variety; every bar, apart from the first and the third, is rhythmically different. The opening ('X') is an ending; an odd, fascinating way to begin indeed. What a wonderful subject this might have been for Beethoven, though he would not have conceived the work in such lyric terms. The transition theme, for all that, has a breadth which recalls the fourth and fifth piano concertos of Beethoven.

EX 10

The metrical displacement of this theme (the bar-lines sound a beat earlier than

soloist, dominant at the keyboard, may unfold the wealth of his instrument and his art, while the orchestra, no longer a mere spectator, may interweave its manifold facets into the scene.' (NZf M, 1839.) This was destined to be Schumann himself. ED

you actually see them) is characteristic of Schumann. It was taken up and developed seriously by Brahms, his greatest 'pupil'.[1]

An off-shoot of the transition theme

EX II

yields this ear-enchanting passage.

EX 12

It gives the lie to those critics who maintain that Schumann was insensitive to piano textures.

The second subject is heralded by a transposed version of the principal theme. How happily this theme now functions in the major mode.

EX 13

I have described this theme as 'haunting', and that is true in a deeper sense. Years later, it reappeared like an apparition in the little-known Introduction and Allegro in D minor (Op. 134).

[1] See, for example, the transition theme in the first movement of Brahms's Second Symphony. See, also, Vázsonyi (p. 79). ED

EX 14

It is as if Schumann were unconsciously reminiscing about his pianistic master-work.

The second subject proper re-creates the main idea, and gives rise to a long, warm stream of melody, the clarinet and piano urging each other on.

EX 15

An orchestral tutti, based on Ex. 11, sweeps forward. As the vigour falls away, the music slips stealthily from C major to C minor, closing the Exposition quietly in the distant key of A flat major.

Hypnotically, in slow 6/4 time, Schumann begins the Development with a new version of what is now *the* theme in tender meditative dialogue with the woodwind.

EX 16

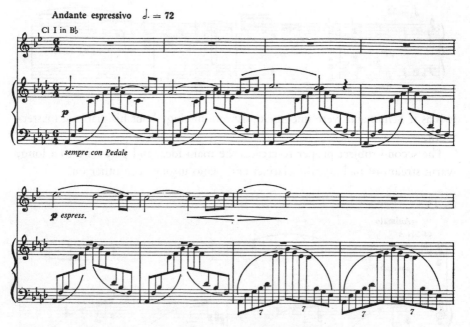

Its chamber-musical aura has been well-described by Sir Henry Wood in his account of a performance of the Concerto, with Paderewski as soloist.

> The moment he was seated he addressed me in the gentlest manner possible: 'Mr Wood, will you permit me to suggest that you move your first clarinet to a position where I can see him?' I made the requested adjustment and Paderewski appeared to devote himself to *accompanying* the flute, oboe and clarinet solos of the Schumann concerto. I do not think that these sections of that beautiful work have ever been played in quite the same manner since . . .

Suddenly the dialogue erupts into vehemence with the startling return of the Introduction—now a reason for fierce argument. Powerful piano octaves sweep everything away into a return, this time marked 'Passionato', of the main theme. Irresistible new eloquence pours from the melody.

EX 17

The sustained *melodic* invention marks out the unconventional nature of this Development, as does the philosophical fall through chromatic harmonies into the Recapitulation.

The Cadenza is one of the most remarkable to come out of the nineteenth century. It is like an improvisation, which is how a good cadenza should feel, even to introducing what appears to be two new ideas, one expressive, the other boldly brassy:

EX 18

It has fine piano writing and sensitive arabesque, yet it is not a virtuoso cadenza; in itself this is unusual for a pianist, and for this period, did we not already know Schumann's dislike of the common bravura of his contemporaries and his scathing comments on their emptiness. The principal subject, beneath right hand trills, brings a hushed atmosphere, and gradually leads to a trill on the dominant in which the orchestra enters, moving headlong into an extended Coda—a speeded-up version of the main idea.

EX 19

The central movement, which Schumann calls 'Intermezzo', with its child-like simplicity and warmth, is set off wonderfully against the strong first movement.

EX 20

Its simple ternary form hides great ingenuity of structure, particularly in this opening, nine-bar sentence. I know of few more mysterious metrical riddles lying beneath such spontaneity and grace. Do you hear this a-symmetrical sentence as 5×4, or as 6×3? The material derives from the rhythm of bracket 'Y', in the Concerto's opening theme (see Ex. 9).

EX 21

The second subject is born quite imperceptibly from the first. Compare Ex. 22 with Ex. 20 bracket 'Z'.

EX 22

Like all great art, the re-creation of the one idea from the other seems perfectly natural and spontaneous. The mood is one of 'recollection in tranquillity', and avoids any overtones of tragedy.

After the return of Ex. 21 we hear a 'cyclic' re-appearance of the Concerto's opening idea, which Schumann uses as an exit into the Finale. The almost archetypal sound of the 'horn-like' fifths comes like magic to the ears.

EX 23

The Finale's main subject is closely modelled on that of the first movement.

EX 24

This movement fairly teems with ideas, and its joyous vitality has a masculine strength and power. An exhilarating transition flies along, with dancing piano figuration, into the famous syncopated rhythm beginning the second group, which has caused the downfall of more than one over-confident conductor.

EX 25

It is yet another case, so frequent in Schumann, of seeing the bar-lines in one place and hearing them in another. The true metre of this passage is 3/2 time ‖: ♩ ♩ ♩.♩: ‖ etc., and that is what the listener hears, unless he happens to observe the 'click' of the conductor's baton marking off the 'missing' bar-lines. The problem becomes quite ticklish when, a few bars later, the orchestra become 'listeners', and the pianist syncopates.

EX 26

Heralding the Development with the first subject, an unexpected fugato appears. Academic dress is not worn for long, however; its attempts at solemnity dissolve into a gay piano and orchestra.

EX 27

There seems no limit to the richness of the Development and the fertility of the ideas. The inter-penetration of the basic shapes 'X', 'Y', and 'Z' into the melodic material appears like a fountain of inspired improvisation.

The 'easy' recapitulation, from subdominant to the second group in the tonic (a practice so beloved of Schubert), is in no sense a symptom of flagging inspiration. It is a carefully calculated manœuvre which throws the subsequent, discourse-sounding Coda into the sharpest possible relief.

EX 28

Even here, the basic idea heard singing its way beneath all the piano figuration clearly springs from Ex. 24. Re-write it like this, and the connection becomes obvious.

EX 29

The touch of the finale is irresistible. One of its secrets lies in the variety of its harmonic rhythm, which traces large spans across the bar lines, alternating with quick changes. Suspensions and dissonances, too, stimulate the ear in a seemingly reckless flow of enharmonic changes that Schubert would have loved. That so much melody has been made to come from so few sources justifies this great concerto being seen as a landmark in Romantic music. It has something to teach us even today.

Concerstück for Four Horns and Orchestra, in F major, Op. 86 (1849)

The year 1849, which was the last Schumann was to spend in Dresden before taking up his ill-fated conducting post in Düsseldorf, must have been an unusual one for him. Free of illness, he composed some thirty compositions, including major works like the Introduction and Allegro Appassionato, the whole of *Manfred,* apart from the Overture written the year before, and the Concertstück for four horns and orchestra. No wonder he referred to this period as 'My most fruitful year'.

The neglect of this noble, high-spirited work is inexplicable. Despite its title, the 'Concertstück' is a fully-fledged concerto, with three linked movements. If Schumann had, in fact, called it a 'Concerto', the work might well have acquired a popular following; the music certainly justifies it. Owing to one of those perversities of history, however, it seems to be cast into limbo, from where it used occasionally to be resurrected by Schumann enthusiasts such as Sir Thomas Beecham; but in recent years it seems hardly to have been performed at all. It is written for the modern chromatic valve-horn, an instrument Schumann may have been inspired to write for by the horn virtuoso Lewy who led the horn section of the Dresden Royal Orchestra. If he felt any qualms about handling the large score, which includes a piccolo, two 'hand' horns, three trombones, and four horn soloists, no sign emerges in the writing. The orchestra plays throughout a rich and varied part, which would have made Wagner think very differently about Schumann had he but heard this work.[1]

The work begins with two introductory chords in the first bar. In come the four horns with the first subject, a splendid and noble fanfare opening.

EX 30

The writing ranges in style from the lyrical to the virtuosic, the quite frequent appearance of top F's (concert pitch) being surpassed at the end of the first movement's recapitulation with this daunting top A.

EX 31

[1] The chances that he did so are, of course, remote. By May 1849 Wagner found himself on the run from the authorities for his part in the Dresden uprising. ED

This movement contains music that has not only enriched the horn repertoire, but the language of music itself. Such textures as the following,

EX 32

a veritable chemistry of singing phrases and skilful design, clearly illustrates Brahms's debt to Schumann.

Schumann calls the second movement 'Romanze'. It is notable for the broad, sensuous melody of its middle section,

EX 33

which turns up again in the finale in this thematic transformation.

EX 34

There are impressionistic images in the finale not far removed from *A Midsummer Night's Dream*, woven together with effortless spontaneity. Nothing stands between the sheer wit of this happy movement and the listener, who cannot but be stimulated by its vivacity. In the closing section there is a wicked cadential flourish which Schumann marks 'Mit Bravour'. And so it sounds!

Although on paper the orchestration seems thick with doubling, in performance the scoring comes off more effectively than one might anticipate. Schumann may be wiser than us with our hindsight. In these days of first-rate horn players the Concertstück should be a common favourite.

Introduction and Allegro Appassionato in G major, Op. 92, for Piano and Orchestra (1849)

It is significant that the Allegro Appassionato was written immediately after *Manfred*. It is possible to go further and say that Schumann could hardly have written the piece at all without the soaking in Byron he gave himself and the inspiration he received from that unique mixture of fantasy and humanism which leaps from Byron's pages.[1] Everything conspired to influence Schumann to materialize his deeper heroic visions, Byronically consummated, into an instrumental work. What more natural instrument than his own—the piano—with orchestra? Sketched between 18 and 20 September the composition fairly flew along, and was completed on 26 September, including the scoring.

Its opening is the very opposite of the introductory flourish of the Piano Concerto, beginning, as it were, as if in a trance, as part of something already happening.

---

[1] Clara's Diary reports that after finishing *Genoveva* in November 1848 Robert began *Manfred*, 'a new work, a kind of melodrama, by Byron, that inspired him extraordinarily'. Shortly afterwards, we find him setting Byron's *Hebrew Melodies* (Op. 95) for voice and piano. It was against this background that the composition of the Allegro Appassionato unfolded.

EX 35

The piano writing throughout is superb. Did Schumann ever compose badly for the instrument?

The lengthy introduction gives way to the Allegro, which begins with a grand, heroic gesture by the full orchestra, answered, concertante-style, by the solo pianist.

The key of E minor suddenly folds into C major, with a caressing melody fore-shadowing the romantic sultriness of Rachmaninov.

EX 36

EX 37

My only criticism of this otherwise spotless composition lies in the cautious scoring of the recapitulation. It is a pity that Schumann does not allow his first violins to soar, in this climactic passage, an octave higher, where they seem to belong at this point. Tchaikovsky would surely not have thrown away such an opportunity!

Robert Schauffler's dismissal of the work as 'one of Schumann's least-inspired compositions'[1] can only be understood if we assume that he had never heard it. Like the other two works I have so far discussed in this essay, I regard it as a key to the mature Schumann, his second period after 1840, when he was battling with varying degrees of success to conquer the high places of symphony, concerto and drama. Its melodic richness and concentrated thought, place it as the first great one-movement work in this genre.[2]

Cello Concerto in A minor, Op. 129 (1850)

If Schumann's Cello Concerto is not flawless, its intuitive lyricism places it among the few 'cello masterpieces that command universal recognition. So much of the work is original and daring for Schumann's time. There is no orchestral exposition; the three movements are linked together; the cadenza is accompanied; there is a 'cyclic' reappearance of the main theme. It is the first great concerto ever composed for the solo 'cello, and that makes it historically important too. Small wonder that Casals, its greatest exponent, thought so highly of it.

> Corredor: Many biographers content themselves merely with noting the existence of the Cello Concerto.
>
> Casals: It must be because they fail to see the interest and the value of this work. It is one of the finest works one can hear—from beginning to end the music is sublime.[3]

Schumann himself described the work as really 'a Concert Piece for 'cello with orchestral accompaniment'.[4] That does not mean that the orchestra is robbed of its rôle of deploying an argument against the soloist in true concerto style; it simply means, as Tovey pointed out, that 'the scoring of this concerto is . . . remarkably free from the dangerous thickness of Schumann's usual orchestral style'.[5] Begun on 10 November 1850 shortly after Schumann's arrival in Düsseldorf, where he went to take up the conductorship of the orchestra, the Concerto

[1] Schauffler: *Florestan: the life and work of Robert Schumann*, p. 429.
[2] Liszt's one-movement concertos came later. ED
[3] J. M. A. Corredor: *Conversations with Casals*, p. 146 (London, 1956).
[4] In his own catalogue of works.
[5] *Essays in Musical Analysis*, Vol. 3, p. 185.

was finished in the remarkably short space of two weeks. Shrouded in mystery is the fact that there is no record of a performance anywhere until 1860, when it was played by Ludwig Ebert at the Leipzig Conservatoire.

The curtains are drawn back with four telling bars in the orchestra, and the solo 'cello begins the narrative.

EX 38

The melody is one of Schumann's finest. Was there an unconscious memory of the Piano Concerto? The opening rhythm is the same. The passionate, downward sweep, after the upward-rising tension of the first two bars, gives the long sentence a sustained eloquence which, towards the end, almost approaches the declamatory character of speech. The second subject is full of Romantic imagery; the 'longing' minor sevenths, the appoggiaturas, and the suspensions were to become the common language of Wagner, and even early Schoenberg.

EX 39

Such a powerful theme, which speaks from the very heart of the 'cello, makes it hard to fathom the criticism, still advanced, that the concerto is misconceived for the instrument.[1] Anyone who has listened to Casals's interpretation knows this observation to be unfounded. True, there are certain awkwardnesses, but

[1] Schumann played the 'cello in his youth. After the accident to his right hand he wrote to his mother from Leipzig on 6 November 1832: 'I am for my part completely resigned. . . . In Zwickau I will take up the violoncello again (for which only the left hand is needed) which besides is very useful for symphonic compositions . . .'

Schumann can hardly be blamed for effectively separating the great 'cellists from those who are merely good. Tovey was surely right in thinking that the days when this work was regarded as a thankless task are long since over.

The Development is full of incident, enough to please any classicist. A triplet figure, first heard in the second group, takes on the sinister quality among violas and second violins, sternly punctuated by the orchestra.

EX 40

The 'cello steps in with a moving plea for peace; and in this play of tensions, a new idea ('Y') enters below the 'cellist's principal subject.

EX 41

The rhythm of 'Y' is hypnotically taken up by the solo 'cello, and spreads menacingly. The horn attempts to revive the principal subject—a beautiful moment this—and the 'cello, reminded, makes a determined effort to recapitulate in F sharp minor. It is violently put off stroke by the orchestra. Another agitated attempt dissolves into groping triplets, literally wandering into the recapitulation which, when it does come is extraordinarily unexpected, as though Schumann had taken himself by surprise! Changes in the transition lead the second group into the tonic major. The coda is left to the orchestra, with the pugnacious triplet figure agitating the atmosphere, but a masterly touch comes with a cyclic return to the 'curtain' chords

EX 42

and the 'cello serenely leads the way into the slow movement. Here is the distilled essence of Schumann. It is a song for 'cello, bringing to the surface the dreamer that is in us all. Deriving from the German tradition of folk-song, its feeling is quite different from that of Schubert and Beethoven, its inwardness betraying the private world of the child.

EX 43

The listener to this tender movement will not find double stops on the 'cello written more simply and with more inward imagination. A haunting interlude in which the first movement is recalled breaks the spell, and the 'cello speeds into the finale. A blunt, strong rhythm in the orchestra is answered by the 'cello with an equally direct gesture, 'Z'.

EX 44

It is in this movement that Schumann's invention falters. The weakness comes in the development section. For a reason probably associated with the terse figure of 'Z', Schumann turned back to a language not his own, but to the sequential clichés and formulae of the eighteenth century. The development begins promisingly enough after a brief tutti which drops from C to B major. The horns enter with an echo of the first movement's principal subject but the 'cello seems wholly obsessed with figure 'Z'. The real interest lies in the orchestra and the curiously classical thinking, meaning also the harmonic progressions. The obsession with figure 'Z' frustrates the instinctive poet and singer that is in Schumann, creating a hard-driven metrical energy with no bloom.

The accompanied cadenza, introduced just before the finale's Coda, is a stroke of great originality which goes far to redeem the rest of the movement. As far as I can discover, it is the first time that a cadenza had ever been placed at this unique structural juncture, and the lesson was not lost on Elgar who followed Schumann's stimulating example when he himself came to write his violin concerto—where the cadenza not only turns up in the finale, but like Schumann's is also accompanied.

EX 45

The finale poses many questions not really possible to discuss here, including the contradictory tendencies we call style, and the possibility of too rapid composition.

Violin Concerto in D minor (1853)

Truth, they say, is stranger than fiction. The mysterious circumstances surrounding the recent discovery of Schumann's Violin Concerto might have been conceived by Hoffman. Yet as we can see now there is no doubting the extra-ordinary sequence of events which brought the work to light from the obscurity in which it had remained hidden for seventy years. The appearance of psychic phenomena makes the story seem even more bizarre, especially to those people who prefer 'material' explanations in life.

Schumann began the Violin Concerto on 21 September 1853. On 1 October he recorded in his diary that 'the concerto for violin is finished' and on 3 October that it was 'completely orchestrated'. Altogether a mere thirteen days! A letter to Joachim shows that the work was written with Joachim in mind.

> Dear Joachim—Herewith you will receive the concerto; may it please you. It seems to me to be easier than the Fantasie and the orchestra has more to do. I should be very glad if we could hear it at our first performance here . . .[1]

Joachim began by greeting the work warmly, but later developed reservations. He certainly influenced Clara by expressing doubts about the finale. In October 1857 he wrote to Clara complaining of 'dreadful passages for the violin' in the last movement. He was clearly referring to problems of violin technique. The next month Clara wrote asking if he—Joachim—would rewrite the finale. What Joachim did was to try the work out at a Gewandhaus rehearsal at Leipzig early in 1858, with disastrous results.

The final decision not to publish the Concerto in the supplementary volume of the *Breitkopf Gesamtausgabe* edited by Brahms is recorded by Schumann's youngest daughter Eugenie.

> Never shall I forget the moment in our home in Frankfurt-on-Main when my mother came in to us and said with deep but suppressed emotion on her face 'I have just settled with Joachim and Johannes (Brahms) that the con-certo is not to be published, not now, or at any time. We are quite agreed on the subject.'[2]

An amazing silence spread over the disgraced work until, on 5 August 1898, Joachim replied to a letter from his biographer Moser, who was enquiring about the 'lost' concerto, that the work was never published because 'it is not equal in rank with so many of his [Schumann's] glorious creations'. He also gave his opinions on the merits and shortcomings of the work. Apart from other reasons,

[1] Moser: *Joseph Joachim*, p. 138, London, 1901. George Schunemann in the preface to his edition of the Concerto (Schott, 1937) confirmed that a copy of the score was found in Joachim's effects and that it had been corrected in several places.

[2] *The Times*, 15 January 1938.

such opinions must be suspect in one who performed the far inferior *Fantasie* with never a word of criticism on record, a work hardly to be ranked as 'glorious'. The manuscript left with Joachim eventually passed to his eldest son Johannes. He in turn sold it to the Prussian State Library in Berlin with the proviso that it was not to be played or published until one hundred years after Schumann's death.

It is very hard for us to look back on such goings-on without feeling wonderment, to say the least, at such authoritarian pomposity and misguided complacency which reflects so much of the moral attitudinizing of the nineteenth century. One does not doubt for a moment Joachim's loyalty to Schumann, but there is every reason to think that the master, very much alive in that part of heaven reserved for dedicated composers, might very well be annoyed, if the rules of heaven permit this, at the fate of the Violin Concerto while the *Fantasie* is alive and—well, at least published.

The events that followed concerned the sisters, Adela and Jelly D'Aranyi, particularly Jelly, both very well known in London's concert life as internationally distinguished violinists. They were also great-nieces of Joachim. When great-uncle Joseph died in 1907, Adela was twenty-one, and Jelly fourteen. Though a number of people knew about the Violin Concerto, and though it is mentioned in Moser's biography of Joachim and Wasielewski's *Schumann*, both girls were completely unaware of its existence. This was stated, and put into writing—a wise precaution in the light of subsequent happenings.

Jelly d'Aranyi had a strong psychic gift, one which a medium would describe as a 'sensitive'. In March 1933, while she was taking part in the well-known game of playing with the glass (consisting of an upturned tumbler in the centre of a circle of alphabetical letters, in which messages purporting to come from the departed spirits are spelt out by the moving glass), a message was received from an unknown sender who declared that he was anxious for Miss d'Aranyi to find, and play, an unpublished work of his for violin. When asked his name, the answer came: Robert Schumann![1] This disconcerting reply created confusion as no one present knew what the work could be. Subsequent enquiries then revealed the existence of the Violin Concerto, but even Tovey (who was consulted) did not know whether it still existed—let alone where it might be found. The

[1] By an odd coincidence, Schumann himself had disclosed an interest in spiritualism. In 1853, he had developed an obsession for 'table-tipping'. He wrote to Hiller on 25 April:

> Yesterday for the first time we tipped tables. A wonderful force! Just think, I asked it how the rhythm of the first two measures of the C minor Symphony went. It hesitated longer than usual before answering. At last it began ♩ ♩ ♩ ♩ | ♩ but at first rather slow. When I told it 'But, dear table, the tempo is faster', it hastened to tap in the right tempo. I also asked it if it could give me the number that I was thinking of, and it correctly gave *three*. We were all beside ourselves with astonishment, as if surrounded by wonders. ED

tumbler, however, was very determined, even spelling out messages in different languages (including Hungarian). After more such experiments, including the purported presence of Joachim (presumably with a guilty conscience), the Concerto was eventually tracked down to the Prussian State Library by Baron Erik Palmstierna the then Swedish Minister in London.[1]

With the Nazi government claiming the copyright, and Eugenie Schumann opposing the enterprise, the first performance planned for 20 October 1937 never took place. After various negotiations, and the first world performance in Berlin,[2] a happy ending sealed it all, the first performance in Great Britain taking place on 16 February 1938, with Jelly d'Aranyi and the BBC Symphony Orchestra conducted by Sir Adrian Boult. The work was not particularly well received. Since Jelly d'Aranyi's time, in fact, the unfavourable verdict of a number of critics has inhibited performances of the Concerto.

It is of special interest therefore to record an almost unknown letter by Donald Tovey printed in *The Times* on 25 September 1937, in which he comes out as a champion of the Concerto. It is too long to quote in its entirety, but some of it is significant.

> I am anxious to publish my detached opinion of the merits of Schumann's Violin Concerto betimes, because I do not see how any posthumous work can appear in circumstances more likely to arouse prejudice . . . Joachim was powerfully moved by Brahms' very strong objection to the publication of posthumous works which might be thought to lower the standard of a great artist's life-work. Brahms habitually destroyed far more of his own works than he ever published, and had a great fear of leaving posthumous works . . . Be that as it may, there is a strong feeling among certain musicians that the production of Schumann's Violin Concerto will be more serviceable to the cause of beautiful music in 1937 than it would be if deferred to 1956 when its production could be only a centenary affair with no effect as reparation for an injustice . . . only a morbid pedantry could decide that this Concerto was inferior to other works published by Schumann in 1853 such as the Fantasie for Violin and Orchestra which Joachim himself and several good violinists of the present day are quixotic enough to play in public. To my taste this Concerto is richer and more attractive than the Fantasie. Being a much larger work it imposes an obviously greater strain upon Schumann's powers of construction and its weaknesses

[1] Who wrote a book entitled *Horizons of Immortality* containing verbatim records relating to the strange sequence of events.
[2] The soloist was Kulenkampff.

are accordingly more obvious . . . I will . . . take the opportunity of asserting strongly and for economy of space dogmatically that there is nothing morbid about any elements of Schumann's latest style. On the contrary, if we look for morbid elements we shall find them where we least wish to cavil, in the best-loved early works, where his epoch-making resources in epigram are often inseparable from a purposeful irrationality like that of Lewis Carroll; and we shall be apt to fall into Schumann's own mistake displayed in his second editions, in which he improved much but tidied away almost as many subtleties of genius as the details he perfected . . . I can think of no more disastrous injustice to Schumann than to suppose that the failure consisted in morbid symptoms, such as Joachim implied in imputing 'Kränkelnder Grübelei' (vexatious ruminations) to the latter part of the slow movement of the Concerto. The theme of the slow movement is said to be identical with the very theme which, during his last illness, Schumann believed to be conveyed to him by Schubert and Beethoven. I think the statement misleading for that theme on which Brahms wrote a beautiful set of variations, is a self-contained and highly organised melody coinciding only in its first six notes with the slow movement of the Concerto. In the Concerto these six notes are part of a much larger scheme that quite legitimately remains unfinished and as Joachim said, rouses itself with an accelerando into the finale as if the composer longed to release himself from his mood of grey reflectiveness.

Joachim's description is very apt, and we cannot but wonder that he should have put it forward as if there was anything unclassical or morbid about what he describes . . .

Tovey's final word in his letter must not be allowed to go by default.

. . . this brings me to a matter on which I dread all manner of misunderstandings. Before the performance of this Concerto a remarkable book will have been published.[1]

The last pages of this book contain a detailed account of spirit messages to Miss Jelly d'Aranyi expressing Schumann's personal wish that this Concerto should be produced. In many minds the circumstances will arouse violent prejudice, for which reason I wish to confine myself to the most agnostic terms on the subject. As Mr Bernard Shaw has wisely said about the Voices which inspired St Joan, the iconography does not matter. Another wise dictum from which I have derived great comfort is that of Sir Frederick Pollock in *For my Grandson* where he refers to the common erroneous belief

[1] *Horizons of Immortality* by Baron Erik Palmstierna.

that personal immortality consists in an existence under improved conditions indefinitely prolonged in Greenwich time. To me, as to many others to whom nineteenth century materialism is as obsolete as the phlogiston theory, it is a mystery how two persons come to understand each other by ordinary human intercourse or by reading and writing. And I am not prepared to find anything more mysterious in other means of ascertaining what the minds of Schumann and Joachim have to say to us now . . . I know how my friend Miss Jelly d'Aranyi has worked at the Schumann Concerto and at other music, and I assert my positive conviction that the spirit of Schumann is inspiring Jelly d'Aranyi's production of Schumann's posthumous Violin Concerto. The sense in which I make this assertion is my own private affair. Greenwich Time is up and you have no more Space.

Yours faithfully,
Donald Francis Tovey

This is a remarkable letter which speaks for itself. It makes mandatory reading for anyone wishing to come to grips with this Concerto.

And what of the music? Critics who are looking at Schumann's Violin Concerto with the justifiably demanding eye of those acquainted with the masterworks of the classical repertoire—far from rich in number, incidentally—might well be jaundiced by his 'failure' to create an equivalent to the classical 'working out' of his subjects, his seeming lack of interest in the dramatic conflict inherent in sonata form. Development here does not take the form of classical 'working out' any more than it does in his Piano Concerto. Schumann is not interested in intensifying rhythmic figures, in magnifying or breaking expectation, in the clash of opposites. He treats his themes as if they were like the characters of a play forming new alignments in varying scenes, but seldom drastically changing their basic personalities. In the feel of the music there is no corrupt over-usage of the melodies—even if it looks so on paper. How misleading paper can be!

The first movement begins with a 'double exposition', in which the orchestra sets out the main points of the argument before the soloist re-states them, classical

EX 46

fashion in violinistic terms. The opening theme projects a note of romantic unease; its spiritual world is close to that of Mozart's D minor string quartet (K. 421).

Schumann has been criticized for failing to grasp the main point of the classical ritornello by letting his orchestral *tutti* anticipate the solo exposition, placing his second subject in the relative major. By the same token, Beethoven (who presumably ought to know better) also fails to grasp this same point in his C minor piano concerto. The observation is surely of no more than academic interest: whether or not music lives has nothing whatever to do with how strongly it conforms to tradition.

EX 47

The soloist's re-statement of this material is imaginative and, at times, original. The opening theme, for instance, re-appears dramatically over this dominant pedal-point. Compare with Ex. 46.

EX 48

Schumann is equally inventive in re-stating his second subject in soloistic terms. At one point, in the recapitulation, he articulates it like this.

EX 49

Such textures are typical of the kind of writing which has been criticized in this Concerto as 'ineffective' and 'awkward'. The above passage is admittedly diffi- cult, lying as it does across the strings; but it does not lie outside a virtuoso's technique. Is any other criterion relevant?

The slow movement is notable for a particularly beautiful theme which resembles the one Schumann claimed was dictated to him by Schubert and Beethoven.

EX 50

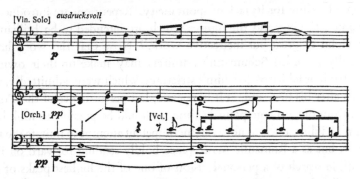

There are few great moments in all Schumann to compare with the inspired idea of recapitulating this theme a third lower—in the minor mode. It takes on an almost unbearably nostalgic hue in its new setting.

EX 51

The Finale is a polonaise. Its main theme runs

EX 52

There are many points of structural interest in the Finale, not least the thematic cross-references to the slow movement (already discussed on pp. 244–45). Technically, it is the most difficult movement in the Concerto and it was heavily criticized by Joachim for its lack of spontaneity. 'Repetitions are introduced until they become fatiguing, and the figures which are intended to be brilliant force the solo violin to great but ineffective work.'[1] Now that the work has been commercially recorded Schumann's admirers may make up their own minds about the truth or falsity of Joachim's strictures, which were, admittedly, written forty years after his first, and, as it happened, last performance of the Concerto.

Today, from our vantage point in time, it should be possible to look back on Schumann's Violin Concerto not as an incompetent attempt to imitate the masters of the past, but as a Romantic masterpiece boldly striding forward on its own lonely path in search of a personal vision of one of the highest peaks of all, the concerto. Like the Piano Concerto it has greatness written on it, and (to paraphrase Tovey) has found its honourable place in Greenwich Time. We look now to its future Space in the repertoire of all good violinists.

[1] Moser: *Joseph Joachim*, p. 140. London, 1901. Joachim was referring chiefly to the development section, and his reactions are exactly what one would expect from someone with his stiff, classical attitude. It upset his expectations. 'There is not the feeling of spontaneity' means there is no dynamic working and contrasting of material. Repetitions become 'fatiguing' because nothing very much has happened in the way Joachim expects. In fact, there is a great deal of variety, some of it far from home. Schumann *aims* at melodic repetition, and, far from being fatiguing, it brings home the work's charm unforgettably. Joachim's criticism in my view is merely pedantic.

CLARA SCHUMANN (*c.* 1880)
a photograph

CHILDREN OF ROBERT AND
CLARA SCHUMANN
(left to right: Ludwig, Marie,
Eugenie, Elise, Ferdinand, Felix)

ROBERT SCHUMANN (1850)
a daguerreotype

ROBERT SCHUMANN
a drawing in 1859 by Bendemann
(after the daguerreotype)

BRIAN SCHLOTEL

The Orchestral Music

Introduction

SINCE Schumann's symphonies and overtures open up a new and unique
world of poetry and romance, the purpose of my essay is, first and foremost, to consider them as works of art in their own right. A more usual approach
has been for writers to compare Schumann's orchestral technique with that of
his contemporaries, particularly Berlioz and Wagner; or else to take the symphonic form as left by Beethoven and to use it as a kind of yardstick against which
to measure Schumann's achievement in this field. This has rarely worked in
Schumann's favour. The intimate style of his expression, which can be seen in
his orchestral works just as clearly as in his songs and piano music, would have
been ill-served had he cloaked it with the virtuoso instrumental brilliance of
Berlioz; while as a symphonist his objectives were different from Beethoven's.

But if Schumann's orchestral works are judged on their own merits they have
many wonders and beauties to reveal, and, considered as a steadily developing
body of work from 1841, when he completed his first composition for orchestra,
to 1853, the date of his last, they have much to tell us about the second half of
his career. Also, the gradual way in which Schumann's attention turned towards
instrumental composition makes a fascinating prelude to the chronological
exploration of his orchestral works. He was thirty when he completed his First
Symphony. But there was nothing unusual in that for Beethoven's symphonic
successors. After all, Brahms was over forty, Elgar over fifty and César Franck
over sixty before they gave the world their first symphonies. But the fact that
Schumann had published only piano music and songs until the age of thirty has
sometimes led to the seeds of his symphonic development being overlooked. But
the seeds were there. As early as 1829, at the age of nineteen, Schumann had
shown his interest in the larger forms by composing a Piano Quartet. Then there

K

was the early Symphony in G minor, which was never finished, but whose first movement was performed in Zwickau on 18 November 1832, then revised and performed again twice in 1833. Schumann continued to work at this early Symphony, but although the second movement was finished, the other two movements remained as sketches. Probably he felt his technique was not yet ready for a symphony and he returned to writing piano music in which he could freely portray his dreams and his surging emotions towards life.

Perhaps it was Franz Liszt who gave the next impetus to Schumann's thoughts about instrumental composition. On 5 May 1838 Schumann received a letter from him, which began by saying with what delight he had been playing the *Carnaval* and the *Fantasiestücke*, op. 12, and continued:

> If I might make a request, I would ask you to write some trios, or a quintet or a septet. It seems to me that you would do that admirably, and for a long time nothing remarkable in that line has been published. If ever you determine to do so, let me know at once, as I should be anxious to have the honour of making them known to the public.[1]

On 5 June 1839 Liszt wrote again to Schumann asking even more emphatically for some ensemble pieces:

> Will you pardon me for pressing this point again? It seems to me that you would be more capable of doing it than any one else nowadays. And I am convinced that success, even *commercial* success, would not be wanting.
> If between now and next winter you could complete some ensemble work, it would be a real pleasure to me to make it known in Paris, where that sort of composition, when well played, has more chance of success than perhaps you think. I would even gladly undertake to find a publisher for it.[2]

In June and July Schumann began work on three Quartets, but nothing came of them. He was striving towards the larger forms of instrumental music, but as yet the time was still not ripe for fulfilment. At this juncture the way forward was pointed out by the first performance of Schubert's 'Great' C major Symphony. For all practical purposes, Schumann had 'discovered' this work which had lain unplayed and unwanted amongst Schubert's posthumous manuscripts for the previous ten years. When Schubert's brother had shown Schumann the

[1] La Mara: *Franz Liszts Briefe*, pp. 18–19. Leipzig, 1893.
[2] La Mara: *Franz Liszts Briefe*, p. 27. Leipzig, 1893.

manuscript, in Vienna in 1838, Schumann had at once realized the Symphony's power and importance, and sent it to Mendelssohn, then the conductor of the Gewandhaus Orchestra in Leipzig, suggesting a performance.[1] Attending the rehearsals, Schumann wrote ecstatically to Clara:

> Leipzig, December 11, 1839
> . . . Oh, Clara, I have been in paradise today! They played at the rehearsal a symphony of Franz Schubert's. How I wish you had been there, for I cannot describe it to you. The instruments all sing like remarkably intelligent human voices, and the scoring is worthy of Beethoven. Then the length, the heavenly length of it! It is a whole four-volume novel, longer than the choral symphony. I was supremely happy, and had nothing left to wish for, except that you were my wife, and that I could write such symphonies myself.[2]

There is no doubt that in the Schubert Symphony, Schumann saw the realization of his symphonic dream of allying romantic spirit with classical form. Here was a new kind of symphony cast in the revered Beethovenian mould on the largest scale, and yet whose heartfelt themes stirred the emotions of deepest romanticism in his own soul.

'. . . That you were my wife and that I could write such symphonies myself.' These, then, were Schumann's ambitions as the year 1840 began, ambitions that were intertwined, for after their marriage at the little village of Schönefeld, near Leipzig, on 12 September 1840, Clara gave Robert the domestic peace he needed to win his way victoriously through the larger forms of musical composition. Already, a year before the marriage, Clara had confided to her diary:

> I believe it would be best if he composed for orchestra; his imagination cannot expand sufficiently on the keyboard . . . His compositions are all orchestrally conceived, and I believe incomprehensible to the public for this reason, for the melodies and figuration are so intermingled that it is very difficult to hear the beauties of the work. . . . My highest wish is that he should compose for orchestra—that is his field! May I succeed in persuading him to enter it.[3]

At the age of twenty-three Schumann had felt obliged to abandon his first

[1] See NZfM 13 (1840). ED
[2] F. G. Jansen: *Robert Schumanns Briefe. Neue Folge*, p. 175. (Leipzig: Breitkopf & Härtel, 1904.)
[3] Litzmann: *Clara Schumann*, Leipzig, 1903, Vol. I, pp. 372–73.

symphonic attempt, but now his art was maturer by seven years of rich experience and he had heard in Schubert's 'Great' C major Symphony the ideal to aim at, and encouraged by Clara's 'highest wish' he was ready. Encouraged by Clara?—yes indeed, although some critics have seen Clara as anything but benign as an influence in turning Schumann's attention away from the piano miniature and the song, in which his genius had been so eminently successful, into symphonic domains. Yet the truth surely is that she, like Liszt, rightly perceived that Schumann's art was maturing, and ready to conquer new worlds; and that the interest he had shown in symphonic composition, long before he was under her influence, was now ready to bring its own fulfilment. By giving Schumann domestic bliss instead of restless life in lodgings, by protecting him from worldly worries, by her sympathy and devotion, Clara let that fulfilment come into its own.

Symphony No. 1 in B flat major (The 'Spring') (1841)

The First Symphony was completely sketched in the remarkably short period of four days: 23 to 26 January 1841; and on 20 February the full score was completed. Both the sketch and score are headed in Schumann's hand 'Frühlings Symphonie' and Schumann acknowledged that the initial inspiration for the Symphony had come from a spring poem by Adolph Böttger. However, when Breitkopf and Härtel published the orchestra parts later in the year they were merely entitled 'Symphony in B flat'. Schumann had also thought of giving individual titles to the four movements: I: 'Spring's Coming', II: 'Evening', III: 'Merry Playmates', IV: 'Full Spring', but he never published these, nor circulated them to audiences of the First Symphony. They are like the many titles for his piano pieces that Schumann thought of *after* the music had been written in order to explain their moods.[1] His picturesque music is always more an expression of feeling than scene-painting. Probably, too, the title of 'Spring Symphony', although it was used by Schumann in correspondence with friends, was withheld from the public because of the possibility that it might be misunderstood. Rather than have the general public expect a work of programmatic scene-painting, Schumann preferred to let the buoyant mood of the Symphony speak for itself. Spring, for Schumann the Romantic, had a special significance at this time; the birth of new life throughout the world of nature, the strengthening sun, the lengthening days—symbolized for him the wonderful springtide in his own life, when the victory of love, and the inspiration and confidence in the future that

[1] See p. 193. ED

he felt his marriage had brought him, pointed forward to new happiness and new achievement.

The opening of the Symphony, which Schumann said he wanted 'to sound as if from on high, like a call to awaken',[1] underwent a series of transformations, and remains a controversial matter for conductors and Schumann connoisseurs. The sketch[2] clearly shows that this was originally thought of, and written down as at Ex. 1a.

EX 1a

This first form would have been brilliant and effective on the natural trumpets and natural horns then in use. But in the original full score this is changed to Ex. 1b.

EX 1b

This was disastrous because the sixth and seventh notes are impossible to play on the natural trumpets and can only be played in a muffled way on the natural horns—as Schumann found out when the Symphony had its first rehearsal with the Leipzig Gewandhaus Orchestra. Mendelssohn, who was conducting, suggested the opening call be transposed up a third, so that it once again came within the horns' and trumpets' natural notes (Ex. 1c).

EX 1c

[1] Letter to the Berlin conductor Wilhelm Taubert, 10 January 1843. F. G. Jansen, *op. cit.*, p. 224.

[2] In the Library of Congress, Washington, together with the original full score.

[3] All the metronome marks used in this chapter are from the first editions of his music that Schumann himself saw through the press. See my essay 'Schumann and the metronome', pp. 109–19.

Schumann agreed, and it was with the opening in this last form that the Symphony was published. But sometimes modern conductors restore Ex. 1b, following Gustav Mahler's edition, which has the advantage of more thematic relevance with the ensuing first subject and the opening of the development. Most performances, however, adhere to the published version, which has the advantage of greater brilliance, with the trumpets and horns in their higher register. The evidence is contradictory about whether or not Schumann finally preferred 'b' or 'c'. By 1850 all the leading orchestras in Europe had valve trumpets and valve horns in their ranks, and Schumann wrote for these in later works such as *Manfred* and *Genoveva*, but he never requested Breitkopf and Härtel to change the published parts, though an opportunity for that might have arisen when the full score was published in 1853. It is possible that by then Schumann preferred the greater brightness of the higher version; but it is equally possible that he did not want to bother Breitkopf and Härtel, the leading German publishers, to whom he was constantly, and most deferentially, offering new works.

This opening motto has an important part to play in unifying the whole Symphony: in the following Allegro it generates the first subject, its rising three-note motif 'x' influences themes in all the other movements of the Symphony, and its insistent rhythm is a rallying point in the finale. In the powerful introduction that follows, the dramatic boldness of the scoring—with thunderclaps for the brass and rushing demi-semiquavers for the strings, gradually giving way to soft woodwind meditations on the opening call—irresistibly reminds one of the mood of stormy winter gradually changing to spring, and, following Schumann's directions for growing vivaciousness and accelerating speed, the whole orchestra bursts in, with terrific impetus and vitality with the first subject (Ex. 2).

EX 2

The song-like second subject makes an admirable contrast (Ex. 3).

EX 3

Starting in A minor, it only gradually settles into F major, the expected 'classical' key for the second subject. The mood of exuberance returns in the codetta and brings the exposition to a spirited close.

The development starts with a vigorous working out of the first subject combined with a new thematic fragment

EX 4

and a new melody.

EX 5

These new themes make excellent foils for the energetic figurations of the first subject, and, since Schumann wisely withholds the fleeting lyricism of his second subject from the development, they prevent any sense of melodic monotony. Forty-four bars of the development section are repeated: but the new keys through which the material is unfolded give a further perspective to the themes (a colouristic device used by Schumann many times in his piano music) and the orchestration has interesting differences, calculated to add to the excitement. Thus, with the ensuing section based on the rhythmic scales of the exposition's codetta, the development as a whole, if the conductor maintains the vigorous motion, gives the listener a sensation of impetuousness and youthful energy, driving on and on until this glorious climax is reached.

EX 6

This splendid peroration for the full orchestra, fortissimo, presents the opening
motto of the Symphony, with the *andante crotchets* of the introduction's first six
bars, augmented to *allegro minims*.

It is at once the end of the development and the beginning of the recapitulation. (Brahms followed a similar structural procedure in the first movement of
his Fourth Symphony, and may well have got the idea from Schumann.) The
first subject does not have a formal recapitulation. For one thing it has been
'used up', so to speak, in the development. More important, it still has vital work
to do after the recapitulation of the second subject. When the latter has taken
place, a new section marked to be played 'faster and faster' is built on bustling
fragments of Ex. 2. Growing in excitement with a prolonged crescendo it leads
to a climax of a completely different kind—a new, long-drawn melody of great
lyrical intensity (Ex. 7).

EX 7

One of Schumann's contributions to the history of symphonic thought is the
way in which he throws the burden of his structures towards the 'episode'. It
used to be considered an 'unsymphonic' thing to do, but later composers (notably
Tchaikovsky and Mahler) were quick to take Schumann as a model.

The slow movements of Schumann's large-scale works are often his most
characteristic utterances. Thus, those of the Violin Concerto and the Cello
Concerto transfigure these works with a rare loveliness, and even the most
hostile critics usually exempt these movements from their strictures on each
Concerto as a whole. Here, too, the rapt poetry of this expressive Larghetto
shows Schumann at his very best. Basically, the plan is a rondo in which the
long-drawn main subject of twenty-four bars

EX 8

appears three times, separated by contrasting episodes conceived in the same mood
of rapt intensity. The three appearances of the subject are orchestrated in entirely

different and remarkably effective ways. The first time it is played by the violins; the next by the 'cellos, soaring through a rich tapestry of sound created by pizzicato first violins and basses, murmuring second violins and violas, and staccato woodwind chords. The final time it is sung by an oboe, doubled an octave lower by the first horn, while the violins simultaneously play a decorated version of the melody.

EX 9

Note that the parts for the violins, as well as the animated figurations for the violas, are carefully provided with rests and marked pianissimo to let the oboe and horn melody come through; while the 'cello part gives a slight pulsation to the bass. But Schumann's master-stroke of orchestration comes at the very end

of this movement. Pianissimo, the three trombones play a solemn chorale
(Ex. 10).

EX 10

It seems like a last fragment of the main melody with darker colouring, and
deepening evening harmonies; but it is, in fact, an anticipation of the main theme
of the Scherzo, which suddenly bursts in *forte*.

EX 11

In this way the two movements are subtly linked by thematic transformation.

The Scherzo, in bold Beethovian rhythms, is structurally important in having
two trio sections. Beethoven and Schubert had each at times required the trio
of their scherzi to be repeated; but Schumann's plan was a symphonic innovation.
The second trio is especially interesting in that it is built on the pattern of three
rising notes which were first heard in the motto (Ex. 12).

EX 12

The coda, with its sudden changes of tempi, its ritardando, its pauses and its
syncopations brings the movement to a close in an aura of fleeting nostalgia
(Ex. 13).

EX 13

The last movement of the Symphony, like the first, is in sonata form. A bold scale in syncopated rhythm, which has an important influence later in the movement, ushers in the first subject, Animato e grazioso. In the classical symphony, F major, the key of the dominant, would be the expected key for the second subject, but Schumann, as in the first movement, starts the second subject in a different key (in this case G minor) and only gradually settles the music into F major.[1] This tonal procedure, although it loosens the classical symmetry, can, in Schumann's hands, be a charming colouristic device. As the second subject progresses, the scale-pattern of the movement's opening becomes more and more prominent, until it generates a splendid new theme in Schumann's most robust vein (Ex. 14).

EX 14

The development ignores the first subject and concentrates on the second subject A quotation from the Symphony's motto (bars 116–117) starts off an excited discussion ranging widely through distant keys.

Soon all the excitement dies down, and a poetic cadenza for horns and flute leads into the recapitulation. The last pages of the Symphony, in Schumann's favourite *poco a poco accelerando* style, with horns, trumpets and trombones in turn insisting more and more on the rhythm of the Symphony's motto, bring the work to a triumphant conclusion.[2]

[1] This became common practice in Schumann. Other examples are found in the Second Symphony.

[2] The 'normal' Schumann orchestra for the purposes of this essay is taken to be 2 flutes, 2 oboes, 2 clarinets, 2 bassoons, 4 horns, 3 trombones, 2 trumpets, timpani and strings. This is the orchestra used, for instance, in the Third and Fourth Symphonies. When significant changes in the size of this normal orchestra occur they will be mentioned, though they are not usually great; for instance, the First Symphony adds a triangle (*ad libitum*, and only used in the first movement), the Second Symphony has only one pair of horns.

The first performance took place in the Leipzig Gewandhaus on 31 March 1841 with Mendelssohn (who had given the work three rehearsals) conducting. This was fortunate, because as one of the most gifted conductors in Europe at the time, he was ideally suited to bring off the work to best advantage, and it seems to have been a definite success, although somewhat overestimated by the Schumanns. Schumann kept a note at the front of his original manuscript score of those performances of the Symphony known to him—including place, date and conductor. His list can still be read: it shows three performances in 1841, eight the next year, and a total of forty-two between 1841 and 1852. The new Symphony was much discussed and brought Schumann's name more prominently before the musical public than any of his previous works. Greatly encouraged by its success he continued to devote his energies, during 1841, to more orchestral compositions: the Overture, Scherzo and Finale (April–May), the first version of the Symphony in D minor (May–September), and finally, in the autumn, a Symphony in C minor, which remained only in sketches.[1]

Overture, *Scherzo and Finale* (*1841, slightly revised 1845*)

The Overture, Scherzo and Finale is characterized as much by its originality of design within the movements as by the originality of its over-all plan, and is unified by vivacious mood, light orchestration and some transfer of themes between movements. Schumann considered calling the work a 'Suite', then a 'Sinfonietta', and finally, a 'Second Symphony'—and under this latter title offered it to the publisher Hofmeister in 1842, without success. It is undeniably slighter than the four Symphonies.

The Overture's introduction

EX 15

contrasts a graceful violin motif 'y' with a bold dramatic utterance on the 'cellos 'z', both of which have an important part to play in the ensuing Allegro, a high-spirited first subject (Ex. 16),

[1] Though the Scherzo of this projected symphony was published as 'Scherzo in G minor'— No. 13 of the *Bunte Blätter*, Op. 99.

EX 16

which is ushered in with a change of key, from E minor to E major. There is little development: the introduction's dramatic motifs jostle with the Allegro's subjects to make a pageant in which Mendelssohnian grace and charm are never far distant. The following Scherzo (Ex. 17)

EX 17

owes something to the spirit of *A Midsummer Night's Dream* music, though more to Schumann's own song *Der Knabe mit dem Wunderhorn*, Op. 30 No. 1, which describes a gay youth, who rides with the speed of the wind, setting the echoes ringing with his silver horn and seeking far-away lands.

The kind of difficulty Schumann sets the conductor is aptly shown in Ex. 17. On the piano a clear crisp start is possible, but the difficulty of getting the orchestra to start neatly a dotted quaver's rest after the upbeat is great. It can so easily fail to come off. (Mendelssohn, thinking far more orchestrally in the Scherzo of his *Midsummer Night's Dream*, brings in the orchestra on the down beat.) Also, the weight of two horns on this soft syncopated part is excessive, and is greatly improved if the conductor asks only one horn to play. Again, the conductor has carefully to guard against the rhythm ♪ ♪ ♩, repeated hundreds of times, degenerating into ♩ ♫, a lapse which is fatally easy after dozens of bars of this unbroken rhythm. These are some of the difficulties—but if it all comes off the effect for the listener is magical. The charmingly lyrical trio appears twice, the second time having an important part to play in unifying the Overture with the Scherzo. A ritardando slows down the Scherzo's motion and leads the listener to expect a coda, but instead motif 'z' ushers in a recapitulation of the trio, and this leads into an extended reminiscence of Ex. 16, which finally ends the movement.

The Finale is remarkable not least for its breath-taking speed. Schumann indicates o = 74, which is eminently playable and suitable for the lively fugato first subject (Ex. 18a) and for the eloquent Mendelssohnian lyricism of the second, and all the play that is made with them until the glorious hymn-like coda (Ex. 18b) built upon an augmentation of the first subject.

EX 18

This could be counted as yet another example of Mendelssohn's influence, which is stronger in the Overture, Scherzo and Finale than in any other of Schumann's orchestral works. For although the boyish enthusiasm of the mood, the original design of the work, and the fascinating developments, built like beautiful coral, are all Schumannesque, the Mendelssohnian influence is seen in the graceful melodies and clear harmonies, and in the lightness of the orchestration, which has only one pair of horns, and trombones *ad libitum*.

Mendelssohn's early-flowering genius and success had a dazzling effect on many of his contemporaries; it was not to be expected that Schumann's genius, although the more original, should not be influenced also—especially as he admired Mendelssohn both as fellow-artist and composer, and as Mendelssohn rendered him singular service as a conductor. The influence was strongest from about 1841 to 1844, while both were resident in Leipzig and in regular contact; thereafter it lessened as Schumann turned again to learning from his principal master, Bach. But the relationship between the two composers was certainly a strange one, because although Schumann's private letters and published articles are full of the most lavish praise for Mendelssohn and his music, remarks about Schumann by Mendelssohn are almost non-existent— although the two composers were in close touch for twelve years, during which time Mendelssohn would have heard and seen most of Schumann's compositions.

Symphony No. 2 in C major (1845–46)

Two critical assessments by noted scholars will serve to show how different the reception of this, the most controversial of Schumann's Symphonies, has been:

> That his mental state at the time was an important factor in contributing to the pathetic failure of this work is not to be gainsaid. Laborious, dull, often mediocre in thematic invention, plodding, and repetitive in argument, the C major Symphony has now fallen into almost complete neglect.[1]

> The characteristic of the C major Symphony is a graver and more mature depth of feeling; its bold decisiveness of form and overpowering wealth of expression reveal distinctly the relationship in art between Schumann and Beethoven.[2]

The sketches of the Symphony are dated December 1845, when Schumann was making a determined attempt to regain his mental and physical health, which had completely collapsed in 1844 following the strain of the feverish artistic activity of the previous years. It is this determination, sometimes fierce, sometimes prayerful, that lends the Symphony its special characteristic, for transmuted by his genius, the Symphony takes on the universal significance of a struggle between light and darkness represented, in part, by the two opening themes marked 'l' and 'k' in the following examples. After periods of conflict and periods of melancholy, the darkness lessens, the light increases, and in the last movement we can feel that the tides of misfortune have been pushed back, while with its final great 'Amen' cadence the Symphony ends on a note of spiritual hope.

Schumann's views on the origin of the work are clearly shown in a letter to Dr D. G. Otten, the Music Director in Hamburg, who had written asking the composer's advice about the interpretation of the work:

> Dresden, April 2nd, 1849
> . . . I wrote my symphony in December, 1845, and I sometimes fear my semi-invalid state can be divined from the music. I began to feel more myself when I wrote the last movement, and was certainly much better when I finished the whole work. All the same it reminds me of dark days. Your interest in a work so stamped with melancholy proves your real sympathy.

[1] Mosco Carner, in the Schumann Symposium edited by Gerald Abraham (1952), p. 221.
[2] Philipp Spitta, Professor of Music History at Berlin University, in Grove's Dictionary of Music and Musicians, first edition (1883), Vol. III, p. 414.

... I was greatly delighted to find that my mournful bassoon in the Adagio was not lost upon you, for I confess I wrote that part for it with peculiar pleasure.[1]

Although the Symphony was sketched in December 1845, the orchestration in which Schumann was constantly interrupted by attacks of tinnitus,[2] was only completed on 19 October, less than three weeks before the first performance, which was conducted by Mendelssohn in Leipzig on 5 November 1846.

The opening of the Symphony consists of the weaving together of two strongly contrasted themes. The one, marked 'l', on the trumpets, a clear and uplifting motto theme, the other, marked 'k', on the strings, hesitant, uncertain, reminding us at once of the 'dark days' mentioned in the letter to Dr Otten.

EX 19

These two themes of light and darkness hold an uneasy balance in the opening pages of the Symphony, and have an important part to play in the work's thematic germination. Often one hears performances in which the brass theme is all too prominent, with the string motif receding to a distant murmuring accompaniment. But conversely, when a conductor gets the violins to sing out their part it can absorb so much of the listener's attention that he may not sufficiently note the brass instruments' motto theme. Getting a just balance is not easy, but it can be done, and then the uneasy partnership with brass and strings, both sounding pianissimo, as Schumann has directed, is gripping, and a portent of the drama that is to come. In Schumann's orchestration the motif 'l' is played by two trumpets, a horn and the first trombone. Not least of the conductor's difficulties is to tone down this vast weight of brass to sound at the pianissimo the composer directed. Significantly, when Gustav Mahler re-orchestrated this Symphony he gave motif 'l' to the two trumpets only, leaving the trombone silent and giving the horns a softly sustained 'C'.

[1] F. G. Jansen, *op. cit.*, p. 300.
[2] Involuntary aural disturbances. Schumann complained of 'singing in the ears'. See p. 410.

EX 20

The silvery tones of the two trumpets playing in octaves, undoubled by the other instruments, are much easier to balance against the dark ruminations of the strings. On the other hand, the Schumann purist might well prefer the great reserve of latent power that can be felt when all four brass instruments are joining in with utmost softness.

The first subject (Ex. 21)

EX 21

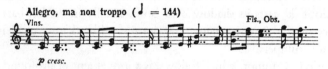

is notable for the aggressive rhythms of its double-dotted notes struggling upwards through a long sustained crescendo towards the second subject, which whirls in, in the unexpected key of E flat major.

EX 22

The conflict of the development is tremendous, reaching climax after climax as the warring elements, gathered in introduction and exposition, are worked and extended against one another. The section ends with a feeling of the great weariness of battle, over a long pedal G, but it has evidently been a battle well worth enduring because the recapitulation bursts in with a splendid new defiance, fortissimo, and with its fierce rhythm spiritedly supported by trumpets and drums. This mood continues through the coda, marked 'con fuoco'. At the height of the excitement trumpets and horns blaze out the opening motto-theme 'l', and the movement ends with a feeling of darkness overcome and determination to strive for victory in the future.

The battle is continued and extended in the following Scherzo, which is pervaded by a mood of restlessness and uncertainty.

EX 23

Schumann, doubtless pleased with the innovation in symphonic form he made by having two trios in the Scherzo of the 'Spring' Symphony, repeats the scheme here. Although both are well contrasted with each other and with the Scherzo, motif 'k' casts its shadow over both. Finally in the last bars the flying semiquavers of the Scherzo theme, still dominated by 'k', are challenged by 'l' on horns and trumpets.

The Adagio in C minor, which follows, is a movement of profound loveliness, tinged with melancholy.

EX 24

Architecturally and orchestrally Schumann is at his best. The movement is constructed in ternary form with subtle hints of sonata development and fugato. Among the happy orchestral touches there are long solos for oboe, clarinet and the 'mournful' bassoon, romantic horn calls and, of paramount wonder, the long chain of trills for violins, high up, in octaves beneath which the woodwind rhapsodizes on the main melody.

EX 25

The movement ends quietly in C major, thus all is ready for the Finale in the same key. (An unusual feature of this Symphony is that all the movements are in the tonality of C. It is difficult to think of a *symphonic* precedent, though some piano sonatas by Haydn have all three movements in the same tonality, and this is the usual key structure for the movements of Bach's suites.)

After this profound reflection, Schumann introduces a Finale which, if it does not bring an absolute and crowning victory, as does the Finale of Beethoven's Fifth Symphony, is yet a fitting completion to Schumann's symphonic argument. The vivaciousness of Schumann 'feeling himself again', is tinged with remembrances of former melancholy thoughts as the second subject is developed out of the Adagio's main melody.

EX 26

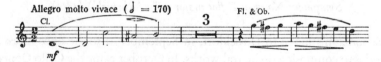

The chief structural novelty of this movement is that the development and recapitulation are telescoped together. There may well be no precedent for what Schumann does here. Development and recapitulation proceed by *alternation*; that is, Schumann moves back and forth, from one to the other, as if to unfold them as simultaneously as possible. There follows a huge coda of over 300 bars, longer than all the rest of the movement. Schumann avoids driving the Symphony to a conclusion of all-out victory. A complete victory over the power of darkness would have been unrealistically optimistic. Instead, Schumann in his coda cultivates a mood of prayerful hope, and it is on that note that this great symphonic Finale ends, the motto 'I' repeatedly sounded by the brass (Ex. 27),

EX 27

with challenging rhythms for timpani, and a great 'Amen' for the whole orchestra.[1]

The neglect that Mosco Carner spoke of[2] was undoubtedly true for much of the Second Symphony's history. Although it had a solitary broadcast in August 1942, over six years then elapsed before it was included in a radio programme again—treatment which compared unfavourably with the other three Symphonies. Further, it did not appear in British gramophone record catalogues until 1949 (although the other Symphonies had been available in the 1930s). Nor was it played at a Henry Wood Promenade Concert until 1961.

This neglect has ended in recent years. It has been no stranger to broadcast concerts, and above all has received a number of superb recorded performances; those of George Szell with the Cleveland Orchestra,[3] of Raphael Kubelik with the Berlin Philharmonic Orchestra[4] and of Georg Solti with the Vienna Philharmonic[5] being especially inspired and doing the highest justice to the Symphony's beauty and greatness.

Symphony No. 3 in E flat major (The 'Rhenish') (1850)

With Schumann's move to Düsseldorf, in September 1850, he once more bent his energies to composing orchestral works. In October came the Cello Concerto, and on 2 November he began work on the Symphony No. 3 in E flat major, laid out on a grand scale in five movements, in which he was to express all his feelings about the Rhine, its scenery, its atmosphere, its legends, and the pageant of German history that had been played out on the river's banks and reflected in its waters. On 29 September the Schumanns had journeyed downstream to

[1] The four bars of timpani solo on the last page of this Symphony so often seem fated to fail in effect at performances: sometimes the player does not synchronize his triplet rhythm with the conductor's accelerating tempo; sometimes the timpani tone is dull; more often, at the end of this long movement, perhaps in a hot hall, they are out of tune. But there is no need for any of these things. The timpanist can carefully check his tuning in one of his earlier periods of rest, and if he plays accurately, with full rich tone, and with the insistent accents that Schumann specifies, the effect can be magnificent and compelling.

[2] p. 291.
[3] Columbia, 33CX 1853.
[4] DGG, LPM 18955. (Later transferred to DGG, 138955.)
[5] Decca, SXL 6487.

Cologne, where the profoundest impression was made on Robert by the great cathedral—a supreme Gothic masterpiece (though in 1850 it was still uncompleted). Here Schumann found the inspiration for the fourth movement of his Symphony. As usual, once the composition was begun, it was completed with rapidity—the full score being finished on 9 December. On 6 February 1851 the first performance took place in Düsseldorf with Schumann himself conducting, and the same year the publisher Simrock of Bonn brought out both the full score and parts of the work.

The Symphony shows Schumann still at the height of his powers in everything except the orchestration, which was by now becoming thick and unhelpful to the music. All Schumann's Symphonies have slow introductions,[1] except the 'Rhenish', which starts off with this extensive, sweeping first subject.

EX 28

The Schumannesque syncopation of the first six bars creates the illusion that the music is in a slow 3/2, but it dissolves in the whirling gaiety of a joyous 3/4 waltz-rhythm from bar 7. The tendency of the later Schumann to use much longer themes can be seen clearly in the *Manfred* Overture of 1848, and here the process stretches much further with an opening theme of twenty bars starting off a vast, seamless first-subject structure of ninety bars. As if to match its breadth, the second subject is equally vast-ranging and its architectural dimensions make it a worthy partner; yet there is an effective contrast of mood here as well.

EX 29

The codetta is in the conventional key of the dominant, so once again this exposition is seen as yet another example of the 'three tier' structure of tonality that Schumann uses also in the first movement expositions of the 'Spring' and C major Symphonies. After the development, the recapitulation abbreviates the material of the exposition, though allowing for the second subject to make its serene contrast in C minor, before re-establishing the tonic key in time for the

[1] Incidentally, all of Schumann's 8 Overtures also have slow introductions, except one: *Hermann and Dorothea*.

coda. In this horns and trumpets are prominent, bringing the movement to a triumphant end with material recalling its exuberant opening.

The second movement is a Scherzo only in name, its easy going tempo having more in common with a Ländler.

EX 30

Formally, its six connected sections show, respectively, elements of the dance with a contrasting trio, of variation form, and of sonata development.

The third movement is a charming intermezzo in which semiquaver watery ripplings in the strings reflecting the Rhine, are never long absent.

EX 31

Although it has the intimacy and the constantly varying iridescent ideas of Schumann's piano music, the movement is emphatically orchestrally conceived with the adventurous horn parts, the writings for solo cello, the warm scoring of the serene theme for divided violas doubled by bassoons. The best performances couple the waywardness of a solo pianist's style with this orchestral language.

The trombones have been kept in purposeful reserve during the first three movements but now they enter, lending their dignity and power to the solemn fourth movement, which shows Schumann's symphonic powers at their most impressive. All his life Schumann studied Bach and learned from Bach. Bach's influence can be seen in the inner contrapuntal lines threading their way through Schumann's early piano music; his influence can be seen again in the longer fugue-like themes that Schumann used in his later works; and here too, in the 'cathedral' movement of the 'Rhenish' Symphony, Bach was the master from whom Schumann learned the polyphonic techniques of canon, augmentation and diminution. However, although the techniques were learned from Bach, the ends to which they were applied were romantic in spirit. Thus entirely Schumann's own are the trombone-dominated scoring and the sequence of romantic E flat minor harmonies, which seem to evoke the dark interior of the cathedral and deep religious emotion.

At the start (Ex. 32)

EX 32

the motif marked 'x', intoned solemnly by the first trombone, is used in diminution by the first violins at their first entry, and it forms an important counterpoint to the theme as the movement unfolds; the speed of 'x' is doubled again in the middle section while, to its counterpoint, the main theme continues grandly on its solemn course. ('x' finally appears in the Finale as a thematic link between the two movements.) From bar 8 the intensity is heightened by the treatment of 'x' in close canon. The contrapuntal masteries displayed here, though, gripping as they are in themselves, are merely the stones with which Schumann builds his cathedral of sound for us—with its powerfully sustained religious mood.

With the Finale we step again into the sunshine and bustle of Rhenish life,

EX 33

and, before the spirited ending, references are made to the Symphony's opening theme and the theme of the fourth movement, but now in joyous E flat major—like a retrospect from afar of the sunlit pinnacles of the cathedral.

Symphony No. 4 in D minor
(Original version 1841, revised version 1851)

When his D minor Symphony was coldly received by the Leipzig public in December 1841, Schumann withdrew it, and seemed in no hurry to get it newly performed. In fact the Symphony lay quietly in his desk for ten years.

Then in December 1851 he decided to revise and re-score the work to bring out at one of his Düsseldorf concerts. In this new form it was completed on 19 December of that year. In 1841, both on the manuscript and at the first concert, the work was referred to as a 'Symphony'. But the 1851 revision at first bore the title 'Symphonic Fantasy'; perhaps Schumann hoped that with this new title the work's remarkable freedom of thought would be more readily accepted. However, before the first performance on 30 December 1852 Schumann changed the title back to 'Symphony'. It is now universally known as the Fourth Symphony, and was published as such by Breitkopf and Härtel.

It is the revised version that is almost always played today, so this will first be examined as it stands, and then a comparison will be made with the original version of 1841.

Three short motifs (Exx. 34, 35 and 36), announced in the introduction, generate most of the melodic material of the entire work. The Symphony is therefore given a powerful unity which overrides the looseness of form that might otherwise result from the profusion of lyrical ideas and the mosaic patterns that Schumann liked to use. In pursuing the course of the Symphony, too, we find that Schumann transforms these three motifs into a wide variety of thematic material, so that although the underlying unity is present there is no sense of monotony. Also the character of the four movements is entirely different—the first being eloquent and passionate, the second a Romance of great charm, the third a vigorous Scherzo, while the Finale, after its majestic introduction, is all exuberance culminating in increasing momentum.

The note 'A' for the whole orchestra, loud but diminishing quickly to pianissimo, immediately arrests the listener's attention at the start of the Symphony. And through the sustained 'A', a melody of deep, but restrained, passion, threads its way.

EX 34

It is driven to a great climax, after which the motifs Exx. 35 and 36 are heard

EX 35

EX 36

and worked together through accelerating speed into the main part of the movement. Schumann evolves his first subject (Ex. 37)

EX 37

from Ex. 36 with a reference to Ex. 34 ('n'). The second subject establishes the orthodox classical key for the second subject—F major, but there is no new thematic material: the D minor first subject is rediscussed in F major. The ensuing development is built on Ex. 37, being worked with ever-increasing excitement through a wide range of keys. Two new themes make their appearance in the development, as a foil for the main subject. Ex. 38

EX 38

is derived from the motif Ex. 35, while the other is a new lyrical melody of exquisite charm, over which the motif 'n' (Ex. 34) casts its influence for a moment (Ex. 39).

EX 39

The excitement caused by the interplay of these three ideas leads to a brilliant climax in D major, which concludes the development and also provides a coda to the movement as a whole. There is no formal recapitulation, though the coda is based on exhilarating variants of Ex. 37.

All the movements are marked to be played without a break between them (an idea Schumann may have got from Mendelssohn's 'Scottish' Symphony of 1842), and the inconclusive single chord on which the first movement ends also creates the expectancy which now ushers in the second movement headed 'Romanze'. As so often in Schumann's major works this slow movement is distinguished by an intense beauty. The key is A minor and after an appealing melody on the oboe, accompanied by pizzicato strings, the opening idea (Ex. 34) makes an impassioned entrance, rising to a full climax, as in its first appearance in the Symphony's introduction. The key changes to D major for the middle section of the movement, which grows from Ex. 34 and thus, as well as giving organic growth to the movement, unites it even more firmly to the structure of the Symphony as a whole. The orchestration here is superb, for while the strings have the main theme, a violin solo weaves poetic figurations above it (Ex. 40).

EX 40

This idea of using a solo violin to provide a delicate contrast in the tone colours was later used by Brahms in the slow movement of his First Symphony.

The vigorous mood of the Scherzo provides a fine contrast. The main theme in the strings (Ex. 41)

EX 41

is an inversion of the motif, Ex. 34; while it is punctuated by woodwind chords, derived from Ex. 35. The contrasting trio section of this movement is also closely linked melodically with what has gone before, because, for all its change of character, it derives its themes from the D major middle section of the previous movement: the strings now have the figurations formerly played by the solo violin, the woodwind hint, with changed rhythm, at Ex. 35. Once again it is impossible not to admire the contrasts, the complete changes of mood, that Schumann achieves although so much of the material is based on the three introductory motifs. Differences of tempo, of rhythm, of key, and of instrumentation all play their part, producing diverse material from the original atoms.

At the end of the Scherzo there is a gradual reduction of speed, no definite final chord, and an imperceptible merging into the slow and impressive introduction to the Finale. The material here consists of a solemn, majestic melody on the brass, derived from the motif Ex. 35, while the strings accompany with impassioned utterances of Ex. 36. These eventually accelerate in speed, as they had done in the introduction to the first movement, and, taking up their juxtaposition from the point they had been left at in the first movement, breathe life into the Finale's first subject, a vigorous, buoyant melody (Ex. 42).

EX 42

The relationship to Ex. 36 will readily be seen, and in bars 285–86 of the first movement just before the coda, these motifs did in fact make their appearance, almost exactly as they are now presented to us in the Finale.

With the other three Symphonies, Schumann himself has given us many clues to their meaning—Spring and its symbolism in the First; his fight against illness in the Second; the Rhenish allusions in the Third. However, the case with the Fourth is quite different; its creation is not discussed in any of the composer's letters that have survived, and the Household Book has almost no elucidating references to it.[1] Most analysts have been content to say that Schumann gave no clues to any poetic meaning behind the music—and leave it at that. This was no doubt Schumann's intention—that it should be received as absolute music—and its appeal is fully satisfying as such.

Schumann regarded his revised version as a great improvement. 'I have instrumented the Symphony afresh altogether', he wrote to his ardent supporter,

---

[1] The possible exception is an entry at the end of March 1841: 'My next Symphony will be called 'Clara', and in it I will paint her picture with flutes and oboes and harps.' (Litzman, *op. cit.*, Vol. II, pp. 30–31.) This may be linked with the fact that Robert gave Clara the score of the original version of the D minor Symphony for her birthday on 13 September 1841.

the Dutch conductor Johannes Verhulst on 3 May 1853, 'and it is certainly better and more effective than it used to be.' But on the other hand Brahms preferred the original 1841 version, and arranged for Breitkopf and Härtel to publish the score and parts over thirty years after Schumann's death.

The difficulty in deciding which version to perform is caused by the fact that the later one contains a number of structural alterations which, though slight, are definite improvements, whereas the re-scoring of the Symphony in Schumann's later, thick style can only be regarded as a tragic blunder, considerably darkening the tone-colours of the work. Other alterations in the revision including changing Italian indications of speed to German ones, and deleting some of the fluctuations in tempo that had appeared in the original. Also the instruction to play the Symphony without a break only appears in the later score. The *structural revisions* which make the 1851 version more effective could be listed thus:

(1) The opening 'A' for full orchestra was extended by one beat—giving it more time to make its effect.

(2) The introduction to the first movement is expanded, and leads far more neatly into the following quick section.

(3) The notation of the first and fourth movement is changed so that each bar now contains twice as much music—in such fast tempi these changes make it much easier for the orchestral players to follow the conductor's beat.

(4) In the introduction to the Finale, the chorale theme is slightly changed and extended.

However, there are also two ideas in the 1841 version which are quite delightful in their effect, but which Schumann did not include in his revision:

(1) The new theme Ex. 39 is accompanied on its appearance by Ex. 36 on the violas—a most pleasing counterpoint (Ex. 43).

EX 43

(2) There is a spirited call for the horns, heard in the second section of the Scherzo (Ex. 44).

EX 44

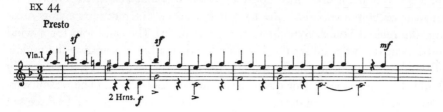

As regards the orchestration, however, almost all the advantages exist in the original: it is reasonably clear and light in its layout with many woodwind solos

EX 45a

—similar in fact to the other works that had preceded it in 1841. But the orchestration of the 1851 version is unremittingly thick and the only advantage it has is that for a bad conductor or an incomplete orchestra it is much easier to perform. To amateur orchestral societies, who have half-a-dozen different instruments missing, the revised Fourth Symphony is a great boon! The only solo for a wind instrument is a little run for the first flute less than a bar in length in the middle of the slow movement. For the rest all instruments have their melodies carefully doubled by someone else, or quite often three or four others. (The reason why Schumann's orchestration deteriorated so much in his later years will be discussed later.) Finally, for comparison, an excerpt from the last movement is given in the original and revised versions (Ex. 45(a) and (b)).

Much that has been said is illustrated here: the clarinet solo of 1841 is given to two clarinets, two bassoons, and the 'cellos, and the melody's second phrase is much more thickly doubled in 1851; also the first violins' light accompaniment to the clarinet solo in 1841 is altered to reinforce the melody and make it even safer still in 1851. On the positive side, though, the 1851 score shows Schumann's greater orchestral experience in violin bowing and his use of the horns.

The Place of the Symphonies in Musical History

Schumann's Symphonies have so far been considered on their own merits, but it is important to see how they fit in with the history of the symphony. If Schumann took the basic form of the symphony from Beethoven, he was nevertheless to accomplish new things with it. Thus the 'Rhenish' Symphony has five movements, like Beethoven's 'Pastoral' Symphony, and the other three have four movements, as was usual with Beethoven. Also adopted from Beethoven was the format of Adagios and Scherzi as the central movements, often cast in sonata form. Beethoven's tempestuous spirit can be seen too as the influence behind such pages as the explosive introduction to the 'Spring' Symphony. Schubert can be seen as Schumann's fore-runner in imbuing symphonic movements with poetic thought. Possibly too it was from Berlioz that Schumann acquired the idea of letting a slow introduction foreshadow the material of a following Allegro, as in the *idée fixe* of his *Symphonie Fantastique*. (This work of Berlioz had been enthusiastically reviewed by Schumann in the *Neue Zeitschrift für Musik* then known to him only in Liszt's piano transcription.)

Schumann's efforts have been justly described as 'the first persistent attempts in a post-Beethovian symphonist to make classical forms serve Romantic ideas'.

Nevertheless, Schumann was conscious of seeking new forms. Even of his early piano sonatas he had written to a friend in 1838: 'I think you would see how many new forms they contain.' As we have seen, his novel ideas for symphony included having two trios in his Scherzi; introducing codas of new lyrical material; making the symphonic form serve ideas of a new melodic type; replacing the dramatic conflict between the first and second subjects with a new plan by which the second subject was presented not in one key, but in two. Most important of all were Schumann's attempts to give *unity* to his symphonies by the use of motifs dominating the whole work and passed from one movement to another. The types of melody that Schumann was using, and the looser, mosaic-type patterns that were evolving as a result, made the question of unity of paramount importance. Although in Beethoven and Berlioz there were precedents for some of Schumann's methods, the ways in which he employed them, and the lengths to which he developed them, constitute an original contribution by Schumann to the history of the symphony.

With later symphonists it is difficult to say how much was due to their own study of the roots of the problem and how much was due to the influence of Schumann. But the practices developed by Schumann became common procedure with many later symphonists. Thus Bruckner and Tchaikovsky used 'motto-themes', Brahms used slow introductions foreshadowing future thematic developments, Sibelius passed themes from one movement to another, while Liszt and Elgar, in their symphonies, took thematic transformation to new lengths. With young composers starting on their careers in the years when the Schumann Symphonies were becoming known in Europe, the influence is even more apparent. Borodin and Tchaikovsky were later to develop highly individual symphonic styles of their own, but in their respective first symphonies (Borodin's was written 1862–67 and Tchaikovsky's in 1866) the use of the Schumann Symphonies as models is easy to see.

As to the standing of Schumann's Symphonies in the unfolding pageant of the symphony's history—here, of course, different generations have their differing tastes and fashions. Philipp Spitta's estimate in the first edition of Grove's *Dictionary of Music and Musicians* was to be frequently quoted, and misquoted, as a rallying-cry not only then but in the arguments and writings of protagonists for the following fifty years and more. What Spitta actually wrote was:

> Schumann's symphonies may without injustice be considered as the most important which have been written since Beethoven.[1]

But that was in 1883 and already in 1908 the second edition of Grove's *Dictionary* had modified Spitta's original statement so that it read:

> Schumann's symphonies may without injustice be considered as the most important in their time since Beethoven.[2]

In the twentieth century new masterpieces of symphony have come from the pens of Mahler, Sibelius, Stravinsky, Hindemith and Shostakovich who have continued to show that the form is always capable of being handled with newness, and remains a vehicle for inspired thought. Yet, during the past twenty years, the ever-increasing number of new recordings and performances of the Schumann Symphonies indicate that they are more firmly fixed in the orchestral repertoire than ever before, not only in Britain, but also in Europe and the USA,

[1] Vol. III, p. 412. [2] Vol. IV, p. 375. (Edited by J. A. Fuller Maitland.)

and that the esteem in which they are held is becoming increasingly more wide-spread.

The Concert Overtures (1851–53)

None of the Concert Overtures of the 1850s approaches the white heat of inspiration that burns in the *Manfred* Overture, nor the vivid romance of the overture to *Genoveva*, though conductors who are sympathetic to them demonstrate that the *Bride of Messina*, *Julius Caesar*, and *Hermann and Dorothea* are well worth an occasional hearing. Schumann is very dependent on his interpreters, and this is shown nowhere more strongly than in these late Concert Overtures: in the wrong hands, or studied on paper, they can seem dull; yet with sympathetic playing, it is remarkable to observe how they can pulsate with life and warmth. Also, these works indicate that, had he lived on in good health, Schumann may well have turned his attention to the composition of the symphonic poem type of orchestral music.

Schumann's diary records that the full score of the Overture to the *Bride of Messina* was written 1 to 12 January 1851. He had read Schiller's play, he says, and felt inspired by it. He also describes his Overture as 'more a theatre overture than a concert overture'. Schumann was, in fact, at this time considering an opera libretto by Richard Pohl, based on the Schiller play, which he only finally turned down in a letter to Pohl a week after the Overture was completed. Thus the Overture might have become the prelude to an opera, and its content is closely linked to Schiller's *Bride of Messina*, which tells how a medieval Prince of Messina had a fantastic dream; an Arab soothsayer interpreted this to mean that the Prince's daughter, Beatrice, would destroy both his sons, Don Manuel and Don Cesar. Beatrice while still an infant is therefore sent to a convent. She comes from the convent, many years later, to attend her father's funeral. Both brothers fall passionately in love with her. In blind jealousy Cesar kills Manuel, and later stabs himself in remorse. The Overture starts with a masterly epigrammatic stroke (Ex. 46),

EX 46

Ziemlich langsam (♩ = 72)

doubtless signifying the curse of fate that hangs over the characters. The first subject falls into two distinct parts, one based on the 'curse' motif,

L

EX 47

the other depicting the two brothers, hostile to each other for most of their lives.

EX 48

The second subject's tender clarinet solo represents the female element in the play, either Beatrice herself or else her mother, who vainly strives to avert the tragic fate lingering over her three children (Ex. 49).

EX 49

The significance of all these themes might have been made more clear if Schumann had gone on to compose the opera; however the Overture, running to some nine minutes, is a fine dramatic piece in its own right, composed in sonata form, but with the dark atmosphere generated by the opening motif never far absent.

Schumann's diary of 2 February 1851 records that the full score of his Overture to Shakespeare's *Julius Caesar* was complete. He was reading a great deal of Shakespeare in the early 1850s. On 24 January he had written in the diary merely the words 'Julius Caesar', but he did not say whether this referred to reading the play or beginning his Overture; perhaps it was both. We may safely conjecture that the Overture is a portrait of Julius Caesar himself, for just as Cassius says of Caesar,

> Why, man, he doth bestride the narrow world
> Like a Colossus; and we petty men
> Walk under his huge legs,[1]

[1] Act I, Scene 2.

—so in the largely monothematic Overture, the 'Julius Caesar' motif, with which it majestically starts,

EX 50

dominates the whole structure, and in the following development seems to be resounding round the whole world, as it is triumphantly echoed by one brass instrument after another.

EX 51

Against this 'Colossus' the other themes are as insignificant as the petty men Cassius describes. The normal Schumann orchestra is enlarged by the addition of a tuba, which enriches the prominent brass writing, and a piccolo, an instrument for whose shrill tones Schumann seemed to have an increasing fondness—though it is used very sparingly in this Overture.

Goethe's play *Hermann and Dorothea* was also a subject that Schumann had considered for a stage work, and in November and December 1851 he was corresponding with the poet Moritz Horn about a libretto. Although nothing was to come of the idea Schumann wrote an Overture, in the same impetuous way that he had written the Overture for *Genoveva* as soon as he had chosen Hebbel's *Genoveva* as the basis of an opera libretto. On the very day that he completed his re-scoring of the D minor Symphony (19 December 1851), Schumann set to work on his *Hermann and Dorothea* Overture, dedicated to 'my dear Clara'. 'Him and her' subjects had always appealed to Schumann, providing a projection of his own feelings about himself and Clara, and here in this miniature 'Carnaval', set in the Rhenish countryside we meet Robert, dressed up as the well-to-do young Burgher, Hermann, with a passionate melody in thirds and sixths (Ex. 52),

EX 52

while Clara is cast as Dorothea, the poor refugee girl fleeing from the French
Revolutionary wars, her beautiful melody showing how worthy she is of Hermann's love and hand in marriage[1] (Ex. 53).

EX 53

The scheme gives the composer a chance to introduce one of his favourite tunes
too, for in the countryside is a detachment of French soldiers, who march and
counter march, complete with military side-drum and jaunty piccolo, to the
strains of the *Marseillaise*.

The last eight bars of the Overture give another example of Schumann's
pianistic thinking setting him almost insuperable problems as an orchestrator.
In Schumann's own piano-duet arrangement the intention is quite clear: a
blurred sound fading into the distance evoked by discords and the available
sustaining pedal. But as orchestrated these bars are thin and need very imaginative
treatment to make them effective. As for the rest, the Overture has all the charm
of Goethe's idyll.

One more work remains for consideration. The Festival Overture, which
Schumann's diary dates as 15 April 1853, was probably written to please the
Düsseldorfers, because the orchestra is joined at the end by a tenor soloist and
men's chorus, who sing the praises of the Rhineland's wine:

> Wreathe with leaves the full and cherished cup and joyfully drain it dry!
> In the whole of Europia there is no longer another such wine to be found.
> Beside the Rhine, there it is that our grapes grow, and blessed be the Rhine,
> [etc.]

The poem *Rheinweinlied*, from which Schumann selected verses, had been written
in 1775 by Matthias Claudius, the poet of Schubert's *Der Tod Und Das Mädchen*,
and was made into a song the next year by Johann André.

Schumann uses André's melody, and this dominates the slow introduction,

---

[1] Goethe's play ends with the betrothal of Hermann and Dorothea.

much of the ensuing Lebhaft and all three choral verses. But the melody is un-distinguished and does not really deserve such treatment, while, alas, there take place no such subtle transformations of theme as Schumann had breathed into the D minor Symphony. The work remains limited to the type of occasion for which it was written.

Problems of Interpretation

Every sympathetic conductor of Schumann knows that there are difficulties in the way of getting good performances, and that these increase with the later works. These difficulties could be summarized as follows:

(1) There are too many cases of 'doubling', particularly of solo instruments. A score by Mendelssohn or Schubert will show a strong contrast here: their orchestral music has many pages with solo melodies felicitously given to flute, oboe, clarinet or horn. Schumann, in his later works, does this less and less. Thus in the Fourth Symphony, except for one bar of flute solo, no woodwind or brass instrument has a single solo melody, while in the first movement of the 'Rhenish' Symphony the melody of the second subject makes both of its appearances on oboes thickly doubled by clarinets. Sometimes, when there *are* melodies for a woodwind instrument, they are obscured by the first violins playing exactly the same melody—for example, in the coda of the second movement of the 'Rhenish' Symphony.

(2) Just as he doubles melodies, Schumann also frequently doubles inner parts—especially in the later works—and this often gives heaviness to the texture. If horns and trumpets were held more in reserve, instead of doubling the middle of the orchestral mass so much, they would make far greater effect at the climaxes.

(3) The bass-line frequently suffers from the same fate of being made over heavy. It would often be effective if Schumann allowed the double basses to rest in the quieter parts, while only the 'cellos sustained the bottom line; but this rarely happens. A relevant example occurs in the opening of the 'Rhenish' Symphony, where the 'cellos are doubled an octave lower by the double basses for the whole of the first 164 bars. This can give a sense of great heaviness to the ear. Yet it is very easy for the conductor to correct, if he wishes to, by here and there giving the double basses a few bars' rest—as at the quiet appearance of the second subject.

(4) The first violins are frequently overworked. In the Third and Fourth Symphonies they introduce most of the thematic material, and are usually in the battle-front of the music's progress. Schumann hardly ever uses the effective device of combining first and second violins, at the unison, or at the octave. Often this would have given much greater force and clarity to the work the first violins are striving to accomplish, as at the opening of the 'Rhenish' Symphony. When Schuman does write for the massed violins at the unison—as in their 34 dashing bars of semiquavers that conclude the Scherzo of the Second Symphony— the effect is electric, and cuts brilliantly through the centre of the chordal accompaniment from the rest of the orchestra.

(5) To some ears, too, the nervous energy of Schumann's frequent use of string tremolo is tiring. If the conductor feels that this device is too overworked for his interpretation, it is again very easy to ask the strings to play some of their passages without tremolo.

As regards the over-thickness: this is not a problem that affects the early works. The 'Spring' Symphony, the Overture, Scherzo and Finale, the Piano Concerto, *Paradise and the Peri*, Faust Part III—all these compositions of 1841 to 1845 were clearly and colourfully scored. The middle period of the Second Symphony and *Manfred* are satisfactory; but the works of 1851 to 1853, his last—and very active —years as an orchestral composer, show him scoring for orchestra much more thickly and far less effectively. Most composers gain in orchestral mastery as their experience of writing works and hearing them played increases, but with Schumann the opposite is the case.

It is possible that his deteriorating mental condition contributed to this directly, but the facts point far more to his steadily increasing difficulties in conducting. At Düsseldorf, with his appointment as Music Director from the autumn of 1850, Schumann was responsible for regular concerts. Before long, diary entries by Robert and Clara speak of increasing problems of absentees at rehearsals, insubordination amongst players, and opposition from committee members[1]— problems with which Schumann was quite unable, temperamentally, to cope. Also at times in the 1850s he seems to have found it physically difficult to conduct. The works of this time tend to be much 'thicker', and are above all scored in a way that would still make them 'safe' to play, if there were absentees, or if the conductor was not fully controlling the proceedings. When a player missed his entry for an important melody, for instance, there were usually others playing the

---

[1] Litzmann, *op. cit.*, Vol. II, p. 240 *et seq.*

same theme and the performance would continue.[1] It is tragic, of course, that posterity has suffered for the sake of temporary expediency.

Mahler's Re-orchestrations

The re-orchestrations of the Schumann Symphonies undertaken by Gustav Mahler (1860–1911) have the advantage of being the work of a romantic composer, who was not only a master orchestrator, but also a conductor of the front rank. There was no doubt about Mahler's sympathy with the music either: he wanted to include the Schumann Symphonies in his own orchestral concerts and for this purpose sought to prepare versions that were more brightly scored and which he felt would be more immediately effective.

Mahler's editions are rarely used for performances, nor have they ever been published. However, seeing the things that Mahler changes makes a fascinating study for anyone interested in orchestration. 'Re-touching' would be an apter description than 're-orchestration', because Mahler never wrote out the Symphonies afresh but merely made alterations, additions and deletions in the published scores. Also, all the Symphonies contain many dozens of pages in which Mahler makes no changes at all. For example, the 'cathedral' movement of the 'Rhenish' Symphony only has a few re-touchings towards its end. Mahler and his copyists have made the modifications in the ordinary scores of the Symphonies as published by Schumann, and these copies are available on hire from Mahler's publishers—Universal Edition. In these the reader will see altered notes, extra expression marks inked in, and many superfluous doublings crossed out, while only rarely has it been necessary for the copyists to paste in blank staves to be filled in again with a fuller type of re-orchestration.

Mahler's changes can be summarized under four headings:

(1) *Greater prominence is given to thematic ideas*. Particularly does Mahler bring help to Schumann's overworked first violins. Thus the opening melody of the slow movement of the 'Spring' Symphony is now given not to the divided first violins only, but to all the violins: the first have the upper octave, the second the lower.[2] This gives the melody much greater clarity. At the same time Mahler divides the violas so that they cover Schumann's original second violin and viola parts.

Also, at the opening of the 'Rhenish' Symphony, the oboes double the first violins in their soaring melody.

[1] See Ex. 45b, above.   [2] See Ex. 8, above.

(2) *Greater orchestral transparency is achieved.* Mahler's re-touching of the
timpani parts is especially interesting, because whereas Schumann is
often content to let his two or three timpani continue to do duty
throughout his quickly-modulating music (causing some blurring in the
process), Mahler requires the timpanist quickly to retune his instruments

EX 54a   (Schuman

[Schumann: Symphony No. 3, 1st movement, bars 397 - 411]

(Mahler)

EX. 45b   Lebhaft

for passages in distant keys. Thus, although Schumann uses three
timpani (tuned to B flat, G flat and F) for the first movement of the
'Spring' Symphony, Mahler also writes rolls on C, D and D flat, and the
only easy way for a timpanist to cope with Mahler's parts is to use
modern pedal-tuned timpani.

But the major way in which Mahler achieves transparency is by
deletion. Often melodies given to two instruments by Schumann are

given to a soloist by Mahler. More particularly, the orchestral weight on heavy bass lines is reduced, and thick doublings of the inner texture by horns and trumpets are cut out. By reserving horns and trumpets for climaxes, Mahler often makes such climaxes more impressive. These points are aptly illustrated by a comparison of bars 403–11 in the first movement of the 'Rhenish' Symphony, showing one of the most extensive of Mahler's alterations (Ex. 54(a) and (b)).

In the eight bars before the recapitulation (letter 'N') Mahler deletes the trumpets and drums altogether; thus, these instruments are held in reserve and, when Mahler again restores them at letter N, the recapitulation starts with much more sense of culmination. Mahler retains the two melodic phrases for the four horns, but drastically cuts out their filling-in notes. This allows the melodic entries of woodwind and strings to be heard much more, and these latter melodic entries are also given greater prominence through the support Mahler gives them from the second violins, and by his bringing down an octave the high tremolos of the first violins. Finally, Mahler cuts out many string tremolos at points where these instruments are making melodic entries (though he allows the glowing incandescence of the violas' melodic tremolos to remain). The result of these changes is greater melodic preciseness, less harmonic thickness, and a far brighter climax at the recapitulation. However, the effect is undoubtedly less Schumannesque.

(3) *Mahler assumes that valve horns and valve trumpets are available*. Thus many chromatic notes not available to an orchestral composer in the early 1840s make their appearance in Mahler's re-touching of the brass parts. Mahler probably goes a good deal too far here for the purist, because the brass technique he uses at times sounds definitely late-nineteenth century in style (Ex. 55).

EX 55

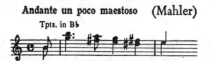

(4) *Dynamics are rethought*. Here Mahler draws on his long experience as an orchestral conductor, and his re-marking of the parts can save a lot of time at rehearsal. He takes full account of the fact that a brass chord marked 'fortissimo' will sound a great deal louder than a simultaneous string passage also marked 'fortissimo', and, if such a string passage is

to be heard, Mahler frequently marks the brass down to 'mezzo forte'. Schumann's practice of writing what he wanted to *hear* in his scores was the usual one with composers up to his time. The conductor thus has considerable work to do in getting a suitable balance, and a certain amount of what the audience hears is always due to his taste. Mahler, following the tradition of later Wagner and Liszt, writes in what he requires the orchestral musicians to *play*. For example, in the second movement of the Fourth Symphony, Schumann had been content to mark the oboe solo and its accompaniments as 'piano'. Mahler leaves the melody as 'piano', but marks all the accompanying instruments down to *ppp*.

Mahler takes infinite care to graduate most lengthy crescendi and diminuendi in much greater detail than Schumann. Often, in order to gain a more striking effect, he does seem to over-exaggerate Schumann's plan. Thus the last four bars of the development in the first movement of the Second Symphony are marked by Schumann '*p* crescendo . . . *ff*'. In Mahler this becomes '*ppp* crescendo . . . *ff*'. And in Mahler marks of '*fff*' as well as '*ppp*' are plentiful, though in the Schumann original these extremes are rare.

When Mahler's marks merely exaggerate what Schum nn wrote they can readily be tolerated—for they simply emanate from trying to render the music in a colourful way. Unfortunately Mahler does not confine himself to this, and at times his dynamics are the complete opposite of Schumann's. For instance, in the 'Rhenish' Finale Schumann had clearly written what he wanted—*forte* from the outset—an effect of brilliant sunshine after the darkness of the cathedral. But Mahler, by marking the first eight bars *piano*, completely loses this.

What Mahler does *not* do is also of interest, especially with the Fourth Symphony. Here it might have been valuable if Mahler had restored some of the felicities of the 1841 version, such as the horn calls in the Scherzo. But he shows no evidence of knowing the 1841 version, and leaves many of the thick textures of Schumann's revision standing, whereas to have restored the original scoring in places would have let the music gain in clarity, yet in a thoroughly Schumann-esque way, for which there was unimpeachable authority. It is surprising to see in Mahler's edition of the Fourth Symphony that those frequent and long passages in which the bassoons double the cellos, the clarinets double the violas, the oboes double the second violins and the flutes double the first violins—are mostly left as they were published in Schumann's 1851 version.

Significantly, Mahler never increases the number of instruments for which Schumann scores.

Schumann's Feeling for the Orchestra

It is in Schumann's own versions that people usually prefer to hear the Symphonies. There are a number of reasons for this. Firstly, his orchestration is usually a good deal more effective in performance than he is ever given credit for. Professional musicians often see faults on paper, and it would indeed be a condemnation if these led to audiences finding their pleasure in the music was marred. But in practice these technical faults get ironed out, and they are not noticeable to listeners. Secondly, there is the important consideration that Schumann's orchestration is appropriate to the type of music he was writing. The relevant comparison is with Brahms, whose 'dark' orchestration undoubtedly suits the sober style of his music. With Schumann the sense of striving for high ideals, which the Symphonies communicate, is in a way echoed by the orchestra striving for effect in those passages that are difficult to 'bring off'. Composers like Handel, Haydn, Mendelssohn, and Elgar knew what they wanted and how to get it. But with Schumann there is always that great sense of the Romantic artist striving for the unattainable, and this gives one of the special flavours so characteristic of his music. Somehow this striving is communicated to the audience if a dedicated conductor works to reveal the vision clearly.

But quite apart from its appropriateness, the many bold effects and poetic colourings that are continually to be met with in Schumann do show that at times he had a wonderful sense of the orchestra. This is only fully seen when the whole range of his orchestral music is examined. Again and again in the major choral and dramatic works the orchestra adds a colouring and a dimension quite impossible of achievement in any other way. In *Faust*, for example, there could be mentioned the resolute five bar solo for trumpet that opens, and repeatedly appears in, the scene of Faust's death; or the chromatic dashes for the flutes, which accompany the mocking gestures of the Lemurs as they dig Faust's grave; or the fervent writing for solo 'cello that appears as an obbligato to the aria of Pater Ecstaticus, or the orchestra's preparation for the entry of the spectres of Want, Guilt, Care and Need. In this the bare octaves of flute, oboe and bassoon are doubled, far above, by the piccolo playing in the highest part of its register, while in the middle of the framework come the strings' mysterious fleeting tremolos (Ex. 56).

EX 56

The *Manfred* music too is remarkable for the colouristic effects of the scoring. In the *Calling of the Witch of the Alps*, Byron describes the scene thus:

> . . . the sunbow's rays still arch
> The torrent with the many hues of heaven,
> And roll the sheeted silver's waving column
> O'er the crag's headlong perpendicular,
> And fling its lines of foaming light along.

Schumann responds with restless watery semiquavers for muted first violins, accompanied in the lightest way by divided second violins, two violas and two 'cellos; while harp harmonics punctuate the pianissimo melody for flute and oboe (Ex. 57).

EX 57

And surely in the long cor anglais solo of the *Ranz des Vaches* in *Manfred* there may occur one of the rare examples of Schumann influencing Wagner—the Shepherd's piping in the last act of *Tristan*. Wagner's cor anglais melody was composed a few years later, and, like Schumann's (Ex. 58(a) and (b)) contains a slow and a fast strain.

In the years 1846 to 1853 the orchestral works show Schumann's style and language continuing to develop: his melodies, as seen in *Manfred* and the opening of the 'Rhenish' Symphony, were becoming far more long-drawn and grandly irregular, and his harmonic language, as in the *Faust* Overture of 1853, was becoming enormously enriched in its individualistic way. But the orchestral works also show that simultaneously the tragedy of his mental illness was progressively marring his maturing genius. It was as though rich farmlands were producing every year a more and more abundant harvest, while at the same time the scourge of blight was getting more and more extensive.

EX 58a

At the very last, with his discovery of the solo violin as an instrument for the expression of romantic passion, Schumann began moving towards a whole new world of emotion and utterance. The vision reaches its strongest in the Violin Concerto of Autumn 1853, but it is clouded: it gives tantalizing glimpses, yet never clearly shows the promised land. It was only with Brahms, who was following along the way pointed out by Schumann, that the new world was entered and gloriously revealed—particularly in the D minor Piano Concerto (composed 1854–57).

But even at the end, in his last major work, Schumann's wonderful feeling for the orchestra can still be heard, even though less frequently than before, and my last examples how show the divided 'cellos start the Violin Concerto's slow movement. *Pianissimo*, and in heavily syncopated phrases, the 'cellos' whispers tell of undreamed-of wonders not far away (Ex. 59).

EX 59

Operatic and Dramatic Music

N
O sadder plight exists for a composer than to spend years toiling away
in pursuit of an ideal only to have it elude him and the results become
unappreciated, fall into neglect and be forgotten. It happened to Schumann's so-
called dramatic works, partly because of their real faults and partly because of odds
supplied by the products of Meyerbeer and Wagner. Dramatic composition held
for Schumann a fatal, siren-like attraction. He could not shake his desire, his
ambition to write music for the stage. Over the years he considered a fascinating
array of subjects: *The Mines of Falun, Till Eulenspiegel, El galan, Der Wartburg
Krieg, Die Niebelungen, Hamlet, The Tempest, Doge und Dogaressa, Bajazet, Abélard
et Héloïse, Atala, The Corsair, Sardanapalus, Maria Stuarta, Ṣakuntala, The Smith of
Gretna Green, King Arthur, Tristan und Isolde* and the *Odyssey*. Eventually,
Schumann rejected them all, devoting himself to Goethe's *Faust*, Hebbel's
Genoveva and Byron's *Manfred*.

Scenes from Faust (1844-53)

Faust was first. Schumann thought about it for nearly ten years, contemplating
in turn an opera and an oratorio. What emerged he called *Scenes from Goethe's
Faust*. It consists of an overture and three largely unrelated sections for soloists,
chorus and orchestra. He began piecemeal in 1844 with the Apotheosis (Part
Three). A year later he wrote to Mendelssohn:

> The scene from *Faust* reposes in my desk. I am absolutely afraid to look at it
> again. The lofty poetry, especially of the final part, moved me so deeply that
> I ventured to begin. I have no idea whether I shall ever publish it.

Yet, in 1847, he recomposed the final chorus as it now stands and, in 1848, completed the large chorus *Gerettet ist*. After a private hearing that year, he wrote to Nottebohm:

> It gave me pleasure. The whole thing impressed me as stronger than the music of the *Peri*—doubtless because the poem is grander.[1]

1849 saw Schumann complete the *Mater dolorosa*, the cathedral scene with its *Dies irae* (Part One), and the *Scene im Garten* (Part One). A triple première of the Apotheosis was arranged simultaneously in Dresden, Leipzig and Weimar on the second day of the Goethe centenary celebration (29 August 1849). A letter written just beforehand reveals Schumann's reactions:

> I only wish I could have Faust's mantle for that day, in order to be everywhere and hear everything. How strange, the piece lay five years in the desk. Nobody knew anything about it, and I myself had almost forgotten its existence—and now in this unusual celebration it has to come to light![2]

In 1850, the three pieces to comprise Schumann's Part Two—*Sonnenaufgang Mitternacht* and *Fausts Tod*—were finished and, in 1853, the Overture (which gave Schumann considerable trouble). The piano score appeared only in 1858; the full score came out a year later. And it was not until 14 January 1862 that the complete work had its première at Cologne under Ferdinand Hiller—five and a half years after Schumann's death.

Faust has appeal for anyone imbued with Goethe's original and, if intelligibility be a criterion of value, seems to have presupposed a thorough knowledge of it on the part of an audience. Schumann selected his text rather curiously, choosing not to set such scenes as the *Walpurgisnacht* (Part One) and *Weitläufiger Saal* (Part Two, Act 1) of Goethe's text—which call for music. The mystical thought and philosophical character of Goethe's masterpiece, not its qualities as a story, entranced Schumann, who felt himself in deep sympathy with it. Thus, he eschewed any attempt at dramatic continuity, handled his text as though it were prose (concentrating mostly upon abstract ideas) and hoped only to escape censure for adding music 'to such perfect poetry'. His theme was the spiritual, saving side of Faust.

The Overture is an involved, motific affair. To judge from nineteenth-century accounts, listeners heard in it hints of the whole of *Faust*—from doubt, temptation, struggle, crime and despair to light, redemption and joy—while judging it less than successful. A few found it 'bewildering'; others 'dull', 'obscure', 'laboured'.

[1] June 1848.   [2] Letter to Härtel.

Certainly, its rhythmic elements conform more to the bar than one might expect, its use of instrumental ranges is somewhat sober and its treatment of sonata form without surprise. Schumann's harmonies, however, are rich and interesting, frequently featuring unprepared suspensions and anticipations. But the prevailing effect is turgid, and the piece seems ill-suited for performance apart from the whole.

As an introduction to what follows, the Overture works quite well. Its short motifs are those of the larger context, especially the following:

EX 1

EX 2

EX 3

EX 4

the principal interval being a major/minor third.

Part One follows, consisting of three scenes: *Scene im Garten, Gretchen vor dem Bild der Mater dolorosa* and *Scene im Dom*. The first, Faust's love-making to Gretchen in the garden, contrasts tellingly with the Overture. Melody and recitative commingle to flow in quavers and crotchets from first to last, consistently and simply. Detractors consider it too smooth, too sweet, and cite its sketchiness, lack of intensity and dramatic development as liabilities. Musically, the scene satisfies, juxtaposed as it is to the Overture. Schumann's mistake lies in following it with something even slower, so that the pace sags.

'Gretchen Before the Mater Dolorosa's Image' is a scene of considerable poignancy, an outpouring of contrition and remorse. As a concert aria it enjoyed a certain, limited popularity in the nineteenth century and, indeed, it may have been more effective out of its static context. Gretchen's cry in octave leaps, 'Help! Save me ere I die!' once proved startling and heart-rending and would still, no doubt, had Schumann supported it with a less obvious chord progression:

EX 5

The cathedral scene ends Schumann's Part One auspiciously. It is very well developed and somewhat theatrical, if not dramatic. The sudden punctuation of the dialogue between Gretchen and the Evil Spirit (who stands behind her, whispering into her ear) by the blazing *Dies irae* is the work's first really exciting idea. Organ-like brass reinforce the choral masses with gigantic effect:

EX 6

The climax, the *Judex ergo*, is particularly shattering, interrupting as it does Gretchen's lament:

EX 7

Part Two opens on an Alpine scene. At Ariel's bidding, beneficent sprites lull Faust to sleep. Schumann, literal to the idea of Goethe's 'aeolian harps', employs harps and violins for an effect intended to be as magical and transparent as anything ever orchestrated along similar lines by Mendelssohn and Liszt. Ariel's solo and the alternation of choral soli with full choir suffer only from Schumann's unhappy syllabic treatment. While this keeps the text maximally clear, it was already used (and to better ends) in the *Dies irae*. Here it seems merely uninspired, and Schumann realizes little of the opportunity for magnificence afforded by the gradual sunrise. But the scene of Faust's awakening, 'Des Lebens Pulse' and its continuation 'So ist es also', though protracted is a fascinating example of Schumann's experiments at composing 'unending melody' after Wagnerian principles—and one of *Faust's* aspects which embroiled the work in a doctrinal dispute that today has meaning only as an object of historical study.

Midnight comes next. Four 'grey women' appear—Want, Debt, Grief and Distress—and Schumann's major/minor third motif is everywhere a part of the texture. Faust's dialogue with Grief paves the way for a chordal perforation in B Major against which Faust utters words which were considered 'golden monuments' of Goethe's genius and especially suited for this kind of setting. If persons of non-German orientation find this music pompous or trite, let them recall the intense spirit of nationalism which bound Schumann and many others to Goethe and his perfectly expressed ideas.

Part Two concludes with Faust's Death, an extended scene between Faust, Mephistopheles and a group of Lemurs. The handling throughout is chordal and syllabic, and lacks contrast between the parts for the two men's voices. Only the Lemurs' *subito* appearances, piano, break up what Schumann could scarcely have intended as monotony.

Part Three is an intricate, elaborate melting of soli and choruses into a series of slow, highly personal expressions. Hanslick admired it tremendously:

> All is heart-felt, warm and simple. Far from Schumann lay the temptation to approach the poem on its brilliant outside. He let it grow warm in his heart, and then gave us, instead of a transcendental scene of triumph, a piece of his deepest and most individual feeling.

And Liszt wrote of it to Schumann:

> This grand and beautiful work has made a most grand and beautiful impression.

The scene is Faust's transfiguration, his apotheosis. Angels escort his soul to heaven—while the Anchorites on the mountains sing hymns of praise. Dramatically, there is only *stasis*. Musically, everything is noticeably moderate, even 'chaste'. No extremes of instrumental range and few of the vocal or dynamic are called for. Six of the seven sections are marked Langsam (slow)—clearly, music of utmost sobriety and well-meant import.

Viewing the entirety of *Faust*, Brahms wrote to Clara in 1859:

> To perform the whole thing (even with orchestra) on one evening seems to me unwise. If I were you, I should try to prevent it rather than encourage it. The third (part) by itself has a better effect than when it follows the first two. Besides which, the pieces rarely have even the faintest connection to each other . . .

And though Clara always staunchly spoke well of the work, she once admitted about Part Two:

> . . . in places I should have liked Faust to have been treated as recitative, where he is merely reflecting, and this would have broken the monotony.[1]

Eventually, she rationalized away every defect of the work:

> I am convinced that this work will some day take its place among the greatest in existence. The second part is at least as great as the third . . .[2]

History has favoured other versions of the Faust legend—notably those of Berlioz, Gounod and Boito. They differ markedly from Schumann's. Berlioz made Mephistopheles his hero, celebrating the arch-fiend's triumph in the damnation of his victim. Gounod confined himself to practicable dramatic limits in the pathetic story of Gretchen. Boito tried to crowd into his opera too much material from both parts of Goethe's *Faust* and failed to achieve dramatic unity, though failing in no other way to supply everything else expected by the operatic public. Schumann's setting, on the other hand, provides nothing of the sort. He never intended it as an opera, and may not have wanted it staged or even performed as an entity.

Genoveva (1847–48)

Schumann's only opera was composed from start to finish in two years, 1847 and 1848. For years his 'prayer from morning to evening' had been 'German Opera'. It was a utopian goal towards which he aspired, a goal his entire generation of

---

[1] Letter to Theodor Kircher, Berlin, 10 May 1858. Litzmann: *Clara Schumann: Ein Künstlerleben* (Leipzig, 3rd Ed., 1906).
[2] Letter to Brahms, Düsseldorf, 25 January 1862. Litzmann: *Clara Schumann—Johannes Brahms Briefe aus den Jahren 1853–96* (Leipzig, 1927).

composers sought to attain. They desired to create a truly national style to compete with those of Italy and France. Though Wagner was working towards it, Schumann believed him still dependent upon foreign influences and thought himself 'called to fulfil the vow'. *Genoveva* would do it, he felt.

A number of composers (including Haydn) had treated the well-known legend of Geneviève de Brabant. Schumann was drawn to it through reading two contemporary dramas made from it: one by Tieck cast 'in the idyllic tones of a fairy tale'; the other, by Hebbel, devised along harsher, more realistic lines. He asked his friend Robert Reinick to fashion a libretto after this latter version, then, uncertain whether to proceed without Hebbel's sanction, Schumann wrote to him:

> In reading your poem *Genoveva* (I am a musician), I was struck by the magnificent material which it offers for music. The oftener I read your unrivalled tragedy—I will not attempt further praise—the more vividly did I see it in its musical form. Finally, I consulted a man living here who is something of a poet. He was immediately impressed by the extraordinary beauty of the poem, and readily consented to try to arrange it as an operatic libretto. . . . But although the adapter has done his best, it is not what I want. It is weak throughout. I very much dislike the ordinary libretto style, and neither can nor will write music for tirades of that sort.
>
> I was almost in despair, when it occurred to me that the direct way might be the best, and I decided to address myself to the original poet, and to ask for his assistance. But do not, dear Sir, misunderstand me. I do not suggest that you should adapt for operatic purposes a work so profound in its conception, so masterly in its form, but that you should look over the adaptation, tell me what you think, and give it an inspiring touch here and there. That is what I have to ask.[1]

Hebbel visited Schumann, who felt honoured in entertaining 'the greatest genius of our day', but Hebbel preferred not to see his work become a libretto and absolved himself of any part of such a project. Schumann then collaborated with Reinick in putting together a libretto based both on Tieck *and* Hebbel. Problems cropped up. Reinick tended to oversentimentalize his parts and Schumann felt forced to write all the words for Act III himself. Neither could agree on how to reconcile the differing views of both poets. Schumann finally decided to shoulder the responsibility of the libretto alone and produced what was to his taste 'a gem'.

[1] Letter to Hebbel, Dresden, 14 May 1847; Storck: *The Letters of Robert Schumann* (London, 1907).

He showed the finished libretto to Wagner, who later related:

> No objection of mine could induce Schumann to discard the unlucky, foolish third act of his version. He grew angry and thought that, by my dissuasion I was trying to ruin his greatest effects.[1]

The libretto stood. Schumann plunged into the Overture, completing it within a few days. His creative fervour spurred him into a crushing schedule. He worked day and night at the opera until he broke down under the strain. Periods of recuperation alternated with furious labour until, on 4 August 1848, the work and its orchestration were finished. Schumann's nerves were bad. He confessed:

> I lost every melody as soon as I had thought of it. What I heard inside my head took too much out of me.

Leipzig accepted the new opera for production. Schumann went there in June of 1849 to help with the preparations. After several delays, the late spring of 1850 was agreed upon for the première, with Schumann to arrive ahead of time in February to assist. But Meyerbeer's *Le Prophète* intervened, pushing *Genoveva*'s first rehearsals into the middle of May. Schumann smarted from this insult particularly, for *Genoveva* had been meant from the start as a protest against Meyerbeer and what he stood for in the world of opera.

The work's full score appeared in print before its first performance that autumn. Mixed reports circulated so effectively that the première was crowded. Gade, Hiller, Moscheles, Reinecke and Spohr were there. Liszt journeyed from Weimar for the great event. Schumann conducted. The first two acts went well; the last two, in Clara's words, 'less well'. The singers and the composer were given only two bows. Two subsequent performances went better, but Schumann remained almost alone in his response to 'the wealth of inner feelings' *Genoveva* contained, and it has seen relatively few revivals since that time.

★   ★   ★

The action takes place in the eighth century. In Act One, Siegfried leaves Genoveva, entrusting her safety to his servant Golo. His estate and household he leaves in charge of Drago, his faithful steward. Surrounded by his troops, Siegfried sets out to join the Emperor Charles Martel in battling the infidels. In Siegfried's absence, Golo's secret love for Genoveva grows uncontrollably and he vows that

[1] Schauffler; *Florestan: the life and work of Robert Schumann*, p. 202, New York, 1945.

she shall be his. A sorceress, Margaretha (in reality Golo's mother), urges him on and promises to help get rid of Siegfried.

In Act Two, Golo comes late at night to tell Genoveva of a reported victory. She is alone, spinning, and longs after her husband. In her joy over the good news, she bids Golo to sing with her. Golo's passion overcomes him. Insulted and indignant, Genoveva spurns him, reminding him of his servile position and—to Golo's horror—bastard's birth. This crushes Golo. His love sours and he plans revenge: he will ruin her. Margaretha is enlisted to spread throughout the household false rumours of intimacy between Genoveva and her chaplain. In the uproar which follows, an incredulous Drago, with Golo's knowledge, agrees to hide in Genoveva's room—to prove to himself that she is innocent. The moment Drago is gone, Margaretha leads the body of outraged servants to Genoveva. Thus confronted, Genoveva pleads in protest, appealing unsuccessfully to Golo for protection. They storm Genoveva's room, find Drago—and Golo murders him on the spot. The plot has worked. Genoveva is dragged away and imprisoned.

In Act Three, Siegfried is on his way home but detained by a wound at Strasbourg—under Margaretha's care (her attempt to poison him failed). Recovered from his wound, Siegfried is impatient to set out again when Golo arrives bearing a letter from the chaplain. It tells of Genoveva's adultery with Drago. Astounded and deeply saddened, Siegfried orders Golo to return and put Genoveva to death. Now, Margaretha has a magic mirror which, she has told Siegfried, will show him Genoveva at home. As he looks into it his suspicions are confirmed: the magic pictures do reveal a growing intimacy between Genoveva and Drago. Infuriated, Siegfried smashes the mirror and rushes away. But the blow to the mirror is fatal to Margaretha's magic, for Drago's spirit rises from the shattered glass and commands her to follow after Siegfried and confess the plot.

In Act Four, Genoveva is led into a rocky clearing overlooked by Siegfried's castle. She is to be put to death. Golo approaches her once more, showing her Siegfried's ring and sword (with which he has been bidden to kill her). He again attempts to win her, promising to spare her life. She prefers death to dishonour. Golo orders his men to carry out the execution, rushes away and falls over a cliff. Genoveva sees a cross among the rocks and clings to it praying. The men are on the verge of tearing her from it when Siegfried, led by Margaretha, appears with his followers. The sun rises on the scene, Siegfried and Genoveva are reunited. She forgives Siegfried and all who were against her. The crowd hails the two lovers.

The deficiencies are several. G. B. Shaw felt them so strongly that he dismissed the story as 'nakedly silly' and 'pure bosh'. Whereas Golo was the strong, central character in Hebbel's original, Schumann chose to centre his plot around Genoveva. Golo, along with Siegfried and Drago, he fashioned as lesser figures. But none of these characters is delineated to anything like his potential. Everyone, including the villain Golo, is sentimental, which lessens their contrast as individuals. Even Genoveva's role is hardly developed beyond that of the others. This, no doubt, was one of Schumann's most noticeable failures, for he always tended to preoccupy himself with the emotional life of womankind. One has only to think of the Peri, the Rose, Gretchen and of the cycle *Frauenliebe und -leben* to realize this. And while Schumann might be forgiven poor character delineation in his males, that he did not provide Genoveva with a friend to sympathize with her, counsel and support her through her tribulation and draw from her at least one aria of innermost personal feeling seems inexplicable. Margaretha and her magic mirror, the objects of Wagner's well-intended warning to Schumann, emerge as especially artificial, old fashioned romantic devices—thoroughly unbelievable and nonsensical (along with the preposterous ghost). That Schumann did not think to have Siegfried surprise Golo in his final appeal to Genoveva—what a trio that would have made!—further supports the suspicion that he lacked dramatic imagination.

The music which Schumann composed for *Genoveva* has always known a higher place in people's opinions than the libretto to which it was married. Its Overture has stood apart and on its own as a standard member of the orchestral repertoire for 120 years. Its first chord, an unprepared chord of the ninth,

EX 8

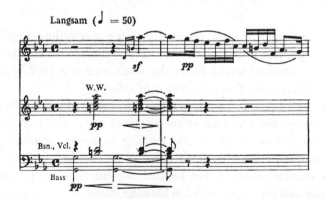

proved as gripping to nineteenth-century ears as had the opening chord of the *Faust* Overture, an unprepared major seventh. But the Faust chord resolves at once quite properly; the *Genoveva* chord is repeated *sfz* and not resolved until the third bar. No trace of hasty workmanship can be found anywhere in this Overture. Its pulse is firmly maintained in juxtaposition with the numerous phrases and motifs of varying lengths (used subsequently in the opera) which occur off the beat. Dovetailing and overlapping of thematic ideas with accompaniment figures leave no gaps in the forward, headlong flow:

EX 9

Harmonies shift unpredictably, constantly, ever a part of the controlled release of musical energy. It is music which *moves* along, the hardest kind to compose. Though cast in standard sonata form, the work excites as do few others and creates great expectations about the drama to follow.

Alas, Schumann's taste forbade him using the devices of successful opera. Not for him the showy effects Meyerbeer knew how to wield with such overwhelming effect—tremendous vocal ranges, flashing orchestral colour, spectacular staging, flamboyant ensembles. Such theatrics lay beyond the boundaries of Schumann's musical morality. He loathed the interruption by applause of dramatic action and almost succeeded in banning 'number' pieces from his opera. Unfortunately, the public was unaccustomed to so homogeneous a blend of recitative with solo, of solo with ensemble, and did not understand or appreciate the uninterrupted stream of continuous music of which Schumann was so proud. Likewise, Schumann's musical characterization lacked variety, a point perhaps sensed only subliminally by the public but which dampens none the less its psychological identification with and empathetic response to those caught up in the course of events. The music Schumann composed for each of his characters might as easily be put into the mouth of any other without the slightest incongruity, a drawback avoided by all the great opera composers.

Margaretha alone stands out from the rest, but unhappily. Schumann depicts her in the orchestra by means of a piccolo. Thus, her orchestral support seems less than appropriate. It provoked a rage in Shaw:

> The witch's music is frivolous and serio-comic, the orchestration sprouting at the top into an outrageous piccolo part which would hardly be let off with mere indulgent laughter if it came from any less well-beloved composer. . . . Instrumentation, as we all know, was not Schumann's strong point; and there is plenty of his characteristic orchestral muddling in *Genoveva*; but I can remember no other instance of his scoring being foolish in intention.[1]

That piccolo is Schumann's single immodest orchestral gesture during the four acts, though other musical faults exist.

Schumann admits no flight of fancy to relieve the endless syllabic style with which he set his text. There is not one cadenza or remotely florid passage, not even one really long-held high note. Demands upon vocal technique are at a minimum. And, sadly, the lines he composed leave little imprint of themselves upon the memory. His choral writing is mostly chordal, syllabic and rhythmically repetitious—in the staid tradition of the *ordinary* nineteenth-century German choral song:

EX 10

[1] G. B. Shaw: *Music in London*, Vol. III, pp. 107–12 (London, 1932).

vor   aus dem Ver — stec — ke ! Un — srer Herr-in die — ses Glas !

vor   aus dem Ver — stec — ke ! Un — srer Herr-in die — ses Glas !

Lest all this seem too severe an indictment of *Genoveva*, let us recall the lofty, idealized goal which Schumann sought—German Opera—and cite an example of *Genoveva*'s most sustained beauty:

EX 11

Adagio (♩ = 60)

O du,   der ü – ber Al – le wacht, der   Al — les wohl ge — macht,   be-

wahr',   o Herr, auch die – se Nacht   die Gu – ten und   die From — men !   In

dei — nen Wil– len leg' ich nun so Seel'._____ wie Leib!

Man¡red (1848–49)

By 1848, Schumann's growing introversion brought him into the perfect frame
of mind to compose *Manfred*. It may be that he felt akin to the character and fate
of the hero of Byron's vast poem. Clara wrote in her diary that the poem 'inspired
Robert to an extraordinary degree', and Wasielewski tells us that once in Düsseldorf, while Schumann was reading it aloud, 'his voice suddenly failed him, tears
started from his eyes, and he was so overcome that he could read no further'. Also,
Mendelssohn's recent death had struck Schumann with great emotional force,
and death began to occupy Schumann's thoughts—possibly heightening his
receptivity to the gloomy atmosphere of *Manfred*. It seems safe to say that Schumann identified with Byron's melancholy hero: they shared a great inward
struggle. Manfred's inner conflict was Byron's own and Schumann saw himself
reflected therein.

So it was that, almost in the same breath with which he ended the torment of
composing *Genoveva*, Schumann plunged into *Manfred*:

> Never before have I devoted myself with such love and outlay of force to any
> composition as to that of *Manfred*.

The work progressed swiftly since much of the text did not have to be set to
music, but music devised to accompany words largely spoken and only occasionally sung—to create a melodrama being far simpler than to compose an opera.
The unique outcome interested Liszt, who suggested staging it at Weimar. He did
so in 1852, the Overture being premièred separately and published that same year.
By 1853, the piano score of the whole appeared, though the full score reached the
public only in 1862.

From the start, the Overture was pronounced a success. 'The most magnificent
thing Robert has done,' declared Moscheles, and Schumann wrote to Liszt, 'I

really consider it one of the finest of my brain-children.' Its special qualities commence with the precipitous first bar, so carefully calculated to furnish no clue as to metre or tempo:

EX 12

The slow introduction is more than just something with which to start. It contains elements of the work's main themes, which finally appear in this form:

EX 13a

EX. 13b

The main body of this Overture, a sonata form, proceeds 'in a passionate tempo'. Schumann characteristically exerts himself here as in the *Genoveva*

Overture by holding taut the reins of musical energy. His rhythm is simply superb: the beat, steadfast, omnipresent; the musical lines, spread across the bars and syncopated. Everywhere that torsion-like pull of two opposing forces, each designed to check the other. Unlike the *Faust* Overture, where phrases coincide too closely with bar lines, the *Manfred* Overture continues to live in the active orchestral repertoire. That it and the *Genoveva* Overture still thrive must be attributed to their ever-interesting, complementary thematic and rhythmic elements. Both pieces were far ahead of their time in that Schumann employed motivic themes throughout and not tuneful melodies; hence their 'modernity' even today. Both arrived in a rush of spontaneous enthusiasm and inspiration (and are the better for it), while the *Faust* Overture had to be contrived without such aid (and is the worse for it). But *Manfred* goes one step further than its dramatic *confrères* by means of a unique coda which resolves the music's drama and makes way for Byron's by telescoping together the three opening chords of Ex. 11 and the two themes of Ex. 12:

EX 14

After the Overture, *Manfred* proceeds through fifteen numbers, six of which are pieces of music complete in themselves, with the rest treated melodramatically. A check against Byron's original reveals that Schumann shortened the dialogue, reduced the seven spirits to four, augmented the number of voices in the Incantation from the one called for by Byron to four and added to the concluding scene the text: *Requiem aeternam dona eis, Et lux perpetua luceat eis.*

M

Manfred is an elaborate piece of artifice on Byron's part, a romantic indulgence in self description and martyrdom of personality. It has no plot; there is no action. Manfred, a special being unlike other men, is laden with a nameless guilt somehow related to the death of Astarte. Escape is denied him—for he cannot die, commit suicide or find refuge in madness. He then calls up an array of earthly and super-natural beings, uses them as sounding boards for his tortured, quasi-philosophical revelations and self explorations—and, in the end, dies. Biancolli puts it, 'He relinquishes his rule over his familiar spirits, lays down his staff like Prospero and and submits to the universal rule of death.' Nothing explains this. It needs no explanation, being surely a literary tragedy, not a real one. But Schumann, for whom the unreal was real, knew all too well Manfred's dilemmas. He did not seek the madness Manfred sought—it sought, found and possessed Schumann. His tragedy was to go mad while desperately trying to cling to sanity and to the art which sanity alone can produce. Perhaps that is why *Manfred* is so curious a creation.

Nowhere does the character Manfred sing. Schumann wrote to Liszt, 'The main thing is . . . the impersonation of Manfred, for whom the music is but a setting.' He speaks alone, against orchestral backgrounds and, at the end, while the choir sings (Schumann indicating in this place the precise rhythms for Man-fred's lines).

Opportunities for other-worldly effects abound as Manfred conjures up spirit after spirit. Schumann is at his best in these places, characterizing each by using different keys, dissimilar orchestral accompaniments and different vocal ranges. In the first piece treated melodramatically, Manfred is confronted with a 'magical apparition of a beautiful female figure' which is depicted musically by means of a theme originating in the Overture. Six repetitions of the line occur, each being given a different treatment. As sphinx-like as 'The Prophet Bird', the figure vanishes:

EX 15

MANFRED. O Gott, ist's so, wenn du nicht Wahn bild, Ver höhnung du nicht

bist, o dann würd'.ich doch noch der Se — lig - ste!

Um-

(Die Gestalt verschwindet)

ar — men will ich dich, und dann

Four bass voices in league with the deeper instruments (bassoons, trombones, violas and basses) colour the Incantation in dark, abnormal hues:

EX 16

Sadly, the effect is too drawn out (fifty-three bars!). A few gleams of light would have made the shadows even blacker—but Schumann was no master of musical chiaroscuro.

The second of the three large divisions of *Manfred* is notable for Schumann's Mendelssohnian attempt to depict a fairy realm:

EX 17

Then follows a hymn sung by the spirits of the lower world to Ariman, their master. Liszt considered the ten-bar introduction too short (it would have been for *him*) and advised Schumann:

> Some sixty to a hundred bars of symphony, such as you understand how to write, would have a decidedly good effect there. Think the matter over, and go fresh to your desk. Ariman can stand some polyphonic phrases, and this is an occasion where one may rant and rage away quite comfortably.

Had Schumann followed the latter half of Liszt's generous advice his chorus would never have degenerated into so unoriginal a chordal trot as this:

The beautiful, lustrous scene between Manfred and Astarte is at Schumann's highest artistic level, its accompaniment being a 'song' for orchestra in Schumann's unique *parlando* style:

EX 19

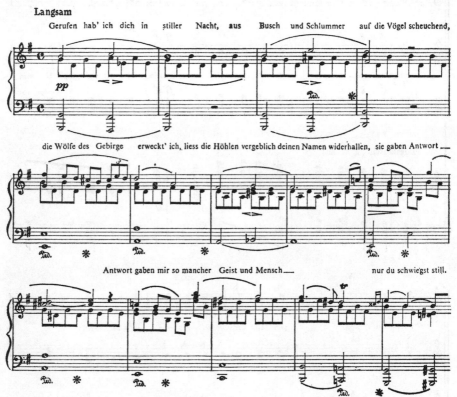

The third section takes us to Manfred's castle. Having renounced the spirit world, Manfred gives himself back to the earth. A kind of peace comes over him for the first time, a kind of repose which Schumann illustrates with remarkable beauty (Ex. 20).

EX 20

Sehr langsam (♪ = 92)

MANFRED. Ein Friede kam auf mich, unsäglich still, wie bis zu dieser Zeit nicht hei – misch war im

Leben, das ich kannte. Wenn ich nicht wüsste, dass Philosophie der eitlen Dinge bunteste Verwirrung, das

leerste Wort, das je aus Schulgewäsch das Ohr bethörte: könnte wohl ich meinen, der Weisen Stein, das vielgesuchte Gut, sei

meiner Seele Fund und Eigenthum. Hält's auch nicht aus, so hab' ich's doch erkannt: es goss ein neu Gefühl in die Gedanken, und

in die Tafeln der Erinnerung möcht' ein ich tragen dies Gefühl. Wer kommt?

ritard.

Manfred closes with the requiem already alluded to. Byron would have sneered at this 'appendix', for it contradicts the poem and repudiates the Catholic doctrine that no requiem is sung for those who reject its blessings. To organ accompaniment the text is heard in double canon at the octave. One voice outlasts the others to linger with Manfred's last words. The section, though lovely, is verbally obscure, since Schumann has seen fit to garble Manfred's role in one language by a four-part chorus singing simultaneously in another language (each part sounding different words at the same time).

EX 21

There has been no drama in the theatrical sense. Just as Goethe's *Faust* was never meant for the stage, Byron's *Manfred* was deliberately contrived to be impossible of dramatic presentation. That Schumann's settings should ever have become thought of as dramatic is regrettable testimony to the errors of history. Schumann's choice of texts, as we have seen, precluded the possibility that *any* musical settings of them could ever deserve the term 'dramatic'. So, Schumann failed in his great dream to become a composer of music for the stage, achieving in *Faust*, *Genoveva* and *Manfred* only what might be termed three dramatic experiments in music.

The Choral Music

MOST musicians regard Schumann as a composer of piano music, solo songs, chamber music and symphonies—probably in that order. A few people will have come across the 'Scenes from Goethe's Faust' for solo voices, chorus and orchestra, a work which receives an occasional performance. But Schumann is not generally thought of as being a *choral* composer at all. In this respect he is unlike many other great masters, including Bach, Handel, Haydn, Mozart, Beethoven, Berlioz, Mendelssohn, Verdi and Brahms, each of whom wrote at least one major choral work which is regularly performed today.

Yet choral music of various kinds figures prominently amongst Schumann's list of compositions. With orchestral accompaniment there are two large-scale and some dozen smaller pieces covering a very wide range of styles—quasi-dramatic works, narrative cantatas and ballads, compositions of a reflective and semi-religious nature, and settings of liturgical texts. He also wrote a fairly considerable number of unaccompanied partsongs for men's, women's and mixed voices, as well as vocal duets, trios and quartets with piano accompaniment.

The neglect of this substantial portion of Schumann's output is all the more astonishing when one considers the masterly treatment of words as seen in his writing of solo songs, his outstanding literary knowledge and talent, and the fact that he spent many years as a choral conductor. Do these works deserve to gather dust, or are we cheerfully overlooking a large number of fine pieces we ought to know?

*   *   *

One of the factors which stimulated Schumann to write choral music was his activity as a conductor. It is no accident that the majority of his choral works, large and small, were written between 1847 and 1853, for it was during this period that he held conducting appointments, first in Dresden and then in

Düsseldorf. When Ferdinand Hiller left Dresden in 1847 Schumann succeeded him as conductor of the *Liedertafel*. He directed this male voice choir for about a year, and wrote a number of pieces for them. In January 1848 Schumann founded his own mixed-voice 'Choral Union'. The choir met on Wednesday evenings, and gave its first concert on 30 April 1848, when the main work was Gade's cantata *Comala*. (The programme also included some of Schumann's partsongs, and Clara played piano solos.) In general, these amateur singers seem to have found Schumann an inspiring conductor. It is true that he was by no means a commanding figure on the rostrum, but the genuineness of his artistic personality made his singers want to give of their best. Professional musicians, however, were much less impressed. 'Schumann never could conduct,' Joachim said.

> In early days he may have beaten time accurately enough, but he made no remarks on the performances. At the rehearsal of *Paradise and the Peri* Clara (at the pianoforte) said: 'My husband says that he wishes this passage *piano*'; and he stood by and nodded gratefully. Repetition without indication. At a performance of one of his own symphonies he stood dreamily with raised baton, all the players ready and not knowing when to begin. Königslöw and Joachim, who sat at the front desk, therefore took the matter into their own hands and began, Schumann following with a smile of pleasure.[1]

In 1850 Schumann moved to Düsseldorf, and again succeeded Hiller as conductor of the choir there. It soon became apparent that Schumann was not fitted for this post. Not only his technical deficiencies but also his declining health led to a serious lowering of the standard of performances. This in turn led to difficulties with the committee of the subscription concerts, and with the choir. That he believed himself to be fully up to his task, however, can be seen in this eye-witness account of his performance of *Messiah*:

> In May, 1853, the Lower Rhenish Music Festival was held in Düsseldorf, and Schumann was called upon to conduct this work. Already very exhausted even at the last rehearsal he was unable to keep together the vast choir, which had assembled from all the surrounding districts. There was no reason for supposing that the performance itself would fare better; in fact, a fiasco was to be feared, and the honour of the entire chorus and orchestra was at stake. Therefore the leader of the Cologne Orchestra (which had joined forces with us at Düsseldorf) persuaded the leaders of the various groups to disregard Schumann entirely and to take their beat from him, from the first violin desk.

[1] Related by Joachim to Frederick Niecks. See Niecks, p. 293.

This so far came off that, apart from a few terrifying moments and a few ragged passages, the performance went off well enough.

Among those present was a certain musician whom Schumann had known in Leipzig. This gentleman, fully realizing the disaster we had so narrowly escaped, at the conclusion leapt into the orchestra, shouting enthusiastically: 'Congratulations, my dear Schumann'. But Schumann, after a moment's hesitation, merely replied quite indifferently: 'Oh! I think you only congratulate expectant mothers.'[1]

This state of affairs clearly could not continue, and eventually the committee persuaded Schumann to hand over most of the conducting to a deputy.[2] Finally, in November 1853, he gave up conducting altogether.

Unaccompanied Choral Music

Schumann's lack of success as a conductor, however, did not deter him from continuing to write a large amount of music for the choral groups with which he was associated. Considering first his partsongs, the majority of these belong firmly to the nineteenth-century partsong tradition—short, simple, largely chordal (with the melody mainly confined to the top voice) and generally strophic settings of verses by some of the same poets he turned to for his solo songs (Rückert, Eichendorff, Heine, Mörike, Goethe, Burns). The more lively partsongs often possess a hearty, outdoor character, whilst in the more introspective pieces we find a gentle vein of melancholy, with sometimes a dash of sentimentality. Doubtless they fulfilled admirably the purpose for which they were written. On occasions Schumann rises above this general level, and then we come across songs of a quality altogether more inspired.

The earliest of these partsongs are the six male voice choruses, Op. 33, written in 1840, the same year as Schumann's great outpouring of solo songs. No. 3 is a setting of Heine's *Die Lotosblume*, a poem which he also set as a solo song, included in *Myrthen*, Op. 25. The male voice piece is not quite in the same class as the celebrated solo song, but it is a gently flowing composition, with rather more textural variety than the average partsong, and with a lovely harmonic progression at the words 'er weckt sie mit seinem Licht':

[1] J. von Wasielewski: *Schumann As I Knew Him*, Musical Opinion, 1956.
[2] Julius Tausch.*

EX I

Schumann's other male-voice works were all written between 1847 and 1849. The most important of them is the motet *Verzweifle nicht im Schmerzenstal* ('Despair not in the vale of woe'), Op. 93, of 1849, a setting of a poem by Rückert

which extols the virtues of patience in adversity. It is laid out for two four-part
choirs of men's voices, each of which has on occasion to supply a group of soloists.
The chief difficulty for any composer writing a fairly extended work for male
voices is to achieve sufficient tonal variety. Schumann overcomes this problem to
some extent by providing plenty of contrast—of speed, rhythm and dynamics—
and he skilfully varies the textures too, sometimes achieving a rich, resonant fabric,
at other times balancing one choir against the other in antiphonal style. Even so,
the writing is not always very well imagined in terms of the chorus. The composer
is too abstemious in the use of counterpoint, which would have provided some
relief from the almost constant chordal writing; the final *alla breve* section is too
drawn out, with an excess of slow-moving chords; and the chromatic writing
makes several passages difficult to negotiate. (It must have been a recognition of
this which prompted Schumann, in 1852, to add an orchestral accompaniment to
support the voices.) But despite these various weaknesses I believe the motet is one
of Schumann's most important shorter choral compositions, and its neglect is
undeserved. This passage from the 'Ziemlich langsam' second section will give
some idea of its quality.

EX 2

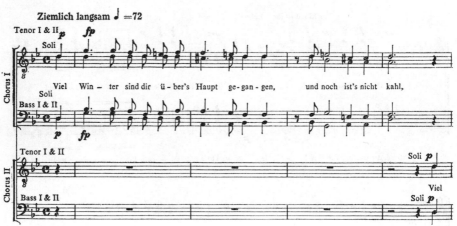

Die Zeit hat dir so

Stür-me ha-ben dir das Laub ge-rüt-telt, und noch ist's nicht fahl. Die Zeit

man — che Lust ge-schenkt, die dir so man-che stahl, und hat__ den

hat dir so man-che Lust ge-schenkt, die dir so man-che stahl,

Kelch mit Bit — ter-keit ge-würzt,__ dass er nicht wer-de schal, und hat den

und hat den Kelch mit Bit-ter-keit ge-würzt, und hat den

The *Ritornelle*, Op. 65 of 1847, a set of seven short pieces for male voices, are of particular interest on account of their indebtedness to Bach. Like Mendelssohn, Schumann had a great admiration for Bach, and on many occasions in the *Neue Zeitschrift für Musik* urged that a complete edition of Bach's works be put in hand. In the early part of his career Schumann had made a careful study of the *Well Tempered Clavier* and continued 'wrestling with fugues' from time to time as an academic exercise. But in 1845 he undertook a really close investigation of Bach's music, with the result that the older master's influence can be seen in much of Schumann's later output. This is most easily detected in such overtly contrapuntal works as the sets of keyboard fugues, Op. 60 and Op. 72, as well as in the *Ritornelle*, which are based on various canonic devices. The most rewarding musically are No. 3, *Blüth oder Schnee!* ('Blossoms or Snow!') for three solo tenors singing in canon accompanied by a four-part chorus; No. 7, *In Meeres Mitten* ('In the midst of the sea') an ingenious strict four-part canon; and No. 5, a canon for four solo voices:

EX 3

In 1849 Schumann composed two volumes of *Romanzen* (Op. 69 and Op. 91) for the women's voices of his choral society. These pieces do not deserve their neglect, for they contain some excellent music. Especially noteworthy are *Meerfey* ('The sea fairy') (Op. 69 No. 5), a setting of a poem by Eichendorff which is more instrumental than vocal in style; *Der Wassermann*, Op. 91 No. 9, a four-part song which shows Schumann at his most charmingly lyrical; and another setting of Rückert's *In Meeres Mitten*, Op. 91 No. 12 (not to be confused with the setting for male voices) in which Schumann uses voices in a bold, sinewy fashion not very typical of him:

EX 4

Prominent amongst Schumann's works for unaccompanied mixed voices are the four volumes of *Romanzen und Balladen*, Opp. 67 and 75 (1849), 145 and 146 (1849–51). As their title would suggest, and like the similarly named collections of solo songs, these are short, simple settings, in German folksong style, of narrative verses. The occasional song stands out as being of more than usual interest—*Im Walde* from Op. 75, with its echo effects; the lively and wholly charming *Der Schmidt* (a setting of the same poem by Uhland which Brahms made famous in his solo song), and *Romanze vom Gänsebuben* ('Story of the Goosechildren'), both from the Op. 145 set; and the delicately expressive *Sommerlied* from Op. 146. Schumann was not the only German Romantic composer to set translations by Robert Burns—others were Loewe, Mendelssohn, Robert Franz and Reger; but he does seem to have been particularly attracted to the Scottish poet, using his verses for nine solo songs, two vocal duets and eight partsongs, including the five pieces for mixed voices comprising Op. 55, composed in 1846. Whereas some of the solo songs from *Myrthen* possess an engaging simplicity which perfectly matches the poems, the Op. 55 partsongs are simple to the point of dullness. The three-part harmony and the static bass line of the third song shows Schumann at his least inspired:

The four pieces of Op. 59 (also dating from 1846) have a little more individuality. The first two songs are fairly substantial, whilst No. 3 in the set, *Jägerlied* ('Huntsman's song'), to words by Mörike, is a piece which only Schumann could have written.

EX 6

Beim Abschied zu singen ('A Song of Parting'), Op. 84, written in 1847, is a slight but attractive piece for mixed voices, mostly in four-part block harmony, a setting of words by Feuchtersleben. Presumably the wind instruments, which do little more than double the voices, were added for performance in the open air.

Many composers have found writing for *two* choirs a stimulus to their imagination, and in the *Vier doppelchörige Gesänge für grössere Gesangvereine* ('Four double-choruses for larger choral societies), Op. 141 (1849), Schumann produced what is by far his most significant music for unaccompanied chorus. As in the Op. 93 motet for double male voice choir Schumann shows his ability to employ eight voice-parts in a number of different ways—only here he has the advantage of exploiting the varied timbres of women's as well as men's voices. The first song in the set, *An die Sterne*, is a setting of a poem by Rückert which is addressed to the stars. Shining serenely in the heavens they comfort mankind with the hope and promise of a better world. The music has a dreamy, almost ecstatic quality rare in Schumann's choral works. Notice his use of antiphonal writing at the opening of this piece, and the spacing of the chords:

EX 7

In the first part of the second song, *Ungewisses Licht* ('Uncertain light'—words by Zedlitz) the poet's comparison of life to a wanderer's journey through a stormy night is set to fierce chordal music, with plentiful use of dotted and triplet rhythms. As the poet goes on to describe a light shining in the darkness (is it a will-o'-the-wisp, or the first rays of dawn? can it be love, or is it death?) the music gradually subsides, and the song ends with the chorus muttering 'Ist es der Tod?' This is not quite such an outstanding song as the first, but it is undeniably effective in performance. *Zuversicht* (also to words by Zedlitz), in which the poet bids troubled mankind to seek comfort from heaven, is similar in mood to *An die Sterne*. Starting serenely, the piece gradually builds in intensity as the voices enter one by one and the chords spread out:

After a series of ebbs and flows, the music fades away in a sixteen-bar coda on a tonic pedal. This beautiful, inspired song is surely Schumann's masterpiece in the field of unaccompanied choral music.

For the fourth song Schumann turned to a poem he had already set as a solo song in 1840—Goethe's *Talismane* (included in *Myrthen*, Op. 25). This hymn of praise from a collection of poems written in the Persian manner gives Schumann the opportunity of writing a brilliant, affirmative piece to complete the set. The continued use of block chordal writing and the insistent dotted rhythms, however, make one long for a little more variety. Schumann does in fact introduce a contrapuntal passage at the words 'Mich verwirren will das Irren', which provides a short breathing space before the last section with its repeated shouts of 'Gottes ist der Orient! Gottes ist der Occident!' The piece eventually subsides into a somewhat ecclesiastical Amen.

These four songs represent Schumann's most successful attempt at writing for unaccompanied chorus. After I had conducted a performance of them I came to the conclusion that their success is due more to the composer's imaginative response to the poems than to the actual quality of the choral writing as such.

In fact, his writing for chorus gives the impression of having been conceived in keyboard terms. This presents no insuperable problems to the singers, provided due allowance is made in performance. After all, there is a great deal of good vocal music which is basically instrumental in style (Bach being the supreme example), just as there is a lot of second-rate music which is superbly realized *technically* in terms of the medium in which it is written.

Accompanied Choral Music

Turning now to Schumann's various concerted voca]pieces with piano accompaniment we discover a different aspect of the composer's output. The duets and trios were mainly intended for domestic consumption, in the days when singing round the piano in the drawing-room not only provided the kind of relaxation nowadays supplied by television, but was considered a useful social accomplishment. Like Schubert, and many other composers before and after him, Schumann was on occasion called upon to write such salon music, and he responded with pieces like the *Mädchenlieder*, Op. 103, four settings of poems by Elisabeth Kulman for two women's voices; the two duets included in the *Liederalbum für die Jugend*, Op. 79; the three duets, Op. 43; and the three trios for women's voices, Op. 114. All these are typical in being technically within the range of amateur performers (the voices generally move together in simple chords), and dealing with homely or mildly romantic subjects.

Of the four duets for soprano and tenor, Op. 34 (1840), the two Burns settings are on a higher level. *Liebhabers Ständchen* ('Lover's Serenade') is a particularly powerful duet, with independent and highly expressive lines for the singers, and a piano accompaniment full of excitement and character:

EX 9

The Op. 78 set of four duets for soprano and tenor (1849) also rises above the merely charming. *Tanzlied* has an infectious dance-like quality which could be considered a little too exuberant for the drawing-room. The three other songs are more conventionally written for the voices. What makes them of especial interest is their piano accompaniment. Common to all there is a restless triplet figuration and a highly expressive use of accented passing-notes not found in much music of this kind. The following example from *Wiegenlied* will illustrate the point:

EX 10

The *Drei Gedichte*, Op. 29 (1840)—settings of poems by Emanuel Geibel—
are more interesting from the formal point of view than for any outstanding
intrinsic merit. The first song is a simple duet, distinguished only by a sequential
passage which carries the music from the home key of G major to D major
through A minor, B flat major and C major. The second piece is a straightforward
trio similar in style to the Op. 114 pieces; and the final number, *Zigeunerleben*, is
scored for various solo voices and a small chorus, with ad lib triangle and tambourine to assist in evoking a gipsy flavour. Rather more ambitious is the *Minnespiel*, Op. 101 (1849), a cycle of pieces from Rückert's *Liebesfrühling* ('Love's
springtime'), which contains four solos, two duets and two quartets. There are
some attractive things in this collection. In the duet *Ich bin dein Baum* ('I am your
tree') the alto and bass voices are given independent flowing lines, which are
characterized by dramatic seventh and octave leaps. Chromatic harmonies are
features of two of the solo songs—*Liebster, dein Worte stehlen* for soprano, and
O Freund ('O friend') for alto. The latter song is especially fine, with accented
passing notes used in the accompaniment in a wholly individual manner. But

taken as a whole I feel that in this cycle Schumann was largely content to re-work ideas which nine years before had been so splendidly fresh and spontaneous.

In 1849 Schumann wrote two more mixed sets of pieces, consisting of settings of Spanish poems translated by Geibel. Although there is nothing idiomatically *Spanish* about these pieces Schumann's imagination was evidently stimulated by the exotic nature of the poems. The *Spanische Liederspiel*, Op. 74, contains ten numbers—three solo songs, five duets and two quartets. A touch of Iberian flavour is discernible in *Der Contrabandiste*, a song for solo bass in which the piano part portrays the strumming of a guitar and the galloping of the smuggler's horse. A dotted guitar-like rhythm is also used in the piano accompaniment of the quartet *Es ist verrathen* ('It is betrayed'), a piece marked 'In Bolerostempo'; whilst the duet *Liebesgram* employs dotted and triplet rhythms and wide leaps to produce an exciting effect:

EX II

küh — ler Er-den, da schläfst du gut und oh-ne Pein; — wirst ru — hig sein,

The use of big leaps in the vocal line, not really characteristic of Schumann's writing for the voice, together with a more than usually florid style, can be seen in two other impressive numbers from this set, *Melancholie* for soprano solo, and *Botschaft* ('Message'), a duet for soprano and alto, in which the following passage occurs:

EX 12

denkt mein Herz an ihn!

denkt mein Herz an ihn!

The *Spanisches Liebes-Lieder*, Op. 138, also has ten numbers, but here the four soloists are accompanied by piano duet (a layout which no doubt influenced Brahms when he came to write his own *Liebeslieder*). Again one finds a mild Spanish flavour (the accompaniment for the *Romanze* for solo baritone is marked 'gleichsam Guitarre'); but the writing is simpler and the general level of invention much less inspired than in the *Liederspiel*. An idea of the quality of the collection can be gained from the opening of the duet *Blaue Augen* ('Blue eyes').

EX 13

Blau – e Au-gen hat das Mädchen, wer ver-lieb-te sich nicht drein!

Sind so reizend zum Ent zücken, dass sie je-des Herz be - stricken,

Sind so reizend zum Ent - zücken, dass sie je-des Herz be - stricken, wis-sen doch so stolz zu

Music for Chorus and Orchestra

The earliest of Schumann's compositions for soloists, chorus and orchestra was *Paradise and the Peri*, Op. 50, written between 1841 and 1843. His attitude to the work can be seen from a letter dated 19 June 1843 to his friend Johannes Verhulst,* the Dutch composer and conductor:

> My chief item of news is that I finished *Paradise and the Peri* last Friday. It is my longest work and, I think, my best. As I wrote *finis* on the last sheet of the score, I felt so thankful that my strength had been equal to the strain. A work of these dimensions is no light undertaking. I realize better now what it means to write a succession of them, such as, for instance, the eight operas which Mozart produced within so short a time. Have I told you the story of the Peri? If not, do make an effort to get it. You will find it in Moore's *Lalla Rookh*. It is simply made for music. The whole conception is so poetic and ideal that I was quite carried away by it. The music is just long enough for an evening performance. I expect and really hope to give it at a concert of my own next winter, and possibly to conduct it myself. *You must certainly come*. I hope my labours may again be rewarded by your kind, approving smile.

Thomas Moore's *Lalla Rookh* was a tremendously popular collection of oriental tales which had been published in 1817. *Paradise and the Peri* is a setting of one of the poems from that collection translated into German by Schumann's school and university friend Emil Flechsig. The Peri is a mythological creature, an angel who has been cast out from Paradise. Far from feeling resentment, and despite the fact that she is free to wander where she wishes amidst the beauties of the earth and sky, the Peri's one desire is to be readmitted to heaven. As she weeps outside the gate the angel tells her that she will be free to enter when she brings 'The gift that is most dear to heaven. Go, seek it now, redeem thy sin.' The Peri's first journey is to India, from whence she returns with a drop of blood from a young hero who died for the liberty of his country. This precious gift is not accepted, nor is the last sigh of an Egyptian maiden who preferred to die in the arms of her mortally sick lover than live a cheerless life without him. What eventually secures the Peri's triumphant return to Paradise is a gift she brings back from Syria—the tear of a hardened sinner who is shamed into repentance at the sight of a small child saying his prayers!

To present-day tastes this story must appear sentimental, but we have to remember that Schumann, in common with many of the early Romantics, was fascinated by the strangeness and beauty of certain aspects of Eastern culture. Furthermore, the writing of cantatas based on themes of this kind was very much in fashion at the time, and Schumann would certainly have come across examples by such composers as Gade, David and Mendelssohn. But although *Paradise and the Peri* belongs to the nineteenth-century Romantic cantata tradition it contains several hitherto untried features. In the first place Schumann broke new ground by making each of the three sections of the work a continuous whole, avoiding formal divisions between solo arias and choruses. He also replaced the traditional type of recitative by a more flowing kind of vocal writing. Something which probably had a bearing on the final character of the work is the fact that when Schumann first came across the story of *Paradise and the Peri* he considered setting it as an opera. When he came to write the work he decided against casting it in dramatic form, describing the piece as 'an oratorio, but for contented people, not for an oratory'; but the colourful scoring, the vivid portrayal of emotion and the vigour of the vocal writing all show to some extent the influence of the early Romantic operas of Weber, Marschner and Wagner.

EX 14

N

There are some very beautiful moments in the oratorio, especially when Schumann is portraying emotion, as in the opening of Part II, where the music expresses to perfection the Peri's longing for heaven as she hastens to deliver her first offering (Ex. 14).

Schumann is also successful when attempting to evoke an oriental flavour, notably in the charming Chorus of Houris at the beginning of Part III. The use of women's voices here, together with the 'eastern' harmonies and rhythms and the simple but highly effective scoring (strings, flute, oboe, horn, triangle, bass drum and cymbals) makes this one of the most appealing passages in the work.

EX 15

As one might expect from his experience as a composer of songs, Schumann's writing for solo voices is often very imaginative:

EX 16

—although the fact that he tends to use a similar vocal style whether for narrative or for personal utterance certainly makes for less variety and reduces the impact of the solo passages. But however interesting the solo writing, and however skilfully the orchestra is handled, the success of a work of this kind must depend ultimately on the way the composer writes for the chorus. There is no denying that it is the choral writing in *Paradise and the Peri* which represents the weakest element in the work. There are some fine moments, notably where Schumann has an opportunity of writing expressive music, as in the chorus which laments the death of the Indian hero in Part I, and the short final chorus in Part II, where the choir joins the Peri in an elegy on the dead Egyptian lovers. But there is too much writing in octaves, and Schumann too readily falls back on slow-moving choral writing in just the places where an exciting climax is called for (at the ends of Parts I and III). Although he makes a few half-hearted attempts to develop a contrapuntal texture, the writing for chorus is often dull and lacking in muscle (see Ex. 17).

These weaknesses could partly be attributed to inexperience; but although at times Schumann produced satisfactory writing for chorus, an uncertain technique in this department remained with him to the end.

EX 17

One sentence from Schumann's letter to Verhulst, quoted earlier, is of special significance—'it is my longest work and, I think, my best'. From this it would appear that Schumann valued *Paradise and the Peri* more highly than *Carnaval*, the C major Fantasy, *Dichterliebe*, the 'Spring' Symphony and the Piano Quintet, to mention just a few of the compositions he had produced before 1843. Although posterity has placed a different value on the work Schumann's estimation of its importance in his output is understandable. Since the beginning of 1841 his ambition (warmly encouraged by Clara) to develop from being a composer of music in small forms, like piano pieces and songs, to a composer of large-scale works had already resulted in the production of the 'Spring' Symphony, the D minor Symphony (in its first version), the *Overture, Scherzo and Finale*, the first movement of the piano concerto, three string quartets, the piano quintet and the piano quartet. In the ten years of creative life which remained to him after writing *Paradise and the Peri* Schumann was to finish his piano concerto, compose two more concertos, two more symphonies, half a dozen overtures, an opera, three piano trios, and some dozen other works for chorus and orchestra.

The first performance of *Paradise and the Peri* took place at the Leipzig Conservatoire on 4 December 1843, and Schumann *did* conduct it (it was his first appearance as a conductor). The work was received so well that it was given another two performances within a few days, one at Leipzig and another at Dresden. Although one or two academic critics objected to the various innovations found in it, the oratorio remained one of the most successful of Schumann's choral works in his own day. That it later went into oblivion was due partly to its defects and partly to a change of taste away from the whole conception of the Romantic cantata. But if the aspirations of a Peri no longer have the power to stir our emotions, lovers of Schumann's music will surely welcome any opportunity of hearing the work, both on account of its fine moments and because of the important part it played in the composer's artistic development.

After completing *Paradise and the Peri* Schumann's creative energies were for some years directed to other forms of composition. But from 1847 onwards, connected with his various conducting appointments, choral music of various kinds began to assume a major role in his output. His next work for chorus and orchestra was *Adventlied*, Op. 71 (1848), a setting of a sacred poem by Friedrich Rückert, which greets the coming of Christ. The music is laid out in Schumann's now familiar manner, with solo passages alternating with sections for chorus (sometimes full, sometimes women's or men's voices only), and one section following another without a break. There is of course no reason why Schumann should have adopted a second-hand, 'religious' style for setting such a text, but the flowing, song-like idiom he actually employs does strike a somewhat incongruous note:

EX 18

In such a context the sudden introduction, towards the end of the work, of passages written in the style of the Lutheran chorale is strangely disconcerting. Schumann adopts a similar procedure in his setting of another religious poem by Rückert, the *Neujahrslied*, Op. 144 (1849–50). Here however the introduction of the well-known chorale *Now thank we all our God* in the final section seems to follow on more naturally from what goes before. True, some of the choral passages are rather square and the contrapuntal writing is predictably somewhat contrived; but this *New Year's Song* has some pleasing and original moments. In the earlier part of the piece there is a tuneful, Mendelssohnian duet for soprano and alto, and some dramatic writing for solo bass including, most unusually for Schumann, a short passage of recitative. Further variety is achieved by the imaginative use of a large orchestra. This is a work which would justify an occasional revival.

★   ★   ★

A much more significant composition is the *Requiem für Mignon*. Op. 98B, with words taken from Goethe's novel *Wilhelm Meister*. This dates from 1849 and is one of a number of works written at that time to celebrate the centenary of Goethe's birth. Schumann was obviously much moved by the story of the strange young girl Mignon, who dedicated herself to Wilhelm Meister after he had come to her rescue. Near the end of the novel Mignon dies, and a 'Requiem' is sung at her burial. Schumann's setting is scored for two soprano and two alto soloists representing the four boys who bear Mignon to her sarcophagus, a baritone soloist, and a mixed choir representing the spirits of the departed. The cantata is in six short sections which follow on without a break. In the first section the spirits ask the children who it is they are bringing to 'the still dwelling'. On learning that 'a tired playmate' is being laid to rest the spirits welcome this youthful addition to their numbers in the following passage, which shows Schumann reflecting the tenderness of the scene not only in the chromatic writing and the sweetness of the harmonic progressions, but also in a more than usually imaginative handling of the chorus:

EX 19

The dialogue between the boys and the spirits continues in the next three sections, with the spirits trying in vain to comfort the children. The orchestral scoring includes many memorable touches—note the use of the harp in this excerpt from the third section:

In the fifth number the baritone soloist appears, and in a short, declamatory passage persuades the children to dry their tears and return to life—sentiments which are echoed by the spirits in the lively final section. Very near the end of the work Schumann interrupts the mainly diatonic proceedings with a few bars of extraordinary poignancy and originality:

EX 21

It is clear that the quasi-mystical quality of Goethe's text awakened in the composer a special response. The *Requiem for Mignon* is by no means a large-scale piece (it lasts only some twelve to thirteen minutes), but it certainly is an inspired work, and must be considered Schumann's finest achievement in the field of choral music.

To the year 1849 belongs another orchestrally-accompanied choral work, the *Nachtlied*, Op. 108. The mystery of night is effectively evoked by sombre orchestral colouring and, as in *Mignon*, the writing for chorus is often very well managed, especially with regard to matters of vocal spacing:

EX 22

quel - len - de, schwel-len-de Nacht,   voll von Lich-tern und Ster - nen

quel - len - de, schwel-len-de Nacht,   voll von Lich-tern und Ster - nen

schwel-len-de Nacht,   voll   von Lich-tern und Sternen

Although short and not particularly important, this is another composition which deserves an occasional hearing, possibly as an opening item in a mixed programme of choral and orchestral works.

It is well known that Schumann's creative life tended to proceed in cycles. He would devote himself energetically to one field of composition for a time, then change to another. We have already noted that most of Schumann's choral music dates from the years 1847–53, that is, the last seven years of his creative life. Towards the end of this period Schumann's increasing mental instability is reflected in a decline in the quality of much of his music. Between 1851 and 1853 Schumann wrote no less than five cantatas, an orchestral overture with a choral ending, and two settings of liturgical texts. In my view, none of these late works really enhances the composer's reputation. The most ambitious of them is *Der Rose Pilgerfahrt* (The Pilgrimage of the Rose), Op. 112 (1851), a fairly large-scale piece which in its general layout is rather on the same lines as *Paradise and the Peri*. But if a modern listener finds it difficult to become in any way involved with the affairs of a fallen angel, how shall he respond to the story of a rose? The sugary poem by the young German poet Moritz Horn, with its fairy queen, its miller's daughter who died of a broken heart, its handsome young forester with whom the rose falls in love, and its choruses of elves and angels, clearly attracted Schumann, however; and although the characters in the tale and the sentiments they utter offered him little opportunity for expressing emotion and drama, some of the numbers contain a great deal of rustic charm. An element of German 'folkiness' can be found in quite a lot of Schumann's music, but in this cantata it completely dominates the score.

EX 23

Having dealt with a folky theme in the *Pilgrimage of the Rose*, and an oriental subject in *Paradise and the Peri*, Schumann turned next to another favourite theme of romantic cantatas, the medieval ballad. His enthusiasm at this late stage of his life for works of this kind resulted in *Der Königssohn* ('The King's Son'), Op. 116 (1851), *Des Sängers Fluch* ('The Minstrel's Curse'), Op. 139 (1852), *Vom Pagen und der Königstochter* ('Of the Page and the King's Daughter'), Op. 140 (1852) and *Das Glück von Edenhall* ('The Luck of Edenhall'), Op. 143 (1853). As one would expect, there is some attractive writing for solo voices and several examples of imaginative orchestral scoring. Furthermore the subject-matter of the poems occasionally prompted Schumann to some bold descriptive strokes. These qualities can be seen at their best in *The Minstrel's Curse*, doubtless because the poem itself (by Uhland, arranged for Schumann by his writer-friend Richard Pohl) offered the composer several opportunities of which he was able to take advantage. Amongst the most attractive items are the Provençal Song, with its delicate accompaniment for harp, woodwind and horns, which the Youth sings at the request of the Queen; the old Minstrel's Ballad 'In der hohen Hall' sass König Sifrid', in which the harp is joined by brass and lower strings; and the duet for the Youth and the Minstrel 'Der Frühling kündet der Orkane Sausen', where the harp is again prominent:

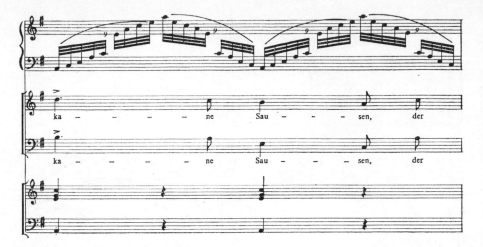

ka — — — — ne Sau — — sen, der

ka — — — — ne Sau — — sen, der

Hee — re Vor — schritt macht die Er — de

Hee — re Vor — schritt macht die Er — de

dröh — — — — nen,

dröh — — — — nen,

Hrn.

At the point in the cantata where the old minstrel curses the king and his palace Schumann rises to the occasion with music of great dramatic power, in a passage notable for its vivid harmonic colouring. But although the work has some fine moments they are hardly sufficient to make one eager to recommend its revival. Despite his extensive knowledge of classical and contemporary literature, and his ability to write articulately about music and other topics, the choice of subjects for these cantatas leads us to the conclusion that Schumann's literary taste was by no means infallible. Will there ever be a re-awakening of interest in musical settings of idealized tales about king's sons, pages and minstrels? No doubt we *would* be prepared to perform these works if they showed sufficient *musical* imagination. But the sad fact is that these ballads, with the possible exception of *The Minstrel's Curse*, belong all too firmly to an outmoded and largely undistinguished genre.

To sum up, I feel that the comparative neglect of Schumann's choral and concerted vocal music is not entirely deserved. True, the major part of it was composed in the later years of his creative life, when the flame of his genius no longer burnt steadily. Much of it, too, was written in musical forms (cantatas, partsongs, vocal duets) and for particular uses (choral societies, domestic performance) which either made lesser demands on his inspiration or no longer form part of our normal musical experience. Also, as I have suggested, Schumann's literary taste, wide-ranging but liable to strange lapses, led him at times to set texts which failed to kindle his imagination. Furthermore, despite his great interest in choral conducting, which resulted in the composition of many of the works discussed in this chapter, his actual writing for chorus is often marked by an uncertainty of technique comparing unfavourably with his writing for the piano, solo voice and chamber instrumental ensembles.

I believe, however, that despite these qualifications, there is some excellent music amongst Schumann's choral output, and several of the works discussed in these pages merit at least an occasional performance.

ERIC SAMS

Schumann and the Tonal Analogue

EARLY all Schumann's music contains or derives from words, whether as texts, titles, programmes or epigraphs. It is also famous for its structure of music *qua* mosaic, an aggregation of small-scale motifs. Now, surely these two basic facts about Schumann—his obviously verbal content, his obviously motivic form—may well be related? He works by way of motto-themes, I suggest, because that is literally what they are—mottoes turned into themes.

In a letter to Clara Wieck[1] he defined his creative procedures thus: 'Everything that happens in the world affects me. . . . I think it all over in my own way, and then it has to make room for itself and find an outlet in music.' Clearly he has in mind a physical or chemical reaction. Music is for him another form of ideas, as steam is another form of water. In his mind the musical stage is of course the higher of the two; more ethereal, less tangible, and composed of small separate entities or droplets of sound.

In describing this transformation Schumann uses one image in particular on which I shall later dwell at some length, because it seems to me beautiful as well as apt and interesting. In general he speaks and writes of his art in terms of words and ideas promoted into music—mottoes in both senses. The musical sense is 'a short and well-defined theme usually occurring at the opening of a composition and used again during its course, in its first form or altered, in the manner of a quotation or an allusion to some definite idea'.[2]

That is Schumann in a nutshell. And for its origin we need look no further than the family tree, and not very far up that. His father was bookseller, publisher, author, editor, librarian, translator, anthologist and bibliophile—altogether a rather bookish man. Like father like son—we can hear the boyish pleasure and

[1] *Jugendbriefe*, p. 282.
[2] Blom: *Everyman's Dictionary of Music*, p. 386, London, 1946.

pride in the early letters:[1] 'I've rummaged through the entire library...', 'I've been allowed to help with the proof-reading...', and so on. No wonder the music took its time to come filtering up through all those layers of print, words, concepts, ideas. No wonder either that it emerged effervescent with utterance and articulation, a new and refreshing spring.

In the world of creation, Schumann's first parents were Schubert and the novelist Jean Paul Richter.* In them, music and letters are not just united, but equated For if in Schubert you can hear how music speaks, in Jean Paul you can hear how literature sounds. His prose is sonorous, not only with rhetoric but literally with puns and other word play; he writes from a quasi-musical imagination. This accounts for Schumann's otherwise puzzling life-long veneration for Jean Paul. They have in common romantic freedom and classic restraint—or (if you like) Florestan and Eusebius. That idea came from Jean Paul of course. In all his novels, as Schumann noted,[2] he presents himself in two contrasting characters, for example Vult and Walt Harnisch in Schumann's favourite novel *Flegeljahre* or 'Salad Days', which also mentions the musical letters, A, C, and H, in their surname. (We shall be hearing more of that pair and their signature tunes.) They symbolize, I suggest, two different aspects of high-mindedness—flights of fancy, lofty ideals. All his life, Schumann *qua* Florestan was imaginative. Again, all his life *qua* Eusebius he was an idealist. All the more reason therefore for believing that his own testimony and practice will be the best guide to the truth about his mind and art.

He testifies repeatedly that for him words and music are different forms of the same thing. For example, he writes: 'When I play Schubert, I seem to be reading a Jean Paul novel turned into music.'[3] The sonorous and the conceptual—where those two realms meet you will find on the border not only Schumann's customs but his actual practice. Music can easily (though exceptionally) be assigned a specific denotative meaning, just as words can, and through exactly the same process of spelling and reading letters. If one were unfamiliar with Schumann's Op. 1, but had absolute pitch, then one could read the name ABEGG aloud just from hearing the first five notes of the theme. One would then be reading music in a novel sense but an entirely valid one. Schumann's theme not only means, but says, ABEGG.

Those variations were written by 1830, when he was studying law at Heidelberg. In August of that year he wrote the 'Abegg' theme in a friend's autograph album with the superscription 'Je ne suis qu'un songe'.[4] Those words 'I am but a dream' are, need one say, a quotation from Jean Paul, where they are spoken by

---

[1] *Jugendbriefe*, p. 16.
[3] *Jugendbriefe*, p. 82.
[2] Bœtticher, p. 159.
[4] Jansen, p. 492.

the noble Liane de Froulay, as she appears in disguise. Meta Abegg was said to have been met at a masked ball. Her title of 'Countess' was a further disguise—a whimsical fancy of Schumann's, like the fancy title of the work itself—*Thème sur le nom Abegg, varié pour le pianoforte, dédié à Mademoiselle Pauline Comtesse d'Abegg*. The music is vividly expressive. The elated outgoing arpeggios of the theme in waltz time clearly embody the feeling of dancing at a masquerade. But this dancing, it seems to me, is going on in Schumann's mind, and nowhere else. Meta Abegg—was there ever such a person? Her title was an invention; the title of her music was an invention; even her theme was an invention: 'je ne suis qu'un songe'.

In the first variation, some would say that Schumann uses only the first two notes of this theme, ABEGG. But in fact all five notes remain audible, if we listen hard enough, even when Schumann uses them in vertical combination, and turns his theme into a chord.

EX 1

An interesting anticipation of serial techniques, perhaps—or merely a trivial coincidence? Hardly the latter, in view of what happens next. In the theme, 'Abegg' had appeared backwards after the double bar: G-G-E-B-A. At the corresponding point in the first variation we again hear the theme verticalized.

EX 2

Much the same happens in Variations 2 and 3 and in the Finale; and then Schumann displays how 'Abegg' can be contained in two chords.

EX 3

Is it possible to doubt that the melody is there being deliberately verticalized? The theme remains perfectly clear and audible, given the idea, even when it is stood on end.

At the same time there is some enigma here. Not just in the extraordinary notation, to which I shall return later, but in the concept as such. Just what kind of theme is this?—composed of arbitrary notes, yet symbolizing a person, and a scene, and a state of mind, and also developed purely technically as music, in some rather unexpected ways? It has perhaps some affinity with the Schönbergian note row, and more with the Wagnerian *Leitmotif,* and more still with the *idée fixe* of Berlioz; but first and foremost it was in every sense the *idée fixe* of Schumann. He called it a 'Papillon'—a word he used in connection with so many of his works.

He actually referred to his 'Abegg' Variations as 'Papillons';[1] the original title of his Op. 2 was *Papillons musicals* (*sic*);[2] he called his Intermezzi, Op. 4, 'Papillons on a larger scale';[3] the Impromptus, Op. 5, were offered to a publisher as 'a second set of Papillons';[4] and, of course, he gave that title to one of the pieces in *Carnaval*, Op. 9. By 'Papillons', I suggest, he means motifs that can appear or disappear, fly forward or backward, and assume an infinite variety of shapes and colours. Let us observe one in *Carnaval*, where it is tantalizingly flaunted in the piece called 'Florestan'. The second theme, which drifts in without comment, 'adagio', in the ninth bar, reappears later marked by Schumann with the singular word 'Papillon' and a question mark.

EX 4

Here, plainly, is another kind of extra-musical reference. The intrusive 'Papillon' in question begins and ends Op. 2, which derives from a chapter in Jean Paul's *Flegeljahre* which begins and ends with Vult Harnisch.

That same theme, at the end of Op. 2 is made to dwindle, note by note, and finally to vanish; while at the end of Jean Paul's novel Vult Harnisch is heard gradually slipping away into the distance until he finally vanishes altogether. The concluding words say that he . . .

took his flute and went, blowing it, out of the room, down the stairs, out of the house and down the road. Walt heard with delight the vanishing tones

[1] Bœtticher, p. 160.   [2] *Jugendbriefe,* p. 155.
[3] *Briefe,* p. 40.   [4] Gertler: *Schumann in seinen frühen Klavierwerken,* 1931, p. 60.

speaking to him; for he never dreamed that his brother was vanishing with them.

This, then, is what Schumann is symbolizing in his Finale; as the music runs out of sight, it runs out of sound, finally reducing almost to vanishing-point in one single note. And shortly thereafter you hear it, in a slightly different guise, disappearing altogether, in a way reminiscent of Ex. 3.

EX 5

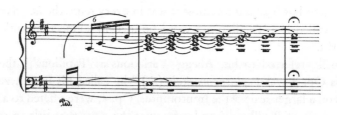

So this theme, I suggest, actually means to Schumann the idea of Vult Harnisch in Jean Paul's novel. On that basis we can easily understand why this Vult Harnisch theme comes into the piece called 'Florestan' in *Carnaval*—for the excellent reason that they are one and the same person or persons. Each is a name for the dynamic out-turned face or mask of Schumann's Janus-like creative mind. If you consider Op. 9, No. 6 as absolute music you may find a certain incongruity, a certain enigmatic quality, in that novel theme of the apparent stranger who comes dancing slowly in at the words 'adagio' and 'Papillon'. But Schumann hardly wrote a note of absolute music in his life. Here as everywhere, his notes are on fire with ideas, so to speak, and so to speak with tongues. One may ask whether on this basis there is in Op. 2 a theme meaning *Walt* Harnisch which appears in the *Carnaval* piece called 'Eusebius', *his* alter ego. One may also wonder whether Vult and Walt, like Abegg, are enciphered on the music to ensure that the idea is stamped all the way through, like Brighton rock. After all, the evidence says plainly that we are in a very strange world in Schumann's very first two works. Both contain passages which have every appearance of meaning disappearance. 'Je ne suis qu'un songe' was Schumann's idea of an apt quotation for Abegg, and those words applied to an apparition in disguise. After the ball, Meta Abegg's image faded; she lost her magic at midnight, like Cinderella. Vult Harnisch vanished as the morning bell struck, like the ghost in *Hamlet*—you can hear that in the music too.

This is Schumann's imagination, not mine; my facts are his fancy. This is what he meant when he spoke of music as a language, and musicians as poets.

Music, for him, was the word given a new freedom by a change of existence from one mode to another, as a chrysalis changes into a butterfly. The change is natural and inevitable, an *élan vital* in each case. The result is small, frail, elusive, colourful, moving and beautiful: *Papillons musicaux*.

It took Shakespeare himself to give us the verbal equivalent of that image— the poet, who gives to an airy nothing a local habitation and a name. It took Schumann to restore the balance for music, to make from the name an airy nothing, an expressive cipher; to develop from 'Abegg' (*ab ovo*, as it were) into a 'Papillon'.

Schumann once compared himself in an unproductive mood to a chrysalis awaiting change.[1] The German word for the larval state, 'Larve', like its Latin and French equivalents, also means a mask. This is the source of all that secondary imagery of masks and dances. 'Larventanz', or masked ball, is the actual name of the chapter in Jean Paul from a reading of which there emerged, according to Schumann, one 'Papillon' after another.[2] This play on words is Schumann's own; he writes those words, 'Larventanz' and 'Papillon', in the same line of a letter home[3] excitedly explaining that there is a direct musical transformation from the one to the other, from masks or larvae to butterflies, And indeed his musico-verbal ideas kept on and on, for years after, emerging from just such masquerades.

Even in his critical writing he related words to music in this same way; several of his reviews take the unusual form of a suite of dances or a ball programme.[4] His music begins with *Abegg*, from the masked ball in Mannheim; proceeds to ASCH and SCHA from *Carnaval* in Leipzig; and continues with similar ideas in *Faschingsschwank aus Wien* ('Carnival Jest from Vienna'), the *Davidsbündlertänze*, and very many others, all 'Papillons'. I suggest that each one was, in a very precise sense, a fancy dress. You may recall how delighted Schumann was at a friend's discovery[5] in the first movement of the early G minor symphony—'Huch! Da fliegt der Schmetterling fort!' said the friend—'Look! There goes the butter-fly!' Fatuous though it may sound to us, Schumann thought this a very poetic idea. Again, in the 'Spring' Symphony, as he wrote to a conductor in later life, there might be a suggestion of a butterfly flying up,[6] which implies that this symphony might contain a 'Papillon', in the sense of a meaningful and unifying motto theme; and so indeed it does. Mosco Carner[7] goes so far as to suggest that every one of the symphonies and the cycles of piano works and songs—all Schumann's best-known and loved works in fact—represent 'a succession of

---

[1] *Jugendbriefe*, p. 200.   [2] *Ibid.*, p. 167.
[3] *Ibid.*, p. 166.   [4] GSK, Vol. I, pp. 201, 256, etc.
[5] Bœtticher, p. 319: as Gerald Abraham has pointed out (*Schumann: A symposium*, p. 193). the theme in question is an analogue of *Papillons* No. 1.
[6] *Briefe*, p. 225.   [7] Abraham, *op. cit.* pp. 191–92.

musical tableaux, whose progress and purpose are chiefly determined by extra-musical thoughts and such general aesthetic considerations as contrast and formal balance'. The reason is that 'Schumann appears to have needed the stimulus of poetic ideas and literary images to bring his imagination to the boil'.[1]

We need not infer that Schumann consciously needed ideas and images to compose; rather that his music is no other thing than the diffusion of those ideas and images into a more rarefied form—a process which the chemist as well as the psychologist might call sublimation. One of his likeliest sources was Jean Paul, who makes a very interesting distinction between two classes of thoughts: daytime ideas, the dayflyers or genus *Papilio*, and the night thoughts or night flyers, otherwise known as 'Sphinxes'.[2] Surely Schumann had read that passage? We have probably all been puzzled by the appearance of 'Sphinxes' in *Carnaval*. We think first of Greek or Egyptian myth. But those Sphinxes asked riddles or kept secrets, whereas Schumann's, on the contrary, answer riddles and disclose secrets; his Sphinxes are not so much myths as moths, or *Papillons de nuit*. And that is what a Sphinx actually is, in its dictionary sense. In English or German, even in French, it means a moth or 'Papillon'. And in *Carnaval* it means a meaning-ful musical idea.

Let me abstract a few examples. Many of us must have wondered what in the world a 'Faschingsschwank', a Carnival Joke or Jest, might be. It pleased Schumann so to entitle two major works: Op. 9, which was later re-styled *Carnaval*, and Op. 26, the *Faschingsschwank aus Wien*. The word will not be found in any German dictionary; it is just an invention by Schumann, I suggest, as an expression of music in which the notes ASCH SCHA occur. The word is built up from those letters in that order as the music is built up from those notes. Surely Schumann is again equating music and letters and joining them in a dance, thus:

EX 6

ASCH—SCHA: *Letters Dansantes* 1830–39

ABEGG   masked *ball* ('Papillons')

INTERMEZZI   ('Longer Papillons')

HARNISCH—   SCHUMANN—   Larven*tanz* ('Papillons')
  | | | | | | | |
FA   SCHINGSSCH WANKE—*Carnaval* ('Papillons' 'Sphinxes')
  | | | | | | | |
FA   SCHINGSSCH WANK   aus *Wien*

DAVIDSBÜNDLER—*tänze*

---

[1] Abraham, *op. cit.*, p. 180.   [2] *Politische Fastenpredigten*, Tübingen, 1817, section V.

There are many other carnival novelties and disguises, as we can see from Op. 9. I said earlier that one of Schumann's first influences was Schubert, who is certainly first on the scene here. *Carnaval* began as variations on a theme which Schumann knew as the *Sehnsauchtswalzer*,[1] or 'longing waltz', part of which is left showing in *Carnaval* as a direct quotation for everyone to hear, in the same key and at the same place.[2] Schumann thus symbolizes an idea, a scene and an emotion. The spirit of Schubert is being invoked, like the spirit of Abegg. Again it is a waltz in masquerade. But it is also perhaps mainly a *Sehnsuchtswalzer* expressing the emotion of longing or yearning—a feeling which in Schumann's case meant principally Clara Wieck. The following lines, in which he refers to her by her pet name, Clärchen, were written only a few years later: 'Egmonts Geliebte Clärchen hiess; O Namen wundersüss'—'Egmont's beloved [in Goethe's play] was called Clärchen; how wondrous sweet that name.'[3] That was the merely verbal mind at work; with no very impressive result, you may think. But the marvellous musico-verbal mind turned *Egmont*, the Goethe play, into *Egmont*, the Beethoven overture. The noble first subject represents the tragic hero himself. So to a mind like Schumann's the following theme would surely mean *Clärchen*, with its voice *dolce* and *piano*, soft and low, an excellent thing in feminine subjects. Next, that mind re-fashions it as a suitable subject for longing for and dancing with in the world of musical imagery.

EX 7

Beethoven Op. 84

Schumann Op. 9

As in the Schubert example, these are the same notes in the same key. So Clara, alias Clärchen, alias the feminine second subject of *Egmont*, slips unnoticed into *Carnaval*, in mask and fancy dress; and is instantly followed by an old friend which, though incognito, is instantly recognizable—the opening and closing theme of *Papillons*: Vult Harnisch, alias Florestan, alias Robert Schumann in his dancing mood. Are we being too fanciful if we hear who was following whom on this occasion and with what expression?

---

[1] GSK, Vol. I, p. 202f.
[2] Cf. *Schubert*, D. 365 (bars 9–10), and Schumann's *Carnaval* (bars 10–11).
[3] Litzmann, Vol. I, p. 255.

EX 8

These ideas cover fully half of Schumann's creative life; the better half, you may think, and not only because it is dominated by Clara. Perhaps it also covers sufficient ground for a hypothesis. Suppose that these motto-themes, these 'Papillons', were in fact Schumann's habitual mode of composition? Then other people ought to have heard them in other works. And so indeed they have. Rudolph Réti[1] has identified the following notes as a linking motif in *Kinderscenen*, Op. 15.

EX 9

The protective colouring of this 'Papillon' is so effective that it has generally been overlooked rather than overheard. But where it is pointed out we can detect its outline plainly enough. We can even sketch further ideas and draw inferences. Thus the piece called 'Schlummerlied' published in the *Albumblätter*, Op. 124, and attributed to 1841, has this same motif in the opening bars, and at the same pitch-level, and hence perhaps first saw the light as a Scene of Childhood. Certainly most of those motifs were of the same birth in Schumann's creative mind or psyche, whether conscious or subconscious. Now let us take those themes of five consecutive notes that go lifting or dipping through all the piano sonatas and the *Fantasie*, Op. 17. These themes are more self-evident, and so, on abundant evidence, is the connection of those works with Clara.[2]

These motifs are unifying, expressive, structural, reversible—in short, 'Papillons'. Many of them have been collected by others over the years, for example by Karl Wörner[3] and Paula Rehberg.[4] Further specimens have been pin-pointed more recently by Roger Fiske[5] in the *Davisdbündlertänze*, Op. 6, a work which according to its composer had special meaning for Clara; it contained wedding thoughts, he said, and other hidden ideas.[6] Dr Fiske's basic Clara theme in B

[1] Réti: *The Thematic Process in Music*, pp. 35–55, New York, 1951. See also pp. 95–99 on the Piano Concerto, and pp. 295–97 on the First Symphony.

[2] Cf. Schauffler: *Florestan: The Life and Work of Robert Schumann*, New York, 1945, pp. 296–317.

[3] *Robert Schumann*, Zürich, 1949, p. 145.

[4] Paula and Walter Rehberg: *Robert Schumann*, Zürich, 1954, p. 476.

[5] 'A Schumann Mystery'. *The Musical Times* (1964), pp. 574–78.

[6] Litzmann, pp. 169, 179, 184.

minor (Ex. 10) can be found throughout Op. 6, for example as melody in the opening bars of Nos. 11 and 13, and as bass at the beginning of No. 4. All this will hardly be unrelated to its extended mirror-image, again in the same key, at the end of No. 2, and again at bars 21 ff. from the end of No. 3, which contains the five-note rising melody found at the beginning of No. 5—and so on.

EX 10

Now if we link all those B minor themes together they form the long pendulum which suddenly appears, swinging backwards and forwards palindromically like other 'Papillons', in the Scherzo of the F minor sonata, in the key signature of five flats—surely as meaningful and deliberate a quotation as the 'Papillon' I have already described in 'Florestan'.

EX II

a)

b)

Scherzo, Op. 14

However this may be, there seems little doubt of the special expressive significance for Schumann of the B minor Clara theme. It is for instance a linking theme in the *Liederkreis*, Op. 24, written for Clara in their marriage year, 1840, for example at the beginning of the second song. It also recurs in the fifth song of the even better known Heine cycle of the same year, *Dichterliebe*—however absurdly appropriate it may seem to find a 'Papillon' poised quivering over the open flower of a lily.

Given these ideas, the next field for their agreeable and harmless pursuit might be the next work after the *Davidsbündler*, namely the *Fantasiestücke*, Op. 12. These pieces too are flights of fancy, as their title shows; again they were meant for Clara; and again we hear 'her' Op. 6 theme in the opening bars. This time, however, it appears in the major, and provides the opening melody of 'Warum' and 'Grillen'

EX 12

and a theme which recurs throughout the cycle; and it duly reappears in its mirror-form in secondary themes throughout, for example in 'Des Abends', 'Aufschwung' and 'Grillen'.

EX 13

All these seem to be unifying themes just like 'Abegg' and 'Asch'. I find it reasonable to suppose that the identifiable and inter-related themes in music dedicated in every sense to Clara will contain themes signifying her, as Schumann repeatedly suggested they did. If so, one of them might well speak her name, as 'Abegg' and 'Asch' did theirs.

Now such a theme would be instantly recognizable; Clara's own features would show through it unmistakably. You need not be a cryptographer to see that just as 'Abegg' can be identified by its melodic shape—five notes, of which the last two will be the same, so Clara too will have a characteristic *Gestalt*—five notes, of which the third and fifth are the same. One example would be the retrograde form of the B minor theme, Ex. 10.[1] One can hear that when its first note is C, its third will be A and its fifth will be A. And anyone can hear that this Clara theme is one of the most famous unifying themes in all music, a *locus classicus* of cyclic construction in Schumann's Fourth Symphony. Less well known, though, is the *locus romanticus* in Clara Schumann's biography where her husband says (in April 1841) that his next symphony will be called Clara and that in it he will depict her.[2] The next was of course the D minor, written a few months later, which has this same theme woven throughout its texture. Is not Schumann depicting Clara as he had depicted Abegg and the rest, namely literally?

[1] Apparently, Erwin Bodky used to tell his students in Berlin between the wars that this basic idea was in fact Schumann's Clara theme.

[2] Litzmann, Vol. II, p. 30.

One can demonstrate that this is indeed so; and further we can infer what cipher systems are being used, and why, and when, and how, and where Schumann found the idea. Given his boyhood and background, of course, it had to be in a book; and there is in fact only one such book—a German manual of cryptography[1] by a professor of Schumann's subject, law, at Schumann's university, Heidelberg, published in the same town, by the same firm, as Jean Paul's *Flegeljahre* (1804–5), the inspiration of *Papillons*; published moreover by suppliers of the Schumann family bookshop, in the year after its foundation in Zwickau (1808). So two of Schumann's favourite works, fiction and non-fiction, could both have arrived in the same consignment. I say favourite works, because of the detailed evidence that Schumann knew Klüber's *Kryptographik* well, and had a copy by him all his life. Its ideas recur in his critical writings and his letters, as well as in his music; and it has a section on how to make a musical cipher by substituting notes for letters.

It also describes codes which use musical symbolism. So did Schumann, for example in the *Études Symphoniques*. The Finale opens with a tune from Act III of Marschner's opera *Der Templer und die Jüdin*, where it is sung to words about the victorious hero Richard the Lionheart, the pride of England.

EX 14

There is general agreement that this was intended by Schumann as a tribute to his admired friend Sterndale Bennett, then in Leipzig. That consensus is fortunate, since in the absence of external evidence the hypothesis I wish to advance might otherwise seem bizarre. For what Schumann did, I suggest, was first to identify Marschner's tune with a few of the words to which it was sung; then, by treating these words as a cryptic reference to his friend, he paid a compliment to Sterndale Bennett. In a sense the idea *is* an old friend. As we can infer from Op. 1 and elsewhere, that upward arpeggio might well have suggested to Schumann an outgoing feeling of ebullient elation, very suitable for a triumphant finale; and it also

---

[1] Johann Ludwig Klüber, *Kryptographik*, Tübingen, 1809. See also my article 'A Schumann Primer?', *Musical Times*, November 1970.

counter-balances the downward arpeggio with which the theme begins. So this
too could be an emotive and structural palindrome, just like 'Abegg'. But the
two differ—and exactly as code differs from cipher. The latter means that each
single symbol is separately replaced by another, for example as letters are replaced by notes in 'Abegg'. In code, a group of symbols arbitrarily represents
some more complex meaning; thus a musical phrase can be feigned by reference
to its words to mean 'Sterndale Bennett.'

Now if this verbal reference is indeed the key to Schumann's use of code we
can try it on his many other musical allusions, for example those to Beethoven's
An die ferne Geliebte heard by Hermann Abert[1] in the *Fantasie*, Op. 17, and by
Mosco Carner[2] in the C major symphony. We expect the melody to refer first of
all to its original words, which will then be given a purely personal interpretation.
They are 'Nimm sie hin denn, diese Lieder'—'accept my songs'; and the music
consequently sings of its own dedication. Similarly, the postlude to a song written
for Clara shortly after their marriage[3] seems to quote a song

EX 15

by Giordani. If so, this quoted melody should refer in the first instance to the
original words—'Caro mio ben / credimi almen / senza di te languisce il cor'—
which puts an agreeable gloss on an otherwise rather wooden work.

It may be hard to understand how the Marschner tune can actually signify
pride and elation, the Beethoven tune humility and devotion, the Giordani tune
simplicity and affection. But it seems to me entirely certain that Schumann
heard such melodies, and the *Marseillaise*, and the *Grossvatertanz*, as encoded
signals. He habitually imagined musical sounds as semantic symbols; which
may explain why his aesthetic and his practice have bewildered everyone, including himself. It is only in modern times that this view of music has become
intellectually respectable, thanks to the theoretical underpinning offered by

---

[1] *Robert Schumann*, Berlin, 1920, p. 69.   [2] *Op. cit.*, p. 229.
[3] 'Der Himmel hat eine Träne geweint', Op. 37 No. 1.

Susanne Langer,[1] who has conferred new status on the symbol itself—quite an achievement. She argues very cogently that works of art embody not an actual emotion, but the pattern, or *Gestalt* of emotional awareness; thus music is for her a tonal analogue of emotive life. This view applied *seriatim* to each separate component of the total pattern, to each small-scale Schumannian analogue or motif, suggests a special case of the general theory. Each such motif corresponds to an emotional equivalent; the symbol sounds like the symbolized feelings feel. Thus 'Abegg', 'Asch', the various Clara themes, are made to sound gay or melancholy as the mood requires.

To pursue that hypothesis, the obvious testing-ground would be the songs. There, if anywhere, one would expect to find direct and definable correspondence between verbal concept and musical equivalent. So I chose at random one of the seventy or so motifs I thought I had heard over the years in Schumann's songs; and then chose—again at random—a group of songs in which to make a spot-check. The analogue chosen was my auditory experience that Schumann in his song-music responds to a poetic mention of the sky or heaven by a tendency to subdominant harmony. The group of songs chosen for test was *Myrthen*, Op. 25, written in early 1840. There is no obvious reason for any such correlation, and a transition to the subdominant is by no means the normal trend of Schumann's harmony at this period; further, one would expect his song modulations to be structural and long-range, rather than a mere local response to a verbal idea. All the more surprising then that, of the twenty times the word or idea of 'Himmel', heaven or sky, occurs in Op. 25, it is associated with the subdominant on no fewer than sixteen occasions, some of them very striking indeed.

EX 16

a)

Widmung, Op. 25, No. 1

mein   Him - mel   du, _____   dar - ein   ich   schwe - be

[1] Notably in *Philosophy in a New Key*, New York, 1942, and *Feeling and Form*, London, 1953.

b)

Venezianisches Lied I, Op. 25, No. 17

In each case the flattened seventh—subdominant occurs for the first time with the appearance of the word 'Himmel'.

Similar analogues have been heard in other vocal music, whether it be in Wagner's operas, or the songs of Schubert, Wolf or Brahms. When it comes to Schumann's songs there is a measure of independent confirmation, for in them such commentators as Wolfgang Bœtticher and Martin Cooper have identified meaningful motifs. Even without an immediate verbal context, such motifs were, as I have shown, audible to Hermann Abert, Erwin Bodky, Mosco Carner, Roger Fiske and Robert Schauffler by sympathetic personal intuition, and to Karl Wörner, Paula Rehberg and Rudolph Réti by analysis. What I have tried to show for my part is that all such motifs essentially exemplify one and the same notion. For even at their most expressive, as in the songs, all these motifs have structural significance; and even at their most arbitrary, as in the enciphered names, they all have emotive significance. It seems that in Schumann's music emotion and structure are somehow inseparable.

This passion for structure as the embodiment of emotion was something

Schumann retained to the end. His was a symbolizing, calculating, chess-playing, ratiocinatory mind. Naturally we often find it puzzling, because it often was—as the music and letters amply testify. But even so, what they show is the merest tip of the iceberg—or perhaps one should say volcano. For even when it neared extinction, that mind still flickered and flared with fires now grown dark and ominous. Shortly before Schumann's final breakdown he wrote to Joachim: 'Between the lines of this letter there is invisible writing which will one day come out.'[1] That idea incidentally is one of the many to be found both in Johann Klüber's book on cryptography and in Schumann's own writing. But it had no other contact with external reality. There was in fact no invisible writing in the letter; there was only the all too visible writing on the wall. Then later in the asylum—think of the comforts about which this stricken man wrote home.[2] Like his father, he was a book-lover first and last. He wanted a copy of his favourite novel, *Flegeljahre*, the genesis of all his 'Papillons'. Then he mentions his English chessbook—no doubt Staunton's *Chess-Player's Companion*, another inexhaustible source of symbols. Then in another letter to Clara he writes 'I still get a lot of pleasure out of the palindrome-riddle Roma—Amor'. The letters still flutter helplessly back and forth in his mind to the last. So his imaginative life ended as it began, with the alphabet. Just before Schumann died, Brahms paid him a visit, and was distressed to see his revered master and friend planning journeys and itineraries. Whole sheets of paper were covered with them. Nothing very upsetting about that, you may think. But what disturbed Brahms was this: all the journeys were by way of towns and rivers beginning first with the letters Aa, then with Ab, and so on.[3] There were ABC guides to the last of his creative fantasies, as to his first. That is all that was left when the music, the psyche, drifted away from him; just the remains of a larva, a mere death mask. Asch, and a Sphinx or two. But what ideas they were when alive and active, those 'Papillons' of his; how colourful and moving!

[1] *Briefe*, p. 391.   [2] *Ibid.*, pp. 397ff.
[3] Johannes Brahms in *Briefwechsel mit Joseph Joachim*, ed. Moser, Berlin 1908, Vol. I, pp. 130–1.

o

SCHUMANN'S ILLNESS

Eliot Slater

AT the time when he made it, in 1906, Möbius's[1] suggestion that Schumann had suffered from 'dementia praecox' was a very reasonable one. It was at that time a very up-to-date diagnosis; since it was not very long after Kraepelin had succeeded in sorting out an important part of the ragbag of ill-understood mental illnesses, and in distinguishing under the name of 'dementia praecox', those conditions which we now call schizophrenic. We now know much more about this group of illnesses, though we are still very ignorant of their causation. At the time Möbius wrote, the principal features recognized were: an onset commonly in adolescence or early adult life; progression by fits and starts, with periods of remission and partial recovery between whiles; symptoms in the form of hallucinations, delusions, unaccountable mood changes, and disorders of behaviour of sometimes a bizarre kind; and eventually successive decline to a state in which the personality is obliterated. All these features seemed to fit the case of Schumann fairly well. He had had nervous symptoms from adolescence onwards; he had had phases of illness and recovery; and finally his illness took a steep downward course to end in dementia and death.

And yet the diagnosis made by Möbius will not do. It did not do in his own day, and its inadequacies were pointed out by Gruhle[2] in 1906. It is still less acceptable now. Gruhle argued that the facts adduced by Möbius, rightly considered, led to a different conclusion, i.e. that during the earlier part of his life Schumann was cyclothymic (manic-depressive), but that his last illness was an organic disease of the brain, most probably general paresis.

Gruhle was one of the pioneers of the 'phenomenological' school of psychiatry, which made a great step forward in the understanding, and especially the diag-

[1] Möbius, P. J. *Über Robert Schumanns Krankheit*. Marhold, Halle, 1906.
[2] Gruhle, W. Brief über Robert Schumanns Krankheit an P. B. Möbius. *Zbl. Nervenheilk.* 29, 805 (1906).

nosis, of schizophrenia, by exact and detailed study of the symptomatology of all mental illness. Symptomatology was linked to the pathological causes where they were recognizable in, for instance, poisoning, infections and diseases of the brain; and, in the 'functional psychoses', to course and outcome. The two principal psychoses, schizophrenia and 'manic-depressive insanity' could be distinguished from one another by these means, and were also found in the main to run true to type in any affected family. Similar methods of study sufficed to distinguish the other main kinds of mental abnormality or disorder, i.e. mental subnormality, the neuroses and the personality disorders ('psychopathy'). This work was all going on at the turn of the century, when also Sigmund Freud was introducing revolutionary new ideas. Gruhle was one of the greatest phenomenologists then engaged in building up a rational taxonomy, one that remains basic for us today. It is not surprising that when he applied to Schumann's case the principles he had done so much to develop, it resulted in a radical reconsideration.

This did not mean the end of the debate. The schizophrenic hypothesis has been revived since Gruhle's day, e.g. by Nussbaum[1] in 1923; and by Wörner[2] in 1949; and a 'congenital schizophrenic-type mental disease which . . . might today be diagnosed as *dementia praecox*' is perpetuated by Joan Chissell[3] in the last edition of her biography of Schumann. But I am not aware of any revival of this hypothesis by a psychiatrist since the paper by Meyer and myself[4] in 1959.

For basic source material we principally relied on the works by Litzmann[5,6] and Wasielewski.[7] We overlooked two important sources: Bœtticher[8] and Erler,[9] which will be mentioned below. Bœtticher, while accepting the manic-depressive view put forward by Gruhle, thinks there is some schizoid admixture,[10] and emphasizes also obsessional symptoms, such as music running on in his head without letting him sleep. Our diagnostic analysis consisted in showing (*a*) that all the nervous symptoms which troubled Schumann in early life and up to the age of, say, forty-two, were characteristically 'cyclothymic', that is, related to the

[1] Nussbaum, F. Der Streit über Robert Schumanns Krankheit. Dissertation, Köln, 1923.

[2] Wörner, K. H. *Robert Schumann: Ein letzter Zukunftsblick.* Atlantis, Zürich, 1949, p. 334.

[3] Chissell, J. *Schumann.* Dent, London, 1967, p. 76.

[4] Slater, E. and Meyer, A. Contributions to a Pathography of the Musicians: 1. Robert Schumann. *Confinia Psychiat. 2*, 65–94, 1959.

[5] Litzmann, B. *Clara Schumann: Ein Künstlerleben,* 5th edition. Breitkopf & Härtel, Leipzig, 1918.

[6] Litzmann, B. (ed.) *Clara Schumann—Johannes Brahms: Briefe 1853–1896.* Breitkopf & Härtel, Leipzig, 1927.

[7] Wasielewski, W. J. von. *Robert Schumann,* 4th edition. Breitkopf & Härtel, Leipzig, 1906.

[8] Bœtticher, W. *Robert Schumann: Einführung in Persönlichkeit und Werk.* Hahnfeld, Berlin, 1941, p. 161.

[9] Erler, H. von. *Robert Schumanns Leben,* Ries & Erler, Berlin, 1887, ii, p. 201.

[10] 'Es fehlt aber bisweilen auch nicht an breiten Übergängen nach der schizoiden Seite hin.

manic-depressive and not to the schizophrenic syndrome; (*b*) that Schumann
survived repeated attacks of this kind of illness without any deterioration of
personality (which was to be expected on the schizophrenic hypothesis); (*c*) that
the last illness which led to his admission to the mental hospital at Endenich began
as a delirium or confusional state, typical of acute organic psychoses but very rare
in schizophrenia; (*d*) that this illness progressed into a form of dementia unlike
schizophrenic deterioration of the personality but typical of organic disease of the
brain; (*e*) that the nature of this brain disease was most probably the late form of
cerebral syphilis called general paresis or G.P.I.

A short explanation of the way in which syphilis affects the central nervous
system may be found helpful at this point. There are three main syndromes:
meningovascular syphilis, *tabes dorsalis* (locomotor ataxia) and general paresis. In
the first condition, which may come on soon after the original infection, or at
any time in later life, the blood vessels and membranes of the nervous system are
principally involved. Symptoms include headaches, convulsions, and a great
variety of pains if the posterior nerve roots are affected. The other two types are
called late or tertiary syphilis, since symptoms appear from ten to twenty-five
years after the infection. In these conditions it is the nerve cells themselves which
are attacked, in tabes the nerve cells of the spinal cord and in general paresis the
nerve cells of the brain cortex, especially in the frontal and temporal regions; the
membranes and small blood vessels are affected also. In tabes, as well as various
forms of unsteadiness of the limbs, leading symptoms are the pains and abnormal
sensations (paraesthesiae). Pains may take the form of severe stabbing, the
so-called 'lightning pains', which may be thought of as rheumatic pain; or girdle
pains; or very severe crises of pain. In a typical case of tabes, with lesions confined
to the spinal cord, mental changes do not occur. In general paresis, mental
symptoms are the leading ones, and take many forms, e.g. a simple dementia, or
a paranoid persecutory psychosis, or onset with an acute confusional or delirious
state progressing later to dementia. Before the days of malarial and other fever
therapies (or nowadays with penicillin), from diagnosis to death the illness usually
only lasted two or three years. Although these three types of condition are distinct, and most patients affected by tertiary syphilis of the nervous system tend
to follow one clinical path or another, combinations are not infrequent. The
combination of tabes with general paresis is recognized as *tabo-paresis*.

Schumann's clinical history was described in some detail by Meyer and myself
(*loc. cit.*), and here can be quite briefly summarized. Covering the varying mood
states which Schumann had all his life, we can draw up the following calendar,
starting when he was eighteen:

1828: predominant mood melancholic.

1829: one and a half years of almost continuous happiness, occasionally interrupted by quite short depressive moods.

1830: recurrence of melancholy in October.

1831: persistently melancholic, psychically inhibited, with phases of agitation. Sudden recovery on 31 December.

1832: excellent spirits throughout.

1833: relapse into depression in the autumn; the fear comes that he might go mad.

1834: by May almost well, and in August elated.

1836: normal spirits pass into elation succeeded by a depressive phase.

1837: depressive state in September.

1838-9: up and down.

1840: marriage, followed by several good years.

1842-3: some months of nervous weakness and incapacity to compose, later passing into elated state.

1844: very melancholic throughout the year, almost without intermission.

1845: some depression in May.

1846: May to July melancholic; then complete remission.

1848: relapse in January and depressive mood predominating for most of the year.

1849: in the best of spirits throughout the year.

1850-1: minor mood changes only.

1852: mild depression.

1853: in good spirits throughout the year.

1854: acute psychotic breakdown.

1856: death.

It is very typical of an 'endogenous' or manic-depressive depression to cause a general slowing up of mental activity. This psychic inhibition, if it is at all severe, makes creative work impossible; and this is strikingly exemplified by Schumann (and even more so in the creative career of Hugo Wolf). The reactive type of depression arising from the losses and disappointments of life does not go so deep, and usually leaves creative powers untouched. In his depressions Schumann became almost incapable of the work of composition; and in 1844, his worst year, nothing was completed at all. He would even take weeks to write a letter. However, the opposite phase of the cyclothymic temperament, that of elation, commonly goes with increased productivity and, in the case of the greatly gifted, with creative work of the best. Very good years for Schumann in terms of prevailing mood state were 1840–41, 1849, and 1853; these years were also his most productive ones, though the quality of his work in 1853 seems to have been far below his best, most probably because of the oncoming organic process.

Schumann's depressions showed other features typical of the 'endogenous', as against the reactive, mood swing: a diurnal rhythm with mood state worst in the morning; feeling of physical malaise with hypochondriacal ideas; insomnia showing itself particularly in early morning waking; though usually gradual transition via a normal mood state, sometimes quite abrupt reversal into an elated phase. In his depressions Schumann would be full of fears and hopelessness, dead to any enjoyment, silent perhaps for days. In an elated phase, on the other hand, he felt full of strength and energy, radiantly happy, with free flow of imagination, wanting to take the world by storm. The elated phase was more likely to terminate by slipping into a depression than by a simple return to normality.

In all the records available to us, we found no evidence of schizophrenic symptoms, e.g. delusions, hallucinations or paranoid symptoms, until the final psychotic phase 1854–56. On the other hand the record is quite typically cyclothymic (manic-depressive), with the colouring of symptomatology which one could have guessed from Schumann's romantic nature.

Premonitory symptoms of organic disease of the nervous system can be suspected in 1843 when there were the first complaints of giddiness, or 1844 when auditory symptoms began in the form of tinnitus, a singing or a roaring in the ears, and a distressing effect by which noises became musical tones. These symptoms would come and go. The commonest cause, Ménière's disease, can be excluded since Schumann never lost his hearing. Otherwise, one cannot be sure how they were caused, though the symptoms are compatible with syphilis of the nervous system.

According to Bœtticher[1] there were painful attacks of 'rheumatism' affecting the feet in 1850, and recurring again in 1852. At the end of August 1852 there were burning sensations at the back of the head, and a succession of prickling nervous sensations, especially in the backbone and the finger-tips. More definite signs that the brain was being affected also appeared in 1852, first with clumsiness of speech and then with what seems to have been a convulsive attack. Schumann had to give up his conducting. In July 1853 he had some kind of attack which was regarded by Nussbaum as a cerebral vascular stroke; congestive attacks, with the clinical features of very temporary strokes, are common in the early stages of general paresis. The physician, Dr Kalt, who saw him seems to have made this diagnosis, since he said he had 'Gehirnerweichung' (brain softening)[2], which was

1 *Op. cit.*   2 Erler, *op. cit.*

the synonym in common parlance. In August there were speech disturbances; and in November more auditory symptoms.

The final psychotic stage, which began with an acute delirium, came on quite abruptly on the night of Friday, 10 February 1854, with an attack of tinnitus, developing in a few days into musical tones and on the night of Friday, 17 February, into angelic music. The next morning the angel voices changed to the voices of devils. They told him he was a sinner and would be thrown into hell. He saw them round him in the shapes of tigers and hyenas. A continuous, or nearly continuous, state of auditory and visual hallucination continued for over a week; consciousness, though presumably clouded, was at least partially preserved and he could recognize and speak to his wife. On Sunday 26th he was rather better, but in the evening said he must go to the asylum, and went and laid out all the things he would want to take with him. The next day he was deeply melancholic and told Clara that he was not worthy of her love. Without the others realizing it, he went out of the house into stormy rain without protection against the weather. An hour later he was brought home again, having thrown himself into the Rhine; he had been seen and rescued.

Clara was not allowed to see him again after this before he was taken to hospital. He left a week later, on Saturday, 4 March, going off with two male nurses without asking after his wife or children. He settled happily into asylum life, and took an immediate liking to his personal nurse. It seems that by this time all delirious symptoms must have passed off, leaving a placid emotional state, and fairly normal affective rapport. However in succeeding weeks he would have periods of agitation in which he would walk up and down his room or kneel and wring his hands. On 31 March Clara recorded with sorrow that Robert asked for flowers, but never for news of her. In April there was another acute psychotic phase with hallucinations and confused talk. At the end of May he was unusually cheerful, and on 21 July Clara received flowers Robert had sent her.

About this time Brahms paid a visit which he describes in a letter to Clara dated 13 August 1854. He found Robert looking well and strong; he was clear and sensible and not confused. Dr Peters told Brahms that he was very changeable and that periods of clarity and confusion followed one another. The day before, while drinking his wine, he had suddenly stopped, said there was poison in it, and had thrown the rest on the floor. He wrote much, but illegibly. The doctor commented on his weakness of memory, and his incapacity to remember what he had done an hour ago.

There seems to have been no consistent change in the winter of 1854–55; musical hallucinations continued to occur. On 23 February 1855 Brahms wrote

Clara a letter describing a second visit, not a very happy one. There were trouble-some defects of memory, an incapacity to recognize or to admit them, patho-logical obstinacy and pathological emotional lability. However it seems his general emotional responsiveness was maintained and natural. On 5 May 1855 Robert wrote Clara his last letter, still affectionate but quite fragmentary and incoherent. By this time intellectual impairment must have reached an advanced stage.

Brahms paid a further visit in April 1856 when Schumann received him with pleasure but could only express himself in single inarticulate words. From this time deterioration was rapid, physically and mentally, and he died on 29 July 1856 after a day of almost continuous convulsion.

A report on the case by Richarz, the medical superintendent at Endenich, in 1873 is quoted by Wasielewski. On clinical aspects, he says that spells of hallucin-ation were repeated again and again. The gradual and progressive impairment of intellectual powers was very slow and never reached an extreme degree. Postmortem examination showed atrophy of the brain, thickening of the lepto-meninges, i.e. the fine membranes wrapping round the actual tissue of the brain, and their adherence to the cerebral cortex in several places. These are the changes one expects with general paresis.

It does not seem possible to doubt the organic nature of the final psychotic phase from 1854 to 1856. The acute delirious state with massive hallucination and prominence of visual hallucinations which came on abruptly on the night of 10 February 1854 must have been due to some physical cause, but could be due to any one of a great range, poisoning, infection, vascular catastrophe, etc. The later slowly progressive course, with numerous ups and downs, is quite a typical course for tertiary syphilis of the central nervous system, i.e. general paresis, and typical of nothing else; other possibilities, not easily to be totally excluded, such as presenile or arteriosclerotic dementia, or brain tumour, rarely run such a wavering course. Kerner[1] suggests arteriosclerosis rather than general paresis as the cause, on the grounds that Clara's pregnancies, apart from one miscarriage, were normal, and that there was no deterioration in the last stages of Schumann's illness. This does not do justice to the facts, and arteriosclerotic syndromes are in any case unlike Schumann's illness in symptomatology or course. The chronic illness is typically organic (i.e. not schizophrenic), with its heavy incidence on

---

[1] Kerner, D. *Krankheiten grosser Musiker*. Friedrich-Karl Schattauer-Verlag, Stuttgart, 1963, pp. 103–26. This book, with pathographies of a number of major composers, is likely to reach a large, musically interested public in German-speaking countries. The Schumann chapter is well informed on the literature, but presents an idiosyncratic theory in a one-sided way. It seems worth while, accordingly, to examine Kerner's thesis more particularly. See Appendix, p. 415.

intellectual capacities, especially memory. Finally the rapid physical deterioration to extreme wasting, with muscular paresis and gross speech disorder, leading to death in convulsions, fit the picture of general paresis as no other disease.

We conclude, then, that, had he been burdened only with the cyclothymic disposition, almost as much of an advantage as a handicap in musical creation, Schumann could have very well lived on into old age and a life of happiness with his family and sustained achievement. But little more than half-way through his life he was smitten down by an organic disease of the brain. This, then, was a kind of accident, an 'act of God', and in no way to be attributed to such a chain of cause and effect which lead us to think of character as destiny. The most likely explanation is that of syphilis, acquired in youth, and manifesting as brain disease in middle age after an interim latent phase of twenty years or so. Schumann did in fact lead rather a wild life as a very young man, and hypomanic mood states which predominated in 1829 and again in 1833 may have been a contributory factor leading to indiscretion. If he acquired syphilis at this time, latency till 1852 would be quite in the order of the day, especially if he had treatment.

It is only if he had treatment that Clara could have escaped infection from him if he had it; but treatment, while rendering him non-infective, would still have left him open to a continuing latency of the infection. In a brilliant piece of biographical research, Eric Sams[1] has shown that the 'injury' to Schumann's finger which he incurred in the early 1830s, and which has long been a mystery, could very well have been a side effect, in the form of muscular paresis, of treatment by mercury, which was the standard treatment for syphilis in that era.

Partially successful treatment could account for the fact that there is no history of stillbirths or miscarriage among Robert and Clara's eight children. Three of them lived to a ripe old age. But did they all escape? It is not very easy to answer this confidently, since we also have to take into account the fact that manic-depression tends to run in families.

There was a family history of mental or nervous illness in Robert's family. His father seems to have had melancholic phases; and his sister Emilie is said to have become mentally ill at seventeen; she is also said to have drowned herself at nineteen.[2] Möbius thought she was schizophrenic, but her illness could quite possibly have been manic-depressive. One of Robert and Clara's eight children, Emil, died in infancy. Felix and Julie both had lung trouble and died in their twenties, Julie dying in childbirth. Ferdinand died after years of ill-health at forty-two. Ludwig, born in 1848, began to show signs of mental illness by the age of twenty, and two years later was regarded as incurable. He died in a mental

---

[1] Sams, E.: 'Schumann's hand injury'. *Musical Times*, December 1971.
[2] However, see footnote 5 on page 3 for an alternative indication of Emilie's death. ED

hospital at the age of fifty-one. He, also, has been regarded as a schizophrenic. But it is highly suggestive that in June 1870 he was diagnosed by his doctors as not only insane but 'Rückenmarkkrank', i.e. suffering from a disease of the spinal marrow.[1] This, then, could conceivably have been a late manifestation of syphilis, this time acquired congenitally.

Of course one will never be able to be quite sure of the nature of Schumann's affliction, since no theory can be submitted to a decisive test. Nevertheless, an obscure and complex problem has yielded little by little to attempts to solve it; and by successive stages from the Möbius–Gruhle debate in 1904-6, we have arrived at a rational and intellectually satisfying explanation of all the facts at our command.

[1] Litzmann, *op. cit.*

Appendix[1]

Kerner considers Schumann's history from a medical point of view, but one which is not in any way instructed psychiatrically. He adopts the hypothesis put forward by H. Kleinebreil (*Der kranke Schumann*, dissertation Univ. Jena, 1943) which was also accepted by W. Schweisheimer ('War Robert Schumann geisteskrank?', *Ärtzl. Praxis*, p. 840, 1959). I have not been able to consult these works, and it is possible that the arguments are stronger there than as they are presented by Kerner. Kerner believes that Schumann was subject to essential hypertension, which eventually resulted in a paranoid-hallucinatory involutional psychosis, schizophreniform in type, which necessitated asylum care for the last years of his life. The physical basis was cerebral arteriosclerosis; and the psychosis was released by a severe conflict situation from which Schumann saw no way out. The conflict situation was not unconnected with Clara, and was also contributed to by his failing musical powers. The affectlessness shown in letters to Clara from Endenich (which has beeen attributed to schizophrenic personality change, but in my view is a typical result of organic changes in the frontal area of the brain) according to Kerner may have had personal causes ('sehr persönliche Ursachen').

Kerner argues against and rejects both schizophrenic and manic-depressive diagnoses. If any children of Robert and Clara succumbed to schizophrenia, this was only because the children of creative personalities are in special danger, as the appearance of a genius in a family often heralds that family's downfall (!). As for the manic-depressive hypothesis, evidence of depression can be accounted for by the many misfortunes of Schumann's life, and also by the romantic sorrow-fulness and suicidal imaginings of the age of Werther.

His diagnosis of essential hypertension is supported by symptoms coming on fairly early in life, such as giddy feelings, attacks of shortness of breath and cardiac anxiety. To the present writer they look more characteristic of simple anxiety states. Kerner does not give any consideration to the history of mood swings throughout earlier life, extending into hypomanic as well as depressive directions, which are so characteristic of cyclothymia.

[1] See footnote, p. 412

Those of Schumann's symptoms which are clearly organic in nature Kerner puts down to cerebral arteriosclerosis, rejecting the diagnosis of general paresis. His discussion is a long one, with much that is not relevant, but reduces itself to the following points: (1) none of the children of Robert and Clara suffered from anything suggestive of congenital syphilis; (2) if Schumann had had an irregularity of the pupil, or unequal pupils, or small pupils, this would have been noticed by the painter Laurens, who portrayed him several times in his last years; (3) Schumann's history does not show progressive impairment of mental faculties. On this last point he quotes from an article Richarz contributed to the Kölnische Zeitung of 15 August 1873: 'Sein Selbstbewusstsein war geknickt, doch nicht zerstört, sein Ich nicht sich selbst entfremdet, nicht umgewandelt. Bis zuletzt behaupteten sich die geistigen Fähigkeiten . . . auf einer verhältnissmässig grossen Höhe.' That is, mental faculties had suffered, but had not been reduced to the lowest level by the time he died. True enough; two days before he died he was able to recognize Clara, though not able to speak a coherent sentence to her. Nevertheless, dementia was quite advanced more than a year earlier, as can be seen from his letter to Clara dated 5 May 1855; and it continued to progress by infinitesimal degrees up to his death.

These arguments, as it seems to me, do not carry much weight. The children could well have been spared a congenital syphilis, if Robert had received medical treatment rendering him uninfective. The point about the pupils is an interesting one. Perhaps the most characteristic of all signs of tertiary syphilis of the brain are pupils unreactive to light but reactive to accommodation, e.g. in focusing the eyes, a sign first described by a Scottish physician, Argyll Robertson (1837–1909). Such pupils are usually small, but may be large, or unequal, or irregular in shape. Kerner says that Schumann's pupils were large; if they were consistently large, even in a good light, this would probably be from loss of the light reflex. This looks like a point in favour of the diagnosis of cerebral syphilis.

Kerner's diagnosis of an essential hypertension causing symptoms about the age of forty calls for a malignant condition which would probably have proved fatal in one to two years. One would have expected more definite symptoms of dizziness and vertigo, severe occipital headaches worse in the morning, and almost certainly eye symptoms, such as scotomata, blurred vision, even partial or one-sided blindness. Cardiac and renal symptoms, as well as cerebral ones, would be expected. On the other hand a benign hypertension would only be expected to produce cerebral symptoms much later; cerebral arteriosclerosis is a disease of later life, and not early middle age. The disease progresses by causing a succession of small or larger strokes, from which recovery is incomplete, so that progress downhill is in a series of steps. Some of these strokes would produce a definite paresis or aphasia; and gross neurological changes, such as would be missed by no competent doctor, would be inevitable. Richarz was certainly competent. His formulation of the case is compatible with general paresis—and this is what he probably thought it was—and not with cerebrovascular disease.

SCHUMANN'S FAMILY TREE

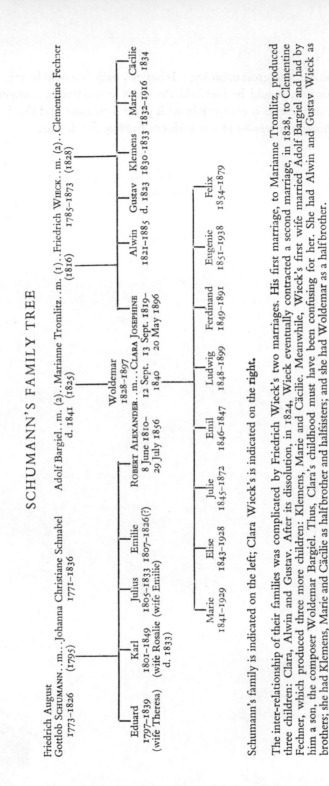

Schumann's family is indicated on the left; Clara Wieck's is indicated on the **right.**

The inter-relationship of their families was complicated by Friedrich Wieck's two marriages. His first marriage, to Marianne Tromlitz, produced three children: Clara, Alwin and Gustav. After its dissolution, in 1824, Wieck eventually contracted a second marriage, in 1828, to Clementine Fechner, which produced three more children: Klemens, Marie and Cäcilie. Meanwhile, Wieck's first wife married Adolf Bargiel and had by him a son, the composer Woldemar Bargiel. Thus, Clara's childhood must have been confusing for her. She had Alwin and Gustav Wieck as brothers; she had Klemens, Marie and Cäcilie as halfbrother and halfsisters; and she had Woldemar as a halfbrother.

ALAN WALKER
_____

A Biographical Summary of Schumann's Life

Childhood and Youth (1810–29)

1810, 8 June. Robert Schumann is born in Zwickau, Saxony, youngest among five children.

1816. He is placed in a private school at Zwickau, run by Archdeacon Döhner.

1817. Starts taking piano lessons from Johann Kuntzsch. His first attempts at composition date from this year.

1820. He is enrolled at the Lyceum in Zwickau, where he remains for eight years. Takes part in frequent musical entertainments given by the Lyceum pupils; at fifteen, plays piano pieces by Moscheles and Herz among others.

1826. His sister, Emilie, who is mentally unbalanced, commits suicide[1]. His father August Schumann dies shortly afterwards, on 10 August. As a result of these bereavements he temporarily succumbs to melancholia.

1828. Graduates from the Lyceum and tours Bavaria with his friend Gisbert Rosen. Accepted as a law-student at Leipzig University. Meets Friedrich Wieck at Leipzig and takes a few preliminary lessons from him; also makes the acquaintance of the nine-year-old Clara Wieck, his future wife.

1829. Tours the Rhine during his Easter vacation, and decides to enrol at Heidelberg University to further his law studies under the great jurist Thibaut. During the summer he visits Switzerland and Italy. He remains at Heidelberg for three terms. Completes the first part of *Papillons* (op. 2).

[1] But see f. 5, p. 3.

At Leipzig (1830–44)

1830. Schumann decides to give up the law and devote himself entirely to music. He returns to Leipzig and again places himself in the hands of Friedrich Wieck who promises to turn him into a virtuoso within three years. Also starts taking theory lessons from Heinrich Dorn, Director of the Leipzig opera. Composes the 'Abegg' Variations (op. 1) and the first version of the *Toccata* (op. 7). First symptoms of his hand injury appear.

1831, December. Publishes his famous article on Chopin ('Hats off, gentlemen, a genius') in G. W. Fink's *Allgemeine musikalische Zeitung*. Finishes the composition of *Papillons* (op. 2).

1832. Hand injury worsens; he seeks medical advice; Resigns himself to giving up his piano studies. Completes his first set of *Six Concert Studies on Caprices by Paganini* (op. 3). Part of his early Symphony in G minor is performed at a concert in Zwickau given by Wieck and his daughter Clara.

1833. Death of his brother Julius. Composes his second set of *Six Concert Studies on Caprices by Paganini* (op. 10). Meets Ernestine von Fricken, a piano pupil of Wieck, with whom he becomes infatuated.

1834. He establishes the *Neue Zeitschrift für Musik* (first edition appears on 3 April), and remains its editor-in-chief for the next ten years. Begins the composition of *Carnaval* (op. 9).

1835. Mendelssohn arrives in Leipzig and takes charge of the Gewandhaus concerts. A close friendship is struck up between the two composers. Schumann completes *Carnaval* and his *Piano Sonata No. 1 in F sharp minor* (op. 11). Meets Chopin in Leipzig for the first time. Breaks off his secret engagement to Ernestine von Fricken.

1836. Death of his mother (4 February). He discovers his love for Clara Wieck. Her father opposes the match and there begins an increasingly bitter feud between the two men which ends in a law-suit three years later. Meets Chopin for a second time. Makes friends with Sterndale Bennett. Composition of the Fantasie in C major (op. 17).

1837. Becomes engaged to Clara, despite Wieck's opposition, who now takes his daughter on tour via Prague to Vienna in an effort to keep the lovers apart. Composes the *Davidsbündlertänze* (op. 6).

1838. Visits Vienna and discovers the manuscript of Schubert's 'Great' C major Symphony in the possession of Ferdinand Schubert which he sends to Mendelssohn. The first performance is given at a Gewandhaus concert in Leipzig under Mendelssohn's baton on 21 March 1839. Composes *Kinderscenen* (op. 15) and *Kreisleriana* (op. 16). Relations with Wieck worsen.

1839. Robert and Clara apply to the Court of Appeal for permission to marry, seeing no hope of overcoming Wieck's violent opposition by orthodox means. The case is postponed and Wieck issues a calumny against Schumann, accusing him of drunkenness and loose living. Death of his eldest brother Eduard. Composes *Faschingsschwank aus Wien* (op. 26) and the *Humoreske* (op. 20).

1840. University of Jena admit Schumann to the degree of Doctor of Philosophy. Meets Liszt for the first time, who visits Leipzig in March. Robert and Clara marry on 12 September, the day before Clara's twenty-first birthday, in the village of Schönfeld, near Leipzig. A great outpouring of composition heralds the event, later called by Schumann his 'song year', including the *Liederkreis* (op. 24), *Myrthen* (op. 25) and *Frauenliebe und -leben* (op. 42) cycles.

1841. Completes his Symphony No. 1 in B flat major ('Spring') which is performed under Mendelssohn's direction at a Gewandhaus concert on 31 March. Birth of Schumann's daughter Marie on 1 September. Symphony No. 2 in D minor (later No. 4) completed in 1st version.

1842. Schumann's 'chamber-music year', in which he completes three string quartets (op. 41), the Piano Quartet (op. 47), and the Piano Quintet (op. 44) which is performed for the first time in Leipzig in December, with Mendelssohn sight-reading the piano part.

1843. Meets Berlioz, January. The Leipzig Conservatory of Music is opened in April, under the direction of Mendelssohn; Schumann is offered a professorship in piano and composition. Wieck, aware of Schumann's growing reputation, attempts to patch up his differences with him. Birth of a second daughter, Elise, in April. Completes *Paradise and the Peri*.

1844. Robert and Clara begin an extended concert-tour, on 25 January, which takes them through Berlin and Königsberg to Russia. Clara plays before the Russian Imperial Court at St Petersburg, and Schumann's 'Spring' Symphony is also given there with Schumann conducting. In May, back in Leipzig, he gives up the editorship of the *Neue Zeitschrift für Musik* and hands over to Franz Brendel. The following month he suffers a nervous breakdown which brings him to the verge of total mental collapse. He rallies sufficiently to begin his *Scenes from Goethe's 'Faust'*. In December the Schumanns leave Leipzig and move to Dresden.

At Dresden (1845-50)

1845. Tries to settle down in Dresden, but complains of the lack of real musical activity there. Frequent contact with Wagner, who is Director of the Dresden Opera, but the two composers fail to hit it off. Makes friends with Hiller. Commences a deep study of Bach and composes his Six Organ Fugues on the name B.A.C.H., and the Four Fugues for piano. Completes the Piano Concerto in A minor. Birth of a third daughter, Julie.

1846. Clara gives first performance of the Piano Concerto in A minor at a Gewandhaus concert on 1 January. Schumann's health deteriorates again. He experiences disturbing auditory symptoms in May, and reports 'a constant singing and roaring in the ears'. Completes his Symphony No. 2 in C major. A fourth child, Emil, is born who dies in infancy.

1847. A summer festival is arranged in Schumann's honour by his native town of Zwickau; he conducts his C major Symphony there and Clara plays his Piano Concerto. Hiller leaves Dresden for Düsseldorf and Schumann succeeds him as conductor of the *Liedertafel*. Begins his opera *Genoveva*, after initial difficulties over the libretto which he now adapts himself. Composes his Piano Trios in D minor and F major. Death of Mendelssohn, on 4 November, throws him into despondency.

1848. In a sustained burst of creative activity Schumann completes *Genoveva* and immediately starts work on the incidental music to Byron's *Manfred*. He gives up the conductorship of the *Liedertafel* and founds his own 'Choral Union'. His fifth child, Ludwig, is born.

1849. Robert and Clara become disillusioned in Dresden, finding its Court-dominated functions restrictive and conventional. The Dresden uprising, in

May, forces them to flee the city and they seek refuge in the village of Kreischa. Hiller gives up the conductorship of the Düsseldorf Orchestra, and offers it to Schumann who accepts it. Schumann composed more than twenty works during this year which he called 'my most fruitful period'. Birth of another child, Ferdinand.

1850. During February and March Robert and Clara undertake a concert-tour of Leipzig, Bremen, Hamburg and Altona. The long-postponed production of *Genoveva* takes place in Leipzig on 25 June but has only a modest reception. The Schumanns finally leave Dresden in September and move to Düsseldorf where Robert takes up his duties as orchestral conductor. Symphony No. 3 in E flat major ('The Rhenish') is begun. Cello Concerto completed.

At Düsseldorf (1851–56)

1851. The first disaffection sets in between Schumann and the Düsseldorf orchestra. The truth slowly dawns on the orchestra that while Schumann may be a distinguished musician, he is not particularly competent as a conductor. Discipline in the choir flags, and attendances at rehearsals fall off. Schumann refuses to accept the Orchestral Committee's valid criticism of him, interpreting it as persecution, and the seeds of a lasting dispute between the Committee and himself are sown. His overture *The Bride of Messina* is received coldly by the Düsseldorfers.

1852. He conducts the first performance of his overture to Byron's *Manfred* at a Gewandhaus concert. Julius Tausch starts to deputize for Schumann at rehearsals. The choir prefer Tausch and a move is made by its more militant members to remove Schumann who is asked to resign by the Committee; there is a quarrel, Schumann's friends rally round him, and the Committee resigns instead. Schumann reluctantly agrees to share his duties with Tausch.

1853. Develops a morbid interest in spiritualism and 'table-tipping'. Brahms visits the Schumanns in September bearing a letter of introduction from Joachim, and he stays with them for several weeks. Schumann recognizes Brahms's genius and writes a laudatory article about him called 'New Paths' which is published in the *Neue Zeitschrift*. His work with the Düsseldorf choir is now regarded by them as so unreliable that he is asked to stop conducting for a while. He reacts by staying away from rehearsals. Undertakes a concert-tour of Holland with Clara in November.

1854. In February the final dissolution of his personality sets in. He is plagued by the sound of an imaginary 'A' ringing in his ears which is later transformed into a continuous stream of music, entire compositions leading into one another without a break. In his distressed state he imagines himself possessed of demons. On 27 February he throws himself into the Rhine, and is rescued by boatmen. A few days later he is taken at his own request to the private asylum of Dr Richarz at Endenich, near Bonn, where he spends his remaining two years. He is visited by Brahms and Joachim. At first, Richarz entertains hopes of a full recovery, but despite lucid moments Schumann's health gradually deteriorates. Clara gives birth to another child (June) called Felix after Mendelssohn.

1855. He is visited by his pupil and first biographer Wasielewski. Bettina von Arnim also visits him and alarms Clara with tales of incompetence among Schumann's doctors, soon dispelled by Joachim. Clara, who is now in serious financial difficulty, receives a large loan from Paul Mendelssohn, in memory of his brother Felix. Brahms becomes a staunch friend of Clara and during the summer the pair spend a walking holiday together in the Rhine Valley.

1856. In order to support her large family, Clara undertakes a three-month concert-tour of England in the spring. She receives a cable from Dr Richarz on 23 July warning her that Robert's death is imminent. She sees Robert on 27 July for the first time in two years and he recognizes her; two days later, on 29 July, he dies in his sleep at four o'clock in the afternoon. He is buried at Bonn on 31 July. Brahms and Joachim act as pallbearers, and Hiller delivers a funeral oration.

ALAN WALKER

Register of Persons

Andersen, Hans Christian (1805–75). Danish poet and author. Creator of famous children's stories. Four of Schumann's Five Songs, Op. 40 (1840), are settings of poems by Andersen in a translation by Chamisso.

Andersen met Schumann in 1844. He relates in his autobiography: 'From Weimar I went to Leipzig, where a truly poetical evening awaited me with Robert Schumann. This great composer had a year earlier surprised me by the honour of dedicating to me the music which he had composed to four of my songs; the wife of Dr Frege, whose singing has enchanted so many thousands, was accompanied by Clara Schumann, and the composer and the poet were the sole audience; a festive supper and a mutual interchange of ideas made the evening all too short.'

d'Arányi, Jelly (1895–1966). Hungarian violinist. She was a great-niece of Joachim. Her violin studies began when she was eight years old, under Hubay, at the Royal Academy of Music in Budapest. She made her debut in Vienna, in 1909, afterwards touring Europe; she settled in London in 1923.

It was d'Arányi who gave the British première of Schumann's D minor Violin Concerto at a BBC Symphony Concert. The circumstances leading to that event were unusual. D'Arányi was interested in spiritualism. In 1933, during a seance, she claimed to have received messages from Schumann and Joachim, who instructed her to go to the Prussian State Library, retrieve the Concerto (where it had lain for eighty years) and arrange the première. These celestial directives appear to have been in flat contradiction to the wishes of Joachim, and possibly Schumann himself, while they were still earth-bound. (See *The Listener*, September 1937, where the background to the première was sketched in by Rollo Myers in an article called 'Finding a lost Schumann Concerto'.)

Arnim, Bettina von (née Brentano) (1785–1859). A powerful literary personality who pushed herself to the forefront of the Romantic movement. She was famous for her egocentricity and for the fervour with which she pursued her enthusiasms, often to the point of dottiness.

As a young woman, she idolized Goethe and enjoyed a famous correspondence with him—and possibly not just a correspondence. In 1811 she quarrelled violently with Goethe's wife, Christina, who sent her packing, after which she married Karl Joachim von Arnim by whom she had seven children. Her interests ranged over sculpture and music, as well as literature, and she knew everybody who was anybody in the world of art.

Bettina's characteristic 'style' comes across in her forthright remarks about the young Clara Wieck's Berlin recital in 1837: 'How pretentiously she seats herself at the piano, and without notes too! How modest is Doehler on the other hand, who has the music in front of him!' She caused a great deal of mischief when she visited Schumann in the asylum at Endenich in 1855 and reported to Clara that his doctors were incompetent.

Bargiel, Frau Marianne (née Tromlitz) (1797–1872). Wieck's first wife, and the mother of Clara. A gifted pianist, she was at first Wieck's pupil; Wieck married her when she was only nineteen. After eight unhappy years of marriage she deserted Wieck, in 1824, and he divorced her. Shortly afterwards, she married another piano pedagogue, Adolf Bargiel. Among the children of her second marriage was Woldemar Bargiel (1828–97) the composer.

Barth, Johann Ambrosius (1790–1851). Book-seller and publisher of Schumann's journal the *Neue Zeitschrift für Musik*.

Bennett, Sir William Sterndale (1816–1875. English composer, pianist, conductor and teacher. He was an infant prodigy, and he entered the Royal Academy of Music, London, before his tenth birthday. At seventeen he was discovered by Mendelssohn who invited him to Leipzig. Here he made a number of lasting friends, including Schumann. After hearing Bennett play his own Piano Concerto in C minor, Op. 9, at a Gewandhaus Concert in 1837, Schumann wrote in the *Neue Zeitschrift*: 'We cannot but marvel at this early-developed master-hand. . . . Here we have to do with an artist of the higher orders. . . .' In 1849, Bennett, who had meantime returned to England, founded the Bach Society; he gave the first English performance of the St Matthew Passion in 1854. He became Principal of the Royal Academy of Music in 1866, and was knighted in 1871.

Schumann dedicated his *Études Symphoniques* to Bennett. The finale contains a musical tribute to his English friend in the form of a quotation from Marschner's opera *Der Templer und die Jüdin*, based on Sir Walter Scott's novel 'Ivanhoe'.

Berger, Ludwig (1777–1839). Berlin pianist, composer and teacher. Henriette Voigt (with whom Schumann enjoyed a romantic friendship in 1833) was his pupil. So was Mendelssohn.

Berlioz, Hector (1803–69). Schumann met Berlioz only once. That was in 1843 when the Frenchman paid a visit to Leipzig. Schumann left an account of him in his diary. 'His face, otherwise so full of charac-

ter, has a certain weakness about the corners of the mouth and chin. Paris has corrupted him. Unfortunately, he speaks no German, so we couldn't have much conversation. I had pictured a more fiery personality.' Despite a fundamental antipathy between the two musicians, whose artistic aims were completely different, Schumann was always generous to Berlioz in print. His analysis of the 'Fantastic' Symphony proves that (*Neue Zeitschrift*, 1835). So does his review of the overture to *Les Franc-juges*: 'When it comes to the compositions of Berlioz, we have not done the usual thing and applied our critical wisdom ten years too late, but announce, in advance that in this Frenchman there is something of genius.'

Böttger, Adolph (1815–70). German poet. Schumann's 'Spring' Symphony was inspired by a poem of Böttger's. Shortly after completing it, Schumann sent Böttger a music quotation from the beginning of the Symphony with this inscription: 'Beginning of a symphony inspired by a poem of Adolph Böttger. To the poet as a remembrance from Robert Schumann. Leipzig, October, 1842.'

Brahms, Johannes (1833–97). Brahms first visited Robert and Clara Schumann in Düsseldorf, in 1853, bearing a letter of introduction from Joachim. From the outset, the Schumanns formed a lasting attachment for Brahms, broken only by Robert's death in 1856, and which, in the case of Clara, survived for more than forty years. Brahms was the subject of Schumann's last major article in Criticism, called 'New Paths', which was published in the *Neue Zeitschrift für Musik* in 1853 a few weeks after their first meeting. 'Seated at the piano, he began to disclose to us the most wondrous regions. It was also the most wondrous playing which transformed the piano into an orchestra of mourning and jubilant voices.' The article brought the twenty-year-old Brahms to fame overnight.

Perhaps this is the place to examine the intimate relationship which sprang up between Clara and Brahms while Schumann was dying at Endenich. On first hearing the news of Schumann's committal, Brahms had hurried back to Düsseldorf to offer what comfort he could to the distracted Clara. He was badly needed. The house was full of well-meaning friends and neighbours who were a perpetual harassment to Clara in her state of grief and shock. Brahms took charge of the situation, restored order, and shouldered the domestic responsibilities, generally making Clara's lot a great deal easier than it would otherwise have been. She, in turn, unashamedly poured out her suffering to him. In such a turbulent emotional atmosphere it would have been surprising if the pair had not eventually developed a strong affection for one another. As it is, the evidence suggests that despite the most honourable intentions on both sides the couple fell in love. It is impossible to say with certainty what degree of intimacy they eventually allowed themselves. Schumann's biographers tend to frown at the suggestion that, after Schumann's committal, Clara and Brahms had sexual relations. Apparently, the dignity of the parties rules it out of order. When two people are as ardent and as closely involved as Clara and Brahms soon became, we shall need more facts than are presently available to us to outweigh the strong circumstantial evidence of a liaison between them. Brahms's letters tell their own story. They start by addressing Clara formally as 'Honoured Lady'; a bit later they progress to 'Cherished Friend'; finally, they have reached 'Most Adored Being', and contain such passages as 'Every day I greet and kiss you a thousand times', and 'Please go on loving me as I shall go on loving you always and for ever'. We are also asked to believe that their walking trips along the Rhine valley, where they were inseparable, and their living together under the same roof at Düsseldorf for several months, at the height of their attachment to one another was purely the expression of platonic feeling. Is this not stretching credulity far?

In later life, they were sensitive about the topic. Brahms threw a large bundle of Clara's letters into the Rhine, hardly the act of a platonic friend with nothing to hide. Clara, for her part, was reduced to writing to her own children, years afterwards, protesting her innocence.

I can truly say, my children, that I never loved any friend as I did him . . . Never forget this, dear Children, and always have a grateful heart for this friend, for a friend he will certainly be to you, too.

Believe what your mother tells you, and do not listen to petty and envious souls who grudge him my love and friendship, and therefore try to impugn him or even to cast aspersions on our relations, which they cannot, or will not, understand.

Within the Schumann family circle, then, there was some gossip, and Clara's letter did not quash it. Certainly the Schumann family behaved very oddly in buying up the complete stocks of a book which appeared in Germany, after Clara's death, which tried to show that Felix (b. 1854) was Brahms's son. The assertion is preposterous, and one is left with the feeling that the family's reasons for wanting the book suppressed had less to do with the question of Felix's paternity (which nobody seriously doubted) than with the infinitely more difficult business of defending Clara's involvement with Brahms. To prove that Felix was not Brahms's son would have been easy; but to draw the inference that Brahms could not therefore have been Clara's lover would have been impossible.

Brendel, Franz (1811–68). German critic and writer on music. He succeeded Schumann as editor of the *Neue Zeitschrift* in 1845, on the latter's retirement from this post. At the same time, Mendelssohn appointed him professor of musical history and aesthetics at the newly-created Leipzig Conservatory of Music. Under his editorship, the *Zeitschrift* gradually shifted its support from the music of Schumann and Mendelssohn, and others of the 'Leipzig School', and became the mouthpiece of the 'Neo-German' School at Weimar, headed by Liszt and Wagner. Later on, Brendel, with a nice sense of history, attempted vigorously to bring the contending parties together under the banner of the *Allgemeiner Deutscher Musik-Verein* (German Musical Union) whose president he was from 1861 until his death.

Breitkopf & Härtel. One of the oldest, and largest, music publishers in the world. It was founded in 1719 by Bernhardt Christoph Breitkopf who set up his printing press in Leipzig. The firm remains there to this day. Härtel joined in 1795, after which 'Breitkopf & Härtel', as it became known, began to publish that great series of complete editions by leading masters for which it is still famous.

Breitkopf & Härtel brought out a complete edition of Schumann's music between the years 1879 and 1888, with Clara Schumann and Brahms as joint editors.

Carus, Karl Erdmann (1774–1842). A Zwickau merchant, and a friend of the young Schumann. He was a keen amateur musician whose house was a rendezvous for local artists. Schumann wrote his obituary notice. 'It was in this house that the names Mozart, Haydn, Beethoven were among those talked of daily with enthusiasm . . . In his house I first got to know the rarer works of these masters . . .'

Carus, Dr Ernst August (1795–1854). Nephew of the above. Professor of medicine at Leipzig University. His wife, Agnes, struck up a close musical friendship with the teenage Schumann. During his holidays, he frequently visited the Carus family in Colditz where Ernst practised medicine from 1824 to 1828.

Chamisso, Adalbert von (1781–1838). German poet, novelist and naturalist of French descent. Schumann's song-cycle *Frauenliebe und -leben* is probably the best-known setting of his poetry.

Chopin, Frédéric François (1810–49). Chopin was the object of Schumann's first essay into musical criticism 'Hats off, gentlemen, a genius!' which was published in the *Allgemeine Musikalische Zeitung* in 1831. It was written before the two composers had actually met. A copy of Chopin's *Là ci darem* Variations had come Schumann's way, and he lost no time in announcing the young Pole's originality to the world. Four years later, in 1835, Chopin was passing through Leipzig, homeward bound from a visit to his parents at Carlsbad, and he took the opportunity to look up Schumann who was at that time living with the Wiecks. According to Clara's diary, he stayed only one day. Clara played to him Schumann's F sharp minor Sonata and two of his own Études. He overwhelmed her with praise, she says, and played her one of his nocturnes. A year later, Chopin returned to Leipzig and this time got to know Schumann him-

self a little better. Schumann wrote to Dorn: 'Just as I received your letter . . . who should come in but Chopin! That was a great pleasure. We spent a delightful day, and yesterday I held an after-celebration . . . I have a new Ballade of Chopin's (G minor). It seems to me his work of greatest *esprit*, and I said to him that it was my favourite of all. After long consideration he said with great emphasis, "I am glad, it is my favourite too." He played besides a number of new Études, Nocturnes, Mazurkas, all incomparable. It is touching to see him at the pianoforte. You would love him very much . . .'

David, Ferdinand (1810–73). German violinist. Pupil of Spohr. In 1836, Mendelssohn, who had been appointed conductor of the Gewandhaus Orchestra, brought in David as his leader, a post he was to hold until his death. Mendelssohn also appointed him violin professor to the Leipzig Conservatory from its foundation in 1843. The publication of David's *Violin School* was a milestone in the history of fiddle technique. Mendelssohn consulted him at every stage of the composition of his Violin Concerto, whose première he gave at a Gewandhaus concert in 1845 with Mendelssohn conducting. Schumann's D minor violin sonata (1851) is dedicated to him.

Davidsbund. The Davidsbund, or 'Band of David', was a fictitious society of musicians, created within Schumann's fantastic imagination, for the express purpose of fighting the Philistines in music. The battle-ground was the *Neue Zeitschrift*, which published a steady stream of critical articles, written by Schumann himself, under such fanciful pseudonyms as 'Florestan', 'Eusebius', 'Master Raro', 'Fritz Friedrich', 'Serpentinus', 'Jonathan', 'Vult', 'Walt', etc., the choice of pseudonym depending entirely on the tone of Schumann's review.

Well might the first readers of the *Zeitschrift* ask, bewildered, who the members of the 'Band of David' were; even today, the identity of some of them is blurred. In 1854, long after he had relinquished the editorship of the *Zeitschrift*, Schumann described the Davidsbund as 'more than a secret society, for it existed only in the head of its founder'. For that very reason, identification of its members is not always easy. One or two stand for Schumann himself; others stand for friends and colleagues. Thus, 'Florestan' and 'Eusebius' represent the twin sides of Schumann's own personality—the passionate man of action and the gentle dreamer respectively. 'Master Raro', on the other hand, is the all-round musician, renowned for the sanity of his judgments; several biographers think he stands for Friedrich Wieck, but this is unlikely in view of the fact that Schumann and Wieck rarely saw eye to eye on matters musical. Riemann made the interesting discovery that if you place Clara's name with Robert's end to end, you get 'claRARObert', which seems to suggest an altogether different derivation. Schumann's rival for Clara's affections, Carl Banck, is appropriately called 'Serpentinus', and one wonders whether he knew about, let alone approved of, a nickname which depicts him crawling on his belly.

Sometimes the Davidsbund turn up in Schumann's music: both 'Florestan' and 'Eusebius' are immortalized in *Carnaval*. At the conclusion of *Carnaval*, in fact, the struggle between the 'Band of David' and the Philistines' is symbolized by the *Marche des Davidsbündler* in which the Philistines are caricatured with a quotation from the then-popular 'Grandfather's dance'—a tune which not only puts them to flight but which, because of its connotation, puts them to shame as well.

Dietrich, Albert (1829–1908). A pupil of Schumann's in Düsseldorf from 1851 to 1854. He collaborated with Schumann and Brahms in the composition of the so-called 'F.A.E.' Sonata, a joint tribute to Joachim, each movement of which uses the notes F–A–E (*Frei aber einsam*—free but solitary), a motto Joachim had adopted. Dietrich wrote the first movement, Brahms the Scherzo, and Schumann the Intermezzo and Finale. Dietrich was one of the pallbearers at Schumann's funeral.

Döhner, Dr (1790–1866). He ran a private preparatory school in Zwickau which Schumann entered at the age of six.

Dorn, Heinrich (1804–92). German conductor, teacher and composer. He was Schumann's theory teacher. After studying at Königsberg, Dorn settled for a time in

Berlin, where he laid the foundations of a distinguished career. He was on terms of friendship with Heine, Mendelssohn, Marx, Spontini, Moscheles and many other musicians who held him in high esteem. Between 1829 and 1832 Dorn was in Leipzig, and it was here that Schumann took counterpoint lessons from him. The encounter was wholly beneficial to Schumann, although at first he complained: 'I shall never be able to amalgamate with Dorn; he wishes to get me to believe that music is fugue—heavens! how different men are.' Later, however, Schumann realized the benefit of Dorn's discipline. 'Dorn, my theory teacher, has advanced me inwardly a great deal. By dint of persevering study, I gained that beautiful clearness of which, indeed, I early had some idea, but which I often lacked.' Schumann kept up a correspondence with Dorn until he died, an indication of the affection in which he continued to hold him. In 1849, Dorn was appointed conductor of the Royal Opera House in Berlin, a post he held until 1868. He was subsequently given the title of 'Royal Professor', and for the next twenty-five years enjoyed a reputation as a teacher and critic. He was musical editor of the 'Post'.

Fink, Gottfried Wilhelm (1783–1846). Theologian and music critic. He edited the *Allgemeine musikalische Zeitung*, in which the twenty-one-year-old Schumann published his famous review of Chopin's 'Là ci darem' Variations containing the imperative: 'Hats off, gentlemen, a genius!' Fink became professor of music at Leipzig University in 1842.

Flechsig, Emil (1808–78). A school friend of Schumann's in Zwickau, and later a fellow-student of his at Leipzig University.

Fricken, Ernestine von (1816–44). In 1838, three years after her engagement to Schumann was terminated, Ernestine married Count von Zedwitz. The following year, she was widowed. She died at the early age of twenty-eight. After Schumann himself died, her letters to him somehow fell into the possession of Marie Wieck, Clara's halfsister, who promptly published them. Clara placed the matter in the hands of lawyers, but it was dropped before it reached the courts.

Schumann left a characteristic souvenir of his attachment to Ernestine in *Carnaval*. He discovered that the letters of her birthplace 'ASCH' yield a musical motif, and that by a happy coincidence they are the same as the musical letters in his own name (see pp.87-88).

Baron von Fricken, Ernestine's father, was an amateur flautist. He composed the theme on which Schumann based his *Études Symphoniques*.

Gade, Niels (1817–90). Danish composer who settled in Leipzig. He took charge of the Gewandhaus Orchestra, in succession to Mendelssohn, from 1844 to 1848. Schumann supported him enthusiastically in the *Neue Zeitschrift*, and once wrote of him: 'I have rarely found anyone who harmonized so well with my views as Gade . . . whom one must love, quite apart from his talent.'

Glock, Dr (d. circa 1860). One of Schumann's student friends at Leipzig University, and an amateur 'cellist who played chamber music with Schumann. He eventually graduated as a doctor of medicine, and became Mayor of Ostheim. He was one of the early group of contributors to the *Neue Zeitschrift*.

Hanslick, Eduard (1825–1904). Viennese music critic. He lectured in aesthetics and musical history at the University of Vienna from 1861, and became a full professor there in 1870. By training and by inclination, Hanslick was a fundamentalist with a highly conservative cast of mind. His enmity towards the music of Liszt and Wagner is well known; so is his championship of Brahms. Hanslick was a brilliant writer whose literary products were noted for their elegance, wit and cogent logic. He spoke his mind fearlessly, and sometimes recklessly. 'The violin is beaten black and blue,' he wrote of Tchaikovsky's Violin Concerto. 'After Liszt, Mozart is like a soft spring breeze penetrating a room reeking with fumes,' was another of his darts. Wagner took a lot of punishment from Hanslick, but repaid him in full by satirizing him in the character of Beckmesser in his opera *Die Meistersinger*. Hanslick's most important book was his *Vom Musikalisch-Schönen* (1854) in which he may be said to have founded a new school of musical aesthetics by arguing, for the first time, the

'integrity' of musical structure. His 'closed world' view of a work of art, in which that work of art is its own meaning, has powerfully influenced twentieth-century music criticism.

Hauptmann, Moritz (1792–1868). German theorist, critic and writer on music. Professor of Composition at the Leipzig Conservatory of Music. Well-grounded in mathematics and philosophy, particularly the philosophy of Hegel, his work culminated in an important book on acoustics called *The Nature of Harmony and Metre* (1853), in which the Hegelian principle of dialectics is applied to music. Hauptmann was regarded as one of the most influential authorities of his day. Schumann, who was for a time also on the staff of the Leipzig Conservatory, knew him quite well. Of the A minor Quartet and the Piano Quintet Hauptmann wrote: 'These compositions are without reservation among the finest that recent times can show in this genre.'

Hebbel, Friedrich (1813–63). German dramatic poet. Schumann based his opera *Genoveva* (1850) on Hebbel's drama of that name. Hebbel objected to his work being carved up as a libretto, and dissociated himself from the project. Schumann, after some difficulty, finally arranged the text of *Genoveva* himself.

Heine, Heinrich (1797–1856). German lyric poet. In his younger days, he was a member of the artistic circle in Paris which included Chopin, Liszt, George Sand and Delacroix. Heine had a sharp tongue. His witticisms about his contemporaries are legend. He once described the nose of Johann Pixis, which was admittedly somewhat large, as 'one of the curiosities of the musical world'. After hearing Kalkbrenner, who was famed for his detachment, play at a concert in 1843, Heine came away and wrote: 'On his lips there still gleamed that embalmed smile which we recently noticed on those of an Egyptian pharaoh, when his mummy was unwrapped at the museum here.' Two of Schumann's greatest song-cycles are settings of Heine: *Liederkreis*, Op. 24 and *Dichterliebe*, Op. 48.

Hiller, Ferdinand (1811–85). German pianist, conductor and composer. Pupil of

Hummel. As a young man, he settled in Paris, and was closely associated with the Romantic movement there during the 1830s; he numbered Berlioz, Liszt and Chopin among his friends. He conducted the Gewandhaus concerts from 1843 to 1844. In 1847, he was appointed conductor of the Düsseldorf orchestra, a post he relinquished in 1850 in favour of Schumann. Hiller had the privilege of seeing Beethoven on his deathbed, and he became one of the early champions of the master's music, giving the first performance of the 'Emperor' Concerto in Paris.

Hirschbach, Hermann (1812–88). Composer and contributor to the *Neue Zeitschrift*.

In June, 1838, right out of the blue, Schumann received two essays from Hirschbach for publication in the *Neue Zeitschrift*. He was instantly attracted by their direct, uncompromising tone. The real test of a musician, Hirschbach argued, was to write music, not to write about it. Schumann promptly asked to see some of his compositions. Hirschbach obliged by sending him three string quartets, a string quintet, and a sonata, together with his 'manifesto' of modern music. Thus began one of Schumann's closest artistic friendships. Hirschbach struck a responsive chord in Schumann. He was a non-conformist, had a progressive outlook on music, and was absolutely sure of his direction. Schumann wrote to Clara: 'There is much of Faust, of the black art, about him. The day before yesterday we were doing quartets of his, deficient in style, invention and endeavour, yet the most colossal to be met with today.'

It is difficult, nearly a hundred and fifty years after the event, to see what Schumann saw in Hirschbach's music. Yet he gave the quartets what amounts to a 'rave' notice in the *Zeitschrift* (1838), describing them as 'the most significant works I have seen for a long time among the younger talents'. For a time, Schumann regarded Hirschbach as the saviour of modern music. His touching faith was not rewarded, however, and today Hirschbach is just a footnote in history.

Hoffmann, E. T. A. (1776–1822). A leader of the Romantic movement in literature, Hoffmann left a far wider legacy to the arts generally. His bizarre, sometimes horrific tales, completely captivated the imagination of the nineteenth century. Each time we hear *Coppélia*, *The Nutcracker* and *The Tales of Hoffmann*, Hoffmann is with us. His short stories can still be read with pleasure today. His essay on Beethoven (1813) pioneered the way for a wider understanding of this master's music.

It was Hoffmann who created the fictional character of Johannes Kreisler, the Kapellmeister, in his collection of stories called *Fantasiestücke in Callot's Manier* (1814–15) These stories inspired Schumann to compose his *Kreisleriana*. 'The title is intelligible to Germans only. Kreisler is a creation of E. T. A. Hoffmann's, an eccentric, wild, clever Kapellmeister. There is much about him that you will like . . .' (Letter to Simonin de Sire, 1839).

Joachim, Joseph (1831–1907). Hungarian-born violinist. An infant prodigy, he made his first appearance at a Gewandhaus Concert when he was only twelve. Later, he studied with Ferdinand David at the Leipzig Conservatoire, laying the foundations of that immaculate technique for which he subsequently became world famous. From 1850 to 1852 Joachim was Liszt's orchestral leader at Weimar. He quickly reacted against the 'New German' School, however, and allied himself with Brahms and Schumann, whom he admired. During the early 1850s he and Schumann enjoyed a regular correspondence. It was for Joachim that Schumann composed (in collaboration with Brahms and Dietrich) the 'F.A.E.' Sonata (see pp. 213–15) based on Joachim's personal motto *Frei aber Einsam* (Free but alone). Joachim was a pallbearer at Schumann's funeral.

Kalliwoda, J. W. (1801–66). Bohemian violinist, conductor and composer, who became Director of the Prague Conservatoire. He was the composer of seven symphonies, several concertos, and a good deal of chamber music. His compositions occasionally featured in the Leipzig Gewandhaus programmes. Schumann thought highly of his Fifth Symphony, and dedicated to Kalliwoda his Intermezzi, Op. 4.

Knorr, Julius (1807–61). One of the founder-members of the *Neue Zeitschrift* *für Musik* and a close friend of Schumann. He was one of Schumann's original 'Band of David', and is referred to in the *Zeitschrift* simply as 'Julius'. Knorr was a pianist of some talent, who made one or two appearances at the Gewandhaus (where he gave the first performance in Germany of Chopin's *Là ci darem* Variations) and then abandoned a public career in favour of teaching. Niecks says of him that in later life 'he distinguished himself more by his billiards than by his pianoforte playing'.

Kuntzsch, Johann Gottfried (1775–1855). Schumann's first piano teacher at the Zwickau Lyceum. In later life, Schumann used to speak of Kuntzsch with gratitude, although there is little to suggest that his teaching was in any way exceptional. When Niecks wrote to Clara, in 1889, requesting some information about him, he received this frosty reply: 'I saw Kuntzsch only once, but I know that my husband thought a great deal of him. He was certainly not distinguished enough to be my husband's teacher, the pupil was superior to the master.' Schumann's own memory of Kuntzsch was highly idealized. When he was twenty, he wrote to his former master: 'You were the only one who recognized the predominating musical talent in me and indicated betimes the path along which, sooner or later, my good genius was to guide me.'

Lind, Jenny (1820–87). Swedish soprano. She received her first singing lessons at the age of nine, having been placed in the school of singing attached to the Court Theatre in Stockholm. She made her début in 1838 at the Stockholm Opera, singing Agathe in Weber's *Freischütz*. Three years later, she travelled to Paris and took lessons from the famous singing teacher Manuel Garcia. Then began a career which brought her European fame. The general consensus of opinion was that she was the greatest soprano of her day, although she made her biggest impact in the concert-hall rather than the theatre. Moscheles heard her in Berlin in 1845. 'Jenny Lind has fairly enchanted me; she is unique in her way . . . perhaps the most incredible feat in the way of bravura singing that can be heard.' She became friendly with the Schumanns about 1845, and subsequently shared several concerts with them. In 1846, when Robert and Clara gave three concerts in Vienna, the first two were dismal failures, and the tour might have ended in total collapse had not Jenny Lind stepped in and helped them out in the third. As Robert Schauffler put it, Schumann 'was embittered through the knowledge that a song by the "Swedish Nightingale" could madden a town which had turned an icy shoulder upon the best that they had to offer'. Her two-year tour of America (1850–52) was a sensation. She acquired £20,000 out of it, together with a husband, Otto Goldschmidt. She ended her days in England, becoming a teacher of singing at the Royal College of Music from 1883 to 1886.

Liszt, Franz (1811–86). As young men in their twenties, full of Romantic ideals, Schumann and Liszt enjoyed a respectful friendship towards one another. Unfortunately, as time wore on, it cooled to a point where they were hardly on speaking terms. When they first met (1840) Schumann wrote to Clara: 'He said yesterday: "I feel as if I had known you for twenty years," and I have just the same feelings towards him.' They had, in fact, already had a cordial correspondence, and Schumann had sent Liszt some of his compositions including *Carnaval*, *Kinderscenen* and the C major Fantasie, Op. 17, which Schumann had dedicated to him. 'The Fantasy', wrote Liszt, 'is a work of the highest kind—and I am really rather proud of the honour you have done me in dedicating to me so grand a composition.' Nevertheless, he never played the work in public. Maybe he was disappointed with Schumann's review of his first concerts in Dresden and Leipzig (March 1840), part of a tour to raise funds for the Beethoven Monument, in which, as a gesture to Schumann, he played ten numbers from *Carnaval*. He got little thanks for his trouble; Schumann seems to have been difficult to please with this work. But whatever Schumann's public attitude may have been, in private he was full of praise. 'I wish you could have been with Liszt this morning,' he wrote to Clara. 'He is really too extraordinary. His playing of the *Novelletten*, parts of the Fantasie, and the Sonata, moved me strangely. Although his reading differed in many places from my own, it was always inspired, and he does not, I imagine, display such tenderness, such boldness, every day. Becker was the only other person present. I think he had tears in his eyes.'

Towards 1850, their friendship deteriorated sharply; it was apparent that they stood for different artistic aims. Clara Schumann did not help matters; she hated everything Liszt represented, and declared him to be a 'smasher of pianos'. Eventually, Schumann moved from Leipzig to Dresden (and later to Düsseldorf), while Liszt settled down in Weimar. As both men were powerful enough to attract support from other musicians, the situation gradually hardened into two rival schools—the Leipzig-Dresden axis versus Weimar. The Leipzig-Dresden côterie included at first Schumann and Mendelssohn (until his death in 1847), together with the academics from the Leipzig Conservatoire, Rietz, Hauptmann, and Ferdinand David; at Weimar there was Liszt, Cornelius, Raff and (closely associated with them) Richard Wagner—the so-called 'New-German' School. In 1852, Joachim, who had been Liszt's orchestral leader at Weimar, defected to Leipzig. Brahms hovered between the two schools for a short time and then closed ranks behind Schumann. Liszt often referred to the goings-on at Leipzig as 'Leipzigerisch'; the Leipzigers retaliated by booing *Mazeppa* when Liszt (in a vain effort to let bygones be bygones) favoured them with a performance of the work in 1857.

It says much for Liszt's breadth of vision that the row between Leipzig and Weimar did not prevent him from performing several of Schumann's works at the Weimar Court Theatre. He wrote to Schumann in 1849 expressing the wish to stage Schumann's *Scenes from Faust* for the Goethe Centenary celebrations; but Schumann sulked and refused to give him a satisfactory answer. Liszt staged it anyway. He also produced *Manfred* and the opera *Genoveva*, the performances of which Schumann declined to attend. A final peace offering from Liszt came in the form of the dedication of his B minor Sonata to Schumann. By this time, however, Schumann had already entered that mental decline to which he eventually succumbed, and a reconciliation never materialized.

Behind the controversy, which is not easy to disentangle, lay the troubled history of the *Neue Zeitschrift für Musik* which Schumann had founded in 1834 and edited for ten years. In 1844 Schumann had resigned the editorship which passed to Franz Brendel, a disciple of Liszt and the 'New German' School. The magazine thus began to champion the cause of Weimar. Schumann was appalled, but had no power to intervene; he saw the organ which he himself had created turned against his own party. Schumann never lived to see the final outcome of the quarrel which was almost unique in the annals of musical history: the publication in 1860 of the 'Manifesto' against the 'New German' School, by Brahms and Joachim, which was drawn up in direct response to the Liszt propaganda of the *Zeitschrift*.

Logier, J. B. (1777–1846). German pianist and piano teacher. He invented the 'Chiroplast', a sort of mechanism for training the hands at the keyboard which caused great controversy during its day. Subsequently, Logier developed a system of piano teaching based exclusively on its use, which allowed him to teach up to a dozen pupils simultaneously. Since they all paid him simultaneously as well, Logier soon became rich, and he proceeded to open 'Chiroplast instruction centres' in several cities, laying the foundations of a reputation as a piano teacher which the results hardly seemed to justify. (Not one pianist of stature was produced by his method.) In 1821, the Prussian Government invited Logier to Berlin to promulgate the 'Chiroplast' there. After a few years, he retired to Dublin where he opened a music shop.

Among the advocates of the 'Chiroplast' was Kalkbrenner whose notorious 'hand-rail' was clearly modelled on Logier's invention. Friedrich Wieck, in his younger days, was a disciple of Logier; later, he reacted against him, claiming that the 'Chiroplast' was a dangerous and damaging contrivance.

Matthäi, Heinrich, August (b. ?; d ?). German violinist. Leader of the Gewandhaus Orchestra from 1827 to 1835. He also founded, and led, a well-known quartet which bore his name. In 1833 Schumann's youthful Symphony in G minor (uncompleted) was performed at Leipzig, with Matthäi leading. After the concert the two men met and Schumann's excitement and confusion were such that he was trapped into an amusing psychological slip. 'When I introduced myself to Matthäi, the leader of the orchestra, the following absurd incident happened. I distractedly said: "My name is Matthäi!" ' (Letter to his mother, 1833.)

Mendelssohn, Felix (1809–47). Mendelssohn's impact on the Romantic era was incalculable. Historians still underrate it. By the time he was in his early twenties he had achieved a position of musical authority from which nobody could dislodge him. He met many of the crowned heads of Europe, and was on terms of intimacy with the English Royal Family. When he died, it was as if a great statesman had passed on, and he was mourned by the whole of Germany.

In 1835, when he was only twenty-six years old, Mendelssohn was appointed conductor of the Leipzig Gewandhaus Orchestra. This marked the beginning of a long association with Leipzig which culminated in Mendelssohn's founding the Leipzig Conservatoire of Music in 1843, one of the finest music academies of the time, to whose staff Mendelssohn appointed such influential teachers as Joachim, David, Moscheles and Schumann.

The warm friendship which existed between Schumann and Mendelssohn in their earlier years cooled off considerably with the passage of time. 'The mere sight of Mendelssohn must make one rejoice,' Schumann wrote to Clara in 1839; 'he is the worthiest artist imaginable.' Within a few years, however, there was a different tale to tell. When Mendelssohn was asked by his friend Klingemann for a letter of introduction to Clara in 1847, he replied: 'I shall not be able to give you a letter of introduction to Frau Schumann; her husband has behaved very ambiguously to me, and has stirred up a very ugly story about me.' What the 'ugly story' was is unclear. It is improbable that Schumann was responsible for it; more likely, Mendelssohn, as Niecks puts it, 'must have rashly lent his ear to idle scandal'. None the less, it rankled with the Mendelssohn family for years, and when the composer's collected correspondence was eventually published, all mention of Schumann was omitted.

Moscheles, Ignaz (1794–1870). German-Bohemian pianist and composer, born in Prague. As an infant prodigy, he came to the attention of Dionys Weber, director of the Prague Conservatoire, who took over his early training and brought him up in the Mozart–Clementi tradition.

Moscheles first came to prominence as a piano virtuoso with his brilliant 'Alexander March' Variations (1815), an early work which he quickly outgrew, but which remained so popular that for years it was requested wherever he went. The young Schumann, who used to play this piece (see p. 2), had a high opinion of Moscheles, which found its natural expression in the dedication to him of the Sonata in F sharp minor, Op. 11.

Moscheles's approach to the piano was strict and classical. At a time when the instrument was becoming the chief tool of romanticism, and was being taken over by the 'thunder and lightning' school of pianists, such as Henselt, Dreyschock and the young Liszt, Moscheles remained coolly aloof. He avoided the sustaining pedal, as far as possible, preferring to produce all his sound with his fingers. He wrote in 1830: 'All effects now, it seems, must be produced by the feet—what is the use of people having hands? It is just as if a good rider wanted forever to use spurs.'

In 1846, Mendelssohn appointed Moscheles Professor of Piano at the Leipzig Conservatoire of Music, a post he held for more than twenty years.

Niecks, Frederick (1845–1924). German scholar and author. In 1891 he was appointed Reid Professor of Music in the University of Edinburgh, a post he held for twenty-three years.

His book *Robert Schumann* (published posthumously in 1925) is a foundation-work on the composer. Niecks was uniquely qualified to write about Schumann. Not only was he on terms of intimate friendship with several of the leading personalities who played a role in Schumann's life, but he was also deeply immersed in the literature of the period.

As a small child, in Düsseldorf, he remembered seeing Schumann walking slowly through the Hofgarten. 'I still see the quiet face, the protruding rounded lips (as if he were whistling, or pronouncing O), and the absorbed, absent look.' In 1889 Niecks interviewed several people in connection with Schumann's life, including Dorn (Schumann's theory teacher) and Clara Schumann herself, which produced basic material to which all subsequent books on Schumann are indebted.

Paganini, Niccolò (1782–1840). Italian violinist. His early childhood was marked by privation. Paganini's mother was fond of relating a dream in which she claimed to have been visited by an angel who had declared that her son was destined to become the greatest violinist in the world. Anxious, no doubt, to reap the financial benefits of this disclosure as quickly as possible, Paganini's father set to work with a will and nearly wrecked everything with his rigorous training methods, which included the administration of generous doses of corporal punishment each time the lad produced a wrong note. From about the age of seven, however, Paganini was a pupil of Giacomo Costa, *Maestro di cappella* of the Cathedral of San Lorenzo, under whose guidance he made such rapid progress that in 1793 he made his début, aged nine. Two years later, there occurred the famous encounter with Rolla, one of Italy's foremost violinists. Paganini had travelled with his father to Parma to visit the distinguished fiddler who, apparently, was ill in bed. He was ushered into an adjoining room, and, spotting Rolla's violin lying on the table, together with a copy of his latest concerto, Paganini picked up the music and read it through at sight. The therapeutic effect on Rolla was remarkable. He leaped out of bed and rushed to the other room, anxious to greet the 'master violinist' who had just despatched his difficult new work; on discovering an eleven-year-old boy instead, he was thunderstruck and is reported to have said that he, Rolla, could teach him nothing. After a suitable interval had elapsed he was prevailed upon to change his mind, and Paganini remained with Rolla for several months.

Such tales are part and parcel of the Paganini legend. He was the supreme violinist who could do anything. Soon, people, unable to account for his miraculous powers, had to invent a reason, and the rumour spread that he was in league with the Devil. Paganini, who was a superb showman, did nothing to deny it, and throughout his professional life the man and his violin where shrouded in mystery and associated with the sinister and the macabre.

Paganini began his travels in earnest in 1828, by playing in Vienna; the newspapers talked about little else for two months. There followed a triumphal tour of Poland, Prussia, Bavaria, Austria and France. Schumann heard him play in Frankfort in 1830. As a direct result of this experience, Schumann transcribed for the piano two sets of Paganini Caprices, Opp. 3 and 10. Paganini also appears in *Carnaval*.

Paganini built a large fortune out of his concerts, much of it in landed estates. On his death he left his son Achillino 2 million Lire (about £80,000).

Paul, Jean. See Richter.

Rellstab, Ludwig (1799–1860). German critic. He was notorious for the malice in his value-judgments. His criticism of the soprano Henriette Sontag in 1826, in which he satirized a respected diplomat, earned him a three-month stretch in Spandau prison. It served only to enhance his reputation. Shortly afterwards, he was appointed to the Berlin paper *Vossische Zeitung*, and he became one of the most powerful critics in Germany. When he first saw Chopin's 12 Studies, Op. 10, he advised pianists not to practise them without a surgeon standing by. He described Schumann's *Kinderscenen* as 'pictures of child life', and wondered whether the composer was joking or in earnest. 'Anything more inept and narrow-minded than Rellstab's remarks about the *Kinderscenen* I have never come across,' wrote Schumann to Dorn. 'He seems to think that I place a crying child before me and then seek for tones to imitate it. It is the other way round.' The musical periodical founded by Rellstab in 1830, *Iris im Gebiet der Tonkunst*, survived until 1842.

Richter, Johann Paul Friedrich (1763–1825). German romantic novelist who wrote under the pen-name of 'Jean Paul'. He was the greatest, single literary influence on Schumann, much of whose writing reflects Jean Paul's highly individual prose-style. The romantic literary theory of double personality runs through his works

—the introspective, inward-looking half of human nature balanced by the extrovert, outward-looking half—and it had its outcome in Florestan and Eusebius, the twin halves of Schumann's own literary character. This is what Schumann meant when he said that he 'learned more counterpoint from Jean Paul' than from any of his music-teachers. Schumann's touching loyalty to Jean Paul was illustrated by Niecks, who tells the following story. 'He was apt to regard as his personal enemies all whose admiration of Jean Paul fell short of his own. A characteristic occurrence, the truth of which is vouchsafed for by Hanslick, took place in 1850, when the musicians of Hamburg gave a banquet in honour of Schumann and his wife. After a toast of the guests, the silent Schumann rose, amid breathless silence, to make a speech—*mirabile dictu!*—and began by remarking the happy coincidence of the day of the festivity, 21 March with the birthday of two of the greatest geniuses of Germany—Sebastian Bach and Jean Paul, the immortal rulers of music and poetry. The toast was enthusiastically drunk, when up rose Grädener, director of the Hamburg *Singakedemie*, who protested against the mention in the same breath of Jean Paul and Sebastian Bach at a gathering of German musicians. Before the speaker had elaborated his thought Schumann rose and left the hall in dudgeon, and it was not till next day that Grädener was able to effect a reconciliation.'

Rietz, Julius (1812–77). German composer and conductor. He was a friend and colleague of the Schumanns during the Leipzig period. Rietz conducted the Gewandhaus orchestra in Leipzig from 1848 to 1860.

Rosen, Gisbert (1808–76). One of Schumann's closest friends at Heidelberg. They were drawn together by a common love for the writings of Jean Paul, and in the spring of 1828 they toured Bavaria together. Rosen, who was a law student, became in later life the chief magistrate of Detmold.

Rudel, Gottlob (b.?; d.?). Schumann's guardian. He was a successful cloth and iron merchant who lived in Zwickau. August Schumann regarded him as a man of integrity. Less flattering was the description given to Niecks: 'A stiff business man who looks as if he had swallowed a ruler'. When August died, in 1826, Rudel appears to have discharged his duties as Robert's guardian in an exemplary manner. Robert maintained a regular correspondence with him during his days as a student at Heidelberg, and his letters are full of references to his parlous financial condition. 'How much you would oblige me, most honoured Herr Rudel, if you were to send me as soon as possible as much as possible!' (1830).

Schubert, Franz (1797–1828). The well-known story that the youthful Schumann cried himself to sleep on hearing of Schubert's death is probably false, but it ought to be true. Schumann felt a great affinity with him ('my only Schubert', he called him) and he eventually became Schubert's greatest successor in the field of Lieder.

In 1838 Schumann stayed for a time in Vienna. Like many musicians before and since, he visited the graves of Beethoven and Schubert while he was there. On his way back from the cemetery, he tells us, the thought occurred to him that Schubert's brother Ferdinand still lived in the city, and he experienced an irresistible impulse to look him up. The visit turned out to be historic. During the conversation, Schumann discovered that Ferdinand still had in his possession a number of Schubert's manuscripts, including the 'Great' C major Symphony. He immediately sent the score to Mendelssohn who gave its first performance at a Gewandhaus concert on 21 March 1839. Schumann tells the story in an article published in the *Zeitschrift* in 1840.

Schumann, Clara (née Wieck) (1819–96). Wife of Robert. From the start, Clara was destined to be a pianist. She was trained exclusively for this profession by her father, Friedrich Wieck. Under his tutelage, Clara's progress was rapid. She made her début when she was nine, in her home town of Leipzig. Two years later, aged eleven, she made the first of her many appearances at a Gewandhaus concert. She began to appear before a wider public when she was about twelve, and in 1831–32 she played in Weimar, Cassel, Frankfurt, and Paris.

During her sixteen-year marriage to Schumann, Clara's lot was not particularly rosy. She was obliged, by her circumstances, to suppress her own career in favour of her husband's; she bore him eight children; finally she took the full brunt of his tragic illness until he was placed in an asylum two years before the end. After Robert's death she courageously gathered together the threads of her former career and made a fresh start. She was still only thirty-six years old.

Clara eventually moved with her young family to Berlin, where she stayed with her mother (who had meanwhile married the musician Adolf Bargiel). From 1863, she adopted Baden-Baden as her headquarters, her foreign tours gradually taking up more of her time. During this period of intensive concert-giving, Clara gradually built up a reputation as the greatest woman pianist of her time. As Hanslick said: 'She could be called the greatest living pianist, rather than merely the greatest female pianist, were the range of her physical strength not limited by her sex. . . . Everything is distinct, clear, sharp as a pencil sketch.' She was the first classical pianist. Her restraint at the keyboard, and her fidelity to the text was regarded as unusual at a time when the bravura pianist was enjoying his hey-day. She never lost an opportunity of playing Schumann's music, and her interpretations came to be regarded as authoritative. For many years she appeared regularly in London, the last occasion being in 1888. From 1878 she was principal piano professor at the Frankfort-on-Main Conservatory of Music.

It is sometimes forgotten that Clara Schumann was also a composer. Her list of works, mostly for the piano, extends to twenty-three opus numbers. Schumann himself occasionally made use of her compositions; for instance, in his Impromptus on a theme of Clara Wieck, Op. 5, and in the Andantino of his Sonata in F minor, Op. 14. (See also entry under 'Brahms'.)

Schumann Family

August (Father: 1773–1826). Bookseller, bibliophile, and author. He married Johanna Schnabel (1771–1836), the daughter of a municipal surgeon, in 1795. They settled in Zwickau, Schumann's birthplace, in 1808. There were five children of the marriage.

Eduard (Brother: 1797–1839). He married Theresa Semmel (1803–87) of Gera.

P

After his death, she married Fleischer, a Leipzig bookseller.

Karl (Brother: 1801–49). He married (1) Rosalie Illing (1809–33), and (2) Pauline Colditz (1818–79).

Julius (Brother: 1805–33). He married Emilia Lorenz (1810–60).

Emilie (Sister: 1807–26). She drowned herself when she was only nineteen years old. Her death, coming as it did, shortly before that of the father, precipitated a bout of acute melancholy in Schumann himself. (However, see p. 3, f. 5.)

Robert (1810–56). The youngest of the family. His marriage to Clara Wieck took place in 1840. There were eight children of the union.

Marie (Daughter: 1841–1929).

Elise (Daughter: 1843–1928).

Julie (Daughter: 1845–72).

Emil (Son: 1846–47).

Ludwig (Son: 1848–99).

Ferdinand (Son: 1849–91).

Eugenie (Daughter: 1851–1938).

Felix (Son: 1854–79). He was born four months after Schumann's committal to the Endenich asylum, and named after Mendelssohn. Brahms was his godfather. The gossip surrounding Clara's friendship with the twenty-two-year-old Brahms at the time of the child's birth led to speculation that Felix was Brahms's son, not Schumann's. (See entry under Brahms.)

Schunke, Ludwig (1810–34). German pianist. Pupil of Kalkbrenner and Herz. Schunke settled in Leipzig in 1833 and found himself lodging in the same house as Schumann. The two musicians quickly became fast friends. 'I could do without all other friends for this one alone,' Schumann wrote to his mother. Schunke, who played in several of the Gewandhaus concerts was, with Schumann, one of the founder-members of the *Neue Zeitschrift*. He died of consumption at the tragically early age of twenty-four. Unable to bear the sight of his friend's slow suffering, Schumann left Leipzig for a time and went back home to Zwickau. 'May heaven give me the strength to lose him . . . How can I bear the thought of giving him up? If he dies for heaven's sake do not tell me, nor let anyone else tell me . . .' Schumann paid a considerable tribute to Schunke's powers as a pianist when he dedicated to him his difficult C major Toccata, Op. 7.

Sire, Simonin de (1800–72). A Belgian landowner and one of Schumann's first foreign admirers. He wrote an appreciative letter to Schumann in 1838, praising his compositions, and thus started a correspondence which lasted for several years. Schumann once explained to him that 'I myself have been robbed by an unfortunate fate of the full use of my right hand, and do not play my things as I have composed them . . ., This has often perturbed me; however, heaven now and then sends me a good idea instead, and so I think no more about the matter.'

Spitta, Philip (1841–94). German writer on music. He is best remembered for his monumental study of J. S. Bach, which remains the foundation work for all research into the composer. Spitta was also a Schumann scholar, however. He wrote a substantial biography of Schumann for the first edition of *Grove's Dictionary of Music* (1889).

Spohr, Louis (1784–1859). Virtuoso violinist, conductor, and composer. He was eminent in all three fields. His chief appointment was as musical director of Cassel, which he held for more than thirty years. His list of compositions is formidable, and includes works of great originality—including a 'Historical' Symphony, a symphony for two orchestras, and quartets for double string quartet. Spohr is credited with being the first conductor to use a baton, and is therefore an important figure in the history of conducting. His *Violin School* (1831) is regarded with respect by violinists.

Schumann was on quite friendly terms with Spohr in the 1840s. When the latter expressed interest in Schumann's newly-composed 'Spring' Symphony, Schumann wrote to him: 'I wrote the Symphony in that flush of spring which carries a man away even in his old age, and comes over him anew every year. Description and painting were not part of my intention, but I believe that the time at which it came into existence may have influenced its shape and made it what it is.' (1842.)

Tausch, Julius (1827–95). German conductor, pianist and teacher. Tausch was one of the central figures in the move (not initiated by him) to oust Schumann from his post as conductor at Düsseldorf. The Düsseldorf music committee, disturbed by Schumann's increasing incompetence as a conductor (which marked the onset of his mental decline, and dated from about 1853), wished to restrict him to conducting his own compositions and to appoint Tausch as his substitute for the other concerts. Clara was bitterly opposed to Tausch. 'Tausch is behaving like a rude, ungentlemanly fellow . . . It becomes increasingly clear that Tausch, seeming quite passive, has manœuvered the chief intrigue.' As Schumann entered Dr Richarz's asylum at Endenich shortly afterwards the difficulty resolved itself, for Tausch was obliged to take over Schumann's conducting work entirely. He retained the Düsseldorf post for more than thirty-five years, not retiring until 1890.

Thibaut, Anton Friedrich (1772–1840). One of the great legal brains of his generation, Thibaut was professor of law at Heidelberg University from 1806 to 1840. Schumann first encountered him when he studied jurisprudence there in 1829 and was mesmerized by his towering intellect. 'Thibaut is a splendid, divine man; my most enjoyable hours are spent with him.' The law apart, Thibaut was also deeply involved in music and aesthetics, which added to his appeal in Schumann's eyes. In 1824, Thibaut published his influential book *Über die Reinheit der Tonkunst*. It is essentially the work of a musical amateur, but it enjoyed a professional following for a time. 'A beautiful book on music is Thibaut's *Purity in Musical Art*,' wrote Schumann in 1851. 'Read it often when you are older.' The eighteen-year-old Mendelssohn shared Schumann's enthusiasm for Thibaut, meeting him at Heidelberg in 1827. 'It is strange . . . I understand more about music than he does —yet I have learned ever so much from him and owe him a great deal . . . What an enthusiasm and glow when he talks.'

Töpken, Theodor (1807–80). A fellow-student of Schumann's at Heidelberg University, and later a doctor of law. According to Wasielewski, Töpken assisted Schumann in the elaboration of technical aids for strengthening his fingers while the two friends were still at Heidelberg. If this is so, Töpken must have viewed with concern a letter Schumann wrote to him three or four years later: 'I am still playing the pianoforte very little; don't be alarmed. I am resigned and regard it as fate—one finger of the right hand is lamed and broken . . .' (see pp. 12–13). Töpken was an early contributor to the pages of the *Neue Zeitschrift*.

Verhulst, Johann (1816–91). Dutch violinist, conductor, and composer. In 1838 he went to Leipzig in pursuit of his studies where he became friendly with Mendelssohn, and, more especially, with Schumann. For four years Schumann and Verhulst were intimates and met regularly at their favourite haunt, Poppe's restaurant, for long discussions. Verhulst returned to Holland in 1842 and was decorated with the 'Order of the Lion'. He eventually became well known as a conductor. Schumann saw Verhulst for the last time in 1852 on a visit to Holland. Afterwards he wrote: 'Goodbye. It delighted me to find you in your old spirits. Unfortunately, you cannot say the same of me. Perhaps my good genius may yet bring me back to my former condition. It delighted me too to find that you have got so dear a wife: in that matter we are both equally fortunate. Give her a nice message from me and take a hearty greeting and embrace for yourself from your old Robert Schumann.'

Schumann dedicated his 'Overture, Scherzo and Finale' to Verhulst.

Voigt, Henriette (1809–39). The wife of Carl Voigt, one of Leipzig's wealthiest patrons; the Voigts gave an endowment for regular performances of Beethoven's Ninth Symphony at the Gewandhaus concerts. Schumann was introduced to Henriette in 1834 by his great pianist friend Ludwig Schunke, a founder-member of the *Neue Zeitschrift*. A close attachment sprang up between Schumann and Henriette, and she became his confidante in the matter of his relations with Ernestine von Fricken. He dedicated his Sonata in G minor to her.

Wagner, Richard (1813–83). Wagner was Director of the Dresden Opera House when Schumann, towards the end of 1844, settled in the city. The two composers met frequently, but failed to establish a real connection. As Niecks shrewdly remarks: 'The most obvious difference between their natures was, of course, the unwillingness of the one to unburden himself and the overwhelming need of the other to do so. Schumann complains that is is impossible to endure for long a man who talks incessantly, while Wagner complains that it is impossible to discuss with a man who will hardly open his mouth.' Both points of view arouse sympathy.

Schumann disliked Wagner's music at first, and he found himself in an awkward position when the irrepressible Richard presented him with an inscribed score of *Tannhäuser*: 'To Robert Schumann as a souvenir from Richard Wagner.' What he said to Wagner is not known. Privately, he vented his true feelings to Mendelssohn: '. . . he is really incapable of conceiving and writing four beautiful bars, indeed *hardly good* ones, in succession. That is where they are all wanting, in pure harmony, skill in four-part chorale writing. What lasting good can come of it? And the score lies before us, beautifully printed, with all the fifths and octaves, and he would like to alter and erase—too late! Now enough! The music is not a whit better than *Rienzi*, is indeed more feeble, more forced. But if one says so, "Oh jealousy," they say; so I say it to you alone, for I know that you knew it long ago . . .' Later, however, after Schumann had seen the work on the stage, he changed his mind. 'About *Tannhäuser* . . . I must withdraw much that I wrote to you after reading the score; on the stage everything works out quite differently. I was greatly affected by much of it . . .'

It was while he was at Dresden that Schumann conceived the opera *Genoveva*. He had great trouble over the libretto, which he was finally obliged to adapt himself. Wagner, in his *Mein Leben*, relates the following incident. 'His society did not inspire me particularly, and the fact that he was too conservative to benefit by my views was soon shown, more especially in his conception of the poem of *Genoveva*. He afterwards invited me to hear him read his libretto, which was a combination of the styles of Hebbel and Tieck. When, however, out of a genuine desire for the success of his work, about which I had serious misgivings, I called his attention to some grave defects in it, and suggested the necessary alterations, I realized how matters stood with this extraordinary person: he simply wanted me to be swayed by himself, but deeply resented any interference with the product of his own ideals, so that thenceforward I let matters alone.' Clearly, the two men were quite incompatible; and after Wagner was forced to flee Dresden during the 1849 uprising, their paths never crossed again.

Wasielewski, Joseph von (1822–96). German violinist, conductor, and author. A pupil of Mendelssohn and Schumann in the Leipzig Conservatory. He played in the Gewandhaus Orchestra until 1850 when Schumann invited him to Düsseldorf. His biography of Schumann, which appeared in 1858, is a source-book on the composer.

Weinlig, C. T. (1780–1842). German organist and composer. Cantor of the St Thomas School, Leipzig, from 1823 until his death nineteen years later. He was a much respected theorist, chiefly remembered as the teacher of Wagner (1831–32) and the author of an important textbook on fugue. Wagner has left a memorable pen-portrait of him in his *Mein Leben*. 'One morning at seven o'clock [*sic*] Weinlig sent for me to begin the rough sketch for a fugue; he devoted the whole morning to me, following my work bar by bar with the greatest attention. At twelve o'clock he dismissed me with the instruction to perfect and finish the sketch by filling in the remaining parts at home. When I brought him the fugue finished, he handed me his own treatment of the same theme for comparison. This common task of fugue writing established between me and my good-natured teacher the tenderest of ties ... Weinlig himself did not seem to attach much importance to what he had taught me: he said, "Probably you will never write fugues or canons; but what you have mastered is independence: you can now stand alone and rely upon having a fine technique at your fingers' ends if you should want it." '

Clara Wieck was also a pupil of Weinlig, and it was partly because of her progress that Friedrich Wieck tried to persuade Schumann to begin a theoretical course with the old Cantor. Schumann preferred to work with the more youthful Dorn (see

p. 429), Director of the Leipzig opera, and musical history has speculated ever since on what advantages, if any, might have resulted had Schumann and Wagner found themselves fellow-students during the most formative period of their lives.

Wenzel, Ernst (1808–80). A pupil of Friedrich Wieck and a friend of Schumann. He was an early contributor to the *Neue Zeitschrift*.

Wieck, Friedrich (1785–1873). Father of Clara Wieck, and a renowned piano-teacher. He was born at Pretzch, a small town on the Elbe, the second of five sons of an impoverished tradesman.

Wieck freely confessed that he was almost entirely self-taught in music. It was not until he was in his late twenties that his interest in the piano suddenly developed. For the rest of his long life, it remained his overriding passion. One of his most distinguished pupils was the young Hans von Bülow who paid him this handsome tribute: 'It was you who, first laying a firm foundation, taught my ear to hear, impressed right rules and logical order on my hand, led my talent out of the twilight of the unconscious up into the clear light of the conscious.' Wieck's piano method is more fully dealt with on p. 10.

Clara, who had much to feel bitter about over her father's interference in her private affairs, never failed to speak up for him as a teacher. She replied in forthright terms to La Mara, who was about to publish a biography of Liszt and was proposing to reproduce an old rumour about Wieck's 'cruelty' to his daughter: '. . . let me call your attention to one or two mistakes. They have reference chiefly to my Father, who, because he himself took art seriously and trained me to do the same, has unfortunately been placed before the world in quite a false light. People do not understand that, if anything of importance is to be achieved in art, one's whole education and course of life must differ from that of ordinary people. My Father always kept physical as well as artistic development in view: in my childhood I never practised for more than two hours, and in later years for three hours a day, and every day I had to walk with him for an equal number of hours in order to strengthen my nerves, and until I was grown-up he always took me away from any party at ten o'clock as he considered it necessary for me to have sleep before midnight. He did not let me go to balls because he said I needed my strength for other things than dancing, but he always let me go to good operas, and even in my earliest days I had constant intercourse with the most distinguished artists. People who cannot understand a serious training of this kind put it all down to cruelty and thought that my execution, which may well have been in advance of my childish years, would be impossible unless I were kept working day and night, whereas it was just my father's genius as an educationalist which enabled him to make me progress as I did, with only moderate work, at the same time carefully training my mind and character. To my sorrow, I must say that my Father has never been accorded the recognition that he deserved. I thank him all my life long for his so-called cruelties' (10 October 1882).

From 1843, Wieck lived in Dresden. There, he was renowned for keeping open house for any and every musician passing through the city, and an evening's music-making at the Wiecks' would be a memorable occasion. Mendelssohn tried hard to secure him as a piano professor at the Leipzig Conservatory, but Wieck refused and the post went to Moscheles instead. Wieck died when he was eighty-eight years old.

Wieck had a reputation for conceit, not entirely undeserved. He was profoundly convinced of the rightness of his views, and of his genius as a piano-teacher. 'I once told Liszt that if only he had had a proper teacher he would have become the first pianist in the world.'

Bibliography

Abert, Hermann Robert Schumann (Berlin, 1920)
Abraham, Gerald (ed.) Schumann: a Symposium (Oxford, 1952)
—— On a Dull Overture by Schumann (Monthly Musical Record, Vol. LXXVI, 1946)
—— Recent Research on Schumann (Proceedings of the Royal Musical Association, 1948–49)
—— Schumann's 'Jugendsinfonie' in G minor (Musical Quarterly, Vol. XXXVII, 1951)
—— Schumann's Opp. 1 and 2 (Monthly Musical Record, Vol. LXXVI, 1946)
—— The Three Scores of Schumann's D minor Symphony (Musical Times, Vol. LXXXI, 1940)
—— Article in Grove V (1954)
Alf, Julius Der Kritiker Robert Schumann (Nieder Rheinisches Musikfest, 1956)
Alley, M. & J. A Passionate Friendship: Clara Schumann and Brahms trans. by M. Savill (London, 1956)
Ambros, A. W. Robert Schumanns Tage und Werke (Culturhistorische Bilder aus der Gegenwart) (Leipzig, 1860)
Basch, Victor Schumann (Paris, 1926)
—— L'esthétique de Schumann (La Revue Musicale, 1935)
—— La vie douloureuse de Schumann (Paris, 1928)
Batka, R. Robert Schumann (Leipzig, n.d.)
Beaufils, M. Schumann (Paris, 1932)
Bedford, Herbert Schumann (London, 1933)
—— Robert Schumann in seinen Beziehungen zu Johannes Brahms (Die Musik, Jg. XXIX, 1937)
—— Ein neuer Marsch von Robert Schumann (Die Musik, Jg. XXXIII, 1941)
—— Robert Schumann: Einführung in Persönlichkeit und Werk (Berlin, 1941)
Bœtticher, Wolfgang Robert Schumann in seinen Schriften und Briefen (Berlin, 1942)
Brion, Marcel Schumann and the Romantic Age, trans. by G. Sainsbury (London, 1956)
Brown, Thomas Alan The Aesthetics of Robert Schumann (New York, 1968)
Bücken, E. Robert Schumann (Cologne, 1940)
Burk, John N. Clara Schumann: a romantic Biography (New York, 1940)
Calvocoressi, D. Schumann (Paris, 1912)
Carner, Mosco Mahler's re-scoring of the Schumann Symphonies (Of Men and Music, London, 1942)
—— Studien zur Sonatenform bei Robert Schumann (1928)
Chantavoine, Jean La jeunesse de Schumann (Paris, 1912)
Chissell, Joan Schumann (London, rev. 1967)
Coeuroy, André Robert Schumann (Paris, 1950)
Colling, A. La vie de Robert Schumann (Paris, 1931)
Dahms, Walter Schumann (6th ed., Stuttgart, 1925)
Davies, Fanny Some Notes on the Interpretation of Schumann's Chamber Music (Cobbett's Cyclopedic Survey of Chamber Music, London, 1930)
Eismann, Georg Ein Quellenwerk über sein Leben und Schaffen (2 vols., Leipzig, 1956)
Erler, Hermann Robert Schumann: aus seinen Briefen (2 vols., Berlin, 1887)
Felber, Rudolf Schumann's Place in German Song (*Musical Quarterly*, Vol. XXVI, 1940)

Fiske, Roger A Schumann Mystery (*Musical Times*, August 1964)

Fuller-Maitland, J. A. Robert Schumann (London, 1884)
—— Schumann: Concerted Chamber Music (Oxford, 1929)
—— Schumann: Pianoforte Works (Oxford, 1927)

Garrison, F. H. The Medical History of Robert Schumann and his Family (Bulletin, New York Academy of Medicine, 1934)

Geiringer, Karl Ein unbekanntes Klavierwerk aus Schumanns Jugendzeit (Die Musik, Jg. XXV, 1933)

Gensel, J. Robert Schumanns Briefwechsel mit Henriette Voigt (1892)

Gertler, W. Robert Schumann in seinen frühen Klavierwerken (Wolfenbüttel, 1931)

Gruhle, W. Brief über Robert Schumanns Krankheit an P. B. Möbius (Zbl. Nervenheilk, 1906)

Hadow, Sir Henry Robert Schumann and the Romantic Movement in Germany (Studies in Modern Music, Vol. 1, London, 1892)

Herbert, May The Life of Robert Schumann told in his Letters (London, 1890)

Homeyer, H. Grundbegriffe der Musikanschauung Robert Schumanns (Dissertation: Münster, 1956)

Hueffer, F. Die Poesie in der Musik (Leipzig, 1874)

Jacobs, Robert L. Schumann and Jean Paul (Music & Letters, Vol. XXX, 1949)

Jansen, F. Gustav Die Davidsbündler: aus Robert Schumanns Sturm und Drang Periode (Leipzig, 1883; 2nd ed., Leipzig, 1904)
—— Briefwechsel zwischen Robert Franz and Robert Schumann (Die Musik, Jg. VIII, 1908–9)
—— Ein unbekannter Brief von Robert Schumann (Die Musik, Jg. V, 1905–6)
—— Auf Robert Schumanns Schulzeit (Die Musik, 1906)

Kohut, Adolf Friedrich Wieck (?)

Kalbeck, Max R. Schumann in Wien (Wiener allgemeine Zeitung, September–October 1880)

Kapp, Julius Schumanns Études Symphoniques, Opus 13 (Die Musik, Jg. IX, 1909–10)

Kerner, D. Krankheiten Grosser Musiker. Friedrich-Karl Schattauer-Verlag. (Stuttgart, 1963)

Korte, Werner Robert Schumann (Potsdam, 1927)

Kötz, Hans Der Einfluss Jean Pauls auf Robert Schumann (Weimar, 1933)

La Mara Robert Schumann (Leipzig, 1911)

Lara, Adelina de Clara Schumann's Teaching (Music & Letters, Vol. XXVI, 1945)

Legge, Robin H. Letters from Brahms to Schumann (Studies in Music, ed. Robin Grey, London, 1901)

Lippman, Edward A. Robert Schumann (Die Musik in Geschichte und Gegenwart, Vol. XII, pp. 271–326)
—— Theory and Practice in Schumann's Aesthetics (Journal of the American Musicological Society, 1964)

Litzmann, Berthold Clara Schumann: Ein Künstlerleben (3 vols., 3rd ed., Leipzig, 1906)
—— Letters of Clara Schumann and Johannes Brahms, 1853–96 (London, 1927)

Macmaster, Henry La Folie de Robert Schumann (Paris, 1928)

Mason, Daniel Gregory The Romantic Composers (New York, 1906)

Mauclair, Camille Schumann (Paris, 1906)
—— La Musique de Piano de Schumann (Le Courier Musicale, 1906)

May, Florence The Girlhood of Clara Schumann (London, 1912)

Meyerstein, E. W. H. A Note on Schumann's Last Composition (Music Survey, 1948)

Möbius, P. J. Über Robert Schumanns Krankheit (Halle, 1906)

Morselli, E. La pazzia di Roberto Schumann (Rome, 1909)

Moser, H. J. and Rebling (eds) Robert Schumann, aus Anlass seines 100 Todestages (Leipzig, 1956)

Newman, Ernest Faust in Music (Musical Studies, London, 1905)

Niecks, Frederick (ed. C. Niecks) Robert Schumann: a Supplementary and Corrective Biography (London, 1925)

Ninck, Martin Schumann und die Romantik in der Musik (Heidelberg, 1929)
Nussbaum, F. Der Streit über Robert Schumanns Krankheit (Dissertation: Cologne, 1923)
Oldmeadow, Ernest J. Schumann (London, 1910)
Parrott, Ian A plea for Schumann's Op. 11 (Music & Letters, Vol. XXXIII, 1952)
Pascal, Dr Les Maladies mentales de Robert Schumann (Journal de Psychologie Normal
    et Pathologique, March–April 1908)
Petzold, Richard Robert Schumann, sein Leben in Bildern (Leipzig, Bibliographisches
    Institut, 1956)
—— Robert Schumann, Leben und Werk (Leipzig, Breitkopf und Härtel, 1941)
Peyser, Herbert F. Robert Schumann: Tone-Poet, Prophet and Critic (New York, 1948)
Pitrou, R. La Vie intérieure de Robert Schumann (Paris, 1925)
Plantinga, Leon B. Schumann as Critic (Yale, 1967)
Pleasants, Henry The Musical World of Robert Schumann (articles, edited and translated)
    (New York & London, 1965)
Pohl, R. Erinnerungen an Robert Schumann (Deutsche Revue, Vol. 2, August–September
    1878)
Redlich, Hans F. Schumann Discoveries (Monthly Musical Record, Vol. LXXX, 1950)
Rehberg, Paula and Walter Robert Schumann, sein Leben und Werk (Zürich and Stuttgart,
    1954)
Reimann, Heinrich Robert Schumanns Leben und Werke (Leipzig, 1887)
Reinhard, W. Die Krankheiten Mozarts und Schumanns. Med. Mschr. 1956.
Reissmann, August Robert Schumann, sein Leben und seine Werke (Berlin, 1879)
Rothe, Hans-Joachim Arbeitsberichte zur Geschickte der stadt Leipzig (No. 13) (Leipzig, 1967)
Sams, Eric Did Schumann use Ciphers? (Musical Times, August 1965)
—— The Schumann Ciphers (Musical Times, May 1966)
—— The Schumann Ciphers: a Coda (Musical Times, December 1966)
—— Why Florestan and Eusebius? (Musical Times, February 1967)
Politics, Literature, People, in Schumann's op. 136 (Musical Times, January 1968)
—— The Songs of Robert Schumann (London, 1969)
—— A Schumann Primer? (Musical Times, November 1970)
—— Schumann's hand injury (Musical Times, December 1971)
Schauffler, Robert Haven Florestan: the Life and Work of Robert Schumann (New York,
    1945)
Schering, Arnold Robert Schumann als Tragiker (Neue Zeitschrift für Musik, 1901)
—— Träumerei (Musikalische Bildung, Leipzig, 1911)
Schnapp, Friedrich Eine unbekannte Rezension Robert Schumanns (Neue Zeitschrift für
    Musik, 1925)
—— Essai de reconstitution de la correspondance de Schumann et de Liszt (La Revue
    Musicale, 1935)
—— Heinrich Heine und Robert Schumann (Hamburg and Berlin, 1924)
Schneider, Louis and Maraschel, Marcel Schumann, sa vie et ses œuvres (Paris, 1905)
Schumann, Alfred (ed.) Der Junge Schumann (1910)
Schumann, Clara (ed.) Jugendbriefe Robert Schumanns (Leipzig, 1885)
Schumann, Eugenie Memoirs, trans. Marie Bush (London, 1930)
—— Robert Schumann (Leipzig, 1931)
—— The Schumanns and Johannes Brahms (New York, 1927)
—— Robert Schumann: Ein Lebensbild meines Vaters (Leipzig, 1931)
Schumann, Ferdinand Ein unbekannter Jugendbrief von Robert Schumann (Die Musik,
    Jg. IX, 1909–10)
Schumann, Robert Briefe: neue Folge, ed. F. Gustav Jansen (Leipzig, 1886)
—— Jugendbriefe von Robert Schumann (Leipzig, 1885)
—— Early Letters, trans. May Herbert (London, 1888)
—— The Letters of Robert Schumann, ed. Karl Storck, trans. Hannah Bryant (London,
    1907)
—— Gesammelte Schriften über Musik und Musiker, ed. F. Gustav Jansen (Leipzig, 1891;
    5th ed, Kreisig, Leipzig, 1914)

—— Music and Musicians, Essays and Criticisms, trans. Fanny Raymond Ritter (London, 1877)

Schwarz, Werner Robert Schumann und die Variation (Cassel, 1932)

Shore, Bernard Schumann's Symphony in D minor (Sixteen Symphonies, London, 1949)

Slater, E. and Meyer, A. Contributions to a pathography of the Musicians: I. Robert Schumann (Confinia Psychiatrica, Vol. II, 1959)

Spitta, Philipp Robert Schumann, ein Lebensbild (Leipzig, 1882)

—— Über Robert Schumanns Schriften (Musikgeschichtliche Aufsätze, Berlin, 1894)

Sutermeister, Peter Robert Schumann: Sein Leben nach Briefen, Tagebüchern und Errinner-ungen (Zurich, 1949)

Tessmer, Hans Der klingende Weg (Regensburg, 1923)

—— Robert Schumann (Stuttgart, 1930)

Tiersot, Julien Schumann et Berlioz (La Revue Musicale, 1935)

Tovey, Sir Donald Analyses of various works in 'Essays in Musical Analysis' (7 vols., London, 1935–44)

Wagner, K. Robert Schumann als Schüler und Abiturient (Zwickau, 1928)

Wasielewski, J. W. von Robert Schumann: eine Biographie (4th ed., Leipzig, 1906)

—— Schumanniana (Bonn, 1883)

Wieck, Marie Aus dem Kreise Wieck–Schumann (2nd ed., Dresden, 1914)

Wolff, Helmut Christian Robert Schumann—der Klassizist (Musica, 1948)

Wolff, V. E. Robert Schumanns Lieder in ersten und späteren Fassungen (Leipzig, 1914)

Wörner, Karl H. Robert Schumann (Zurich, 1949)

Young, Percy M. Tragic Muse: The Life and Works of Robert Schumann (London, 1957)

COMPLETE CATALOGUE OF SCHUMANN'S WORKS

KEY

1. KEYBOARD MUSIC

(a) Solo Piano Music

OP. NO.	TITLE	DATE OF COMPOSITION	AGE	DATE OF PUBLICATION	DEDICATION
1	Theme on the name ABEGG with Variations	1830 (January)	19	1831 Kistner	'Pauline, Countess d'Abegg' (Meta Abegg of Mannheim)
2	Papillons	1829–31	19–21	1832 Kistner	Theresa, Rosalie and Emilie Schumann
3	6 Studies on Paganini Caprices (Set I) See op. 10 for Set II	1832	22	1832 Hofmeister	
4	6 Intermezzi	1832	22	1832 Hofmeister	Johan Václav Kalliwoda
5	Impromptus on a theme by Clara Wieck	1833 rev. 1850	23	1833 Hofmeister	Friedrich Wieck
6	Davidsbündlertänze. 18 Characteristic Pieces	1837	27	1838 Friese	Walther von Goethe
7	Toccata in C major (Orig. in D major and called 'Étude fantastique en double-sons')	1830 rev. 1833	20–23	1834 Hofmeister	Ludwig Schunke
8	Allegro in B minor (Orig. intended as first mov. of a Sonata)	1831	21	1835 Friese	Ernestine von Fricken
9	Carnaval: Scènes mignonnes sur quatres notes (Orig. 'Fasching': Schwänke auf vier Noten von Florestan') 1. Préambule 2. Pierrot 3. Arlequin 4. Valse noble 5. Eusebius 6. Florestan 7. Coquette 8. Réplique 9. Sphinxes	1834–35	24–25	1837 Breitkopf & Härtel	Carl Lipinski

Solo Piano Music (cont.)

OP. NO.	TITLE	DATE OF COMPOSITION	AGE	DATE OF PUBLICATION	DEDICATION
	10. Papillons				
	11. A.S.C.H.–S.C.H.A. (Lettres dansantes)				
	12. Chiarina				
	13. Chopin				
	14. Estrella				
	15. Reconnaissance				
	16. Pantalon et Colombine				
	17. Valse allemande				
	18. Paganini				
	19. Aveu				
	20. Promenade				
	21. Pause				
	22. Marche des 'Davidsbündler' contre les Philistins				
10	6 Concert Studies on Paganini Caprices (Set II) See op. 3 for Set I	1833	23	1835 Hofmeister	
11	Sonata No. 1, in F sharp minor	1833–35	23–25	1836 Kistner	Clara Wieck
12	Fantasiestücke 1. Des Abends 2. Aufschwung 3. Warum? 4. Grillen 5. In der Nacht 6. Fabel 7. Traumes Wirren 8. Ende vom Lied 9. ★ ★ ★	1837	27	1838 Breitkopf & Härtel	Anna Robena Laidlaw
13	Études en forme de variations (Symphonic Studies) (Orig. 'Etüden in Orchester Charakter')	1834–37 rev. 1852	24	1935 (Schweizerische Musikzeitung) 1837 Haslinger	William Sterndale Bennett

14	Sonata No. 3 in F minor (Concert sans orchestre)	1835–36 rev. 1853	25–26	1836 Haslinger	Ignaz Moscheles
15	Kinderscenen 1. Vom fremden Ländern und Menschen 2. Curiose Geschichte 3. Hasche—Mann 4. Bittendes Kind 5. Glückes genug 6. Wichtige Begebenheit 7. Traümerei 8. Am Camin 9. Ritter vom Steckenpferd 10. Fast zu ernst 11. Fürchtenmachen 12. Kind im Einschlummern 13. Der Dichter spricht	1838 (April)	27	1839 Breitkopf & Härtel	
16	Kreisleriana—8 fantasies	1838	28	1838 Haslinger	Chopin
17	Fantasie in C major (Orig. entitled 'Obolen auf Beethovens Monument: 1. Ruinen. 2. Trophaen. 3. Palmen. Grosse Sonate f.d. Pianof. Für Beethovens Denkmal')	1836	26	1839 Breitkopf & Härtel	Liszt (Orig. Clara Wieck)
18	Arabeske in C major	1839	29	1839 Spina	Frau Majorin F. Serre
19	Blumenstück in D flat major	1839	29	1839 Spina	Frau Majorin F. Serre
20	Humoreske in B flat major	1838–39	28–29	1839 Spina	Frau Julie von Webenau
21	8 Novelletten	1838 (March)	27	1839 Breitkopf & Härtel	Adolph Henselt
22	Sonata No. 2, in G minor	1833–38	23–28	1839 Breitkopf & Härtel	Henriette Voigt

OP. NO.	TITLE	DATE OF COMPOSITION	AGE	DATE OF PUBLICATION	DEDICATION
	Solo Piano Music (cont.)				
23	4 Nachtstücke	1839	29	1840 Spina	E. A. Becker
26	Faschingsschwank aus Wien: Fantasiebilder	1839	29	1841 Spina	Simonin de Sire
	1. Allegro				
	2. Romanze				
	3. Scherzino				
	4. Intermezzo				
	5. Finale				
28	3 Romanzen	1839	29	1840 Breitkopf & Härtel	Count Heinrich II of Reuss-Köstritz
	1. B flat minor				
	2. F sharp major				
	3. B major				
32	Clavierstücke	1838–39	28–29	1841 Schuberth	Fräulein Amalie Rieffel
	1. Scherzo in B flat major				
	2. Gigue in G minor				
	3. Romanze in D minor				
	4. Fughetta in G minor				
68	Album für die Jugend (Orig. 'Weihnachtsalbum')	1848	38	1851 Schuberth	
	Part 1: Für Kleinere				
	1. Melodie				
	2. Soldatenmarsch				
	3. Trällerliedchen (Orig. 'Kinderstückchen')				
	4. Ein Choral				
	5. Stückchen				
	6. Armes Waisenkind (Orig. 'Armes Bettlerkind')				
	7. Jägerliedchen				
	8. Wilder Reiter				
	9. Volksliedchen (Orig. 'Volkslied')				
	10. Frölicher Landmann				
	11. Sicilianisch (Orig. 'Zwei Sizilianische')				

12. Knecht Ruprecht
13. Mai, Lieber Mai (Orig. 'Mai, Schöner Mai')
14. Kleine Studie
15. Frühlingsgesang
16. Erster Verlust (Orig. 'Kinderunglück')
17. Kleiner Morgenwanderer
18. Schnitter Liedchen
Part II: Für Erwachsenere
19. Kleine Romanze
20. Ländliches Lied
21. * * *
22. Rundgesang
23. Reiterstück
24. Ernteliedchen
25. Nachklänge aus dem Theater
26. * * * *
27. Canonisches Liedchen (Orig. 'Canon')
28. Erinnerung (in memory of Mendelssohn)
29. Fremder Mann
30. * * *
31. Kriegslied
32. Sheherazade
33. 'Weinlesezeit—Fröhliche Zeit!'
34. Thema
35. Mignon
36. Lied italienischer Marinari (Orig. 'Schiffer-lied')
37. Matrosenlied
38. Winterszeit I
39. Winterszeit II
40. Kleine Fuge
41. Nordisches Lied (Gruss an G) (The theme is on the notes 'G.A.D.E.')
42. Figurierter Choral
43. Sylvesterlied (Orig. 'Zum Schluss')
Additional pieces published in 1924
    Kuckuck im Versteck

1924
Schott

Solo Piano Music (cont.)

OP. NO.	TITLE	DATE OF COMPOSITION	AGE	DATE OF PUBLICATION	DEDICATION
	Lagune in Venedig				
	Haschemann				
	Kleiner Walzer				
72	4 Fugen	1845	35	1850 Whistling	Carl Reinecke
	1. D minor				
	2. D minor				
	3. F minor				
	4. F major				
76	4 Märsche	1849 (12–16 June)	39	1849 Whistling	
	1. E flat major				
	2. G minor				
	3. B flat major (Lager-Scene)				
	4. E flat major				
82	Waldscenen	1848–49 (Dec.–Jan.)	38	1851 Senff	Fräulein Annette Preusser
	1. Eintritt				
	2. Jäger auf der Lauer (Orig. 'Jägersmann auf der Lauer')				
	3. Einsame Blumen				
	4. Verrufene Stelle (Orig. 'Verrufener Ort')				
	5. Freundliche Landschaft (Orig. 'Freier Ausblick')				
	6. Herberge (Orig. 'Jägerhaus')				
	7. Vogel als Prophet				
	8. Jagdlied				
	9. Abschied				
99	Bunte Blätter	Composed at different times (1838–49)	28–29	1852 Arnold	Miss Mary Potts
	1–3 Drei Stücklein				
	4–8 Fünf Albumblätter				
	9. Novellette				
	10. Präludium				
	11. Marsch				
	12. Abendmusik				

	13. Scherzo (Orig. the trio of a projected symphony, op. 76)				
	14. Geschwindmarsch				
111	3 Fantasiestücke (Orig. 'Cyclus für Pianoforte') 1. C minor 2. A flat major 3. C minor	1851	41	1852 Peters	Frau Fürstin Reuss-Köstritz
118	3 Clavier-Sonaten für die Jugend 1. G major 2. D major 3. C major	1853	43	1854 Schuberth	Schumann's daughters Marie, Elise and Julie
124	Albumblätter 1. Impromptu 2. Leides Ahnung (Orig. a variation on Allegretto from Beethoven's 7th Symphony; see unpublished solo piano works) 3. Scherzino 4. Walzer 5. Fantasietanz 6. Wiegenliedchen 7. Ländler 8. Lied ohne Ende 9. Impromptu 10. Walzer 11. Romanze 12. Burla 13. Larghetto 14. Vision 15. Walzer 16. Schlummerlied 17. Elfe (Orig. one of 'Papillons', later altered to fit into 'Carnaval') 18. Botschaft 19. Fantasiestück 20. Canon	1832–45	22–35	1854 Arnold	Alma von Wasielewski

Solo Piano Music (cont.)

OP. NO.	TITLE	DATE OF COMPOSITION	AGE	DATE OF PUBLICATION	DEDICATION
126	Sieben Clavierstücke in Fughettenform	1853	43	1854 Arnold	Rosalie Leser
	1. A minor				
	2. D minor				
	3. F major				
	4. D minor				
	5. A minor				
	6. F major				
	7. A minor				
133	Gesänge der Frühe	1853	43	1855 Arnold	Bettina Brentano
	1. D major				
	2. D major				
	3. A major				
	4. F sharp minor				
	5. D major				

Other Solo Piano Works

(unfinished, unpublished, without opus numbers, etc.)

OP. NO.	TITLE	DATE OF COMPOSITION	AGE	DATE OF PUBLICATION	DEDICATION
	Waltzes (later used in 'Papillons')	1829	19		
	Sonata in A flat major (first mov. and Adagio only)	c. 1830	c. 20		
	Andante in G major ('Mit Gott', Variations on an original theme)	1831–32	21–22		
	Prelude and Fugue	1832	22		
	Burlesken	1832	22	(one publ. as op. 124, No. 12)	
	'Phantasie satyrique, (nach Henri Herz)' (unfinished)	1832	22		
	'Fandango', in F sharp minor (later used in 1st movement of op. 11)	1832	22		Wilhelm de la Lühe

'Exercice fantastique'	1832	22		Johann Gottfried Kuntzsch
Sketch for a movement in B flat major	c. 1832	c. 22		
Sketch for a fugal piece in B flat minor	c. 1832	c. 22		
Sketch for a canonic piece in A major	c. 1832	c. 22		
'Fugue No. 3' (intended as a finale to op. 5?)	c. 1832	c. 22		
'Sehnsuchtswalzervariationen' (Scènes musicales sur un thème connu de Fr. Schubert. Also known as 'Scènes mignonnes')	1833	23		Henriette Voigt
'Etüden in Form freier Variationen, über ein Beethovensches Thema' (Allegretto of 7th Symphony) (One variation appeared as op. 124, No. 2)	1833	23		Clara Wieck
Sonata No. 4, in F minor (unfinished)	1833–37	23–27		
Andante in F major	1833	23		
'Variations sur un nocturne de Chopin'	1834	24		
Sonata mov., in B flat major	1836	26		
Canon on 'To Alexis', in A flat major	?	?		
'Scherzo und Presto Passionato' (The 'scherzo' was originally intended for op. 14; the 'presto' the rejected finale from op. 22)	1835–36	25–26	1866 Kahnt	
'Thema mit Variationen', in E flat major (Schumann imagined that angels had dictated this theme to him. It is related to the slow movement of the Violin Concerto. Brahms later used it for his Variations for Piano duet, op. 23)	1854 (17 Feb.)	43	1939 Hinrichsen	
Five Short Pieces	1837–38	27–28		
1. Notturnino (unfinished)				
2. Ballo				
3. Burla				
4. Capriccio (unfinished)				
5. Écossaise (unfinished)				
'Romanza' in F minor (unfinished)	?			
Allegro in C minor (lost)	1839			

(b) Piano Duets, two pianos, organ, etc.

OP. NO.	TITLE	DATE OF COMPOSITION	AGE	DATE OF PUBLICATION	DEDICATION
	Pianoforte Duets				
—	Eight Polonaises	1828	18	1933 Universal	Eduard, Charles and Jules Schumann
—	Variations on a theme of Prince Louis Ferdinand of Prussia (Lost)	1828	18		
66	Bilder aus Osten, 6 Impromptus	1848	38	1849 Kistner	Frau Eduard Bendemann
85	Zwölf vierhändige Clavierstücke für kleine und grosse Kinder	1849 (10 Sept.– 10 Oct.)	39	1850 Schuberth	
	1. Geburtstagsmarsch				
	2. Bärentanz				
	3. Gartenmelodie				
	4. Beim Kränzewinden				
	5. Kroatenmarsch				
	6. Trauer				
	7. Turniermarsch				
	8. Reigen				
	9. Am Springbrunnen				
	10. Versteckens				
	11. Gespenstermärchen				
	12. Abendlied				
109	Ballscenen	1851	41	1851 Schuberth	Henriette Reichmann
	Nine characteristic pieces for piano duet				
	1. Préambule				
	2. Polonaise				
	3. Walzer				
	4. Ungarisch				
	5. Française				
	6. Mazurka				
	7. Écossaise				
	8. Walzer				
	9. Promenade				

No.	Title	Composed		Published	Dedicatee
130	'Kinderball' Six easy dance pieces 1. Polonaise 2. Walzer 3. Menuett (1850) 4. Écossaise 5. Française 6. Ringelreihe	1853	43	1853 Breitkopf & Härtel	
	TWO PIANOFORTES				
46	Andante and Variations in B flat major (See also Chamber Music)	1843	43	1844 Breitkopf & Härtel	Harriet Parish
	PEDAL PIANOFORTE				
56	'Studien für den Pedal-Flügel' Six pieces in canon form	1845	35	1845 Whistling	Johann Gottfried Kuntzsch
58	'Skizzen für den Pedal-Flügel'	1845	35	1846 Kistner	
	ORGAN				
60	'Six Fugues on the name of 'BACH'' for organ or pedal piano	1845	35	1847 Heinze	
	HARMONIUM				
39	Piece in two movements, F major (unpublished)	1849	39	—	

2. SONGS

No.	Title	Composed		Published	Dedicatee
24	Liederkreis (Heine) Vol. 1: 1. Morgens steh' ich auf 2. Es treibt mich hin 3. Ich wandelte unter den Bäumen 4. Lieb' Liebchen 5. Schöne Wiege meiner Leiden 6. Warte, warte, wilder Schiffsmann 7. Berg' und Burgen schau'n herunter	1840	30	1840 Breitkopf & Härtel	Pauline Garcia

458

OP. NO.	TITLE	DATE OF COMPOSITION	AGE	DATE OF PUBLICATION	DEDICATION
	Songs (cont.)				
	8. Anfangs wollt' ich fast verzagen				
	9. Mit Myrthen und Rosen				
25	Myrthen	1840	30	1840 Kistner	Clara Schumann
	1. Widmung (Rückert)				
	2. Freisinn (Goethe)				
	3. Der Nussbaum (J. Mosen)				
	4. Jemand (Burns)				
	5. Sitz' ich allein (Goethe)				
	6. Setze mir nicht (Goethe)				
	7. Die Lotosblume (Heine)				
	8. Talismane (Goethe)				
	9. Lied der Suleika (Goethe) (the poem has been attributed to Marianne von Willemer)				
	10. Die Hochländer-Witwe (Burns)				
	11. Mutter! Mutter! (Rückert)				
	12. Lass mich ihm am Busen hängen (Rückert)				
	13. Hochländers Abschied (Burns)				
	14. Hochländers Wiegenlied (Burns)				
	15. Mein Herz ist schwer (Byron)				
	16. Rätsel (Catherine Fanshawe)				
	17. Leis rudern hier (Thomas Moore)				
	18. Wenn durch die Piazzetta (Moore)				
	19. Hauptmanns Weib (Burns)				
	20. Weit, weit (Burns)				
	21. Was will die einsame Träne (Heine)				
	22. Niemand (Burns)				
	23. Im Westen (Burns)				
	24. Du bist wie eine Blume (Heine)				
	25. Aus den östlichen Rosen (Rückert)				
	26. Zum Schluss (Rückert)				
27	Lieder und Gesänge, Vol. I	1840	30	1849 Whistling	
	1. Sag' an, o lieber Vogel mein (Hebbel)				
	2. Dem roten Röslein gleicht mein Lieb (Burns)				

	3. Was soll ich sagen? (Chamisso)				
	4. Jasminenstrauch (Rückert)				
	5. Nur ein lächelnder Blick (Zimmermann)				
	(See also opp. 51, 77 and 96)				
30	Drei Gedichte (Geibel)	1840	30	1841 Bote & Bock	Frau Josephine Baroni-Cavalcabo
	1. Der Knabe mit dem Wunderhorn				
	2. Der Page				
	3. Der Hidalgo				
31	Drei Gesänge (Chamisso)	1840	30	1840 Cranz	Frau Gräfin Ernestine von Zedwitz
	1. Die Löwenbraut				
	2. Die Kartenlegerin				
	3. Die rote Hanne				
35	Zwölf Gedichte (Kerner)	1840	30	1841 Klemm	Dr. Fr. Weber in London
	1. Lust der Sturmnacht				
	2. Stirb, Lieb' und Freud				
	3. Wanderlied				
	4. Erstes Grün				
	5. Sehnsucht nach der Waldgegend				
	6. Auf das Trinkglas eines verstorbenen Freundes				
	7. Wanderung				
	8. Stille Liebe				
	9. Frage				
	10. Stille Tränen				
	11. Wer machte dich so krank?				
	12. Alte Laute				
36	Sechs Gedichte (Reinick)	1840	30	1842 Schuberth	Frau Dr. Livia Frege
	1. Sonntags am Rhein				
	2. Ständchen				
	3. Nichts Schöneres				
	4. An den Sonnenschein				
	5. Dichters Genesung				
	6. Liebesbotschaft				
37	Gedichte aus 'Liebesfrühling' (Rückert)	1840	30	1841 Breitkopf & Härtel	
	1. Der Himmel hat eine Träne geweint				
	2. Er ist gekommen				

OP. NO.	TITLE	DATE OF COMPOSITION	AGE	DATE OF PUBLICATION	DEDICATION
	Songs (cont.)				
	3. O ihr Herren				
	4. Liebst du um Schönheit				
	5. Ich hab' in mich gesogen				
	6. Liebste, was kann denn uns scheiden				
	7. Schön ist das Fest des Lenzes				
	8. Flügel! Flügel! um zu fliegen				
	9. Rose, Meer und Sonne				
	10. O Sonn', o Meer, o Rose!				
	11. Warum willst du And're fragen?				
	12. So wahr die Sonne scheinet				
	(Nos. 2, 4 and 11 are by Clara Schumann)				
39	Liederkreis (Eichendorff), Vol. II	1840	30	1842 Heinze	
	1. In der Fremde				
	2. Intermezzo				
	3. Waldesgespräch				
	4. Die Stille				
	5. Mondnacht				
	6. Schöne Fremde				
	7. Auf einer Burg				
	8. In der Fremde				
	9. Wehmut				
	10. Zwielicht				
	11. Im Walde				
	12. Frühlingsnacht				
40	Fünf Lieder	1840	30	1842 Schuberth	H. C. Andersen
	1. Märzveilchen (Andersen) ⎫ trans.				
	2. Muttertraum (Andersen) ⎬ Chamisso				
	3. Der Soldat (Andersen) ⎭				
	4. Der Spielmann (Andersen)				
	5. Verratene Liebe (Chamisso)				
42	Frauenliebe und -leben (Chamisso)	1840	30	1843 Heinze	Oswald Lorenz
	1. Seit ich ihn gesehen				
	2. Er, der Herrlichste von allen				

Op.	Title				
	3. Ich kann's nicht fassen				
	4. Du Ring an meinem Finger				
	5. Helft mir, ihr Schwestern				
	6. Süsser Freund, du blickest				
	7. An meinem Herzen				
	8. Nun hast du mir den ersten Schmerz getan				
45	Romanzen und Balladen, Vol. I	1840	30	1844 Whistling	Ferdinand Hiller
	1. Der Schatzgräber (Eichendorff)				
	2. Frühlingsfahrt (Eichendorff)				
	3. Abends am Strand (Heine)				
	(See also opp. 49, 53 and 64)				
48	Dichterliebe (Heine)	1840	30	1844 Peters	Wilhelmine Schröder-Devrient
	1. Im wunderschönen Monat Mai				
	2. Aus meinen Tränen spriessen				
	3. Die Rose, die Lilie				
	4. Wenn ich in deine Augen seh				
	5. Ich will meine Seele tauchen				
	6. Im Rhein, im heiligen Strome				
	7. Ich grolle nicht				
	8. Und wüssten's die Blumen				
	9. Das ist ein Flöten und Geigen				
	10. Hör' ich das Liedchen klingen				
	11. Ein Jüngling liebt ein Mädchen				
	12. Am leuchtenden Sommermorgen				
	13. Ich hab' im Traum geweinet				
	14. Allnächtlich in Traume				
	15. Aus alten Märchen winkt es				
	16. Die alten, bösen Lieder				
49	Romanzen und Balladen, Vol. II	1840	30	1844 Heinze	—
	1. Die beiden Grenadiere (Heine)				
	2. Die feindlichen Brüder (Heine)				
	3. Die Nonne (Fröhlich)				
	(See also opp. 45, 53 and 54)				
51	Lieder und Gesänge, Vol. II	1840–46	30–36	1850 Whistling	—
	1. Sehnsucht (Geibel)	1840			
	2. Volksliedchen (Rückert)				
	3. Ich wand're nicht (Christern)				

OP. NO.	TITLE	DATE OF COMPOSITION	AGE	DATE OF PUBLICATION	DEDICATION
	Songs (cont.)				
	4. Auf dem Rhein (Immermann)	1846			
	5. Liebeslied (Goethe)	1840(?)			
	(See also opp. 27, 77 and 96)				
53	Romanzen und Balladen, Vol. III	1840	30	1845 Whistling	—
	1. Blondels Lied (Seidl)				
	2. Loreley (Lorenz)				
	3. Der arme Peter (Heine)				
	(a) Der Hans und die Grete				
	(b) In meiner Brust				
	(c) Der arme Peter wankt vorbei				
	(See also opp. 45, 49 and 64)				
57	Belsatzar (Heine)	1840	30	1846 Siegel & Stoll	—
64	Romanzen und Balladen, Vol. IV			1847 Siegel & Stoll	—
	1. Die Soldatenbraut (Mörike)	1847	27		
	2. Das verlassene Mägdelein (Mörike)				
	3. Tragödie (Heine)	1841	21		
	(a) Entflieh mit mir				
	(b) Es fiel ein Reif				
	(c) Auf ihrem Grab				
	(duet for soprano and tenor)				
	(See also opp. 45, 49 and 53)				
74	Spanisches Liederspiel	1849	39	1849 Kistner	—
	Nine songs for one, two and four voices, translated from the Spanish by Geibel. The items for one voice are:				
	6. Melancholie (S.)	1840	30		
	7. Geständnis (T.)	1850	40		
	(See Vocal Duets and Vocal Quartets)				
77	Lieder und Gesänge, Vol. III	1840–50	30–40	1851 Siegel & Stoll	—
	1. Der frohe Wandersmann (Eichendorff)				
	2. Mein Garten (Fallersleben)				

Op.	Title	Date		Publisher
79	3. Geisternähe (Halm)	1850	40	
	4. Stiller Vorwurf (Wolff?)	1840	30	
	5. Aufträge (L'Égru)	1850	40	
	(See also opp. 27, 51 and 96)			
	Liederalbum für die Jugend	1849	39	1849 Breitkopf & Härtel
	1. Der Abendstern			
	2. Schmetterling ⎫			
	3. Frühlingsbotschaft ⎬ (Hoffmann von Fallersleben)			
	4. Frühlingsgruss ⎭			
	5. Vom Schlaraffenland (Fallersleben)			
	6. Sonntag			
	7. Zigeunerliedchen (Geibel)			
	8. Des Knaben Berglied (Uhland)			
	9. Mailied (Anon.)			
	10. Das Käuzlein (Des Knaben Wunderhorn)			
	11. Hinaus in's Freie! (Fallersleben)			
	12. Der Sandmann (Kletke)			
	13. Marienwürmchen (Des Knaben Wunderhorn)			
	14. Die Waise (Fallersleben)			
	15. Das Glück (Hebbel)			
	16. Weihnachtslied (Andersen)			
	17. Die wandelnde Glocke (Goethe)			
	18. Frühlingslied (Fallersleben) (duet)			
	19. Frühlingsankunft (Fallersleben)			
	20. Die Schwalben (Anon.)			
	21. Kinderwacht (Anon.)			
	22. Des Sennen Abschied (Schiller)			
	23. Er ist's (Mörike)			
	24. Spinnlied (Anon.)			
	25. Des Buben Schützenlied (Schiller)			
	26. Schneeglöckchen (Rückert)			
	27. Lied Lynceus des Türmers (Goethe)			
	28. Mignon (Goethe)			
83	Drei Gesänge	1850	40	1850 Schuberth
	1. Resignation (J. Buddeus)			
	2. Die Blume der Ergebung (Rückert)			

OP. NO.	TITLE	DATE OF COMPOSITION	AGE	DATE OF PUBLICATION	DEDICATION
	Songs (cont.)				
87	3. Der Einsiedler (Eichendorff)				
	Der Handschuh (Schiller)	1850	40	1851 Whistling	
89	Sechs Gesänge (von der Neun)	1850	40	1850 Kistner	Jenny Lind
	1. Es stürmet am AbendHimmel				
	2. Heimliches Verschwinden				
	3. Herbstlied				
	4. Abschied vom Walde				
	5. In's Freie				
	6. Röselein, Röselein				
90	Sechs Gedichte (Lenau) und Requiem	1850	40	1851 Kistner	
	1. Lied eines Schmiedes				
	2. Meine Rose				
	3. Kommen und Scheiden				
	4. Die Sennin				
	5. Einsamkeit				
	6. Der schwere Abend				
	7. Requiem (old Catholic poem)				
95	Drei Gesänge (Byron)	1849	39	1851 Simrock	Fräulein Constanze Jacobi
	1. Die Tochter Jephthas				
	2. An den Mond				
	3. Dem Helden				
96	Lieder und Gesänge, Vol. IV	1850	40	1851 Whistling	
	1. Nachtlied (Goethe)				
	2. Schneeglöckchen (Anon.)				
	3. Ihre Stimme (August, Count Platen)				
	4. Gesungen (Neun)				
	5. Himmel und Erde (Neun)				
	(See also opp. 27, 51 and 77)				
98(a)	Lieder und Gesänge aus 'Wilhelm Meister' (Goethe)	1849	39	1851 Breitkopf & Härtel	
	1. Kennst du das Land?				
	2. Ballade des Harfners				

		Composed	Age	Published	Dedication
	3. Nur wer die Sehnsucht kennt				
	4. Wer nie sein Brod mit Tränen ass				
	5. Heiss mich nicht reden				
	6. Wer sich der Einsamkeit ergiebt				
	7. Singet nicht in Trauertonen				
	8. An die Türen will ich schle:chen				
	9. So lasst mich scheinen				
98(b)	See Choral Works				
104	Sieben Lieder (Kulmann)	1851	41	1851 Kistner	To the memory of the poet Elisabeth Kulmann
	1. Mond, meiner Seele Liebling				
	2. Viel Glück zur Reise				
	3. Du nennst mich armes Mädchen				
	4. Der Zeisig				
	5. Reich' mir die Hand				
	6. Die letzten Blumen starben				
	7. Gekämpft hat meine Barke				
107	Sechs Gesänge	1851-52	41-42	1852 Luckhardt	Fräulein Sophia Schloss
	1. Herzeleid (Ulrich)				
	2. Die Fensterscheibe (Ulrich)				
	3. Der Gärtner (Mörike)				
	4. Die Spinnerin (Paul Heyse)				
	5. Im Walde (Müller)				
	6. Abendlied (Kinkel)				
117	Vier Husarenlieder (Lenau)	1851	41	1852 Senff	Heinrich Behr
	1. Der Husar, trara!				
	2. Der leidige Frieden				
	3. Den grünen Zeigern				
	4. Da liegt der Feinde				
119	Drei Lieder (S. Pfarrius)	1851	41	1852 Schuberth	Fräulein Mathilde Hartmann
	1. Die Hütte				
	2. Warnung				
	3. Der Bräutigam und die Birke				
125	Fünf heitere Gesänge	1850-51	40-41	1853 Schuberth	
	1. Die Meerfee (Buddeus)				
	2. Jung Volkers Lied (Mörike)				
	3. Husarenabzug (Candidus)				

Songs (cont.)

OP. NO.	TITLE	DATE OF COMPOSITION	AGE	DATE OF PUBLICATION	DEDICATION
127	Fünf Lieder und Gesänge	1840–50	30–40	1854 Heinze	
	4. Frühlingslied (Braun)				
	5. Frühlingslust (Heyse)				
	1. Sängers Trost (Kerner)				
	2. Dein Angesicht (Heine)	1840			
	3. Es leuchtet meine Liebe (Heine)				
	4. Mein altes Ross (Strachwitz)	1850			
	5. Schlusslied des Narren (Shakespeare)	1840			
135	Gedichte der Königin Maria Stuart (tr. G. Vincke)	1852	42	1855 Siegel & Stoll	
	1. Abschied von Frankreich				
	2. Nach der Geburt ihres Sohnes				
	3. An die Königin Elisabeth				
	4. Abschied von der Velt				
	5. Gebet				
142	Vier Gesänge	1840	30	1858 Rieter–Biedermann	Frau Livia Frege
	1. Trost im Gesang (Kerner)				
	2. Lehn' deine Wang' (Heine)				
	3. Mädchen—Schwermut (Lily Bernhard) (?)				
	4. Mein Wagen rollet langsam (Heine)				

Other Songs

(unfinished, unpublished, songs without opus numbers, etc.)

	TITLE	DATE OF COMPOSITION	AGE	DATE OF PUBLICATION	DEDICATION
	'Verwandlung' (Schulze) (unpublished)	1827	17	—	
	'Lied für ✱✱✱' (Schumann) (unpublished)	1827	17	—	
	11 Songs	1827–29	17–19	1933	Schumann's sisters-in-law Therese, Rosalie and Emilie

Song			
1. Sehnsucht (Robert Schumann)[1]			1933 Universal Edition
2. Die Weinende (Byron)			
3. Erinnerung (Jacobi)			
4. Kurzes Erwachen (Justinus Kerner)			
5. Gesanges Erwachen (Kerner)			
6. An Anna (Lange harrt' ich) (Kerner)			1893 Schumann-Werke suppl.
7. An Anna (Nicht im Thale) (used in slow movement of op. 11) (Kerner)			
8. Im Herbste (used in slow movement of op. 22) (Kerner)			
9. Hirtenknabe (used in Intermezzo op. 4, No. 4) (Ekert)[2]			
10. Der Fischer (Goethe)			
11. Klage (Jacobi)			NZfM 1933
'Vom Reitersmann'	?	?	
'Maultreiberlied'	1838	28	
'Ein Gedanke' (Ferrand)	1840	30	1942 (Musical Quarterly)
'Der weise Hirsch' (Uhland) (sketches)	1848	38	
'Frühlingsgrüsse' (Lenau)	1851	41	1942 (Musical Quarterly)
'Soldatenlied' (Fallersleben)	?	?	1845
'Die Ammenuhr'	?	?	
'Das Schwert' (Uhland)	?	?	
'Glockentürmers Töchterlein' (Rückert)	?	?	
Die Nächtliche Heerschau (Zedlitz)	1840	30	1922
Der Reiter und der Bodensee (Schwab)	1840	30	1922

[1] and [2] Both of these songs were attributed to 'Ekert' by their first editors. But the words of *Sehnsucht* appear in a collection of *Schumann's* own early writings called *Allerley aus der Feder Roberts an der Mulde.* So perhaps 'Ekert' (and Eric Sams's 'Ebert' in 'The Songs of Robert Schumann') are misreadings of 'Robert'.

3. CHAMBER MUSIC

(a) Instrumental (Quartets, Sonatas, etc.)

OP. NO.	TITLE	DATE OF COMPOSITION	AGE	DATE OF PUBLICATION	DEDICATION
41	Three String Quartets	1842	32	1843 (parts) 1849 (score) Breitkopf & Härtel	Mendelssohn
	1. A minor				
	2. F major				
	3. A major				
44	Piano Quintet in E flat major for piano, two violins, viola and 'cello	1842	32	1843 Breitkopf & Härtel	Clara Schumann
47	Piano Quartet in E flat major for piano, violin, viola and 'cello	1842	32	1843 Whistling	Count Grafen Mathieu Wielhorsky
63	Piano Trio No. 1, in D minor for piano, violin and 'cello	1847	37	1848 Breitkopf & Härtel	
70	Adagio and Allegro in A flat major for horn and piano (or 'cello, or violin and piano)	1849	39	1849 Kistner	
73	'Fantasiestücke' for cl. and piano	1849	39	1849 Luckhardt	
80	Piano Trio No. 2, in F major for piano, violin and 'cello	1847	37	1850 Schuberth	
88	'Fantasiestücke' for piano, violin and 'cello	1842	32	1850 Kistner	Frau Sophie Petersen
	1. Romanze				
	2. Humoreske				
	3. Duett				
	4. Finale				
94	'Drei Romanzen,' for oboe and piano	1849	39	1851 Simrock	
102	'Fünf Stücke im Volkston' for 'cello and piano	1849	39	1851 Luckhardt	Andreas Grabau

Op.					
105	Sonata No. 1, in A minor for violin and piano	1851	41	1852 Hofmeister	
110	Piano Trio No. 3, in G minor for piano, violin and 'cello	1851	41	1852 Breitkopf & Härtel	Niels Gade
113	'Märchenbilder', four pieces for viola and piano	1851	41	1852 Luckhardt	J. von Wasielewski
121	Sonata No. 2, in D minor for violin and piano	1851	41	1853 Breitkopf & Härtel	Ferdinand David
132	'Märchenerzählungen', four pieces for cl., violin and piano	1853	43	1854 Breitkopf & Härtel	Albert Dietrich

Other Chamber Works

(unfinished, unpublished, works without opus numbers, etc.)

	Piano Quartet in C minor	1829	19		
	Sketches for two string quartets (lost)	1838	28		
	Piano Trio in A minor (material transferred to op. 88)	before 1842	before 32		
	Andante and Variations for two pianos, two 'cellos and horn (orig. version of op. 46) See Two Pianos	1843	33		
	Violin Sonata No. 3 (two movs. only)	1852	42	Complete Sonata published in 1956, Schott	Joachim
	'F.A.E.' Sonata for violin and piano (second and fourth movements only; Dietrich and Brahms wrote the other two)	1853	43		
	Piano accompaniments to six 'cello sonatas by Bach (unpublished)	1853	43	—	
	Piano accompaniments to Paganini's Violin Capricci	1853–56	43–46	1930	
	Piano accompaniments to six violin Sonatas by Bach	1853	43	1854 Breitkopf & Härtel	
	Five Romances, for 'cello and piano (lost)	1853	43		

(b) Vocal (vocal duets, vocal quartets, etc. with piano accompaniment)

OP. NO.	TITLE	DATE OF COMPOSITION	AGE	DATE OF PUBLICATION	DEDICATION
29	'Drei Gedichte' (Geibel) 1. Ländliches Lied (2 Sops.) 2. Lied (3 Sops.) 3. Zigeunerleben (S.A.T.B.)	1840	30	1841 Brietkopf & Härtel	
34	'Vier Duette für Sopran und Tenor' 1. Liebesgarten (Reinick) 2. Liebhabers Ständchen (Burns) 3. Unter'm Fenster (Burns) 4. Familien—Gemälde (Grun)	1840	30	1841 Klemm	
43	'Drei zweistimmige Lieder', for vocal duet 1. Wenn ich ein Vöglein wär' (Anon.) 2. Herbstlied (Mahlmann) 3. Schön Blümelein (Reinick)	1840	30	1844 Simrock	
64 (No. 3)	'Aufihrem Grab', (Heine), for vocal duet (see also Songs)	1847	37	1847 Siegel & Stoll	
74	'Spanisches Liederspiel' (Geibel, trans. from Spanish) 1. Erste Begegnung (S.A.) 2. Intermezzo (T.B.) 3. Liebesgram (S.A.) 4. In der Nacht (S.T.) 5. Es ist verraten (S.A.T.B.) 6. Melancholie (S.) 7. Geständnis (T.) 8. Botschaft (S.A.) 9. Ich bin geliebt (S.A.T.B.) 10. Der Contrabandiste (Bar.)	1849	39	1849 Kistner	
78	'Vier Duette für Sopran und Tenor' 1. Tanzlied (Rückert) 2. Er und sie (Kerner) 3. Ich denke dein (Goethe) 4. Wiegenlied (Hebbel)	1849	39	1850 Luckhardt	

79	No. 24 'Spinnelied' (vocal trio) No. 9 'Mailied' (vocal duet)	1849	39	1849 Breitkopf & Härtel
101	No. 18 'Frühlingslied' (vocal duet) 'Minnespiel' (Rückert, from 'Liebesfrühling') 1. Lied (T.) 2. Gesang (S.) 3. Duett (A.B.) 4. Lied (T.) 5. Quartett (S.A.T.B.) 6. Lied (A.) 7. Duett (S.T.) 8. Quartett (S.A.T.B.)	1849	39	1852 Whistling
103	'Mädchenlieder' for vocal duet (Kulmann 1. Mailied 2. Frühlingslied 3. An die Nachtigall 4. An den Abendstern	1851	41	1851 Kistner
114	'Drei Lieder für drei Frauenstimmen' 1. Nänie (Bechstein) 2. Triolett (L'Égru) 3. Spruch (Rückert)	1853	43	1853 Simrock
138	'Spanische Liebeslieder' (Geibel, trans. from Spanish) 1. Vorspiel (piano) 2. Lied (S.) 3. Lied (T.) 4. Duett (S.A.) 5. Romanze (Bar.) 6. Intermezzo (piano) 7. Lied (T.) 8. Lied (A.) 9. Duett (T.B.) 10. Quartett (S.A.T.B.)	1849	39	1857 Rieter- Biedermann

472

Other vocal chamber works
(without opus numbers)

OP. NO.	TITLE	DATE OF COMPOSITION	AGE	DATE OF PUBLICATION	DEDICATION
	Vocal Duets				
	'Sommerruh' (Schad)	1849	39		
	'Liedchen von Marie und Papa' (Marie Schumann) (unacc)	1852	42	1942 (Musical Quarterly)	
	Vocal Quartet				
	'Die Orange und Myrte' (Schumann)	1853	43		

4. ORCHESTRAL MUSIC

OP. NO.	TITLE	DATE OF COMPOSITION	AGE	DATE OF PUBLICATION	DEDICATION
38	Symphony No. 1, in B flat major ('Spring' Symphony)	1841	31	1841 (parts) 1853 (score) Breitkopf & Härtel	King Friedrich August of Saxony
52	Overture, Scherzo and Finale in E major	1841	31	1846 Kistner	
61	Symphony No. 2, in C major	1845–46	35–36	1848 Whistling	
97	Symphony No. 3, in E flat major ('Rhenish' Symphony)	1850 (Oct.)	40	1851 Simrock	J. H. Verhulst
100	Overture to Schiller's 'Die Braut von Messina', in C minor	1850–51	40–41	1851 Peters	Oscar I, King of Sweden
115	Overture and Incidental Music to Byron's 'Manfred'	1848–49	38–39	1852 (Overture) 1862 (Complete score) Breitkopf & Härtel	

120	Symphony No. 4, in D minor	1841 (as No. 2; revised 1851 as No. 4)	31	1853 (parts) 1854 (score) Breitkopf & Härtel	—
123	Overture on the 'Rheinweinlied' (see also Choral Works)	1853	43	1857	
128	Overture to Shakespeare's 'Julius Caesar', in F minor	1851	41	1855 Litolff	
136	Overture to Goethe's 'Hermann und Dorothea', in B minor	1851	41	1857 Rieter-Biedermann	Clara Schumann

Other Orchestral Works

	Symphony in G minor (3 movs. only)	1832	22
	Symphony in C minor (complete sketches for 2 movs.)	1841	32
	Overture to Goethe's 'Faust' (See Choral Works)		

5. CONCERTOS, etc.

54	Concerto in A minor, for piano and orchestra	1841 (1st mov.) 1845 (complete)	31	1846 (parts) 1862 (score) Breitkopf & Härtel	Ferdinand Hiller
86	'Concertstück' in F major, for four horns and orchestra	1849	39	1851 Schuberth	
92	'Concertstück' (Introduction and Allegro appassionato) in G major, for piano and orchestra	1849	39	1852 Whistling	
129	Concerto in A minor, for 'cello and orchestra	1850	40	1854 Breitkopf & Härtel	

OP. NO.	TITLE	DATE OF COMPOSITION	AGE	DATE OF PUBLICATION	DEDICATION
		Concertos (cont.)			
131	Fantasie in C major, for violin and orchestra	1853	43	1854 Kistner	Joachim
134	Introduction and Allegro in D minor, for piano and orchestra	1853	43	1855 Senff	Brahms

Other Concertos

(unfinished, unpublished, without opus numbers, etc.)

OP. NO.	TITLE	DATE OF COMPOSITION	AGE	DATE OF PUBLICATION	DEDICATION
	Concerto in D minor, for violin and orchestra (first performance given in London in 1937, by Jelly d'Aranyi)	1853	43	1937 Schott	
	Concerto in F minor, for piano and orchestra (unfinished)	1829	19	—	
	Concerto in F major, for piano and orchestra (unfinished)	1830	20	—	
	Introduction, Theme and sketches for four variations (B mi) on a theme of Paganini, for piano and orchestra. (Vars. 3 and 4 used in opp. 4 and 8)	c. 1830	20	—	
	Concerto in D minor, for piano and orchestra (unfinished)	1833	23	—	

6. CHORAL MUSIC

(a) With Orchestra

OP. NO.	TITLE	DATE OF COMPOSITION	AGE	DATE OF PUBLICATION	DEDICATION
50	'Das Paradies und die Peri' for solo voices, chorus and orchestra (translated and adapted from Thomas Moore's 'Lalla Rookh')	1841–43	31–33	1843 Breitkopf & Härtel	

71	'Adventlied' (Rückert), for sop. solo, chorus and orchestra	1848	38	1849 (pno reduction) 1866 (score) Breitkopf & Härtel	
84	'Beim Abschied zu singen' (Feuchtersleben) for chorus and wind instruments	1847	37	1850 Whistling	
98(b)	'Requiem für Mignon' (Goethe) for solo voices, chorus and orchestra	1849	39	1851 Breitkopf & Härtel	
108	'Nachtlied' (Hebbel) for chorus and orchestra	1849	39	1852 Simrock	Friedrich Hebbel
112	'Der Rose Pilgerfahrt' (Moritz Horn) for solo voices, chorus and orchestra	1851	41	1852 Kistner	
116	'Der Königssohn' (Uhland) for solo voices, chorus and orchestra	1851	41	1853 Whistling	
123	Festival Overture on the 'Rheinweinlied' (Müller) for orchestra with chorus	1853	43	1857 Simrock	
139	'Des Sängers Fluch' (Richard Pohl, after Uhland) for solo voices, chorus and orchestra	1852	42	1858 Arnold	Brahms
140	'Vom Pagen und der Königstochter' (Geibel) for solo voices, chorus and orchestra	1852	42	1858 Rieter-Biedermann	
143	'Das Glück von Edenhall' (Hasenclever, after Uhland) for solo voices, chorus and orchestra	1853	43	1860 Rieter-Biedermann	
144	'Neujahrslied' (Rückert) for chorus and orchestra	Dec. 1849–50	39–40	1861 Rieter-Biedermann	
147	Mass for chorus and orchestra	1852	42	1862 (piano red.) 1863 (score) Rieter-Biedermann	
148	Requiem for chorus and orchestra	1852	42	1864 Rieter-Biedermann	

Other Choral Works with Orchestra
(unfinished, unpublished, works without opus numbers, etc.)

OP. NO.	TITLE	DATE OF COMPOSITION	AGE	DATE OF PUBLICATION	DEDICATION
	'Scenen aus Goethe's "Faust"'	1844–53	34–43	1858 (piano red.) 1859 (score) Friedländer	
	Psalm 150 (unpublished)	1822	12	—	
	Overture and chorus (unpublished)	1822	12	—	
	'Tragödie' (Heine) (basis of op. 64, No. 3)	1841	31	—	

6. CHORAL MUSIC
(b) Partsongs

OP. NO.	TITLE	DATE OF COMPOSITION	AGE	DATE OF PUBLICATION	DEDICATION
33	'Sechs Lieder', for male voices 1. Der träumende See (Mosen) 2. Die Minnesänger (Heine) 3. Die Lotosblume (Heine) 4. Der Zecher als Doktrinär (Mosen) 5. Rastlose Liebe (Goethe) 6 Frühlingsglocken (Reinick)	1840	30	1842 Schuberth	Dr Karl Stein
55	'Fünf Lieder', for mixed voices (Burns) 1. Das Höchlandmädchen 2. Zahnweh 3. Mich zieht es nach dem Dörfchen hin 4. Die gute alte Zeit 5. Hochlandbursch	1846	36	1847 Heinze	Leipziger Liederkranz
59	'Vier Gesänge', for mixed voices 1. Nord oder Süd (Lappe) 2. Am Bodensee (Platen) 3. Jägerlied (Mörike) 4. Gute Nacht (Rückert)	1846	36	1848 Whistling	Raimund Härtel

No.	Work	Date	No.	Publisher	
62	'Drei Gesänge', for male voices 1. Der Eidgenossen Nachtwache (Eichendorff) 2. Freiheitslied (Rückert) 3. Schlachtgesang (Klopstock)	1847	37	1848 Whistling	
65	'Ritornelle' (Rückert), seven canons for male voices 1. Die Rose stand im Tau 2. Lasst Lautenspiel und Becherklang 3. Blüt' oder Schnee 4. Gebt mir zu trinken! 5. Zürne nicht des Herbstes Wind 6. In Sommertagen 7. In Meeres Mitten	1347	37	1849 Breitkopf & Härtel	Ruckert
67	'Romanzen und Balladen', Vol. I, for mixed voices 1. Der König in Thule (Goethe) 2. Schön Rohtraut (Mörike) 3. Heidenröslein (Goethe) 4. Ungewitter (Chamisso) 5. John Anderson (Burns) (See also opp. 75, 145 and 146)	1849	39	1849 Whistling	
69	'Romanzen', Vol. I, for female voices 1. Tamburinschlagerin (Eichendorff) 2. Waldmädchen (Eichendorff) 3. Klosterfräulein (Kerner) 4. Soldatenbraut (Mörike) 5. Meerfey (Eichendorff) 6. Die Capelle (Uhland) (pno ad lib)	1849	39	1849 Simrock	
75	'Romanzen und Balladen', Vol. II, for mixed voices 1. Schnitter Tod (Old German) 2. Im Walde (Eichendorff) 3. Der traurige Jäger (Eichendorff) 4. Der Rekrut (Burns) 5. Vom verwundeten Knaben (Old German)	1849	39	1850 Whistling	
91	'Romanzen', Vol. II, for female voices 1. Rosmarin (Old German)	1849	39	1851 Simrock	

OP. NO.	TITLE	DATE OF COMPOSITION	AGE	DATE OF PUBLICATION	DEDICATION
	Choral Music (cont.)				
	2. Jäger Wohlgemut ('Des Knaben Wunderhorn')				
	3. Der Wassermann (Kerner)				
	4. Das verlassene Mägdelein (Mörike)				
	5. Der Bleicherin Nachtlied (Reinick)				
	6. In Meeres Mitten (Rückert) (pno *ad lib*)				
93	Motet: 'Verzweifle nicht im Schmerzenstal', (Rückert), for double male chorus (Organ *ad lib*)	1849 (orch. 1852)	39	1851 Whistling	
137	'Jagdlieder'. Five Hunting songs (Laube), for male voices (4 horns *ad lib*) 1. Zur hohen Jagd 2. Habet Acht 3. Jagdmorgen 4. Frühe 5. Bei der Flasche	1849	39	1857 Rieter-Biedermann	
141	'Vier doppelchörige Gesänge', for mixed voices 1. An die Sterne (Rückert) 2. Ungewisses Licht (Zedlitz) 3. Zuversicht (Zedlitz) 4. Talismane (Goethe)	1849	39	1858 Kistner	
145	'Romanzen und Balladen', Vol. III, for mixed voices 1. Der Schmidt (Uhland) 2. Die Nonne (Anon.) 3. Der Sänger (Uhland) 4. John Anderson (Burns) 5. Romanze vom Gänsebuben (Malsburg)	1849–51	39–41	1860 Arnold	
146	'Romanzen und Balladen', Vol. IV, for mixed voices 1. Brautgesang (Uhland) 2. Bänkelsänger Willie (Burns) 3. Der Traum (Uhland)	1849	39	1860 Arnold	

4. Sommerlied (Rückert)
5. Das Schifflein (Uhland) (Flute and Horn)
(See also opp. 67, 75, 145)

Other Partsongs
(without opus numbers)

'Zum Anfange' (Rückert) for male voices (lost)	1847	37	—
'Der deutsche Rhein' (Becker) Patriotic Song, with solo voice (piano)	1840	30	—
Three Partsongs	1848	39	1913 (Revue Musicale)
1. Zu den Waffen (Ulrich)			
2. Schwarz-Rot-Gold (Freiligrath)			
3. Freiheitssang (Fürst) *wind band ad lib*			
'Wenn zwei auseinandergeh'n (lost)	1850	40	—

7. OPERA AND THEATRE MUSIC

81	'Der Corsair', opera Libretto by Oswald Marbach, after Byron (unfinished)	1844	34	—
	'Genoveva', opera in 4 acts Libretto by Reinick (modified by Schumann) based on the dramas of Ludwig Tieck and Friedrich Hebbel	1847–48	37–38	1850 (score) 1851 (pno red.) Peters
115	'Manfred'. Overture and Incidental music to the dramatic poem by Byron	1848–49	38–39	1852 (Overture) 1853 (pno red.) 1862 (score) Breitkopf & Härtel

Index of Schumann's Works Discussed in this Volume

[main page entries are in italics]

General Index

[An asterisk (*) indicates 'See Register of Persons']

main page entries are in italics